Between Worlds

DATE DUE			

Between Worlds

Interpreters, Guides, and Survivors

Frances Karttunen

Rutgers University Press
New Brunswick, New Jersey

Library of Congress Cataloging-in-Publication Data

Karttunen, Frances E.
    Between worlds : interpreters, guides, and survivors / Frances Karttunen.
      p.   cm.
    Includes bibliographical references and index (p.   ).
    ISBN 0-8135-2030-4 (cloth) — ISBN 0-8135-2031-2 (pbk.)
      1. Translators—Biography.   2. Linguistic informants—Biography.
    3. Intercultural communication.   I. Title.
    P306.9.K37   1994
    418′.02′0922—dc20
    [B]   93-8366
                                          CIP
British Cataloging-in-Publication information available

This book is dedicated to my aunt Esther Ulrika Gibbs,
in admiration of her indomitable strength and loyalty.

Contents

Acknowledgments

I owe a debt of gratitude to many friends and colleagues. My thanks to all, and especially to the following:

Doña Concepción Hernández de Villanueva and her family for their hospitality and willingness to tell me about Doña Luz, and Joe Campbell for facilitating our conversations.

The Charlot family and curator Nancy Morns for sharing two decades of Doña Luz's letters and Jean Charlot's vision of Luz in his diaries, paintings, and prints.

Senni Timonen, Paraske's biographer, for her generosity and help at the Finnish Literature Society, and Ritva and Markku Henriksson for aiding me in many ways.

Leslie O'Bell, who helped me with Russian source material.

R.M.W. Dixon, who sent me the recorded life stories of Chloe Grant and George Watson so I could hear their voices for myself.

Eunice Pike, who helped me with the final years of María Sabina; Rachel Saint, who brought me up to date on Dayuma; and Evelyn Pike, who sent me a collection of Huaorani texts including Dayuma's.

Fred Ellison, who gave me his copy of Laurinda Andrade's autobiography.

James Lockhart, who introduced me to Mexico and its Indian heritage and provided me with a model for historical writing about individuals. My debt is boundless.

Laura Gutierrez-Witt and the staff of the Benson Latin American Collection, whose good will and helpfulness have sustained me through many years.

The Departments of Linguistics and History at the University of Hawaii for providing me with space, facilities, and collegial support as I finished the writing.

Alan Ross, who listened to some of these stories and encouraged me.

Helpful readers, including Monica Barnes, Jerry Bentley, Margot

Beyersdorff, Anne Boyer, John Charlot, Inga Clendinnen, Amy Conger, Catherine Fowler, Ascensión H. de León-Portilla, Jane Hill, Svatava Jakobson, Susan Milmoe, Deborah Tannen, Rosemary Stubbs, Edward Tripp, and Merle Wachter.

Mary and Robert Erler, Jorma and Eine Tulkku, Liisa and Erkki Hannu, Olli and Hilkka Kiviluoto, and Liisa and Reino Kurki-Suonio for their enduring friendship.

Jaana and Suvi Karttunen with love and affection.

And Al Crosby, without whom nothing would be possible.

Introduction

This is a book about individuals, many of them women, who have served as interpreters, translating their languages and also their cultures for outsiders. Some were guides and scouts who worked, voluntarily or involuntarily, for soldiers and explorers. Others had careers as assistants to missionaries and as professional civil servants, while others worked as what anthropologists and linguists call "native informants." They functioned as conduits through which information flowed between worlds in collision, translating more than just words and bringing comprehensibility to otherwise meaningless static.

As the twentieth century draws to a close, the language of international aviation is English. I recollect seeing the same bright yellow "Follow Me" sign on the back of little vehicles guiding aircraft to their gates in Helsinki, Moscow, Mexico City, Barcelona, Frankfort—regardless of the national language or its writing system. I feel certain that in Tokyo and Cairo and Bangkok it is the same cosy "Follow Me" that precedes the anxiety of baggage claim, the wariness of customs inspection, and the ultimate hubbub of the street and negotiation of taxi fares.

It has not always been so. In the grand scheme of human history it was just a little while ago that some of us learned to use the oceans as thoroughfares and initiated what is known as the Age of Discovery. On the shores of the Canary Islands and the west coast of Africa, in the Caribbean and on the mainland of the Americas, and finally on islands across the Pacific, the lack of a common language reduced voyagers and local folks to crude pantomime as they sought to communicate. Inland, as newcomers traversed continents, matters were no better. Everywhere guides and interpreters were needed, and we will see how some of them were literally dragged into the role.

Incompetent and wholly unwilling interpreters didn't last long. Given the least opportunity they fled for their lives, or lost them in violent encounters when negotiations failed. The famous ones are the individuals who had some aptitude for living in two worlds and who survived to tell about it. Their biographies, especially their autobiographies, should give us all pause as we prepare to enter a new century, well aware that the "Follow Me" signs around the globe take us only just so far, and beyond them still lie worlds and yet more worlds where we are dependent on interpreters. How shall we regard the individuals who do this work? Do we comprehend why they do it and what price they pay for what they do?

What follows is not and cannot be a theory about interpreters in the abstract. It does not pretend to be a sociological study based on a balanced subject pool. Instead, this book presents in detail the life experiences of nine extraordinary individuals and more briefly sets forth those of another seven. The last chapter touches on some obvious parallels despite the circumstance that these women and men lived at different times and in different places around the globe. And since many of them had families, there is an epilogue about what happened as their children sought places for themselves in one or the other of their parents' worlds.

We are about to meet fewer than twenty people, individuals who are included here because records of them happen to exist and are accessible in languages that I happen to be able to read. Yet despite these limitations, I think we may ask as we read, why do people do this? And then: why was it these particular individuals who did it?

From their stories we may learn at least as much about what it is to be a misfit as about what it is to be an Amerindian or an Australian Aborigine, an Azorean or a Karelian, for within their own communities these were unconventional people. However much they have to tell us about their particular societies, from their positions on the edge they have at least as much to tell us of the special perspective of the marginalized.

There are two kinds of material to be found in these pages. The biographical sections are as accurate as sources permit and as I think I know what to make of them. On the other hand, the last sections of chapters 1–3 and all of chapter 5 are my own meditations on the experiences of the people included here. These parts of the book are to be understood as suggestive, not as reasoned anthropological or psychological arguments. I have no theoretical points to score and invite readers to their own conclusions, whether they agree with mine or are very different indeed.

This is a book full of names and words from unfamiliar languages. The forms of such names in use among English speakers are often poor approximations of the way they were actually pronounced, but the purpose here is not instruction in the pronunciation of foreign names. Against the impulse to put in every one, I only give the name of an individual if that person will be coming up again. Otherwise I provide a brief description of who they were, what they did, or why they are relevant, and I do the same for place names. As for foreign words, if I think I must use one, I provide an English equivalent or explanation immediately afterwards: *barrio* 'neighborhood' or *kantele*, 'a stringed instrument'. In sum, I have tried to observe three sometimes contradictory principles: follow the original sources, be consistent, and avoid confusion.

Today the people Lewis and Clark called the Minnetaree are known as the Hidatsa. But the Lewis and Clark usage will prevail here for the sake of consistency with quotations from their journals. For the same reason, I have written Chippewa instead of Ojibway, Sioux instead of Dakota. The great lord of the Aztecs appears here as "Montezuma," the form of his name familiar to English-speaking readers, rather than the Spanish "Moctezuma" or his own Nahuatl "Moteuczoma." The Shoshone interpreter for the Lewis and Clark expedition appears as "Sacajawea," although a case has been made for "Sacagawea." The Andean who wrote a devastating report to the Spanish king signed himself "Guaman Poma," and so it is here, although "Huaman Poma" and "Waman Puma" are both more suggestive of the Quechua pronunciation of his name. It is a close call between "Shoshone" and "Shoshoni," and between "Waorani" and Spanish-style "Huaorani," and in these cases I have been guided by the spelling that predominates in the sources I quote. I do not add accent marks to names in indigenous languages where Spanish spelling uses accents, because Spanish pronunciation often displaces the stress. Naturally, I do write the accent marks in Spanish words.

"Indian" is a word I would like to avoid. The name and the idea were both mistakes imposed on the diverse peoples of two immense continents. But it forces itself upon us, because the Spanish sources use the word *indios* constantly. Likewise Lewis and Clark and Sarah Winnemucca write of "Indians," and for Charles Eastman—a Santee Sioux trying to come to terms with the rise of the Ghost Dance, the massacre at Wounded Knee, and the consequences of the doctrine of Manifest Destiny—the abstract idea of "the Indian" became a source of strength and comfort in a desperately discouraging world. Five hundred years ago, when the Americas (not yet so called) were inhabited by millions of people living in groups great and small, speaking vast numbers of different languages, sustaining themselves in many different ways, and calling themselves by their own names, it was misguided to regard them as all undifferentiated "Indians." Now that their descendants have survived near extermination and found common cause among themselves, "Indian" has a positive meaning, at least for some people in some places. In this book "Indian" is used to mean an indigenous person of the Americas just as "Aborigine" is used to mean an indigenous person of Australia.

While peoples of the Americas were being labeled Indians, Europeans were saddled with the senseless label "Caucasian." Very few of us have our roots in the mountains between the Caspian and the Black Sea, yet the term persists. The Irish, French, and Scandinavians would not willingly identify themselves as "Anglo," and as for "European," it hardly applies to people of European descent who were born, lived their lives, and died on other continents.

The labels "white" and "black" are as spurious as "Indian" once was, but I will use them here, since they are omnipresent in books by and about the people we are soon to meet. I considered capitalizing "white" and "black" to emphasize that they are labels, but since the sources do not, I have not either.

Throughout I have deferred to others in matters of translation, using my own only where no other English version is available or where it seems to me that the existing English version does not quite capture what the original language says.

Autobiographies were the original inspiration for this book. I thought at first to write only about women from traditional cultures who had become engaged in one way or another with academic investigators and who later wrote or dictated their autobiographies. But my vision expanded to people whose circumstances did not permit the spinning out of their own life stories from beginning to end. If autobiography were not a criterion, then the door was open to that most famous of interpreters, Doña Marina. And finally, Theodora Kroeber's sensitive portrayal of Ishi's last years and V. K. Arsenjev's account of Dersu Uzala showed me that the issue was not gender. In the end I wrote of both men and women, some who left autobiographies and others who did not, some who worked for academics, others for missionaries, and yet others for explorers and military men who wrote about them. The unifying theme is that they all became bridges between their own worlds and another, unfamiliar one.

Welcome now to lives between worlds.

Between Worlds

Three Guides

TO THE VALLEY OF MEXICO: *Doña Marina, "La Malinche" (ca. 1500–1527)*

As our Captain wished to be more thoroughly informed about the plot and all that was happening, he told Doña Marina to take more chalchihuites [gem stones] to the two priests who had been the first to speak, for they were not afraid, and to tell them with friendly words that Malinche wished them to come back and speak to him, and to bring them back with her. Doña Marina went and spoke to the priests in the manner she knew so well how to use, and thanks to the presents they at once accompanied her.

—*BERNAL DÍAZ DEL CASTILLO*[1]

Doña Marina and Hernán Cortés came together on the coast of the Gulf of Mexico, and they have remained inseparable in popular imagination to this day. According to Bernal Díaz del Castillo, one of the chroniclers of the conquest of Mexico, they had known each other for hardly a month when their portraits were painted. Montezuma sent emissaries to the Spaniards while they were still on the coast, and with them, the emissaries brought painters to capture the likenesses of Cortés and his retinue, including the woman who was interpreting for him in the language of the Aztecs. From that day to this, Doña Marina and Cortés have been depicted together in countless ways. They can be seen painted in delicate colors on pages of paper made from pounded fig bark. They appear in the illustrations of a work known as the *Florentine Codex* and again and again in scenes copied from a colonial-period painting commissioned by the city council of Tlaxcala. Looking for all the world like a prosperous couple out for a walk, they stroll down a road on a painted map. Countless times they are to be found in murals, on calendars, in comic books.

Characters in pageants performed throughout Mexico and Guatemala wear Cortés and Doña Marina masks. In the ubiquitous Mexican velvet paintings of an Aztec warrior standing guard over an unconscious woman who is often blonde, usually voluptuous, and scantily clad, the watchful warrior and the unconscious lady are personifications of the two volcanoes on the eastern side of the Valley of Mexico: Popocatepetl 'the smoking mountain' and Iztaccihuatl 'the white woman'. Folklore has it that the lady is Malintzin, and the smoking mountain is a great ruler who would marry her if only she would wake up. East of the volcanoes another mountain is known as Malinche.

Doña Marina, Malintzin, Malinche—all are names by which people know the Indian woman who accompanied Cortés in the high adventures of the conquest of Mexico. Throughout history she has been imagined as beautiful and desirable, an Indian princess. As an old man writing a half-century after the events at which they were both present, Bernal Díaz recalled her as an excellent woman, of obviously noble birth and bearing. He also described her as "good looking and intelligent and without embarrassment."[2] The illustrations of the *Florentine Codex* represent her as an Indian matron in the decorated *huipil* blouse of a noblewoman, her hair bound in the way of Aztec women. But in the bark-paper illustrations drawn at about the same time, her hair flows loose, and with her lovely huipil she wears European shoes, while all the other women are barefoot.[3] The loose-haired image is the one that has lived on in popular imagination, and as beauty has come to be equated with deficiency of pigment, her image has evolved into that of a pink-cheeked, blue-eyed blonde with the proportions of a Hollywood starlet.

To say that Mexican attitudes toward this woman are ambivalent would be an understatement. As "Malinche," she is perceived as the ultimate traitor, the collaborator who betrayed the indigenous peoples of the New World to the Spaniards. She is the mistress of Cortés, a woman driven by lust for the white man, who is resentfully called *gachupín*. She is identified with La Llorona, a ghost in the form of a beautiful woman who leads men to death in dark out-of-the-way places and is heard weeping loudly in the night. La Llorona appears already in the *Florentine Codex,* as one of the omens of the fall of Mexico, wailing and lamenting the coming fate of the Aztecs.

In the popular imagination Malinche is fair but dangerous. Behind that facade lurks a hag. Even when she is depicted as beautiful, her face is sometimes decorated with lizards, and in some dances she carries a snake that bites people. She has been linked in people's minds with Eve and with the ferocious Mesoamerican female deities, women who one way or another have sinister and intimate associations with snakes.

In another aspect, she is indigenous intelligence personified, the equal of the great Cortés, the person without whom he would have been led into traps and defeated. Hers is indigenous beauty that captivated the European conqueror. In folklore about Iztaccihuatl, she goes to sleep rather than submit to being married, and as long as she sleeps, she protects her people. In the conflict of the Dance of the Conquest, she and Cortés are the ultimate winners, and together they bring Christianity to the people of the New World.

In the most extreme cases, Malinche and Cortés fuse. As Bernal Díaz explained, "In all the towns we had passed through, and in others where they had heard of us, Cortés was called Malinche. . . . The reason why he was given this name is that Doña Marina, our interpreter, was always in his company, particularly when any Ambassadors arrived, and she spoke to them in the Mexican language. So that they gave Cortés the name of 'Marina's Captain' and for short Malinche."[4] In some dance-dramas, only Malinche appears, and in others a dancer wears a two-faced mask, Cortés on one side, Malinche on the other.

Despite the twentieth-century depiction of her as the Barbie-doll mistress of the swashbuckling Spanish conquistador, the figure of Doña Marina through the course of four and a half centuries is undeniably powerful. The compelling idea of her has spawned poetry, plays, romantic novels, dubious histories, emotional defenses, and also scholarly biographies that have sought to rescue her from the morass of collective imagination. But the biographers have their own cultural biases, and from the perspective of a few decades, some entirely serious attempts to explain how things came about as they did seem breathtakingly sexist and racist. For instance, a woman writing in the 1940s asks, "In order to comprehend this mystery, should we not first put aside those sentiments peculiar to the Christian way of life? Because for those young Indian women, so animal-like in their approach to sex, the idea of chastity or virginity had no meaning at all. Moreover, would they not have looked upon the Spaniard as a kind of god, even as the Spaniard himself doubted whether such women could be really human? This mutual feeling of strangeness, as strong in one as in the other, must have lent the erotic experience entirely new facets and an emotional aspect we can only faintly imagine."[5] Two decades later another biographer, a man writing a work of sober scholarly intent, gives in to a similar mind-set: "Doña Marina loves a man for the first time, and logically subjugates herself to his will; it is a law of biology. In the sexual union of a male and female, the stronger, the male, dominates, and the female yields her will to powerful sexual desire in the interest of conserving the species."[6]

Although it is not literally true, this is yet another potent element of the tradition: that the child born to Cortés and Doña Marina was the first mestizo, the foundation of a new race and of the modern Mexican nation.

At the root of this towering construction of myth, with its sentimental themes of the physical beauty of Doña Marina and her love for Cortés and its darker themes of unbridled female sexuality and racial betrayal, there is a real woman. She left no written record of herself, but she was a major participant in the events of the conquest of Mexico. Other people who were present, both Spanish and Indian, recorded her part in it.

We do not know exactly how old she was when she was baptized by Father Bartolomé de Olmedo in March 1519. Bernal Díaz simply says that she was young. And we do not know exactly how or when she died. Much later, her daughter testified in court that it was in 1527. In the intervening eight years Doña Marina interpreted for Cortés during his Mexican campaigns and bore him a son in 1522. She was married to a Spaniard named Juan Jaramillo in 1525 at the outset of an expedition to Honduras on which she again served as interpeter for Cortés, and bore Jaramillo a daughter in 1526. She was nowhere near middle age when her life ran out.

Her son, consigned during her lifetime to the care of a male cousin of Cortés and taken to Spain by his father when he was six years old, hardly had a chance to know her. If she died in 1527, her daughter was only a year old and would have had no memory of her at all. Jaramillo remarried immediately, providing the little girl with a Spanish stepmother.

As for Cortés, on the eve of his marriage to a Spanish noblewoman he successfully petitioned to have three of his natural children, including his son by Doña Marina, legitimized, and thence went on to sire yet more children, legitimate and illegitimate. He lived out his full life and died in 1547, more than two decades after he had handed Doña Marina on to Jaramillo. According to his biographer Francisco López de Gómara, at the time of his death he had sired three daughters and a son by his wife, one son by Doña Marina, a son by a Spanish woman to whom he was not married, and three more daughters, "each by a different mother, all Indians."[7] One of these Indian mothers was a daughter of Montezuma.

Before she passed into Spanish hands and became Doña Marina, the first part of the life of "La Lengua" ('the interpreter', literally 'the tongue') was played out in an area at the base of the Yucatan peninsula, a coastal stretch that lies across the modern Mexican states of Veracruz, Tabasco, and Campeche. Bernal Díaz relates that she was born to local rulers in the Nahuatl-speaking area of Coatzacoalcos, and that after her father's death and her mother's remarriage, she was deliberately given away to people from Xicalango, a coastal town farther to the east.[8] They passed her on to yet other nearby people who lived in the area between. These places are not far apart, but once away from Coatzacoalcos, she was among Maya-speaking people, whose language she learned before she was given away once again. This time the Chontal Maya people of Tabasco gave her to Cortés.

Cortés had come to the Tabasco coast after sailing from Cuba to Cozumel Island and the Caribbean coast of Yucatan and then rounding the peninsula and coming down the Gulf of Mexico side. With him he brought a recently rescued Spaniard, Jerónimo de Aguilar, one of two survivors of shipwreck and enslavement by the Yucatecan Maya. The other survivor, Gonzalo Guerrero, who had married a Maya woman, fathered children, and found a place for himself in Maya society, declined to rejoin his fellow countrymen. Aguilar, who had taken holy orders and continued to live by them as much as he could under the circumstances, gladly returned to Spanish society and, having become fluent in Maya during his captivity, began to serve at once as interpreter for Cortés.

The Chontal Maya of the Tabasco coast had been friendly in an earlier encounter with a Spanish expedition, but this time they attacked the outnumbered forces of Cortés. Despite their advantage, the Maya were unable to prevail against the Spanish horses and weapons, and switched to a strategy of appeasement, sending Cortés male slaves, food, cloth, gold ornaments, and twenty women to cook for them and look after whatever other needs these strangers might have. (For a brief time the mainlanders were uncertain about what sort of food the Spaniards might eat, whether the horsemen were separable from their horses, and whether they could be wounded, but the Spaniards made it clear from the first that they had a thoroughly carnal interest in Indian women.)

The Spaniards set up a cross, had Aguilar interpret a sermon by Father Olmedo about the Christian faith, and baptized the women. In writing of the events of this day, the Spanish chroniclers say that the woman destined to be Aguilar's professional colleague was given the baptismal name "Marina."[9] In the speech of Nahuatl-speaking Indians her new name took the form "Malintzin," but for her Spanish-speaking contemporaries, and for her son and daughter, she was "Doña Marina." The one time that Cortés himself mentions her by name in his dispatches to the king of Spain, he refers to her as "Marina"; writing in 1526, he did not favor her with

"Doña." In an earlier letter, written in 1520, he refers to her only as "my interpreter, who is an Indian woman."[10]

"Malintzin" does not seem much like "Marina," but it makes sense in terms of how Nahuatl speakers borrowed Spanish words into their own language. Nahuatl replaces Spanish *r* with *l*, and "Marina" becomes *Malina*. To this is added an ending *-tzin*, which expresses respect and honor in much the same way as Spanish *Doña* does when it is put in front of a name. Thus, the equivalent of "Doña Marina" is *Malina-tzin*, and losing a vowel it becomes "Malintzin."

Spanish borrowed "Malintzin" back from Nahuatl. Just as Nahuatl speakers could not pronounce Spanish *l*, Spanish speakers could not pronounce Nahuatl *tz* and changed it to *ch*. They didn't hear the often-whispered Nahuatl *n* at the end of the word either, and the result was "Malinche." Something more than precision of pronunciation was lost in this reborrowing, because Spanish speakers had no idea of the politeness of Nahuatl *-tzin*. In time, Spanish "Malinche" came to be used in ugly ways impossible for Nahuatl "Malintzin." In Mexico the words "Malinche" and "gachupín" both reverberate with overtones of racial resentment. (Some people believe that *gachupín* is from Nahuatl, meaning 'someone who kicks people with his shoes on'. Since Indians typically go barefoot, it would be Spaniards who "shoe-kick" people.)

It has become part of the myth of Doña Marina that her pre-baptismal name had been "Malinalli," a Nahuatl word for grass one can twist into rope by rolling it on one's thigh. It is not a particularly lovely name, but part of one that a person might receive by being born on a certain day determined by the pre-Columbian Mexican calendar. According to this explanation of her name, "Marina" was a Spanish approximation to Nahuatl "Malinal-tzin." Yet this is giving credit to Father Olmedo for powers of communication and linguistic sensitivity that he scarcely could have possessed. The women were baptized as soon as they were given to the Spaniards, amidst a swirl of other events, and it is unlikely that Olmedo would seek to learn through Aguilar each woman's personal name in order to find a Spanish near-equivalent.[11]

On the day of the baptism, Cortés was not yet aware of Doña Marina's special claim to usefulness—that she spoke both Maya, a language she shared with Aguilar, and Nahuatl, a language she shared with Montezuma.[12] He turned the newly baptized women over to his lieutenants. Doña Marina he gave to Alonso Hernández de Puertocarrero. A month later he had taken her back, and she and Aguilar were working together as his interpreters.

In the meantime the expedition had sailed further west along the Gulf coast and finally put in to shore, where they found themselves in Nahuatl-speaking territory. Aguilar was unable to interpret, but according to chroniclers, Doña Marina was observed speaking to members of the Indian delegation and pointing out Cortés to them as the leader of the Spaniards, whereupon Cortés set her immediately to work mediating between Montezuma's emissaries and Aguilar. Aguilar, in turn, conveyed to Doña Marina what Cortés wished to say to Montezuma's chief representative.

Soon thereafter the expedition encountered Totonac Indians, whose language was unknown to both Doña Marina and Aguilar. Among these people, however, there were interpreters who spoke Totonac and Nahuatl, and so a chain of interpreters was formed. The Totonacs' interpreters translated Totonac to Nahuatl for Doña Marina. She translated from Nahuatl to Maya for Aguilar, and he translated from Maya to Spanish for Cortés. And then the exchange was reversed: Cortés to Aguilar to Doña Marina to the interpreters to the Totonacs. The wonder of it is that any vestige of communication survived the transmission back and forth through four languages.

Shortly the Spaniards were presented with more women. This time they were noble ladies with their own female servants, daughters of local rulers. Theirs was a different situation from that of the first women given to Cortés, for they were given to cement strategic alliances between the Spaniards and the rulers of the Veracruz coast. In no way were they to be looked upon as servants. Cortés again required Christian baptism, and he once again distributed the women among his men. Cortés himself accepted the daughter of the local ruler. Puertocarrero received another properly baptized woman. In July Puertocarrero departed for Spain, and a month later the expedition under Cortés set out toward the interior. Along the way they accumulated yet more women.

According to accounts, Cortés was already using the services of Doña Marina and Aguilar to manipulate Montezuma's officials. On the coast he had put on raw demonstrations of horsepower and artillery, but in the Totonac city, he engaged in a fine piece of double-dealing when Montezuma's tax collectors arrived to upbraid the Totonac nobles for consorting with the Spaniards. Doña Marina explained to Cortés what was going on, and he prevailed upon the resentful Totonacs to take the Aztecs prisoner. At night he had two of the Aztec prisoners secretly freed and brought to him and his interpreters. Through Doña Marina he expressed ignorance of their imprisonment and outrage at the Totonacs for their bad behavior. Pledging his friendship to Montezuma, he had the two given safe passage out of Totonac territory. In the morning he blamed the Totonacs for allowing two prisoners to escape and insisted on taking custody of the remaining ones himself. Placing the Aztecs on his ship, he represented himself to them as their rescuer. If we are to believe the accounts, as interpeter Doña Marina was instrumental to the entire ruse.

It took some weeks for the Spanish expedition to make its way to the city-state of Tlaxcala. Although they shared a common language, the Tlaxcalans were enemies of the Aztecs, and unlike the Totonacs, they did not pay taxes to them. It took most of the month of September for the Tlaxcalans and the Spaniards to get past bloodletting to negotiation. During the process, Doña Marina reportedly informed on a group of Tlaxcalans who, under guise of delivering food to the Spaniards, were reconnoitering in order to inform their lord of the best moment to attack. Acting on her tip, Cortés rounded them up, cut off the hands of some and the thumbs of others, and sent them back.[13]

Thirty-three years later, in 1552, after the conquest and the establishment of colonial rule in Mexico, the municipal government of Tlaxcala commissioned a large painting or wall hanging to show the events of the arrival of Cortés in Tlaxcala and the subsequent war against the Aztecs in which the Spaniards and the Tlaxcalans were allies. The painting was to be sent to Spain, but a copy, now lost, was kept in Tlaxcala. We know it only from copies that are not exact, but which agree in overall detail. Doña Marina figures prominently in a number of the eighty-seven scenes from this *Lienzo de Tlaxcala*, as it is known.

Four of these scenes also appear on loose pages from what must have been a large book. The written Nahuatl captions for the pictures and the detail in the paintings themselves show that they were done around the same time that the big painting was commissioned, within living memory of people who had been eyewitnesses to the events they portray. In the first of the surviving scenes, Doña Marina stands interpreting between Cortés and a Tlaxcalan emissary on the road, Cortés still mounted at the head of his troops. In the next, Cortés has dismounted and removed his hat. He stands grasping the hand, or more precisely the wrist, of the Tlaxcalan lord Xicotencatl, while Doña Marina continues to interpret. Then the two men are seated in Spanish folding chairs in the palace of Xicotencatl. Doña Marina remains standing, facing them and translating. To the right of the palace stand a group of Tlaxcalan nobles, and to the left the men of Cortés, dismounted. Two of their horses are tethered and have been given fodder. Spread out before the palace are the turkeys and quail and eggs and baskets of maize and of baked tortillas that the Tlaxcalans presented to the Spaniards. In the fourth and last surviving scene, Cortés remains seated in his chair with his men behind him. Facing him, Xicotencatl and other Tlaxcalan noblemen stand as they give a group of noblewomen to the Spaniards. Doña Marina faces the richly dressed women and makes the finger-pointing gesture that usually accompanies speech in such drawings, while behind her a Spaniard holds a spear in one hand and makes the same pointing gesture with his free hand. This may be a rare acknowledgment of the presence of Jerónimo de Aguilar. It is at this point in the train of events that Bernal Díaz remarks that all the Indians called Cortés "Malinche" because of the inseparableness of the captain and his Nahuatl interpreter. In both the indigenous record and the Spanish chronicles, Aguilar recedes into the background and Doña Marina moves to center stage.

One of the five nubile noblewomen presented to Cortés was the daughter of Xicotencatl himself. In the baptism that followed, she received the name Doña Luisa. Then Cortés gave her to Pedro de Alvarado, a man noted for impetuousness in the conquest of Mexico and later notorious for his severity in Guatemala, a man who came to be known in Nahuatl as *Tonatiuh* 'the sun'. Taking leave of her home, Doña Luisa accompanied Alvarado into Montezuma's city, survived a disastrous retreat from that city, and lived to bear him a son and a daughter.

Leaving Tlaxcala, Cortés set his route to the city-state of Tenochtitlan, where Montezuma ruled, via yet another city named Cholula. The Tlaxcalans sent a large company of men along to protect the Spaniards and the noble Tlaxcalan ladies from the Cholulans, who were perceived as allies of Montezuma, hence mortal enemies of the Tlaxcalans. None of the city-states that Cortés visited was anxious to receive him. They tried buying him off, and they urged him to pass on. Cholula was no exception, and it took some days of negotiations and the dismissal of many of the accompanying Tlaxcalans before Cortés achieved his intention of entering the city.

At this point, there was a great assembly of people in and about Cholula. The city itself was full of spectators. Cortés still had with him his Totonac allies from the coast, and the Tlaxcalans were nearby. According to reports, a large force of Montezuma's soldiers was in the vicinity as well. Distrust ran high among these groups. Cortés was warned by his allies that the Cholulans, in order to divert and maim his men's horses, had erected barricades in the streets and had dug stake-lined pits, and that once the Spaniards were caught within the walls of Cholula, Montezuma's men would fall upon them.

Now, according to the chroniclers, Cortés engaged in another of his schemes. He detained two of Montezuma's ambassadors, and he had some Cholulan priests brought to him. Through Doña Marina he spoke gently to these men and offered gifts, encouraging them to serve as intermediaries between himself and the rulers of the city, from which he said he intended to depart very soon.

Then he had Doña Marina privately take more gifts to the priests and speak persuasively with them. He urged them, again through Doña Marina, to be truthful as priests should be, whatever gods they served, and they confirmed that there were Mexican forces waiting to fall upon the Spaniards as the Cholulans brought them out of the city through a narrow and barricaded route.

The chroniclers and Cortés himself tell us that at this point, having received intelligence about the situation at hand from his allies and from the Cholulan priests, Cortés received confirmation of the details for a third time via Doña Marina. A noblewoman of the city urged her to save herself from certain death by coming over to the Cholulan side and being married on the spot to her son. Doña Marina pretended to go along with this suggestion, asked for details of the Cholulans' plans, and reported all to Cortés.

Cortés assembled the Cholulans in a walled plaza of the city and placed armed soldiers at the exit. There he confronted them and condemned them for treason. The Spaniards then fell upon the trapped Cholulans, and soon the Tlaxcalans arrived to take over the carnage. Cortés now summoned the ambassadors of Montezuma, showed them the price of resistance, and sent them back to their city-state with the scarcely veiled message that their city of Tenochtitlan was next.

Here lies the crux of the issue of Doña Marina as traitor. If we accept the accounts of the chroniclers, when given an opportunity to join the Cholulans against the Spaniards, she instead informed on the Cholulans. However, she was not herself a Cholulan, and moreover, according to the account of Bernal Díaz, the offered deal involved union with yet another man she did not know. And if it happened as the chronicles relate, how could she have known whether such an offer was trustworthy or simply a ruse on the part of the Cholulans to separate Cortés from his interpreter?

Having used Cholula to set a terrifying example to the citizens of Montezuma's Tenochtitlan and the other cities of Central Mexico, Cortés once again sent word that in spite of all Montezuma's bribes and his courteous excuses for not receiving them, the Spaniards were implacably on their way to his city. The route they took was up over the saddle between the volcanoes Popocatepetl and Iztaccihuatl, through pine country where the air is thin and cold. It is a place where exertion makes the lungs ache and where rest from exertion brings on chills. Moreover, Popocatepetl was in full eruption. In spite of the smoke and flames and the pumice raining down, some of the men had climbed to the crater's rim, and from there Tenochtitlan, Montezuma's great city in the middle of the lake, lay in sight.

According to Bernal Díaz, one road over the mountain pass had been blocked with felled trees, and another was swept clean and made inviting. Cortés, wary of intended ambush, chose the closed route. He ordered the tree trunks removed, "and some of them still lie by the roadside to this day," wrote the chronicler many years after the fact. The Nahuatl account of the same event says that the way was blocked not with tree trunks but with maguey plants that the Spaniards, oblivious to the dagger-sharp spines, just kicked aside.[14] Coming down the far slope, they set out toward the edge of the great lake that lay in the basin of the Valley of Mexico and the causeways that led over the water to Tenochtitlan. Still Montezuma's emissaries kept arriving with excuses, and finally Montezuma himself arrived, borne on a litter.

Doña Marina was at the side of Cortés as interpreter for this extraordinary meeting, the likes of which was not to be seen again.[15] Montezuma's speech to Cortés was elaborate, constructed according to his culture's rules of polite rhetoric. To be polite in Nahuatl, one says things very indirectly. In fact, one sometimes says quite the opposite of what one means.[16] To make sense of the words Montezuma addressed to Cortés, Doña Marina had to command an understanding of what was known in Nahuatl as "lordly speech." That she was competent to do so supports the chroniclers' assertions that she was a daughter of Nahuatl-speaking nobility. That she dared to address herself directly to Montezuma in order to translate for Cortés bespeaks raw courage, for none of his own courtiers "dared even to think of looking him in the face, but kept their eyes lowered with great reverence." If the Nahuatl text of this exchange that appears in the *Florentine Codex* is even remotely accurate, Doña Marina returned to Montezuma the speech of Cortés in a style utterly devoid of the special language of politeness. Never in his life would Montezuma have heard such a thing. And moreover, the Nahuatl account in the *Florentine Codex* reports that Cortés and his company stared frankly at the greatest lord of all and touched him with their hands. Bernal Díaz continues, "Those great Princes who accompanied Montezuma held back Cortés by the arm so that he should not embrace him, for they considered it an indignity."[17]

Perhaps Cortés and his men did not appreciate how they were assaulting the sensibilities of all around them, but Doña Marina knew full well, and yet she was not paralyzed by the terror her situation surely must have inspired. To bear up to the events of this day and the days that followed required nerves of steel. Cortés and his company indisputably possessed such nerve, but Doña Marina, sharing the language and culture of Montezuma, understood the enormity of it more than they could, and there is no record that she ever faltered.

The Spaniards and their retinue, including a Spanish woman who had come with them and the Indian women given to them along the way, began a tour of Tenochtitlan like none that would take place again. They looked with admiration on the gardens and canals and palaces at every side, the markets and the zoological gardens and the aviaries of exotic birds. Simultaneously they were appalled by the bloodied, skull-bedecked monuments of the Aztec religion.

They were given every sort of food and fragrant flower, and gifts were heaped before them. Thinking back on it later, Bernal Díaz wrote, "It was indeed wonderful, and, now that I am writing about it, it all comes before my eyes as though it had happened but yesterday. Coming to think it over it seems to be a great mercy that our Lord Jesus Christ was pleased to give us grace and courage to enter into such a city."[18] Cortés in his second letter to the king writes at great length about the city, giving an inventory of the goods sold in the market places and describing the temples and the figures within them, the palaces and the causeways. He concludes that despite the fact that the Aztecs are something quite different from decent Christians, their way of life otherwise compared favorably with that in Spain and was outstanding in its civic orderliness. This state of affairs was not to survive much longer.

If Montezuma imagined that by taking Cortés into his city, he would impress the Spaniards with their own vulnerability, he was mistaken. Although they were surrounded on all sides by crowds of people, in short order they simply took over. Cortés announced his desire to set up a cross and a chapel of the Virgin Mary on the pyramid temple of the Mexican gods Huitzilopochtli and Tlaloc, and he aggressively set about relaying through Doña Marina the message of Christian salvation to a less-than-receptive Montezuma.

Aztec hospitality soured, as their visitors took to knocking down walls in their quarters (thereby stumbling into a royal treasury) to put up a cross and altar for the celebration of Mass. The Spaniards were not being provisioned as generously as at first, and the Nahuatl account, complete with illustration, says that Doña Marina got up on a parapet and harangued the Aztecs, ordering them to bring food and fodder and criticizing their ill temper.[19]

To protect themselves, the Spaniards considered taking Montezuma hostage, and a report from the Veracruz coast gave them the pretext for doing so. Six Spaniards and a horse had been killed in an attack by

Montezuma's men, and the coastal cities had turned against the garrison he had left there. Cortés laid responsibility for the attack on Montezuma personally, and said that under the circumstances the ruler had to accompany him to the Spaniards' quarters. Montezuma offered yet more bribes and members of his family as hostages, but Doña Marina counseled him that if he did not cooperate, he was a dead man.

Despite Montezuma's captivity, his retinue continued to serve him, and he and the Spaniards passed time by playing a local game of chance, at which, according to Bernal Díaz, Pedro de Alvarado habitually cheated. The Spaniards built a sailboat and took their hostage out on the lake, far outdistancing his people in their canoes, yet another demonstration of Spanish power in the guise of entertainment. Cortés kept up his unnerving game, threatening Montezuma with death while simultaneously fawning over him through his interpreters, now assisted by a Spanish boy named Orteguilla who was picking up Nahuatl as quickly as Doña Marina was acquiring Spanish.

Montezuma turned over to Cortés the leaders of the Aztec attack on the Spaniards at Veracruz, and Cortés burned one of them alive, yet another grisly example of the consequences of resistance. Aztecs, Tlaxcalans, Totonacs, and their neighbors all participated in the burning of excised human hearts as part of their religious rituals, but the burning of a live human being from the feet up appalled them.

Unwilling to have combat take place within his city, Montezuma informed on the Texcocans, his allies in a city to the northeast, when they threatened to liberate Tenochtitlan from the Spaniards. Together Montezuma and Cortés managed to imprison the Texcocan nobles and install a ruler of their own choice. Finally Montezuma gave in and made a declaration of fealty to the Spanish king, in token of which he delivered a huge amount of luxury items.

Having effected this capitulation, Cortés turned to the issue of human sacrifice. In cities that had become allies, the Spaniards had prohibited it, but it had continued in Tenochtitlan. Now Cortés insisted it be stopped. Again he asked that a cross be put up and a chapel to the Virgin Mary be established at the great temple of Huitzilopochtli and Tlaloc, a demand met with stony resistance. The Spanish boy Orteguilla reported to Cortés that Montezuma, in great agitation, had said things to him in Nahuatl that he could not follow. Doña Marina confirmed that they would probably be attacked for this ultimate provocation. The boy's nerve broke, and he could not keep from crying.

The arrival of Spanish forces on the coast may have saved Cortés from immediate attack. Word came to Montezuma together with a painting of the new fleet, for his artists were busy again. This force, under the leadership of Pánfilo de Narvaez, had as interpreters three disgruntled soldiers of Cortés who had learned some Nahuatl. Through them Narvaez made it known that he was no friend of Cortés. Montezuma kept this information to himself, but when Cortés saw the painting, he suspected the intent of Narvaez. He and Doña Marina announced to Montezuma that Cortés would go to the coast to meet with his countrymen. Montezuma expressed great sadness that Cortés was leaving, but it was hardly necessary for Doña Marina to assure Cortés that the sentiment was feigned. What could have been more propitious than to have one Spanish force engage another, solving Montezuma's problem for him?

Leaving Alvarado in charge of Tenochtitlan, Cortés set out to deal with the challenge. Through spies and bribes, Cortés learned that Narvaez had caused considerable distress among the Totonacs. Attacking his rival, Cortés defeated Narvaez and took over his forces and ships. With that, he set out on the road back to Tenochtitlan with the new men and their supplies as reinforcements.

There were three consequences of this interlude, and their relative importance in the long run turned out to be quite different from how they may have appeared at the time. First, that Cortés now brought many more Spaniards to Tenochtitlan must have seemed to strengthen his position enormously, but this turned out not to be so.

The reason that their increased numbers were of no real significance has to do with the second consequence. During the absence of Cortés, Alvarado had launched an attack on celebrants at a religious ceremony, an attack much like the attack in Cholula, with people being hacked to pieces in a walled plaza. However, whereas the Cholula attack could be understood as a calculated piece of strategy to terrorize Montezuma, this attack served only to convince the residents of the occupied city that they had nothing left to lose.

Cortés, who had told the soldiers of Narvaez of the beautiful, populous, wealthy, and well-ordered city, found it nearly empty of its inhabitants. The markets were not operating, and there was a scarcity of fresh water. There were signs of insurrection on all sides. Spaniards were harrassed when they went out and about, and they were beseiged in their quarters. Bridges and causeways had been damaged to make retreat difficult.

Their position no longer tenable, Spaniards and their Tlaxcalan allies had to leave as best they could. Montezuma was thrust forward to negotiate the Spanish withdrawal and soon was dead. The Spaniards claimed he was killed by stones thrown by his own subjects, while indigenous accounts hold the Spaniards responsible for his death (which of course they ultimately were, no matter who actually struck the fatal blows).

The Spaniards attempted to leave the city under cover of darkness and rain. Their numbers were many, they had heavily laden horses, and it was impossible that their retreat should not be detected at once. Attacked, the withdrawal turned into total rout. Cortés, who had gone on ahead out of the city, turned back to help, but he could not accomplish much. The survivors were pursued by the Aztecs back to Tlaxcala where, in relative safety, they took stock of who had been lost and who had escaped.

Doña Marina, Doña Luisa, some of the brothers of Doña Luisa, and the Spanish woman, María de Estrada, had survived. Other Indian women accompanying the Spaniards, including daughters of the Tlaxcalan lords and of Montezuma, and the indigenous noblemen the Spaniards had tried to take with them as hostages, had perished. Elsewhere, other Spanish women who had accompanied the Narvaez forces were also killed during this week of bloody uproar.

Resting and recovering in Tlaxcala, the Spaniards and their allies began to lay plans for attacking Tenochtitlan over water in boats. Groups of Spaniards continued to arrive from the coast to augment the tattered forces of Cortés, and while the final assault was being devised, they occupied themselves with raiding around the central valleys, taking women, children, and goods from defeated towns. According to Bernal Díaz, a great deal of squabbling went on about the women, and a decision was made to sell them at auction with the best-looking going for the highest bids.

And now the third consequence of the Cortés-Narvaez contretemps. The men of Narvaez joining up as reinforcements of Cortés had been less advantageous than the Spaniards might have hoped, because by the time he brought them back to Tenochtitlan, things had gotten out of hand, and many of them died in the retreat. Had Cortés not left the city to begin with he would not have added them to his forces, but possibly he would have been able to prevent the insurrection that proved so lethal; thus it is likely that these two consequences canceled each other out. But the third consequence was smallpox, and, given just a little time, it proved a more powerful ally than armed men and horses. As Bernal Díaz, in hindsight, describes it, "Let us return now to Narvaez and a black man whom he brought covered with smallpox, and a very black affair it was for New Spain, for it was owing to him that the whole country was stricken and filled with it, from which there was great mortality." [20]

The Spaniards had been ejected from the city in the lake, but smallpox settled in. Montezuma had been replaced as ruler by a nobleman who very shortly died of it and was replaced by another nobleman, Cuauhtemoc ('He who descends like an eagle'). His fate was to survive both pestilence and defeat as the last Aztec ruler and then to die at the hands of Cortés. But it was not only in Tenochtitlan that smallpox took its toll, but on all sides, just as Bernal Díaz tells it. The peoples of Mexico, who had no experience of the disease, died at an appalling rate. Even as a water-borne attack on Tenochtitlan was being prepared from their city, the Tlaxcalans were beginning to die. When the Spaniards entered Texcoco, they met no resistance. Various other cities sent messages that they would give up the fight. Advised by Doña Marina and Aguilar, Cortés now sent a message to Cuauhtemoc that further resistance on his part would mean destruction of the city, and the Spaniards were true to their word. The boats were built, and desperate efforts to burn them failed. More and more neighboring towns capitulated. Many were found to be deserted. Combining cannon attack with blockade, the Spaniards closed in on the center of Tenochtitlan, blowing up and burning the margin as they came, pushing the people still remaining into the central temple enclosures. Aguilar and Doña Marina were on hand to interpret between Cortés and the allies who kept arriving from area cities to support his campaign of destruction.

Finally, with his city completely destroyed, Cuauhtemoc was seized by the Spaniards, and Cortés began again the same fatal sport he had taken with Montezuma. Calling Doña Marina and Aguilar to his aid, he spoke what seemed to be consoling and flattering words while affectionately embracing Cuauhtemoc and paying him every gesture of respect.

It was midsummer 1521. Tenochtitlan no longer existed. The beautiful city that had so impressed the Spaniards upon their first entry had been reduced to flooded rubble heaped with corpses. Work began immediately to level what was left and to build a Spanish city, Mexico City, in its place.

Doña Marina had survived. She had seen it all, been in the thick of everything, called on at any hour to interpret between Cortés and the most intimidating people one could imagine. She had not been taken prisoner and sacrificed at the top of a pyramid, as some of the Spaniards had been. She had not been killed in the flight from Tenochtitlan. She had not drowned in the lake. She had not died of smallpox. Now she was (or soon would be) pregnant by Cortés.

But Cortés had a wife in Cuba, and with the fighting over and a Spanish city coming into being, she came to join him in his palace at Coyoacan, south of the massive construction site. Doña Catalina Suárez arrived in August 1522. Before the end of the year she was dead, and Cortés was under suspicion of murdering her, although charges were not brought against him until seven years later, in 1529, after Doña Marina, too, was dead. Although there is much in the way of popular tradition, it is not in fact known how Cortés managed this difficult domestic aftermath of his victory over Tenochtitlan.

Nor do we know about the circumstances in which Doña Marina gave birth in 1522 and how she lived for the next two years. When not engaged in interpreting, she does not appear in the chronicles, but various sources tell us of people and events connected with her past life and her future.

María de Estrada, the Spanish woman who with Doña Marina had escaped from Tenochtitlan in the great rout, was already noted for her readiness to take up arms with the men. After the fall of Tenochtitlan, she participated in an attack on a mountain town in the foothills of Popocatepetl. Charging on horseback with lance in hand and shouting the war cry of Santiago, enemy of the heathen, she frightened the defenders out of their wits. In recognition of her valor, certified by Cortés, she and her husband were awarded a grant of Indian service there.

Back in Spain, Puertocarrero, the first Spaniard to whom Doña Marina had been given, died in prison, the victim of political intrigue. Another connection to her past: one of the conquerors, returning to the Tabasco coast, found Coatzacoalcos no longer friendly to Cortés. After some negotiations, he seized the city by force and captured the noblewoman who ruled it. In the not-so-distant future Doña Marina would pay the city a visit.

And on the very heels of the fall of Tenochtitlan, friars arrived to evangelize the peoples of what was now known as New Spain. First came three Flemish Franciscans, and nine months later they were joined by twelve more members of their order. The fate of two of these Franciscans was soon to be tragically entangled with those of Cortés, Doña Marina, and Cuauhtemoc.

And now began the last dramatic episode of Doña Marina's life, one that would, if Bernal Díaz is to be believed, reunite her with her relatives, carry her back into the land of the Maya, join her in legitimate matrimony with a Spanish husband, and after a year of brutal deprivations, send her pregnant in a ship back to Mexico City.

Cortés had sent his lieutenant, Cristóbal de Olid, to search for a strait through Panama to the Pacific. Instead, Olid used his provisions to set up an independent colony in Honduras. Having first sent emissaries to find out what Olid was up to, Cortés grew impatient and decided to head a punitive expedition of his own, taking Cuauhtemoc and other noble hostages along to guarantee his safety. Sentiment was against this risky and expensive project, and efforts were made to dissuade him from the undertaking, but Cortés was obdurate. (Unknown to him, Olid was already dead, and the expedition was, indeed, unnecessary.) Doña Marina was called to service as interpreter.

Two Flemish Franciscans also joined the expedition. Juan de Tecto left behind the Nahuatl catechism he was composing, and he never returned to finish it. A fellow countryman completed it for him, and eventually it was published both in Europe and in Mexico, while Juan de Tecto's bones rotted in a swamp.

Although the conventional way to Honduras was by sea to Cuba and then down the Caribbean coast of Yucatan (the course Olid had taken), Cortés was determined to make a land march through uncharted territory. The first destination on this route was Coatzacoalcos. Here let Bernal Díaz tell his story:

> When Cortés was in the town of Coatzacoalcos he sent to summon to his presence all the Caciques [rulers] of that province . . . and among the Caciques who assembled was the mother of Doña Marina and her half-brother, Lázaro.
>
> Some time before this Doña Marina had told me that she belonged to that province and that she was the mistress of vassals, and Cortés knew it well. . . . In such a manner it was that mother, daughter, and son came together, and it was easy enough to see that she was the daughter from the strong likeness she bore to her mother.
>
> These relations were in great fear of Doña Marina, for they thought she had sent for them to put them to death, and they were weeping.
>
> When Doña Marina saw them in tears, she consoled them and told them to have no fear, that when they had given her over to the men from Xicalango, they knew not what they were doing, and she forgave them for doing it, and she gave them many jewels of gold and raiment, and told them to return to their town, and said God had been very gracious to her in freeing her from the worship of idols and making her a Christian, and letting her bear a son to her lord and master Cortés and in marrying her to such a gentleman as Juan Jaramillo, who was now her husband. That she would rather serve her husband and Cortés than anything else in the world, and would not exchange her place to be Cacica of all the provinces in New Spain.[21]

Is this a true story or a sentimental fabrication of Bernal Díaz? Or some wishful thinking embroidered around a core of fact? Like all his writing, its fine detail has the appealing air of eyewitness reporting.

Doña Marina was newly married to Juan Jaramillo. The wedding had been performed as the expedition got under way. López de Gómara, the biographer of Cortés, claims that Jaramillo was drunk when the wedding took place and that Cortés was criticized for permitting it.[22] Bernal Díaz, with atypical brevity, merely mentions that the marriage of Doña Marina and Jaramillo took place. Scholars have speculated about the oddity of the place and timing of this union, but there is nothing in the original sources to enlighten us.

Beyond Coatzacoalcos, the lords of Tabasco and Xicalango provided a map showing an overland trading route all the way to Nicaragua. The expedition set out for the Chontal Maya land of Acalan, building bridges and mucking through swamps with their horses and pack animals and pigs along a route intended for canoes. There was quicksand. Men and animals drowned. Some towns were found deserted. Provisions were not readily available. Finally the towns of Acalan were reached and the first round of miseries were behind.

Doña Marina had assumed Aguilar's former position, interpreting for Cortés in Maya. But she also continued as Nahuatl interpreter, since Cortés had brought along Cuauhtemoc, other Aztec noblemen, and several thousand commoners from Mexico City to serve as bearers. In Acalan Cortés decided to execute Cuauhtemoc and two of his closest associates. Accounts differ on the details, but they generally agree that Cuauhtemoc, seeing how people were drowning and dying of hunger, had some hope of taking advantage of the Spaniards' disarray to lead a revolt against them and be done with them once and for all. López de Gómara repeats the account Cortés himself gave of the incident, that the plot was betrayed by one of Cuauhtemoc's men, who showed Cortés a piece of paper written in hieroglyphs revealing the plot. Bernal Díaz claims that two Aztec lords came forward to expose the conspiracy. The Chontals claimed that their ruler, Paxbolonacha of Acalan, personally warned Cortés of Cuauhtemoc's intention. And Don Fernando Cortés, seeking to maximize her role in the conquest, claimed that it was his grandmother, Doña Marina, who revealed the plot.

The Chontal account states that on the third day of the inquiry Cuauhtemoc was baptized before execution. With Marina assisting the Franciscans in commending their souls to God at the end, he was hanged with one or two associates, according to the Spanish sources. The Chontal claim he was beheaded.[23] In any case, Cortés had once again set a terrifying example. The Chontal Maya were properly frightened, and the rest of the people brought from Mexico City considered themselves lucky to get off with their lives. The several thousand bearers were so hungry and exhausted they posed no threat.

Before his execution, according to Bernal Díaz, Cuauhtemoc had reproached Cortés for all the expressions of friendship and respect Cortés had heaped upon him, when in fact Cortés had taken from him the chance of a decent death and instead led him through years of captivity and physical and spiritual torture to a degrading end far from home. Both Bernal Díaz and López de Gómara agree that Cortés was criticized for thus executing Cuauhtemoc.

And now the expedition set out again, this time toward the Itza Maya city of Tayasal. Like Tenochtitlan, Tayasal was a lake city far from any coast. It was so inaccessible that although they were visited by Cortés in the mid-1520s, its inhabitants did not surrender to the Spaniards until 1697. In the interim, in 1618, two Franciscan evangelists paid a visit and were appalled to find a stone idol of a horse at Tayasal. One of the friars smashed it to bits, to the outrage of their Maya hosts. Seeing that they were making no progress with conversion, the friars moved on.

The model for the idol, which the Maya called "thunder horse," was a lame animal Cortés left in the care of the Itza in 1525. He never returned for it, and after its death the Itza continued to faithfully attend to its image until the bad-tempered Franciscan destroyed it.

In Tayasal Doña Marina interpreted between Cortés and the local ruler, who bore the name Canek (as did successive Maya rulers). The fact that Chontal Maya and Itza Maya are sometimes considered separate languages seems to have posed no difficulties for her. In his report to the Spanish king, this is the only occasion on which Cortés refers to her by name. He says that Canek inquired whether Cortés might be the Spaniard who had passed through Tabasco six or seven years previously, and he told Canek that indeed he was, as Canek could confirm by asking "the interpreter with whom he was speaking, Marina, who traveled always in my company after she had been given me as a present with twenty other women. She then told him that what I had said was true and spoke to him of how I had conquered México and of all the other lands which I held subject and had placed beneath Your Majesty's command."[24]

Canek told Cortés that there were, indeed, Spaniards on the Caribbean coast, and that the easiest way for Cortés to reach them would be to go directly from Tayasal to the coast and then to proceed by boat, because the land route was over difficult terrain. But Cortés again rejected the idea of traveling by water, and the expedition continued its trek. The rainy season was at its height, and they trudged through deluges. The way became difficult with mountains and unfordable streams, and horses died in appalling numbers. Hunger, thirst, and relentless heat took their human toll as well. Towns emptied out at the news the Spaniards were coming, and it was hard to find provisions or guides.

Back in Mexico City the rumor had long since taken root that Cortés and Doña Marina had perished, and people claimed to have seen their ghosts burning in flames where the temple of Huitzilopochtli and Tlaloc had stood.

There was political turmoil among the Spaniards. But amidst all the misery, injury, and death in the rain forests, mountains, and savannas they passed through, Doña Marina, Cortés, and Jaramillo as well were once again survivors. Reaching the Caribbean coast, they learned that the insurrectionist Olid was long since dead.

Cortés purchased and reconditioned a ship that came by, and with it he explored along the coast, finding deserted towns, swampy river deltas, and clouds of mosquitos that gave no one rest. At one town that was inhabited, there was a noisy rally going on that worried the Spaniards. Doña Marina was sent to find out what it was all about and was told it was a celebration, but the Spaniards were suspicious and spent the night out in the pouring rain before attacking the town at dawn. Further along the coast of Honduras they came to towns where Nahuatl was spoken, and, according to López de Gómara, "the messengers were very glad to talk with Marina, because their language and that of the Mexicans are not very different, except in pronunciation."[25]

Now Cortés began sending invalids back by ship, carrying messages to Mexico City. Word returned to him from the city that he had better return immediately to put down the unrest there, and so he too returned by ship via Cuba, the easy route he had rejected on the outward leg of his journey.

Doña Marina was pregnant. Returning from the Honduras expedition in 1526 she gave birth to Jaramillo's daughter, who was baptized María. Apparently Doña Marina did not survive the birth by more than a year.

When she was grown and married, Doña María Jaramillo went to court to defend her right to land she claimed as the only child and heir of Doña Marina and Juan Jaramillo. In 1547, she testified that her mother had died twenty years before. It was her father's second wife, Doña Beatriz de Andrada, with whom Doña María and her husband were in contention over the land. Considerable testimony was given that agrees that Doña Marina had been dead for over twenty years and that Doña Beatriz had been married to Juan Jaramillo for almost as long.

The belief that Doña Marina had a long and prosperous life is sadly mistaken. The tradition that she accompanied Jaramillo to Spain and was a celebrity at court is baseless, as are reports of her still being alive in the 1530s. They seem to arise from a confusion with two other women sharing the same baptismal name: one a daughter or granddaughter of Montezuma and the other Doña Marina Gutiérrez de la Caballería. The latter, together with her children, were heirs to the estate of her husband, Alonso Estrada, in the 1530s, and official documents concerning this inheritance have been mistaken to refer to "Doña Marina, la lengua," the interpreter of Cortés.

Beyond the fact that she took part in all the extraordinary events of the conquest of Mexico and survived, there were not many rewards for Doña Marina. During her whole life she had been treated as disposable property. If we are to believe Bernal Díaz, it was her own mother who gave her to the people of Xicalango. They gave her to the Chontal Maya, who gave her to Cortés, who gave her to Puertocarrero. When Cortés observed her potential usefulness, he took her back and kept her for several years. Then he married her to Jaramillo. Although Octavio Paz writes, "It is true that she gave herself voluntarily to the conquistador,"[26] only in the last case is there a possibility that she might have had any choice in the matter, and there is no evidence either way. Nor is it likely she had any choice about sexual activity or bearing children, so it is just as well that she appeared to Bernal Díaz to be "without embarrassment."

She had no people and nowhere to flee. Her best hope of survival was to accept whatever situation was assigned to her and to try to make herself useful and agreeable, a strategy at which she already had practice among the Chontals. From the accounts of the Spanish chroniclers of the conquest, she was cheerful, sociable, ever willing to answer questions.

She worked hard. In addition to interpreting for Cortés, she also interpreted for the friars and taught others to interpret. In 1597 a daughter of one of the soldiers who accompanied Cortés claimed that in addition to everything else, Doña Marina tutored her father, Juan Pérez de Arteaga, in Nahuatl, so that he was the first of the Spaniards to understand it for himself.[27]

Above all else, she distinguished herself through absolute reliability from the unpredictable Indians the Spaniards met at every turn. There is no record of her ever giving Cortés and his company cause for distrust. As López de Gómara put it, "She and Aguilar were the only trustworthy interpeters between our men and those of the country."[28] Moreover, she is cited repeatedly as helping to uncover plots against Cortés and his company. In the testimony of her grandson, who sought to give the greatest possible amplitude to her services, this may be an exaggeration, but it is hard to see what Bernal Díaz stood to gain from according her so much credit.

As interpreter Doña Marina had a role unlike that of any of the many other indigenous women the expedition accumulated. It would seem that she succeeded to a remarkable degree in making herself one of the men.

Soon after reaching Yucatan, the Spaniards had captured two Maya men and tried to use them as interpreters, but one died and the other ran off. In any case neither had the competence of Aguilar. Cortés also had along a man captured on an earlier voyage who did not speak Maya, which meant that he could not communicate with Aguilar or anyone else in anything but the rudimentary Spanish that he had acquired. Doña Marina outshone all these men through her reliability and her multilingualism. The historian Fernando de Alva Ixtlilxochitl engages in hyperbole when he claims that she learned Spanish in the course of a "few days,"[29] but she did eventually—and a lucky thing that was for Cortés.

OVER THE CONTINENTAL DIVIDE:
Sacajawea (ca. 1790–1812 or 1884)

The two interpreters were George Drewyer and Toussaint Chaboneau [sic]. The wife [Sacajawea] of Chaboneau also accompanied us with her young child, and we hope may be useful as an interpreter among the Snake Indians. She was herself one of that tribe, but having been taken in war by the Minnetarees, she was sold as a slave to Chaboneau, who brought her up and afterward married her.
—*MERIWETHER LEWIS*[30]

Sacajawea was a Shoshone Indian woman who accompanied the Lewis and Clark expedition from the Missouri River over the Continental Divide and on to the Pacific coast in 1805. As the hundredth anniversary celebration of the expedition approached, she was memorialized as the intrepid guide of Lewis and Clark, the person who revealed to them the way through the mountain passes. She was made the heroine of a book about the expedition. Mountains and lakes were named for her. Statues of her were erected, and paintings done. Historical markers have been placed near her presumed birth and burial places, at the summit of the mountain pass she is said to have led the men through, and on the spot where she was believed to have been reunited with her own people.

She was held up as a patriotic heroine, and her biographer became president of the Sacajawea Statue Association. An appeal was made to American women's organizations for money, and they responded by selling buttons and spoons to raise funds for the sculptor's commission. This effort was especially significant for members of the National-American Woman's Suffrage Association, which held its 1905 annual meeting in Portland, Oregon, to coincide with the Lewis and Clark Centennial Exposition.

The Suffrage Association had grown out of an organization formed by Susan B. Anthony in the 1860s. Her address at the 1905 annual meeting was one of her last public appearances. The octogenarian feminist spoke of the statue unveiled in Portland as the first tangible recognition of the active role a woman could and did play in American exploration and discovery. Within a year Anthony died and was laid to rest.

In 1884 another very old woman had been found dead in her home. Her body was wrapped and sewn into skins and taken by horse to the cemetery of the Wind River Shoshone reservation, where a large gathering of people, Shoshones and others, attended her burial. In the mission register the deceased was identified by a recently arrived Welsh clergyman only as "Bazil's mother." Later, he and many others came to share the belief of the Wind River Shoshones that Bazil's mother was the very woman who had accompanied Lewis and Clark to the Portland area in 1805, fifteen years before the birth of Susan B. Anthony.

If this is so, the life of the suffragists' heroine and the life of their past president had overlapped for a sixty-four-year stretch of American history. Sacajawea had been an elderly woman taking part in community councils when Anthony, as a middle-aged woman, had organized the Suffrage Association. They had both led active lives in arenas traditionally closed to women and reached old age secure in the respect of their associates.

Yet the part of her life for which Sacajawea received recognition as a model for American women was not the part that paralleled Anthony's own. It was not as wise counselor and coequal with male elders for which she was honored but as guide for Lewis and Clark, a role she did not choose and for which she did not receive much reward.

Officially she was not guide but only the Indian wife of the expedition's Canadian French interpreter Toussaint Charbonneau, and not his only wife at that. Charbonneau had arrived at the expedition's base camp with two adolescent Shoshone wives, one with a toddler and the younger one in the last weeks of pregnancy. On February 11, 1805, after difficult labor, Sacajawea gave birth to a son. Before he was quite two months old, she started the trek west with the baby strapped to his cradle board on her back. Her co-wife and the toddler, who was undoubtedly too heavy to carry and too young to hike, were left behind.

The Shoshone girls had not become Charbonneau's wives by choice. Lewis described the two women as "prisoners from the Rock [Rocky] mountains, purchased by Chaboneau."[31] As they traveled west, Sacajawea identified a place where the expedition made camp as the spot where five years before she and other Shoshones had been pursued and taken captive in an attack by Minnetaree Indians.[32] Lewis was struck by the unemotional way in which she described her capture, remarking, "She seems to possess the folly or the philosophy of not suffering her feelings to extend beyond the anxiety of having plenty to eat and a few trinkets to wear."[33] After a while she had been passed, as a piece of property bought or won, from the Minnetarees to Charbonneau, who over the years demonstrated an unquenchable taste for very young Indian women, marrying many as he had Sacajawea and her co-wife.

In 1805 Sacajawea's life was not her own. When she became part of the expedition, she was an enslaved pregnant adolescent, not what would come to mind as the ideal role model for young American womanhood. When it was over, she was still Charbonneau's property and further bound to him because he was the father of her son. Like Doña Marina, she coped with her inescapable situation by being cheerful, cooperative, and an untiring worker. At the outset Lewis seemed to take this as constitutional indifference, the sort of thing that set primitive peoples apart from more refined white folk, but later he was to change his mind about Sacajawea and to some extent about Indians in general. On the return trip east they were importuned to treat a chronically ill man, and Lewis observed, "This strong evidence of feeling is directly opposed to the received opinion of the insensibility of savages, nor are we less struck by the kindness and attention paid to the sick man by those who are unconnected with him; which is the more surprising, as the long illness of three years might be supposed to have exhausted their sympathy."[34]

Lewis and Clark were painstaking scientists. They measured, recorded, and identified everything they came across, sending back maps and physical samples of everything imaginable to support their written observations. Yet they were also men of their times. Throughout their journals they intersperse their descriptions with ethnocentric commentary on the indigenous peoples they met on their travels. After pages of details about clothing, ornaments, and hairstyles of men and women of the Pacific coast communities, Lewis remarks, "Nor have we seen any more disgusting object than a Chinnook or Clatsop beauty in full attire. Their broad, flat foreheads, their falling breasts, their ill-shaped limbs, the awkwardness of their positions, and the filth which intrudes through their finery—all these render a Chinnook or Clatsop beauty, in full attire, one of the most disgusting objects in nature."[35]

They were hardly more charitable to men, and they dismissed whole ethnic groups as filthy, unreliable, and sneaky. On the return trip, tired and worn down by malnutrition, they began to threaten uncooperative Indians with beatings and executions. But despite their determination to shoot if provoked, in the course of the whole year they killed just one Indian outright and wounded another in a fight when some of their weapons were stolen. They executed no one.

As for sexual use of women along the way, Lewis and Clark could not keep the men of their expedition from consorting with Indian women, although they would have preferred that the men remain abstinent for the year. The peoples of the Pacific coast had been in touch with traders and crews of ships for some time, and venereal disease was already present and spreading. It disabled one or two of the expedition's men. Lewis credited the poor diet on which they all existed over the winter of 1805–6 for protecting them from worse ravages. They were simply too weak and hungry to be predatory about women.

Such sexual activity as there was seems to have arisen from Indian practices of hospitality and from enterprise on the part of women themselves. Lewis and Clark did not accept women and distribute them among the men, and they did not record any instances of the forcible taking of women by the men under their command. The Lewis and Clark expedition was quite a different thing from that of Cortés in Mexico, although the end result—the dispossession of indigenous peoples and their decimation through infectious disease—was, sadly, much the same.

Lewis wrote that Indian women were treated as property and that women themselves sometimes had only their own bodies as assets. He felt the station of Indian women was miserable, a condemnation to drudgery and abuse. Yet he also observed that certain women in the Shoshone communities he visited were held in high respect (as, according to later Shoshone tradition, Sacajawea herself was). He concluded that in general, the more women contributed to the community economy, the better they were treated, while in communities where they were considered a burden, their treatment was likely to be cruel and exploitive.

If Lewis and Clark could be scathing in their descriptions of Indians, they were equally generous with contempt toward Charbonneau, whom they abused repeatedly in their journals. Even before they set out, they noted that he tried unsuccessfully to negotiate an arrangement whereby he was not under their orders. Once underway he was criticized for incompetent boatsmanship, for being careless about his wife's health, as a craven coward who left it to Clark to rescue his wife and baby from a flash flood, and as a wife beater. He seems to have been the all-occasion scapegoat and whipping boy of the expedition. Nonetheless, he stayed with Lewis and Clark to the end, and when they parted in the summer of 1806, they paid him his wages, offered to take him to St. Louis, and allowed that "this man has been very serviceable to us."[36]

As the members of the expedition set out in boats up the Missouri River, they took along provisions, medicine, scientific equipment, books, gun powder and lead for shot, spare parts, writing desks, a violin, a large dog, and a great load of goods to give as presents to Indians or to use in trade with them. Among the things they had for the Indians were tailored coats, bandanna handkerchiefs, knives and hachets, looking glasses, beads, flags, and medals bearing the likeness of President Thomas Jefferson, the patron of the expedition. All along the way Lewis and Clark dispensed the medals and flags while extolling the virtues of their president and country. They explained that the purpose of their exploration was to find the best way to transport merchandise through the territory and to provide the local people with whatever they might need.

The uniform jackets, woven cloth, steel blades, mirrors, and beads were attractive to the Indians, but they had another motive for cooperation as well. As in Mesoamerica, so too in North America some of the peoples saw the newcomers as potential help against their local enemies. Already familiar with firearms but poorly equipped, they hoped soon to be able to buy guns and ammunition. Lewis and Clark did not say that this was an impossibility, but they consigned arms trading to some indefinite time in the future. In the meantime, they gave medals as tokens of alliance. Once the leader of a Cheyenne community tried to return his to Clark on the grounds that he and his people were afraid of anything that white people gave to Indians. His prescience was to no end. Clark talked him into keeping the medal and, won around by Clark's assurances, he requested that traders come to the Cheyennes.

On the one occasion when they killed an Indian, Lewis and Clark took back the flag they had given to his group, but they left around the dead man's neck the medal they had given to him so that other Indians seeing it "might be informed of who we were."[37] Compared to the terrorism practiced by Cortés, this was mild business. But in the grand scheme of things, the prospects for Indian groups to form strategic alliances with whomever it was that Lewis and Clark represented (someone obviously powerful and rich), combined with the expedition's ready supply of exotic goods, put the expedition in the same sort of charmed circle that had protected Cortés and his forces in a land where they were greatly outnumbered and dependent on local people for provisions and protection.

In both cases the people perceived monolithically as "Indians" were in fact many different groups without a sense of unity against the newly arrived whites. This was crucial to the survival and success of the expeditions. So too their flags and Jefferson medals and their call to Indian leaders to become friends of the government in Washington must have seemed as strange to the peoples of the Northwest as did the message of cross and crown to the peoples of Mesoamerica nearly three centuries before.

And like Cortés, Lewis and Clark had an Indian woman with them. One of Sacajawea's biographers remarks more than once that her presence with an infant clearly signified that the expedition was not a war party and that this was as important as anything she did in the way of guiding them.[38] But this view of things gives her too little credit, for although she was not acknowledged in the roster as an equal partner with the interpreters George Drouillard and Charbonneau (and at expedition's end was not paid for her services, either), she performed crucial translation tasks from the very outset, and, what is more, she kept everyone from starvation during a very difficult year. There were countless encounters with grizzlies, and the expedition sometimes seemed more likely to be eaten by mosquitoes than by the bears. But the greatest threat and the most constant companion of the explorers was unremitting hunger.

The men all hunted and fished, but they were no more consistently successful in this than Shoshone men had ever been. Sacajawea knew the Shoshone woman's skills of collecting roots and berries. Many of the edibles that she located and prepared were unknown to the men she fed, and they would never have struck upon them on their own. She not only collected plants as they grew but also knew how to locate the underground caches of small animals that had already done the work of collecting the food; Sacajawea simply dug it up. She cracked animal bones and extracted nourishing marrow, and, although it was repulsive to her, she cooked dog and horse meat for the men. One of the deliciously scandalous stories the old woman on the Wind River reservation told many years later was of feeding white men dog meat.

Finding enough to eat was a struggle through all the sixteen months it took to cross to the Pacific coast and return again to the Missouri. The other dangers were sudden and over in a matter of moments, almost before anyone could grasp what was happening. It took quick wits to evade charging bears and striking rattlesnakes. In one of the early near-disasters, Charbonneau lost control of the rudder of one of the boats. The boat was swamped, and the boxes and bales stowed on it began drifting away. In the chaos of men trying to keep the boat from capsizing altogether while shouting abuse at Charbonneau, Sacajawea is given credit for retrieving what washed overboard. Two days later, with things dried out and repacked, they were on their way again.

A little over a month later, they learned about flash floods. Clark often walked on shore with Charbonneau and Sacajawea. On a summer's day at the very end of June, he and the two of them, accompanied by his servant York, set out on such a walk. Sacajawea, as ever, carried her baby on his cradle board. When a storm came up, they took shelter from the rain in a ravine. The rain turned to downpour, and suddenly the ravine was filled with rushing water, mud, and tumbling boulders. They clambered up and out to safety, Charbonneau pulling Sacajawea, and Clark pushing them all from behind. Clark managed to hang on to his gun with one hand while pushing with the other. Charbonneau lost his gun, and the baby's cradle board and bindings were torn away, but the baby himself remained safe in his mother's arms. A moment later all of them would have been washed away and drowned. York, who had not gone into the ravine with them, found them drenched and shaken.

Between these two near brushes with drowning, Sacajawea had survived another threat to her life. Early in June she had become desperately sick, and the course of the infection, whatever it was, lasted two full weeks. Lewis and Clark treated the illness by bleeding her, laying on poultices, and having her drink some sort of bark tea. When things seemed to get only worse, Lewis resorted to opium. The situation was critical not only for her but for the baby, who at four months was entirely dependent on breastfeeding. With no wet nurse on hand to help, his mother's death would have meant death for the child as well.

Lewis had a further concern, noting that Sacajawea was "our only dependence for a friendly negociation with the Snake Indians, upon whom we depend for horses to assist us in our portage from the Missouri to the Columbia River."[39] The illness ran its course, and Sacajawea appeared to be on the mend. She was able to eat nourishing food again and to get up, but before she was pronounced completely recovered, she had a relapse for which Charbonneau was blamed. Less than a week later, she was on foot, carrying her baby for herself, and keeping up with the men when they were caught in the storm that nearly drowned them.

Lewis himself had been ill and had been doctoring himself with chokecherry bark, and around this time others also fell ill. Yet the expedition moved onwards, their leaders making and writing up observations, often in lyrical prose. In mid-June Lewis wrote that he had seen "one of the most beautiful objects in nature."[40] They had reached the great falls of the Missouri River. Above the falls, they were in country abundant with buffalo and prickly pear cactus. For the moment there was plentiful meat. On the other hand, everyone was footsore and busy sewing double soles onto their moccasins for protection.

Through the month of July and on into August they traveled southwest, hoping to meet Shoshones in a land so empty that they met absolutely no one. Only with horses could they continue to carry everything they had brought with them, and they depended on finding horses with the Shoshones.

At the end of the first week of August Sacajawea recognized a land-mark and assured the men that her people were not far away. Lewis took three companions and struck out in the direction in which she said the Shoshones might be found. The Missouri River was now more of a brook. They found an Indian road up into the mountains and began to encounter fresh hoof prints and to see Indians from a distance. The road crested the Continental Divide and brought them among the Shoshones.

The first people they met were an old woman and a little girl. Saca-jawea was not there to interpret, but she had instructed them to carry red paint with them to paint the cheeks of people they met. This was under-stood as a sign of peaceful intention, and Lewis and his men were led to the main group of Shoshones. One of the men who accompanied Lewis was competent in the sign language used in the area and interpreted for Lewis while they awaited Clark, Sacajawea, and the rest of the expedition.

The main leader of the Shoshone group was a young man named Cameahwait. Through the sign interpreter, Lewis attempted to convey to him that the rest of the expedition was coming with a Shoshone woman to speak for them. After some days Lewis managed to get the Shoshones to accompany him back in the direction from which he had come, in order to hasten the meeting. Two days later the groups met. Sacajawea had been walking out ahead of Clark when she dropped all reserve and began to gesture joyfully. She was immediately recognized by a woman who had also been a captive of the Minnetarees for a while, and there was general rejoicing at her return.

But according to Lewis and Clark's *History of the Expedition*, an even more emotionally charged reunion was to take place. Sacajawea was called away from her friends to begin work. Lewis and Clark were already smoking with Cameahwait when Sacajawea joined them, sat down, and began to interpret. Looking up at the man she was addressing in Shoshone and realizing that it was her brother, "she instantly jumped up, and ran and embraced him, throwing over him her blanket, and weeping profusely. The chief was himself moved, although not in the same degree. After some conversation between them she resumed her seat and attempted to inter-pret for us; but her new situation seemed to overpower her, and she was frequently interrupted by her tears."[41]

So much for the perception that Sacajawea was a simple little woman whose passions were limited to her daily bread and a bit of adornment. What Lewis and Clark had seen before was the mask of a woman practic-ing day-to-day survival. Here they saw what separation from her com-munity had meant to her.

Returned to the Shoshone, she found her brother in mourning and learned that most of her immediate relatives were dead. Left with two brothers and an orphaned nephew, she declared herself responsible for the boy, although she could not take him along with the expedition to the coast.

Her open-hearted joy may have been met with less reciprocity than she expected. Her brother was more reserved than she at first meeting, and a week later Sacajawea warned Charbonneau, who tardily passed the information along to Lewis and Clark, that Cameahwait was about to depart and leave them stranded without horses for the trip west. Lewis summoned him and demanded to know why he planned to go back on his word to sell horses to the expedition and help carry their goods over the mountains. Cameahwait accepted full blame and once again pledged himself to the original agreement. By informing on him, Sacajawea had clearly identified her own best interests with the expedition rather than with the surviving fragments of her family.[42]

One of her biographers writes, "Although she doubtless could have stayed with the Shoshonis, she chose to remain with Charbonneau and the expedition."[43] Perhaps this is, after all, open to some doubt. Added to the coolness of her powerful brother, another experience may have convinced her that she could not rejoin her people. Lewis writes:

> The infant daughters are often betrothed by the father to men who are grown, either for themselves or for their sons, for whom they are desirous of providing wives. The compensation to the father is usually made in horses or mules; and the girl remains with her parents until the age of puberty, which is thirteen or fourteen, when she is surrendered to her husband. . . . Sacajawea had been contracted for in this way before she was taken prisoner, and when we brought her back her betrothed was still living. Although he was double the age of Sacajawea and had two other wives, he claimed her; but on finding that she had a child by her new husband, Chaboneau, he relinquished his pretensions and said he did not want her.[44]

When they purchased horses for the overland part of the journey, they gave Charbonneau the means to acquire one for Sacajawea to ride. For two weeks the horse dealing went on and preliminary explorations were made, while in the evenings the men of the expedition entertained the Indians by dancing figures to the music of the violin. At the beginning of September the Shoshones and the expedition parted ways, the Indians going to hunt buffalo for their winter store of meat, and Lewis and Clark seeking to get through the mountains before winter weather set in. It was a difficult trip made more difficult by insufficient food and by early snow. Yet they managed to cross the Rocky Mountains with all their baggage and come down on the western side among the Nez Perce Indians.

The Nez Perces were initially frightened by the bearded men's appearance, but they overcame their anxiety and were helpful and cooperative, offering food of various sorts. The hungry men welcomed whatever they could get, but the local root diet apparently disagreed with them, because many suffered incapacitating intestinal cramps. Nonetheless, by early October they had managed to build new boats and load up for the downstream trip to the Pacific. They buried some things to be picked up on the return trip, and they left their surviving horses in the care of the Nez Perces.

And so the journey continued, Lewis and Clark handing out medals and flags to everyone they met and the men entertaining with violin music and square dancing. Early in November they portaged around the falls of the Columbia River and met the incoming tide from the Pacific.

They built Fort Clatsop, their winter camp up a small river from a bay. During December they built cabins surrounded by a palisade, and there they waited out a northwest Pacific winter—four months of steady rain. The men were often on the coast itself, exploring and hoping to meet a ship. A coastal station was set up and several men were put to work there evaporating seawater to supply the expedition with salt, an activity that kept them occupied where they could watch for sails. To their disappointment, none came.

Time hung heavy during this damp and gloomy period. They passed their time in visiting with local people, who were already accustomed to dealing with traders and ships' crews. There were gambling parties, and prostitutes arrived, one with the name "J. Bowman" tattooed on her arm. How long-standing the contact between seamen and the coastal Indians had been became evident when Lewis and Clark encountered among the Clatsops a red-haired, freckled man already about twenty-five years old, who clearly had been fathered by a white man.

Commerce in services, provisions, robes, and sea otter pelts was an occupation in which the coastal Indians had long experience. They held back part of their merchandise, sought high prices, and sometimes would not trade at all. The expedition's trading wares were not so exotic to them as they had been to the people of the interior, and the blue beads most prized in trading had already been expended. Because the Indians were not interested at all in selling to members of the Lewis and Clark expedition any of their highly valued sea otter skins, these furs came to represent an irresistible challenge. Lewis and Clark engaged repeatedly in efforts to buy some but only succeeded once, when they traded Sacajawea's own belt of blue beads for a beautiful sea otter robe.

The robe was not for Sacajawea. Lewis and Clark compensated her for her belt with a blue cloth coat. Apparently she harbored no hard feelings toward Clark, because she made him two rather significant presents. Joining in the Fort Clatsop Christmas gift giving, she gave him two dozen white weasel tails. On another occasion she presented him with a piece of bread she had been carrying for months with the intention of giving it to her baby when he was old enough to take solid food. The bread had gotten wet and probably was not fit for the baby, but Clark willingly ate it and was grateful.

Early in January some Indians arrived with food for sale. They brought the usual roots and berries and three dogs. The prospect of eating dog, once unappealing, was now welcomed by the meat-hungry men. But even more interesting was that the traders brought some blubber from a whale that was beached down the coast. Assured by the Indians that it was excellent food, they cooked and ate it and found it comparable to both pork fat and beaver. They immediately decided to go see the remains of the whale itself and to try to buy some more blubber.

At this point Sacajawea spoke up for herself. Lewis writes, "As soon as this resolution was known, Chaboneau and his wife requested that they be permitted to accompany us. The poor woman stated very earnestly that she had traveled a great way with us to see the great water, yet she had never been down to the coast, and now that this monstrous fish was also to be seen, it seemed hard that she should be permitted to see neither the ocean nor the whale. So reasonable a request could not be denied; they were therefore suffered to accompany captain Clark."[45] After three days of walking, the group reached the whale to find it already stripped to its skeleton, which Lewis and Clark reported to be 105 feet long. (Decades later, the old woman on the Wind River reservation told stories of this monstrous fish to the Shoshones who, utterly ignorant of whales, did not take her seriously.) In nearby villages everyone was engaged in boiling oil out of the blubber. No one was anxious to sell it, and the expedition had to settle for less of it than they wanted and at what they considered an exorbitant price.

Much of the food that the members of the expedition ate while at Fort Clatsop did not agree with them. Their meat went bad, and a diet of dried fish rehydrated with salty water was blamed for the prevalent diarrhea among them. There was also the misery of unremitting respiratory infections, and they were bedeviled in their cabins by fleas. They gave up all hope of contacting any ships and turned their minds to retracing the route by which they had come. As soon as there were some signs of spring in late March, they closed Fort Clatsop and headed back upstream toward the mountains.

All along Clark had been doctoring himself and treating illness in the expedition's members. The reputation of his practice had spread and many Indians came to him for help. The weakness and malnutrition of wintering over swamped him with patients and slowed the progress of the return trip to the Nez Perce area where they hoped to acquire horses. One of the places they stopped was at the mouth of the Walla Walla River where they received a warm welcome even before they began to look after the sick.

Among the people there they met a Shoshone woman prisoner. Sacajawea explained the purpose of the expedition to her, and the prisoner in turn translated the message for her captors. According to a later description of the details of such an interpreting chain, "It was not without difficulty . . . that we were able to convey all this information . . . much of which might have been lost or distorted in its circuitous route through a variety of languages; for in the first place, we spoke in English to one of our men, who translated it into French to Chaboneau; he interpreted it to his wife in the Minnetaree language; she then put it into Shoshone, and the young Shoshone prisoner explained it to the Chopunnish in their own dialect."[46]

One evening there was an exchange of entertainment, the men first dancing to the violin for the Indians and the Indians then singing and dancing for them. Clark's treatment of Indian patients earned them much good will and the gift of several good horses. Leaving the Walla Walla, they soon located the Nez Perces just as a May storm of wind-driven snow and hail descended on them. As it turned out, earlier arrival at the mountains would have been pointless, because the spring melt had not yet taken place.

While there was a positive side to Clark's practice of rudimentary medicine, it was also exhausting for everyone to have to deal every day with so many importunate people, people whose intentions were not always clear. Nerves wore thin. In April for the first time Lewis had beaten an Indian caught stealing from the camp. He addressed all the Indians present and warned them that he had it in his power to fight them, kill them, and burn their houses. A couple of weeks later a derisive Indian, observing the white men eating dog meat, threw a puppy at Lewis. Lewis lost his temper, slammed the puppy back in the Indian's face, and threatened him with his tomahawk.

Nonetheless, there was hardly an alternative but to continue to try to help all comers and to play the violin and dance. The most common complaints about which Indians consulted Clark were sore eyes and skin diseases. Clark did not have much confidence in his remedies and tried to give to the Indians things that would at any rate not be harmful, such as "eye water" and liniment. He was sparing in his administration of opium to Indians, thereby reserving the small supply of it for emergencies among members of the expedition.

Another patient they were treating was Sacajawea's child. He was now fifteen months old, no longer an infant, at an age of cutting teeth, eating solid food, and learning to walk. He must have been much heavier to carry than on the outbound trip, harder to keep still, problematical to feed. In late May he was stricken with a sore throat, swollen salivary glands, high fever, and diarrhea. The illness lasted more than two weeks and probably subsided in spite of rather than because of the cream of tartar, sulphur, resin, beeswax, bear oil, and hot onion poultices Clark applied to him.

The child was named Jean Baptiste, but the pet name used for him on the expedition was Pomp. One of Sacajawea's biographers claims that Pomp is a Shoshone word for "first-born,"[47] but Pompey is a name that was often patronizingly given to African slaves in the late eighteenth and nineteenth centuries. Clark named a rock formation on the Yellowstone River "Pompey's Pillar" in honor of the child.[48] There is no way to know for sure, but the nickname Pomp may have been as unthinkingly racist as if they had called the baby Sambo.

With the baby well again and the snow now melting away, the expedition followed the Indian road back up and through the first range of mountains. Then it was decided that the group would divide. Lewis would take some men to explore a short northern route back to the falls of the Missouri, while Clark, accompanied by the rest of the men, Charbonneau, Sacajawea, and her baby, would retrace the route they had taken west the previous summer, then cut across to the Yellowstone River and follow it up to the Missouri. With good luck, they would rendezvous with Lewis where the rivers meet.

Once the groups had parted, Sacajawea came into her own as guide. The Indian road they had been following petered out, but she was in familiar childhood surroundings. She led them across the plain to a place where they could see a gap. From the top of the gap, she told them that their next landmark would be a snowy mountain. In two days, following her directions, they reached the place where the previous year they had cached goods and canoes. Some days later, faced with two gaps to choose from, Clark accepted Sacajawea's advice to take the southerly one, and they passed through it into the valley of the Yellowstone.

Now they built new boats and sent off their remaining horses to be traded to the Mandan Indians in the area. Sailing down the Yellowstone, they came to a prominent rock, the vertical faces of its cliff carved with petroglyphs. On the top, accessible from only one direction, there were rock cairns. Clark went up for the view and added his name and the date—July 25, 1806—to the inscriptions. This was the formation he named Pompey's Pillar.

A week later the boats reached the confluence of the Yellowstone and the Missouri, and they set up camp where they had been in late April the year before. Unfortunately, the mosquitos, which had not been in evidence on an April day, proved unbearable in August. Leaving a note for Lewis, they proceeded downriver, fleeing the insects. Sacajawea's child's face was puffed and swollen from their bites, and no one could sleep or work or hunt.

It took another nine days for Lewis's party to catch up with them. Lewis hadn't gotten the note, but his party had come on downstream anyway. Lewis lay wounded in the bottom of one of their boats, the victim of a hunting accident the previous day.

At this point the expedition was really over. They made a triumphal cruise down the Missouri, greeted by crowds of Indians who had seen them off in 1805. There were meetings with chiefs along the way, with Clark carrying on the ritual tobacco smoking while Lewis recovered from his wound. Discussions were held in which the president of the U.S. was referred to as the Great Father and the Indians as his red children, whose chiefs should travel with Lewis and Clark to Washington "to hear in person the counsels of their Great Father, who can at all times protect those who open their ears to his counsels, and punish his enemies."[49] The chiefs of the various groups all expressed their deep desire to visit Washington but made excuses for not doing so.

Since no Minnetarees could be prevailed upon to make the trip to Washington, Charbonneau asked to be paid off and released from service. He was no longer needed as interpreter and he preferred to remain among the Indians. On August 17 Lewis wrote, "This man has been very serviceable to us, and his wife was particularly useful among the Shoshones. Indeed, she has borne with a patience truly admirable the fatigues of so long a route, encumbered with the charge of an infant, who is even now only 19 months old. We therefore paid Chaboneau his wages, amounting to $500.33, including the price of a horse and a lodge purchased of him."[50]

That might have been the last ever heard of Sacajawea and her child, except that Clark wanted the little boy for himself. On the day they paid off Charbonneau, Clark—with his idiosyncratic spelling and punctuation—wrote in his journal: "I offered to take his little son a butifull promising Child who is 19 months old to which both himself & his wife wer willing provided the child had been weened. they observed that in one year the boy would be Sufficiently old to leave his mother & he would then take him to me if I would be so freindly as to raise the Child for him in Such a manner as I thought proper, to which I agreed, &c." [51]

Clark then left for St. Louis, but Harold Howard quotes a letter he wrote to Charbonneau from downriver three days later in which he acknowledges the value of Sacajawea's services and expresses regret that they had not rewarded her adequately. He writes, "As to your little son (my boy Pomp) you will know my fondness for him and my anxiety to take and raise him as my own child. I once more tell you if you will bring your son, Baptiste, to me, I will educate him and treat him as my own child." He then goes on to offer to set Charbonneau up as a farmer or to become a partner with him in a trading venture. In any case, he says, if Charbonneau would accept, his wife "had best come along with you to take care of the boy until I get him." He closes the letter: "Wishing you and your family great success, and with anxious expectations of seeing my little dancing boy, Baptiste, I will remain your friend." [52]

And here Sacajawea's history bifurcates. In the tragic version she lived only six years more, dying miserably at twenty-five of "putrid fever" at a riotous trading outpost—apparently in the absence of Charbonneau—leaving a baby girl to the compassion of the trading company's clerk.

Charbonneau, who had refused to accompany Lewis and Clark to St. Louis because he felt he had no way of earning a living there, had apparently changed his mind. In 1807 the government awarded each of the men under the command of Lewis and Clark, including Charbonneau, 320 acres of land. In the fall of 1810 he bought some more land from Clark on the Missouri River near St. Louis. Then after a few months, he sold it back to Clark, bought supplies, and set out upriver with an Indian wife and an official of the Missouri Fur Company. Henry Brackenridge was a passenger on the same river boat and wrote of Charbonneau and his Shoshone wife, saying that they had both accompanied Lewis and Clark to the Pacific and that the woman was now sickly and anxious to revisit her "native country." The next we hear of a wife of Charbonneau is on December 12, 1812, from John Luttig, clerk at Fort Manuel, a trading station far up the Missouri. He wrote that Charbonneau's Shoshone wife, a woman about twenty-five years old, had died at the fort, leaving an infant daughter.

The fort was abandoned late in February, and Luttig went to St. Louis, where he applied to be appointed guardian for two children of Toussaint Charbonneau: a baby girl named Lizette and a ten-year-old boy named Toussaint. The father was said to be deceased. In August 1813 the court issued a document granting this guardianship, but Luttig's name is crossed out and William Clark's written in its place.

Sometime between 1825 and 1828 Clark made a list of the members of the expedition and their subsequent fates. He recorded Sacajawea as dead. The name of Toussaint Charbonneau, who had not, after all, been dead, is followed by the cryptic abbreviation "Mand," which has been interpreted to mean that he was once more living among the Mandan Indians, where he had lived in the past.

Clark really did get Sacajawea's son for himself. There are recorded payments by Clark on behalf of "J. B. Charbonneau" for educational expenses in St. Louis. But apparently the boy subsequently returned to his father. In 1823 the young Prince Paul of Württemberg, touring up the Missouri, met Jean Baptiste in the company of Toussaint Charbonneau and prevailed upon him to go to Germany with him. Upon his return six years later Baptiste—now proficient in German as well as French, English, and one or more Indian languages—became a guide for other visiting royalty and traders. Throughout the 1830s there are notices of this polyglot man who had been to the Pacific coast with his parents and Lewis and Clark. At least once the story was garbled, and he was identified as Clark's own son. Notices continued through the 1840s, and the death of a person believed to be the same Jean Baptiste Charbonneau was reported in the 1860s.

But there are inconsistencies in this version of events that have fueled debates throughout most of the twentieth century. Charbonneau was a polygamist. He had left behind a Shoshone wife and her child when he and Sacajawea and Jean Baptiste set out with Lewis and Clark. Did he find them and take them back after Lewis and Clark paid him off and departed? We don't know the name of this woman's child, and neither Brackenridge nor Luttig gives the name of the Shoshone wife of Charbonneau. Brackenridge says that the sickly woman he met was the woman who went with Charbonneau to the Pacific coast, but to some investigators involved in the controversy it has seemed unrealistic that Charbonneau would really take an ailing Sacajawea all the way back to Shoshone country.

It is natural to assume that the wife of Charbonneau who was in failing health in the spring of 1811 is the same woman who died a year and a half later. But the unnamed Shoshone woman who died in December 1812 had recently given birth. Luttig identified Charbonneau as the father but believed him to be dead. Had Charbonneau taken Sacajawea to St. Louis and back to Indian country, then impregnated and been separated from her? It is possible. But it is also possible that more than one Shoshone wife is involved in this series of events.

All bets are off as to what we might consider appropriate behavior. For instance, we might think that Charbonneau would be too embarrassed to turn up in St. Louis with two Indian wives or with some wife other than Sacajawea, especially in view of Clark's specific invitation to him to come with Sacajawea and Jean Baptiste. But from Clark's journal entry and his letter to Charbonneau it is clear that it was the boy Clark wanted, at practically any cost. He was not concerned with keeping mother and child together. In 1806 he wanted the baby and could wait a year until he was weaned. If they came earlier, Sacajawea could care for Jean Baptiste "until I get him." Under the circumstances it may not have made much difference to Clark what woman or women accompanied Charbonneau then or later, so long as the child was delivered to him.

None of this would matter much if it were not for the second history of Sacajawea. The Shoshones said that the woman who was buried on the Wind River reservation told of having been married to a Frenchman and accompanying white men to the Pacific, of feeding them dog and horse meat, and of seeing seals and an impossibly big fish. In retrospect the Shoshones were certain that the old woman was Sacajawea. Not only were there the convincing details of her stories, but moreover the Shoshones told of a collection of important government papers and a large silver Jefferson medal that she had in her possession. Sometimes she wore the medal, and other times one or the other of her sons did.

The woman thought to be Sacajawea had settled at Wind River in 1871 with a son named Bazil, and after a while they were joined by another son, Baptiste. There they finished out their lives together. She died in 1884, Baptiste the following year, and Bazil the year after that. The important papers were buried with Bazil.

Bazil's body was exhumed by a Dartmouth-educated Sioux named Charles Eastman. Eastman was a physician by training, but bureaucratic infighting had prevented him from practicing medicine among the Sioux. That he spoke to them in their own language had made him an effective physician, but it evoked deep suspicion in Indian agents who did not speak the language of the people on their agencies. Time after time Eastman was accused of troublemaking. After decades of frustration, he finally concluded his sporadic association with the Bureau of Indian Affairs by serving as an inspector, traveling to sites where trouble had already been made in order to ascertain the facts and report them back to Washington.

One piece of trouble had to do with the conflicting stories of Sacajawea's life subsequent to the Lewis and Clark expedition. A proposal had been made to erect a statue commemorating her death at Wind River. Historians who believed that she had died in 1812 objected vociferously. Eastman took on the task of investigating the conflicting stories, beginning on New Year's Day 1925, and submitting a report three months later. In the meantime, he had taken testimony from Shoshones, Comanches, and

Minnetarees in three states. He consulted material provided to him by Grace Hebard, the woman who wished to have the statue put up, and also interviewed her opponents. Working from the interviews he had conducted, Eastman concluded that the woman who died on the Wind River reservation was Sacajawea, although this did not satisfy the people who thought she was not.

Piecing together the oral tradition assembled by Eastman and Hebard, how did Sacajawea pass her life from 1806 until she arrived at Wind River in 1871? The Minnetarees said that Charbonneau took both his Shoshone wives with him to St. Louis a year or so after the expedition ended. Around 1820 Charbonneau took a Minnetaree girl from among them to be his wife and set off back to St. Louis. After a while Sacajawea was discovered to be living at a nearby town with two sons, Bazil and Baptiste. Charbonneau combined his two families and they all lived and traveled together for a while, passing among Wichitaws, Comanches, and Utes.

From the Utes Charbonneau took yet another wife. This led to an argument between him and Sacajawea. He beat her and she left. Bazil and Baptiste were away at the time and did not see her again for years. The group continued traveling, but the Ute woman eventually went off with some of her relatives. By a circuit northwards and then down the Missouri, Charbonneau and his remaining wife returned to Minnetaree country where he continued to acquire and lose women. Charbonneau was getting old and feeble, and sometime after 1839 he died, a man in his eighties.

Sacajawea, in the meantime, had come to rest among the Comanches, assumed the name of Porivo, and married a man by whom she had five children and eventually grandchildren. But widowed and grief-stricken, she had left the Comanches. They assumed that she was dead until Comanche and Shoshone children met at an Indian boarding school, compared stories, and concluded that the grandmother of some of the Comanches was the great-grandmother of one of the Shoshones.

For some years she lived as a transient, catching free rides with stages and eating at stage stations. According to the tradition, she returned to the Nez Perces, whom she had met in the company of Lewis and Clark, and lived with them for a time, and she also visited the Blackfeet and the Bannock Indians. One of the interviewees said that during this time she was greatly respected by whites and given food and money everywhere she went. By the mid-1860s she had settled near a station named Fort Bridger, and it was common knowledge among whites and Indians in the area that she had been on an expedition with white men.

There were Shoshones in the area, and two of the interpreters at Fort Bridger were Bazil and Baptiste, who interpreted between English, French,

Shoshone, and other Indian languages as well. By 1868 they had been reunited with their mother after a long separation.

The occasion that fixes Sacajawea/Porivo at Fort Bridger in 1868 was a meeting called by the Shoshone leader Chief Washakie with officials from Washington. She was recalled as having assumed equal standing with the men in speaking before the Shoshone council. The subject was clearer definition of Shoshone territory, which was suffering incursions of other groups of Indians and of the white settlers and traders that these Indians were trying to move away from.

Definition of borders alone did not settle the problem of population pressure, and over the next four years Washakie requested United States army protection. The reservation soon had a local police force, a reservation agent, a white Supervisor of Agriculture, and log-cabin housing. Bazil and his mother moved into one of the new houses and provided interpreting services to the agent. Eventually Baptiste joined them.

To the Shoshones the old woman was now known mainly as Bazil's mother. People agreed that she had come from among the Comanches, and to some people she told stories of much earlier times, of the expedition with the white men, the eating of dog flesh and horse meat, the Pacific coast and the whale skeleton. Many people told of her medal and the papers. She was also credited for personally introducing the Sun Dance to the northern Shoshones, and her grandson was leader of the dance at the time Eastman conducted his interviews. Eastman had written about the Sioux version of this dance, and he had considerable personal interest in the information that it had been introduced to the Shoshones by a woman.

The only thing left to do was to find out what the papers buried with Bazil said. Bazil's son directed Eastman to his father's burial place and gave permission for exhumation. The body was there with the leather pouch containing the letters, but the documents that might have settled the controversy, having lain buried for nearly forty years, were too decayed to be read. Bazil's remains were reinterred next to those of his mother in the Shoshone cemetery. In 1963 a chapter of the Daughters of the American Revolution placed a marker at the cemetery stating that the woman buried there was Sacajawea and that she had died in 1884.

And so we are left with the two histories. According to one, Sacajawea, like Doña Marina, did not long survive her adventure with a company of white men. In the other she is the toughest of survivors. Most of the people who subscribe to the idea that she died young are white men, while many of the people who are attached to the idea that she lived a very long life and died in dignity among her people have been women and Indians.[53]

It is easy to understand the emotional investment shared by American women and Indians in the oral tradition's depiction of long life and public service. It is less obvious why passions should run high on the other side. The librarian of the Missouri Historical Society (a woman) felt that a historical marker on the grave at Wind River would be a "travesty," [54] and Harold Howard quotes Will G. Robinson of the South Dakota State Historical Society: "I, for one, am much better pleased with a feeling that this truly great woman died at Ft. Manuel . . . rather than try to follow the vague and nebulous wanderings of a woman who had many husbands, followed the hard life of a drudge among the fur traders and died wholly unrecognized." [55]

The opposing views find their places in two biographies of Sacajawea written in the 1970s. Howard says of the people who knew firsthand the woman on the Wind River reservation, "The sincerity of the people who interviewed her has never been questioned, but they may have been gullible." [56] He suggests that some other wife of Charbonneau may have appropriated Sacajawea's stories for herself. Moreover, he discredits the interviews conducted by Eastman and Hebard on the grounds that "the Indians had no written language and could only report their recollections orally." [57] Finally, he concurs with Robinson that it is more pleasing to think that Sacajawea died young, saying ambiguously of Robinson's statement, "Certainly this seems a reasonable conclusion." [58] (Which conclusion, one might ask: Robinson's conclusion drawn from the evidence, or an appropriate way for Sacajawea's life to conclude?)

Ella Clark and Margot Edmonds, writing a few years after Howard, take the opposite view. They point out that tribal historians are trained to accomplish phenomenal feats of memorization and that interviews with people who had known the woman thought to be Sacajawea were carried out in languages comfortable to the interviewees and often certified by community interpreters. [59]

All of Sacajawea's most recent biographers have to twist and turn around the contradictions, inconsistencies, and unanswered questions within both the written and the oral records. Who was Bazil, for instance? Was he the nephew Sacajawea adopted when first reunited with the remnants of her family on the westbound leg of the Lewis and Clark expedition? Was he the son of her Shoshone co-wife who was left behind when the expedition set out? Was Jean Baptiste sometimes called "Toussaint" or was that his older half-brother? Did the elder Toussaint misrepresent another Shoshone wife as the one who had been with him to the Pacific? Did another Shoshone woman assume Sacajawea's identity after Sacajawea died? Nothing can make all the pieces fit together.

What Lewis and Clark tell us about Sacajawea in their expedition notes is the most authentic window we have on the woman. But we encounter her there through their eyes, and they were men of their times. Their unquestioned sense of superiority to Indians is evident in everything they wrote, including their wry references to Clatsop "beauties" and Chinook "damsels." They habitually referred to Sacajawea as "the squaw," and although they came to admire her fortitude and usefulness, they would undoubtedly have found very strange the romance and sentimentality written into early twentieth-century accounts of her. In their own telling of her request to see the coast and the whale, there is an unmistakable implication of servitude. They make it clear that she could only do so with their permission, and that it was generosity on their part to let her come along.

In his journal note at the end of the expedition and in his subsequent letter to Charbonneau, Clark directs his request for Sacajawea's child to the child's father and refers to the baby with an easy sense of possession as "my boy Pomp." Charles Eastman, writing in 1925, rejected the idea that Sacajawea could have been induced to leave behind a five-year-old Jean Baptiste in St. Louis to make the trip upriver where Brackenridge met Charbonneau with a Shoshone wife. In his report he wrote, "She could not have permitted (herself) to be separated from her child of that age." [60] But how realistic is it to imagine that she could have refused to give her child up to Clark or insisted on remaining with him after he was weaned?

From the point of view of Clark's contemporaries there were two societies, Indian and white. Charbonneau had gone over to the Indians and become a squaw-man. If Jean Baptiste were to remain with Charbonneau and Sacajawea, he would grow up no different from the freckled redhead they met on the Pacific coast who "was in habits and manners perfectly Indian." [61] Clark, who had lost his heart to the child, wanted to save him from this fate, which to Clark could not have appeared to be anything other than a life of degradation. The only way to prevent this was to get the child away from his parents before he was ruined.

In the course of their long trek Lewis and Clark had perceived Sacajawea first and always as an Indian woman. They registered that she was cheerful, hard-working, and useful, and otherwise they seem to have taken her mostly for granted. Weeks went by when they made no mention of her in their journals. Mainly they noticed when she did something unexpected. A few days before they traded away her belt of blue beads, Clark remarked of the usually agreeable Sacajawea, "Squar displeased with me." [62] In January 1806 they recorded in full her heartfelt complaint that she had been kept from seeing the ocean she had walked so far to get to. And they kept up a running commentary on her condition during the week when it seemed that she might die before she could serve them in horse-trading with the Shoshones.

But the most telling vignette is the moment on the westward trek when "Captain Clark saw Sacajawea, who was with her husband 100 yards ahead, begin to dance and show every mark of the most extravagant joy, turning round to him and pointing to several Indians, whom he now saw advancing on horseback, sucking her fingers at the same time, to indicate that they were of her native tribe."[63] This is the first expression of open emotion attributed to Sacajawea. She acted as though she had wakened from a long, dark dream.

In mid-August 1805 began a week that opened in that joy and perhaps ended in disillusionment. There were Shoshone women who welcomed her back, but it was men who held her fate. Her brother was cool toward her, and her intended husband no longer wanted her. At this point she may have realized that she had no choice but to continue with Charbonneau and the expedition. Months later, when she and the Shoshone woman captive met beside the Walla Walla, they did their interpreting business and moved on. There is no suggestion of joy or comfort in their meeting. The emotional attraction of the Shoshone oral tradition is that Sacajawea finally did reunite with her people many decades later when she was no longer in servitude to a French husband, a company of white explorers, and a nursing infant.

Once the Lewis and Clark journals close, we cannot be sure whether the glimpses we catch of Shoshone women accompanying Charbonneau are of Sacajawea. The woman Brackenridge met with Charbonneau was "a good creature of mild and gentle disposition."[64] Of the woman who died the next year, Luttig wrote that she was "the best woman in the fort."[65]

The deceased woman Luttig praised cannot be the same woman who grew old on the Wind River reservation, but the descriptions are much the same. The elderly woman was described by people who had known her as "a good-natured woman, always jolly," a "smart and active woman," "very bright and gay," multilingual, and an excellent rider despite her age.[66]

She was also remembered as a consistent advocate of the policies of white government and a person liked and respected by white people. She was credited with having been of great help in negotiations at Fort Bridger. Her medal and documents, said to have been presented to her by great white chiefs, gave her high status in frontier society.

Perhaps Sacajawea separated from Charbonneau, grew old, success-fully rejoined the Shoshones after many adventures, died among her people, and was buried at Wind River. Or she died very young, and some other Shoshone woman assumed her identity, spreading her stories widely among the Comanches, the Minnetarees, and the Nez Perces, as well as among her own people.

Long before, people had called both Doña Marina and Cortés "Mal-intzin," not separating the identity of the man from the woman who interpreted for him. In an analogous way, "Sacajawea" could have both died in 1812 and lived until 1884. People with a narrow view of history would dislike such a scenario muddling the clean course of documented evidence, and for them putting up a memorial to an impostor would indeed be a travesty. For others more sympathetic to oral history and the sacred role of impersonation among Indians of North America it is a rather lovely notion: that another gifted woman may have rescued Sacajawea's stories, perpetuated them, and lived for her the life she might have had.

FROM THE GREAT BASIN TO THE HALLS OF CONGRESS: *Sarah Winnemucca (1844–1891)*

Sir I am the daughter of the Chief of the Piutes I am living at Camp McDermit and have been in this employ of the U.S. Government for nearly three years as interpreter and guide I have the honor to be, Sir, your

MOST OBEDIENT SERVANT
SARAH WINNEMUCCA [67]

Sarah Winnemucca was a celebrity equally at home before audiences in San Francisco theaters and New England churches. Her autobiography, edited by Horace Mann's widow, was published in Boston and New York in 1883. She was well known on the East Coast lecture circuit, and she twice met with presidents of the United States. From her letters we can see that, contrary to what her contemporaries sometimes claimed, she wrote with a clear hand and a mastery of English spelling and punctuation that was a good deal better than average and much better than that of William Clark. In the photography studios that sprang up in the years after the Civil War, she had publicity and family pictures made that show us what she and her associates looked like. We can read published testi-monials to her good reputation as well as affidavits of pure character assassination from her enemies, respectful newspaper interviews and disparaging reviews of her theatrical appearances. We know the names of her relatives, how long she lived, and the date, place, and circumstances of her death. Thanks to the prolific writing of the nineteenth century, we can know Sarah Winnemucca as a person on much more intimate terms than Doña Marina or Sacajawea.

Her eventful life can be related in three parts. During the first part, which lasted until her mid-teens, she was deeply influenced by her grandfather. Because of him, Sarah entered the world of white society and learned to speak, read, and write English. His death and the refusal of a California school to continue her education marked the end of this period. From that point until Sarah was nearly forty, her life centered around her work as interpreter at the Indian agencies and army camps of Nevada, Oregon, and Washington. In 1883 began the final period, when the Bostonian sisters Mary Mann and Elizabeth Palmer Peabody made it possible for Sarah to lecture in the cities of the East Coast, lobby in Washington on behalf of her people, and establish a school for Paiute children in Nevada.

She was born around 1844 in Nevada, received a Paiute name meaning 'Shell-flower', and lived out the rest of the 1840s with her parents, entirely among the Paiutes. In her autobiography she recalls fearing white people long before her first encounter with them. Once, panicked by rumors that whites were killing Indians, her mother and other Paiutes fled, leaving Sarah and another child buried up to their necks in sand and covered over with brush. The next day the adults returned to rescue the children, but the trauma was indelible.

While her parents and the other people with whom they lived were terrified of the white people streaming into their area, Sarah's grandfather had a long positive association with them. He had served as a guide for the first settlers crossing the Great Basin on their way to the Pacific coast and had taken the English name Captain Truckee. When Sarah was an infant, her grandfather was away with the United States army fighting against the Mexicans in California.

So began a three-generation family enterprise of guiding and interpreting, although Sarah's father, Chief Winnemucca, was less enthusiastic about the work than his father or his children. Unlike Sarah, her brother Natchez, and her half-brother Lee Winnemucca, who all worked for the army, he spent much of his life trying to avoid white people.

Captain Truckee and the Winnemuccas were influential within their community, although Chief Winnemucca was probably not the undisputed top authority over all Paiutes, as Sarah claimed to her audiences. She knew that white people thought in terms of great chiefs and Indian princesses and took care to give them what they expected when she was seeking their sympathy and support.

Captain Truckee died when Sarah was in her mid-teens, and later she wrote of his central importance in her life and of her belief that he was the key to the Paiutes' coexistence with whites. Saying that she perceived his death as a light going out and the world growing cold, she concluded, "I was only a simple child, yet I knew what a great man he was. I mean great in principle. I knew how necessary it was for our good that he should live. . . . And now, after long years of toil and trouble, I think if our great Father had seen fit to call me with him, I could have died with a better opinion of the human race."[68]

Sarah's allegiance to her grandfather's principles had taken time to develop, however. When he came back from the army at the end of the 1840s, he was on a recruiting trip to take Paiute families to California to work on the ranches of white settlers. He claimed that the white people were their kindly brothers to whom the Paiutes owed generosity. In return they could acquire many good things from them. Certainly his blue cloth uniform jacket with brass buttons and the gun he was carrying were impressive, and the opportunity to acquire horses was more attractive still. Yet Sarah recalled sharing her parents' suspicion of white men, whose strange whiskered faces and light eyes seemed as terrifying to the Paiutes as they had to the Nez Perces when the men of the Lewis and Clark expedition first appeared among them.

Captain Truckee managed to convince some families to go with him, while the rest of the Paiutes went about collecting their traditional foods and storing them for winter. Like their relatives the Shoshones, the Paiutes lived largely on roots, seeds, and berries collected by the women. (A derogatory name the whites used for Indians who lived this way was "Diggers.") The women dug camas bulbs and other roots and shelled pine nuts from piñon trees. To these staple foods the men added game from the mountains and fish from the rivers and lakes of the area. This sort of subsistence could support a thin population distributed over a wide area, but it required constant migration from digging fields to piñon groves to fishing waters and mountain forests. When the men went to hunt and fish by themselves, the women, children, and old people were left alone and vulnerable.

Their food stores were vulnerable too, because they cached their roots, nuts, and dried fish unattended, to use when everyone came together in their winter camps. At about the time Captain Truckee was making his California recruitment trips, a white expedition wantonly destroyed a winter food cache. Information reached the Paiutes that these same people were subsequently trapped by snow in the mountain passes and resorted to cannibalism in the last weeks before all perished, confirming the Paiutes' suspicions about the appalling nature of white people.

Around 1850, Sarah began a decade of close contact with white people, during which she mastered English and learned some Spanish as well. She received a little schooling, and learned to read and write. These skills that she acquired between the ages of about six and sixteen years old served her well in her future work as interpreter, lecturer, lobbyist, and writer. She also became comfortable with other aspects of white culture of the mid-1800s. She rode sidesaddle, went to square dances, learned dressmaking, and became skilled in making ladies' hats and gloves. On people who met her then she made an impression of intelligence and vivacity.

Her experience with white people had not begun auspiciously. It was at the height of the California gold rush that Captain Truckee returned to the Paiutes to take Sarah's mother and her children to work in California, and they departed with very little protection. Sarah's father, who had two wives and two sets of children, let them go and stayed behind with his other family.

In her autobiography Sarah portrays herself in a state of sustained terror during the journey to the world of the white people, crying, hiding, and bitterly blaming her grandfather for what he was doing to them. When he reproved her and told her not to be afraid, she says, "I told him that they looked so very bad to me I could not help it."[69]

Upon first meeting with white settlers, Sarah's brothers and sisters were given sugar, a practice she repeatedly mentions in her autobiography. Virtually everywhere the first act of white contact with Indians was the giving of sugar, especially to Indian children. Indians often suspected that what seemed at first a novel treat was in fact poison employed by the white people against them, and they were not so mistaken. Paiutes had been fond of sweet plant sap, but it was whites who addicted them to white sugar just as surely as they introduced them to alcohol. Sugar was offered for comforting children, treating the sick, and easing the misery of the dying. When cavalry soldiers found an abandoned Indian baby after a skirmish, Sarah reports that they fed her sugar, water, and gingersnaps. It is no wonder that as an adult woman Sarah would complain that her starving people were being deprived of sugar and coffee, although it was meat and flour that would have saved their lives.

The sugar that the whites gave to her brothers and sisters distracted young Sarah from her tantrums. At Stockton, California, she began to take an interest in the wonders of a town with multistory buildings and a steamboat. And then it seemed that sugar brought disaster upon her. Her brother shared some cake with her, and soon after, she was prostrated by violent fever and chills and a face so swollen that she could not open her eyes. Her mother told Captain Truckee in her hearing that the child had been poisoned by the cake and was going to die. According to Sarah, he pointed out that they had all shared the cake, and that if it were poisoned, they would all be dying. This is the first of several stories she tells in which her grandfather offers logical arguments against Paiute suspicions.

As it turned out, being stricken soon after eating the sugary cake was coincidental. The swelling with fever was a severe case of poison ivy. A white woman tended her through the misery, and this experience with a gentle, compassionate person won Sarah around to her grandfather's optimistic view of white society.

The Winnemuccas were placed for work at a ranch, and the adult men went off to herd cattle, leaving mother and children to learn the domestic skills of cooking, cleaning, and sewing for a white establishment. As soon as the Winnemucca men had gone, the white men on the ranch tried to carry off Sarah's older sister Mary, and the owners had to move mother and daughters into the ranch house for their protection. Sarah's mother wanted to take her children and leave, but travel was too dangerous. Living indoors, Sarah became fascinated with the furnishings of white households.

After the work season Captain Truckee's group returned to Nevada, where there had been an epidemic among the Paiutes. Again they suspected that the whites were poisoning them, and again Captain Truckee intervened with a logical refutation, pointing out in this case that if the whites had poisoned the river, the whites as well as the Paiutes would be dying.

Striving to instill in the Paiutes army-style patriotism, Captain Truckee had taught them to sing the U.S. national anthem. Later, at a tense moment when troops were conferring with the Paiutes, the soldiers' commanding officer assembled his men and said, "We will sing the Star-spangled Banner." Sarah comments in her autobiography, "It was not a bit like the way my grandfather used to sing it, and that was the first time I had heard it sung by the white people."[70]

This surprise became a model for many of Sarah's future experiences. White people rarely turned out to be what her grandfather had said they were, seldom were what they represented themselves to be, and almost never did what they claimed they were going to do. Sarah's acquired irony about Christian morality and civilization became a major unifying thread running through her lectures and writing.

After the first season on the ranch Sarah continued to work as a child domestic for white families in California, acquiring at some point her Christian name as well as her language skills. She had contact with Catholicism, Mormonism, and Methodism and as an adult considered herself a Methodist, although she also retained respect for the traditional Paiute religion.

In 1857, at the age of about thirteen, she was sent with her younger sister Elma to live with the family of Major William Ormsby on the Nevada side of the mountains. The Paiute girls, separated from their mother and other relatives, kept house for the Ormsbys, worked in the their business enterprises, and were companions for their nine-year-old daughter. Prominent members of the local community visited constantly at the Ormsby home, where Sarah could observe them and interact with them. This seems to have been a happy time for her and was probably when she acquired her white social skills and all the schooling she was ever to get.

Frederick Dodge, the first United States Indian agent for the area, was a frequent visitor to the Ormsby establishment. He made a report on the area Paiutes, giving the number in each group and the name of their leader. At this time Sarah began representing her father as the leader of all of them and continued to claim ever after that he was the chief of the Paiutes. Dodge found that settlers had invaded the traditional Paiute lands and requested a reservation at Pyramid Lake as a refuge from the latest immigrant influx.

As silver-ore discoveries in Nevada brought in a new flood of whites, Chief Winnemucca called Sarah, Elma, and Natchez to him. A traveler who met fifteen-year-old Sarah at this time of transition found her "highly intelligent and educated" and fluent in English.[71] Her commanding intelligence, commented on by many others who met her in the years that followed, together with the education and the manners she had acquired in white households and her ferocious tenacity of will, were the resources with which she now began a life of adult responsibility.

The 1850s were ending in conflict. The Paiutes had suffered through difficult winters with a diminished food supply, sharing their fisheries with Bannock Indians who had been forced off their hunting grounds. There was debate in the Paiute councils about whether to switch over to agriculture or to try to withdraw farther from the white settlers and to continue traditional life, even though it meant abandonment of places sacred to the Paiutes.

News of yet another offense against the Paiutes disrupted the deliberations. Two girls had been found confined in a cellar. The Paiutes killed the white men who lived in the house and burned it to the ground. Settlers in the area believed that this was the beginning of an Indian uprising, and Major Ormsby, whom Sarah described as "our dear good friend,"[72] led a force of white men to put it down. Sarah's cousin Young Winnemucca led the Paiute resistance, and in an ambush Ormsby was killed. Sarah had lost her white home forever.

The Paiutes retreated into the mountains, and a fort was built on what they considered their land. In negotiations about going to Pyramid Lake, Young Winnemucca pointed out that northern California Indians had been put on a reservation, not provisioned, and then massacred for stealing cattle. Nonetheless, Chief Winnemucca was convinced to come back, a treaty was made, and the reservation established.

It was in October of 1860, during the pine nut gathering season, that Captain Truckee died, and Sarah, deprived of both her Paiute grandfather and her white foster father, perceived the world growing dark and hopeless. Her grandfather had made a dying request that Sarah and Elma be taken back to California to be educated by the nuns at the Academy of Notre Dame in San Jose, but the parents of white students at the school objected, and the girls were sent away almost as soon as they arrived.

The first governor of the Nevada Territory, appointed by Abraham Lincoln in 1861, visited the new Pyramid Lake reservation, where Chief Winnemucca ceremonially received him. The celebration was capped by a dance in which soldiers and Paiutes took part together, much in the same spirit as the men of the Lewis and Clark expedition dancing with their Indian hosts by the Walla Walla River. This was the precursor of many theatrical events featuring Sarah's father that would be staged in years to come.

Finding white settlers illegally on the reservation, the governor ordered them off, but this action proved ineffective, and other disasters befell the subsistence economy of the Paiutes as well. A stage road had been put through the reservation, and the piñon trees on which they depended were cut down. Chief Winnemucca and Natchez denied rumors of unrest among the neighboring Bannocks, but the traditional food sources of both the Paiutes and the Bannocks were disappearing, and the United States government was not providing anything in their place.

In 1864 Chief Winnemucca, his daughters Sarah and Elma, and some of his men made a series of stage appearances, hoping to raise money for relief of the Paiutes at Pyramid Lake. Their first booking was at a music hall in Virginia City, Nevada. Before the performances, they rode through the streets of town, Chief Winnemucca in epaulets and feathers. Then, with Sarah interpreting for him, he addressed the crowd that gathered.

The gist of what he had to say was that the Bannocks had asked him to join his people with theirs against the whites, but he steadfastly refused to do that. Then the hat was passed for contributions for the Paiutes, and Sarah gave a newspaper interview.

The troupe then moved on to a theater in San Francisco, where they once again rode through the streets before performances. A newspaper review of their stage program described it in three parts. First a white man read a lecture about Indian life, probably written by Sarah with white popular sensibilities in mind. The second part was a series of Indian dances and tableaux about Indian life, and the third part was the address by Chief Winnemucca interpreted by Sarah. Despite the generally deprecatory tone of his article, the reviewer was impressed by Sarah's English.

This effort on the part of Sarah and her father was not particularly successful; after expenses had been met, not much cash was left for the benefit of the Paiutes. But it was the beginning of Sarah's lifelong career of making emotional public appeals on behalf of her people.

Sarah and her father were absent when a troop of cavalry made a quixotic attack on the Winnemuccas the next year. There were only women, old men, and children at the encampment when the soldiers destroyed it. Sarah's baby brother was killed, her older sister Mary the only person to escape to tell what had happened. Then or soon after Sarah's mother and Mary both died.

Sarah had now lost grandfather, mother, sister, and brother, and she withdrew entirely from white society to live with her brother Natchez at Pyramid Lake. A detractor who wrote about her during this period described her with unwashed face and matted, uncombed hair, as though that were a moral failing on her part. But she was in mourning, and she might have looked a great deal worse; in her autobiography she describes Paiute mourning practices that included hacking off the hair and making long cuts through the skin to produce copious bleeding.

Sarah's father, stricken by the murder of his infant son, once again went off into the mountains and was not seen for a long time. Elma took another escape route. First joining a white family in California, she soon married a white man and settled with him in Idaho. She never returned to the Paiutes.

Conditions had become insupportable. Whites attacked Indians wherever they encountered them. It was not safe to leave the reservation, but on the reservation there was relentless hunger, since there were no provisions from outside. Settlers ran their cattle onto Indian lands, trampling the digging fields. A sawmill to provide boards for building houses on the reservation was promised but never delivered. Land was taken for a railroad right of way, and the squatters who had been evicted by the governor had returned.

Sarah and Natchez took it upon themselves to head off violence, making frantic nighttime rides between one faction and another and enlisting the aid of the cavalry (under a different captain from the one who had led the massacre at the Winnemucca camp). The commanding officer, finding the Paiutes starved and unprovisioned, rebuked the reservation's agent and distributed food. He asked Sarah about her father's whereabouts and pointed out that it was dangerous for him to be off in the mountains. Settlers were continuing to harass, pursue, and kill Paiutes.

In 1868 Sarah and her brother went to work for the army. Natchez was paid five dollars a day to go with the cavalry to find his father. Sarah was engaged for sixty-five dollars a month to serve as interpreter at Camp McDermit. The fact that the Paiutes at the army camp were well clothed and fed convinced Sarah and Natchez to try to get their father to join them in order to avoid conflict with other whites who were dealing with Paiute groups very harshly.

Chief Winnemucca came to the camp with close to 500 Paiutes, and the army provided clothing to them. When the chief encouraged his people to remain at least partially self-sufficient by supplementing their army rations with game, the army gave ammunition to the Paiutes for hunting.

Army discipline must have been as alien to most of the Paiutes as anything they had yet met with among the whites, but Sarah, the daughter of the old army scout Captain Truckee, took to it with enthusiasm. The army issued canvas tents to the Indians and provided daily rations before dawn. As Sarah describes it, "Each woman came to me each day with her basket, and her number on a tag, fastened to a leather thong around her neck, and told me the size of her family and took what she needed from me; and everything was recorded, for that is the way things are done in soldiers' camps."[73] This sounds chillingly like refugee camps of our century, and it is hard to appreciate Sarah's enthusiasm, but she concludes, "It is this generosity and this kind care and order and discipline that make me like the care of the army for my people."

It was a situation in which no one could escape criticism. In her autobiography Sarah acknowledges that some Paiutes resented the alliance of the Winnemuccas with the army: "It is said that I am working in the interest of the army. . . . It is not so; but they know more about the Indians than any citizens do, and are always friendly."[74] On the other hand, the white settlers were vociferously critical of the army's humanitarian treatment of the Indians.

At the same time that Paiutes were gathering in the army camps, the ones at Pyramid Lake began drifting off because of hunger and disease there. The railroad had now been built across what had been part of the reservation, and the Paiutes took to the rails as the Shoshone tradition says Sacajawea did. Trains had replaced horses as the means of Indian mobility, but the trains only took the Indians between white towns, with their alcohol and card games and racism.

After the Civil War, military men replaced civilian Indian agents for a time. The new Nevada superintendent of Indians contacted Camp McDermit with questions about the Paiutes. Sarah responded in a letter critical of the reservation system, arguing that Indians needed allotments of land and protection from whites in order to become farmers. Her letter was forwarded on to the Commissioner of Indian Affairs in Washington, D.C., where it was circulated and published. This was the beginning of Sarah's national celebrity and elicited the first salvo of personal vilification. The writer mentioned above who claimed that she was guilty of poor grooming also complained that she was the beneficiary of army coddling. Major Henry Douglass, who had sent the original questionnaire to Camp McDermit, made a visit there to meet Sarah and wrote a measured rebuttal, pointing out that she was neither the idealized Indian princess that the Easterners imagined, nor the verminous creature she was made out to be by her attacker, but a woman of intelligence and good language skills who was at home in both cultures. This pattern of personal attack and countering testimonial was to dog Sarah the rest of her life.

Douglass made plans for improving the area reservations and attempting to bring back to them the Indians who had left. One of the attractive features was to be schooling for Paiute children with Sarah appointed as instructor. But before this could be accomplished, there was once again a change in Indian policy. Now the agents of the reservations were to be personnel from the Baptist Home Mission Society.

As the 1870s opened, a new agent was coming to Pyramid Lake, and there was a rumor that Camp McDermit was to be closed. Sarah now wrote directly to the Commissioner of Indian Affairs, asserting herself to be the foremost expert on the Paiutes and expressing her concern that if the soldiers were withdrawn and the Paiutes deprived of protection and rations, hostilities would break out. She also gave a newspaper interview in which she solicited schoolbooks for her to use in educating Paiute children at the army camp.

She was now twenty-six years old and about to make the first of several ill-fated unions. In January of 1871 she and First Lieutenant Edward C. Bartlett of Camp McDermit traveled all the way to Salt Lake

City to be married by a justice of the peace, because Nevada laws prohibited interracial marriage. It was a disaster from the start, for it estranged Sarah from her father and brother Natchez, and it took a long time for Sarah to win her way back into her father's graces. From the first it was apparent that Bartlett was a charming, irresponsible alcoholic, and Natchez came to their Salt Lake City hotel to intervene. Within the year Bartlett resigned from the army, but Sarah went on working at Camp McDermit. Over a period they had some contact with each other, but five years after they were wed, Sarah finally initiated divorce proceedings. She testified that her husband had pawned her jewelry and then spent all the money. Bartlett did not appear to contest the proceedings, and the divorce was granted.

At about the time that Sarah was getting herself resettled at Camp McDermit after her elopement to Salt Lake City, a Baptist minster named George Balcom arrived to take over Major Douglass's position at Pyramid Lake. He employed Natchez as interpreter and planned a day school for the reservation children. In his sermons to the Indians he preached the Second Coming of Christ and the day of judgment, which resonated with a nascent religious movement beginning to take form among the Paiutes. Aghast at the destruction of their traditional culture, they were receptive to the message of a Paiute shaman who prophesied the return of all the Paiute dead. This was the first stirring of the Ghost Dance religion that spread to many other Indian groups during the next twenty years.

Troubles continued between settlers and Indians, and Balcom was unable to cope with the intrigues swirling around him. Nor could he manage his own bookkeeping, greatly overspending his budget for improvements at Pyramid Lake, including a salary for a teacher and a school with desks and a blackboard. Sarah, campaigning in Nevada and San Francisco to keep Camp McDermit open, said she thought Balcom's school facilities should not have had priority over provisions for starving Paiutes, who had once more moved off the reservation looking for food.

In a short time, Balcom was joined by a second Baptist minister named Bateman. For a while they coexisted, hurling accusations back and forth, but ultimately Balcom pulled out and Bateman stayed on for years. Bateman saw, as Balcom apparently did not, that the Paiutes could not feed themselves at Pyramid Lake, because the area no longer provided enough in the way of traditional staples. He tried to undo the damage done by Balcom, but he did not consult with Sarah or Young Winnemucca, thereby losing potential supporters. Young Winnemucca, a gifted leader, was dying of some untreated chronic disease, possibly tuberculosis, and was soon gone.

The Ghost Dance was gaining strength. Indians from Idaho, Oregon, and the Great Plains were drawn to it. The movement would spread and finally culminate in the massacre of the Sioux at Wounded Knee, where Charles Eastman, just appointed to his first post as physician to the Sioux, would tend to the survivors.

Eventually the soldiers at Camp McDermit ceased feeding the Paiutes, but the camp itself was not closed. Sarah continued to work there until 1873, assisting the camp physician as hospital matron. Then, not getting along with the commanding officer and still estranged from her father, she moved south to one of the railroad towns, ironically named Winnemucca. Back in white society after a long absence, she supported herself by making gloves and hats and doing some interpreting.

It was a period in which the stress in her life began to take its toll. She had fallen out with the commanding officer at the army camp where she had worked for so long and had bitterly criticized Agent Bateman over inequities of distribution of food and clothing to various Indian groups. In a newspaper interview she was outspoken about her husband's alcoholism and the fact that her father would not see her. She got into a street fight with another Indian woman and then a brawl with a white man. After this second fight Sarah apparently suffered some sort of nervous collapse and took to bed.

It was known that Chief Winnemucca was once again away from Camp McDermit, and Sarah had implied in her interview that he might join the Modoc Indians who were fighting against efforts to return them to a reservation in northeast California. The Modocs had their own version of the religion of resistance and believed that all Indians must resume their traditional life and reject every aspect of white society. Their uprising was suppressed, and the Modocs were sent far away to Indian Territory. Chief Winnemucca was obviously sympathetic but escaped involvement.

Natchez, who had distinguished himself as an arbitrator, interpreter, and generally influential Indian (rather like Bazil among the Shoshones), nonetheless found himself in trouble in the mid-1870s. Like Sarah, Natchez was unsparing in his criticism of how goods were distributed to Indians, and this got back to his employer, Agent Bateman. Bateman threatened Natchez and then had him taken off to Alcatraz prison, but this piece of intimidation backfired. There was an uproar in the newspapers. Petitions were circulated on behalf of Natchez, and Bateman, caught up in the controversy, circulated a petition of his own attacking the integrity of Natchez. Early in 1874, Natchez was released from Alcatraz and returned home a hero, proclaiming that he had been treated with respect and dignity by the soldiers on the prison island.

The Winnemuccas had first taken an appeal for their people to General John M. Schofield in San Francisco in 1871. While at Alcatraz Natchez had refreshed his acquaintance with the general, and in 1875, Natchez, Sarah, and Chief Winnemucca sought aid from Schofield again. The Paiutes were no longer being fed by the army and were unwilling to live on a reservation if that involved dealing with agents. Chief Winnemucca asked for a land allotment near Camp McDermit, protection by the soldiers there, farming implements and seed, in order for his group of Paiutes to become farmers. Schofield again, as he had in 1871, said he had no authority.

When the Winnemuccas returned to Camp McDermit to ask the military for provisions, they again were told that they were appealing to the wrong authority. The incredulous Indians were told to go to the reservation, where they would receive food and clothing. On an afterthought, the commanding officer offered bacon to the Paiutes. Sarah explained that she would eat pork, but even in the face of starvation, she could not induce the Paiutes to do so. (It seemed to take a long time for the Paiutes to reconcile themselves to accepting pork as something they could trade for other things. Sarah pointed out that on a previous occasion they had thrown it into the creek.) Sarah warned that the desperate Paiutes would be driven to an uprising, which would prove as costly to the government as the Modoc rebellion had been. This time, she said in a burst of anger, she would put off the trappings of civilization and join her people against the whites.

She then returned to the town of Winnemucca, became involved in more street fights, and was jailed for cutting a man with a knife. Although the charges were dropped, Sarah and Natchez used the occasion to give an interview on their dim view of white justice.

Later in 1875 Sarah visited her father, with whom she was at last reconciled. While she was with him, the agent at the Malheur reservation in Oregon, which included the military fort Camp Harney, asked her to become interpreter there for a monthly salary plus housing. Sarah's brother Lee spoke well of the agent, S. B. Parrish, and his management of the reservation, so Sarah accepted the job and soon found much to admire in Parrish's work at Malheur. The Paiutes, with few exceptions, willingly joined in communal labor, which in 1875 included digging an irrigation ditch, building a road for hauling winter supplies, and cutting hay. Parrish frequently consulted with the Paiutes in council and paid people for labor done for him or the agency.

Relations between Paiutes and agent on the reservation were generally good, although there was a dissident named Oytes who resisted Agent

Parrish and tried to intimidate the Paiutes by claiming power to resist bullets and to bring disease on people. Oytes shared in the ideas of the Ghost Dance religion, expecting the return of the Paiute dead and the undoing of all wrongs to Indians. He threatened to kill Agent Parrish, but Parrish faced him down. Oytes was to continue to foster conflict for years and was blamed for Paiute participation in an uprising by the Bannock Indians.

The agent's brother Charles with his wife and family joined him at Malheur, and by 1876 a school had been built and the agent's sister-in-law and Sarah hired to teach in it. Sarah carefully observed Annie Parrish's teaching methods and incorporated what she saw into her own concept of how to teach Indian children. They were paid a visit by General O. O. Howard (for whom Howard University in Washington was named) and his daughter, a recent Vassar graduate. Like so many others who met Sarah, they were both impressed with her, and Howard became an enduring supporter.

After Howard's visit, an anonymous letter critical of Agent Parrish appeared in the local newspaper. Parrish wrote a rebuttal and sent it to General Howard, but President Grant appointed a man named W. V. Rinehart to replace Parrish at the Malheur reservation. The Paiutes were apprehensive. According to Sarah's autobiography, Agent Parrish explained to her that he was being replaced because he was not a practicing Christian. (In her writing Sarah betrays some fascination with non-Christian white men, once listing which soldiers in a company were not Christians.) Sarah, her father, another Paiute chief named Egan, and the otherwise resistant Oytes traveled to Camp Harney to plead to keep Parrish. The commanding officer said he would write to Washington about the matter, but there was little he could do. When Rinehart arrived, Parrish gave him a tour of the reservation and departed.

From the first, Agent Rinehart contradicted every part of Parrish's policy in dealing with the Paiutes. He set up issues of clothing on the company-store plan. Instead of paying the Paiutes for work they did for him, he made them take their pay in clothing at inflated prices. He issued vouchers instead of clothing or food, and he told the Paiutes they could leave Malheur if they did not care for his ways. Starvation again loomed.

In mid-November 1876 Sarah married again. She and a man named Satwaller were wed in the home of Charles Parrish, in the presence of Annie Parrish and the Parrish children. Then, within days of the wedding, Sarah, Egan, and other Paiutes were again on their way to Camp Harney, this time to complain about Agent Rinehart. The commanding officer felt that Rinehart was doing no wrong and counseled the Paiutes to send their children to the reservation school and to work for their goods and clothes. But Rinehart had fired Sarah and closed the school. Sarah had also been fired as interpreter and replaced by one of her male cousins. In a letter to General Howard, Rinehart blamed Sarah for keeping the Paiutes stirred up. Sarah left the Malheur reservation to live with her husband, but this marriage was not a success either. Sarah does not even mention Satwaller in her autobiography, and we do not know how long they remained together nor what were the circumstances of their parting.

In the second half of the decade, Chief Joseph of the Nez Perces led his people in war to resist reservation life in northern Oregon. Many Paiutes returned to the Malheur reservation to seek safety from retaliatory attacks by whites, but Chief Winnemucca stayed away. Earlier he had been rumored to have joined the Modocs; now it was said he was with the Nez Perces, but Natchez sent a telegram to San Francisco that his father was not in Oregon at all but in Idaho. And in fact he really was in Idaho, being feted by the governor of the state. But returning to Oregon, Chief Winnemucca ran into trouble with Oytes, whose sympthies lay with Chief Joseph. Agent Rinehart wanted the chief of the Paiutes on his reservation, but Winnemucca wanted a reservation of his own away from Oytes.

Once again Natchez and his father appeared in San Francisco to talk with the army about reservation matters. Apparently never grasping that the U.S. Army and the Bureau of Indian Affairs that administered reservations were bureaucratically separate (and in fact at odds with each other), they asked the army for land with cavalry protection and seed and stock for farming. Inevitably the military referred them back to Rinehart. Chief Winnemucca did stop briefly at the Malheur reservation after this trip, but he did not stay. White settlers with their horses and cattle had invaded Malheur, just as they had done at Pyramid Lake. They were taking over the digging fields and had gotten timbering rights on Indian land.

By 1878 Sarah was no longer living with Satwaller and instead was sharing the home of a white woman, where she was approached by some of the Malheur Paiutes and asked to speak on their behalf at Camp Harney yet again. She went to Malheur and learned that there were now many Bannock Indians on the reservation. As usual the Paiutes were not getting issues of food and clothing, and they were hungry as ever. Once more there was a rape and murder. This time the rape victim was a Bannock girl caught out digging, where women were always at their most vulnerable, and her brother had killed a white in retaliation. The Bannocks, knowing what the consequences would be for them all, turned him in immediately only to learn that all their horses and guns had been confiscated, making it impossible to hunt for their food. They asked Sarah to write about the matter to Washington, but the Paiutes went a step further. They collected about thirty dollars for her expenses and asked her to go to Washington in person on their behalf. But as she set out in a wagon to catch a train, the Bannock War was already erupting in southern Idaho. Sarah found herself in the midst of an uprising and unable to reach the railroad.

The Bannocks at Malheur and some sympathetic Paiutes, including Oytes, held Chief Winnemucca and his people prisoner, although Natchez managed to escape. Told that her father and relatives were in the hands of the Bannocks, Sarah volunteered as a scout and received a letter of safe conduct from the army. She was offered $500 (which she eventually did receive) to bring her people back from the Bannocks, and she set out with two Paiute men to accomplish this. On the way she met her brother Lee. Together they entered the Bannock camp and brought their father and relatives out under cover of darkness. This was the beginning of Sarah's close companionship with her sister-in-law Mattie, who had once been a student in Annie Parrish's school at Malheur and who was now wife of Lee Winnemucca. From this day on the two Paiute women stayed together until Mattie died.

When the escape of the Winnemucca group was discovered, they were pursued by the Bannocks, and Sarah and Mattie rode on hard ahead to bring army protection. General Howard sent soldiers, who brought Chief Winnemucca and about forty Paiutes to safety at Camp Mc-Dermit. Sarah writes a gripping account of this whole adventure in her autobiography.

Chaos reigned among the white settlers, many of whom blamed Agent Rinehart for driving the Paiutes into league with the Bannocks by his mistreatment of them at the Malheur reservation. Most of the Paiutes were, indeed, with the Bannocks, except for Chief Winnemucca's people and some who managed to escape during subsequent battles. Sarah and Mattie continued serving together as army scouts and interpreters, staying with General Howard's command, where they were sometimes taken by civilian whites to be prisoners of the soldiers rather than employees. The two women were present in the midst of combat, which Sarah enjoyed. Decribing one battle, she advances the idea that the Indians and soldiers were playing at war without the intention of doing each other much damage:

> Sometimes I laugh when I think of this battle. It was very exciting in one way, and the soldiers made a splendid chase and deserved credit for it; but where was the killing? I sometimes think it was more play than anything else. If a white settler showed himself he was sure to get

a hit from an Indian; but I don't believe they ever tried to hit a soldier,—they like them too well,—and it certainly was remarkable that with all these splendid firearms, and the gatling gun, and General Howard working at it, and the air full of bullets, and the ground strewn with cartridges, not an Indian fell that day.[75]

What was singularly horrible to Sarah and Mattie, however, was the murder of Chief Egan by Umatilla Indians who had been paid by the army to get him away from the Bannocks. Egan had been severely wounded in an earlier attempt to escape the Bannocks and was defenseless. The Umatillas decapitated him, and word got out that the army had recovered his head and sent it to a museum in Washington. This was more than Sarah and Mattie could bear, and Sarah later incorporated her outrage into her public lectures about the abuses against Indians. While Egan's head was not inventoried in Washington, the head of another man decapitated by the Umatillas was officially received, so Sarah's charges were by no means fanciful.

In pursuit of the Bannocks Sarah was constantly finding cast-offs along the trail. Once it was a clock, another time a violin that she carried with her for a while. After one skirmish, a baby was found, the little girl to whom the soldiers fed gingersnaps. Sarah took responsibility for her for three months until her parents were located. By then the child might have grown unrecognizable even to her mother, but Sarah had taken care to preserve the clothes she had been wearing when found. The parents took the baby back and gave her Sarah's name. This is as close as Sarah herself ever came to having a child, and perhaps, recalling the time she had been left buried in sand, she identified more with the terrified abandoned child than with the Indian mother.

In the midst of the campaign there were moments both serene and frantic. One day Sarah came upon Sam Parrish, and they had a quiet ride and conversation together. Later she would have a similar meeting with his brother and sister-in-law. On another occasion, alone in the country-side, Mattie and Sarah were threatened by soldiers. There ensued a wild ride to escape, and they had the satisfaction of seeing the men dismissed from the army. At Camp McDermit Sarah was reunited with her father and Natchez and Mattie with her husband. Sarah, Mattie, and Lee continued to serve as army couriers as the Bannock War died out.

And now Sarah and Mattie found themselves involved in a betrayal. An order came that all Paiutes from the Malheur reservation who were at Camp McDermit were to be taken north to Camp Harney. Sarah and Mattie were in the employ of the soldiers taking them from one camp to the other in early October. The suspicious Paiutes doubted that they were really going to be taken back to the Malheur reservation for the winter, and they were right. Instead, they were to be escorted much further north across the Columbia River to the Yakima reservation. The trip through the mountains was to be made in winter. Sarah, having gotten them to Camp Harney, had led them into a trap. In her autobiography she says that she could hardly go on working. She quotes Mattie as saying, "Well, sister, we cannot help it if the white people won't keep their word. We can't help it. We have to work for them and if they get our people not to love us, by telling what is not true to them, what can we do? It is they, not us." Sarah says that she replied, "Our people won't think so because they will never know that it was they who told the lie. Oh! I know all our people will say we are working against them and are getting money for all this."[76]

As groups of Paiutes kept running away, Sarah and Mattie were sent out to bring them back. Mattie's horse slipped in the snow and fell on her, and, taken to Yakima in a wagon, she never recovered from her injuries.

The trip of 350 miles to Yakima was made in the snow, and the Paiutes did not have much in the way of winter clothing. The Paiute men got coats from the army, but there was nothing for the women and children. All along the way they died and were left unburied—old people, women who gave birth on the trail, their babies. During the trek Charles Parrish and his wife joined them and were distressed for the Paiutes they had known so well. Sarah begged them to help, but Charles Parrish said there was nothing he could do.

The Yakima agent James H. Wilbur was unprepared for the arrival of the Paiutes. Nothing more than a large shed was built to shelter the 500 or so who had survived the march, and the Yakima Indians saw the miserable Paiutes as fair prey. They stole their horses and won away the army coats in card games with the Paiute men. Paiutes kept on dying. Sarah writes, "At first Father Wilbur and his Christian Indians told us we could bury our dead in their grave yard; but they soon got tired of us, and said we could not bury them there anymore."[77] In the early spring there was an issue of clothing as meager as any of Agent Rinehart's had been at the Malheur reservation. Mattie, having received no medical treatment for her injuries in the winter, was unable to assist Sarah in distributing what little there was, and she died at the end of May.

To the south Chief Winnemucca and Natchez worked for the return of the Paiute prisoners from Yakima. Agent Rinehart, embarrassed at finding himself administering a reservation with no Indians, tried to bribe and intimidate the chief and his son to come live there with their small group of relatives. They refused, and white squatters moved in.

In mid-1879 Natchez gave an interview in San Francisco in which he said Sarah was teaching school in Yakima and had sixty Paiute students. During that summer Agent Wilbur planned a religious revival meeting with prominent visitors from the East, including a bishop from Boston. According to Sarah, he told her to keep the Paiutes away, but instead she staged a confrontation, putting the thin, poorly dressed Paiute children in the front row and interpreting the bishop's sermon to them.

About this time Sarah received substantial back pay for her earlier army service, and for at least the third time, she set out for Washington to make a plea on behalf of her people. (When she and her father made their first benefit appearance in San Francisco, they said that they were on their way to Washington, but they used what little money they cleared that time to buy flour and blankets instead. Her second attempt to go to Washington had been blocked by the Bannock War.) In the meantime, the Ghost Dance religion had ebbed but was to resurge with a new generation. The railroad that carried Sarah across the continent to the East, would soon carry other Indians spreading the message of a better day coming.

Sarah began her trip by going to Portland, where some twenty-five years later Susan B. Anthony would preside over the unveiling of a statue to Sacajawea. From there Sarah took a boat down the coast to San Francisco to join Natchez in giving lectures and interviews. In covering these appearances, one reporter exaggerated how many times Sarah had been married to white men, and she issued a rebuttal. Although she was in her mid-thirties, reporters persisted in referring to her as an "Indian girl." They also perceived her as "Nature's child."[78] Agent Rinehart, in reaction to all her publicity, wrote a vicious letter to the Bureau of Indian Affairs claiming that she was given to lying and gambling. He also wrote that no credit should be given to anything General Howard might write.

Just as in street fights, Sarah could give as well as she got at the lecture podium. She made savage verbal attacks on Agent Rinehart as well as tearful appeals on behalf of the Paiute prisoners at Yakima. She circulated a petition to have Agent Parrish or someone like him appointed at Malheur and the Paiutes returned there. She gave her closing public lecture in San Francisco at Christmas, and then she and Natchez went to Winnemucca to pick up their father. A special agent from the Interior Department, J. M. Haworth, was sent to interview them and make arrangements for their trip to Washington. They were to be four: Chief Winnemucca, Sarah, Natchez, and another Paiute called Captain Jim.

The train trip began in mid-January 1880 and took a whole week. It appears that the Interior Department did not provide them with sleeping berths. In her autobiography Sarah writes that at the end of their stay in

Washington, when they were about to start back, she told Haworth, "I am not going back as I came here." And he responded, "All right; you shall have a sleeping car."[79] But in Omaha he gave them three dollars for the rest of the trip home and abandoned them.

Unknown to Sarah, Agent Rinehart had collected a set of affidavits attacking her in the crudest terms. In them she was again represented as much-married and adulterous as well, a liar and a bad influence on Indians. To these old charges were added a new one, that she was an alcoholic and that she would prostitute herself for a bottle of whiskey. These statements, several of them from Rinehart's business associates, may not have arrived in Washington until after Sarah had concluded her visit and departed, but they came to rest in a file there to cause trouble later.

Sarah and her group found their time in Washington so scheduled that they had no free contact with the public. When not in meetings, they were taken on carriage tours, always in the company of Haworth. There was a valid concern that in public gatherings they might become infected with smallpox, but there was also the unconcealed intent to block Sarah from the press and to keep her from making her appeals. She tried her tearful approach with the first bureaucrat she met at the Interior Department and was curtly warned not to "lecture." Then she was taken in to meet the Secretary of the Interior himself, Carl Schurz, who appeared interested and sympathetic, according to Sarah.

Despite Haworth's watch-dog vigilance, Sarah managed to give a newspaper interview, and one day she and the other Paiutes dug in their heels and refused to go sightseeing. Sarah still planned to speak publicly in Washington when she was called in by Secretary Schurz and rebuked for inappropriate behavior and ingratitude. He pointed out that the government was paying the expenses for her group's visit and told her that if she wished to give public lectures she should do so on a subsequent visit, which is what she ultimately did.

At the conclusion of their series of meetings, Schurz gave Sarah an official letter which said that the Paiutes at Yakima were free to leave there and rejoin their people. They were equally free to stay where they were. Paiutes at the Malheur reservation were to get 160-acre allotments for each head of family so they could farm. Schurz told Sarah to get her people settled at Malheur before coming to Washington again.

In the letter there were two fatal clauses that Sarah did not grasp at the time. The first was that the Paiutes at Yakima were free to return to their families, but the government would not pay for their move. And second, the Paiutes at Malheur were to get land allotments to farm but no government support. However, Schurz did promise immediate shipment of a hundred canvas tents for Sarah to distribute.

Then the Paiutes were taken to the White House to be received by President Rutherford B. Hayes. It was a disappointing experience. The president simply came in to ask Sarah whether she had gotten what she wanted for her people. She had only a moment to give a qualified "yes" before he left again. The Winnemuccas left Washington with a new suit of clothes for Chief Winnemucca and an appointment for Sarah as interpreter at the Malheur reservation.

Back in Nevada they were met by a large group of Paiutes, and they waited for the tents, which didn't arrive. Chief Winnemucca gave away the suit he had been given. When Sarah read Secretary Schurz's letter to the Paiutes, it was met with derision. They felt that the Great White Father, that ideal supreme authority that Lewis and Clark had promoted, was no better than any of the others. None were to be believed. Sarah telegraphed Schurz asking for provisions for the gathered Paiutes, and his response was that she should take them to the Malheur reservation, which would have involved another trip through winter snow over mountains. The disillusioned Paiutes scattered to find whatever food they could. Some showed up on other reservations, passing themselves off as Shoshones and disavowing the Winnemuccas.

In the meantime Sarah, unaware of Agent Rinehart's affidavits, was appalled at the spreading newspaper characterizations of her as a drunkard and went to court about them. Rinehart blocked her appointment as interpreter by writing to the Indian Commissioner that she had worked in a house of prostitution in the town of Winnemucca. He also reiterated the claim that she was untruthful and an alcoholic. To Sarah, however, he only said that she could not have the job she had been appointed to in Washington because there were no Paiutes at the Malheur reservation for her to interpret for. Taking him at his word, she set out to bring the Paiute prisoners back from Yakima.

Low on funds in northern Oregon and believing that she would have a paid position at the Malheur reservation when she returned with the Paiutes from Yakima, Sarah borrowed money against her letter of appointment. And once more she happened to meet Charles Parrish and now told him of the deaths at Yakima of Mattie and the other students Annie Parrish had taught in her school.

When Sarah arrived at the Yakima reservation, Agent Wilbur said he had received no communication from Washington about the Paiutes. She presented him with her letter from Secretary Schurz and, according to her autobiography, he in turn offered her a bribe and a job as interpreter at Yakima if she would not show it to the Paiutes. Sarah bluntly pointed out that she had never received the pay due for her previous interpreting at Yakima.

After some delay and the arousal of suspicion among the Paiutes, Sarah interpreted the letter to them. There was general elation, and the Paiutes began preparations to leave. Agent Wilbur threatened Sarah with prison for inciting the Indians and refused to request a military escort to protect them on their trip back to Malheur. Moreover, he sent a telegram to the Interior Department asking them to rescind the terms of the Secretary's letter. Wilbur said Sarah was guilty of unspecified offenses and had proved incorrigible, and he concurred with Agent Rinehart that she was unreliable and deceitful. A return telegram from Washington told him to hold the Paiutes at Yakima. Sarah also received a telegram. Hers claimed that the Paiutes could not leave Yakima because without an army escort they would be at risk on their way back to Malheur.

Unable to take the Paiutes to Malheur and work there as an interpreter and banned from the Yakima reservation, Sarah was in debt and unemployed. With no money to return to Nevada, she wrote to General Howard, who gave her a job at Vancouver Barracks as interpreter and teacher for Bannock prisoners there, fifty-three in all including eighteen children. She immediately wrote to the Secretary of the Interior to ask for land allotments for the Bannocks so they could farm and become self-supporting, and she also requested a shipment of clothes for the women and children (who always had problems at army camps, since the army only had men's jackets available). There came no response from Washington.

Now Sarah at last received the five hundred dollars she had been promised as reward for bringing her father and his band back from the camp of the hostile Bannocks. When the Bannocks were moved away from the Vancouver Barracks and her duties there ended, she used some of the reward money to go to visit her sister Elma in Idaho. It was their first reunion since her sister's marriage, and together the sisters made a trip to Winnemucca, Nevada. News came to them there that some of the Paiutes at Yakima had managed to slip away and return to Oregon, but not to the Malheur reservation. Later more attempted an escape but were returned to Agent Wilbur.

At the end of 1881 Sarah made her last marriage. Her new husband was Lewis Hopkins from Virginia, and they were joined by a justice of the peace in San Francisco. After the wedding they announced that Sarah would go to the East on a lecture trip. But Hopkins had gambled away Sarah's earnings from her teaching post at Vancouver Barracks and what was left of her reward. They had to raise money all over again, and for part of that time they withdrew to Elma's home in Idaho. It took a year for Sarah to recoup.

Chief Winnemucca was now very old, though in recent years he had still appeared in costumes at the head of street processions of Paiutes. His last defiant act in the face of age and infirmity was to marry a young woman who already had a small child. When he fell ill, this hapless woman and her baby were killed by the Paiutes, who believed she was to blame. Chief Winnemucca died anyway. Sarah had been present at her grandfather's death, but she was not there when her father died, nor has she anything to say about his death in her autobiography. It would have been difficult to explain to the Easterners whose hearts she now sought to move on behalf of the Paiutes.

When Sarah finally arrived in Boston in the spring of 1883, it was to begin an extraordinary relationship with the influential sisters Elizabeth Peabody and Mary Mann. Elizabeth, the older of the two, was seventy-nine years old but possessed of the same stamina that sustained Susan B. Anthony and Elizabeth Cady Stanton. These women, all powerful figures of the second half of the nineteenth century, were indefatigable fundraisers and organizers, and Elizabeth Peabody turned her talents to setting up public lectures for Sarah. Through her efforts, Sarah made appearances at churches, YMCAs, and local meetings of the Indian Association throughout the eastern states. She also spoke at Vassar College, where General Howard's daughter had been educated. Sarah was now in the same circle of earnest reformers and idealists that fostered young Charles Eastman and was about to send him off to Dartmouth College. She was meeting all the influential people of Boston, New York, Baltimore, and points in between.

Encouraged by Elizabeth Peabody and Mary Mann to write, and provided with a place to do so, Sarah set down her autobiography in order to carry her lecture topics to a broader audience. The result, *Life among the Piutes: Their Wrongs and Claims*, is a long work incorporating information on the traditional culture of the Paiutes, Sarah's own life experiences, and a condemnation of Indian agents and the wrongs they had done to the Paiutes and to Indians in general. It is a work by turns sentimental, ironic, and vituperative, yet the linear narration of Sarah's life holds its parts together. It reads like an adventure book as much as a polemic, both of which it is.

The book interweaves a selection of appealing vignettes of Paiute traditional life, a justification of Sarah herself, and a denunciation of white hypocrisy. Her articulate account of the Bannock War has much in common with the letters about the conquest Cortés sent to Spain; both are eloquent eyewitness narratives that are also self-serving and written with attention to persuasion and audience appeal.

Among the ethnographic details are a story of the separation of human beings into dark and light people and another about how the Paiute ancestors drove cannibals into a cave and destroyed them with fire. The life of women is traced from spring song-and-dance festivals where girls met young men, through menstruation rituals and marriage, to the role of women in marriage, councils, and war. Hunting magic is represented in an account of the charming of antelope. Although Sarah tells of men who styled themselves shamans and claimed to be able to bring illness and death to people, she omits mention of the Ghost Dance or the killing of marginal people such as her father's last wife and stepchild, topics that would have troubled her white audience.

Sarah's last lecture in Nevada before she left for Boston had been criticized as disorganized, but her autobiography is not. Perhaps it owes its coherence to sound editorial advice, but in her preface Mary Mann asserts that she had limited herself to standardizing Sarah's spelling and punctuation. She also added very few footnotes.

Gretchen Bataille and Kathleen Sands, in their book *American Indian Women: Telling Their Lives*, write of Sarah's "inflated Victorian prose style," saying that it "reveals no apparent mark of her first language or of traditional oral technique."[80] This seems to be missing the point, since Sarah was writing directly to her white audience, seeking, as she did in her public lectures, to engage its active support on behalf of the Paiutes. The book is a calculated work in her public's own language, providing pieces of folklore at just the right moments and interspersed with gripping narratives to temper what is essentially a sustained howl of outrage.

Sarah knew her audience's tastes and expectations and played to them, but this hardly renders her autobiography inauthentic. When Sarah wrote her book, she was well on her way to death at age forty-seven, worn out by a lifetime of hardships. The factualness of what she writes has been documented by her biographer, Gae Whitney Canfield: her service with the army, her employment records, her newspaper interviews, her correspondence with authorities, her marriages, and all the rest, and Sarah emerges as a truthful person. As for the abusive Indian agents Sarah railed against, hindsight shows us that she was generally on target. When she writes about breaking down in helpless tears, as she very often does in her autobiography, it may seem to us maudlin nineteenth-century sentimentality, but we should recall that Sacajawea exhibited just this behavior among the Shoshones. And looking at the destruction of the Paiutes' means of life, we might well ask what perceptive human being would not be blinded by tears at the magnitude of human suffering.

Sarah often took the risk of offending her audiences with her denunciations of individual agents, her sarcasm about Christian morality, and her allegations of corruption at high levels in Washington. She also had to bear the charges that she was on the lecture circuit to enrich herself and that she was the tool of the army in the competition between the Department of War and the Interior Department for jurisdiction over the Indians. Publication of the affidavits Agent Rinehart had sent to Washington in 1880 fueled the fire, and she now had to cope with a new slander that she was a prostitute in the army camps.

All this was too much for some of the people who knew her personally in Nevada. They themselves might abuse her in print, but it was another thing to have a public figure from home held up for ridicule in the East. Published rebuttals came from Nevada, and Sarah also received letters of testimonial, mostly from army officers, that were published as an appendix to her book. Her own statement on the mudslinging (nineteenth-century yellow journalism at its most flamboyant) was that character assassination is something that cannot be disproved, and that her real friends knew and trusted her.

Unfortunately for Sarah, her husband Lewis Hopkins did as much harm to her efforts in both the short term and the long run as her declared enemies could. Hopkins carried on research for Sarah at the Library of Congress and at the Boston Athenaeum. He introduced her at her lectures and generally seemed supportive as Sarah worked at a superhuman pace through the summer and the fall. In Baltimore alone, she spoke sixty-six times. After the lectures she signed books, and Hopkins handled correspondence and mail-order sales. The profits from her lectures were going into an account to found a school for Paiute children. But in midsummer of 1884 she found that she had on her hands an invalid husband who was also a compulsive gambler. He had tapped into the school account and lost all the profits from the lectures and the book sales. She covered the overdrafts and paid his medical bills and was left once again back at the starting point. To make matters even worse, the story of the Paiutes' murder of Chief Winnemucca's wife and her baby began making the rounds, and now even Sarah's staunchest supporters had reason to pull back.

At this time Sarah received news that other Paiutes had finally managed to escape Yakima and return to Oregon. Agent Wilbur had retired, and no effort was made to bring them back this time. Sarah tried lobbying for turning over Camp McDermit to the Paiutes as a reservation under military administration, but instead the Paiutes were told to go to Pyramid Lake and be under the Secretary of the Interior. However, there was no longer room for new people at Pyramid Lake, which had been taken over by white settlers and Chinese fishermen.

Hopkins had gone off, and Sarah was unable to accomplish more in

Washington. With hardly anything to show for all her efforts in the East, she could not face the Paiutes. Instead she returned to Elma's home in Idaho. Her last money went to settle a debt for Natchez.

Elizabeth Peabody and Mary Mann would not give up the fight. They maintained constant pressure on Washington to have the squatters and fishermen removed from Pyramid Lake and told Sarah to go and settle her people there. But she found that the agent at Pyramid Lake did not want the additional Paiutes, and the squatters were already back. The Paiutes simply could not fit in. Sarah, waiting for some resolution, was taken ill and never completely recovered. For the rest of her life she suffered from malaria-like chills and fever.

Elizabeth Peabody was not one to make allowances for infirmity, and she pledged ten dollars a week to keep Sarah at Pyramid Lake to observe what happened next. A new agent arrived but would not employ Sarah as either teacher or interpreter, pointedly hiring one of Sarah's cousins as interpreter instead, and installing his wife as school mistress. Elizabeth Peabody was now caught between Sarah's actual situation and the assumption of Sarah's supporters in the East that Sarah was gainfully employed and that Congress had taken care of the Paiutes' needs. The Paiutes, for their part, did not wish to settle at Pyramid Lake. They preferred the solution for which Sarah had lobbied without success, that they should remain at Camp McDermit and be provisioned by the army during the winters.

Sarah gave up hope for the adult Paiutes, who now seemed lost to drink, gambling, prostitution, and despair. The only hope seemed to be in educating the Paiute children so they could be something more than hired men and house maids. Sarah, who never relinquished her ambition to be a teacher, decided to hold school for Paiute children on her brother Natchez's property in Lovelock, Nevada. Her intention was to have Indians taught by Indians, not separating them from their families, culture, or language. This was diametrically opposed to the entrenched boarding school philosophy embodied at Eastern schools for Indians such as Hampton Institute and the Carlisle School, where the teachers were white, and use of Indian languages was prohibited.

The octogenarian Elizabeth Peabody moved to Washington to keep up pressure on the new administration of President Grover Cleveland. Donors sent gifts of farm equipment, seed, and tents to Nevada. In the summer of 1885 Sarah began teaching Paiute children in Lovelock. Hers was a bilingual method, explaining everything in both Paiute and English, using the childrens' native language to teach them English. She employed songs and rhythm, blackboard work, and copybooks, and she sent samples of the children's work to Boston. There was constant fundraising in the East and a flow of cash and goods to Nevada to support both the school and Natchez's farming enterprise that hosted it.

But problems ground everyone down. Natchez had difficulty getting enough water for his land, construction of the school building was behind schedule, Sarah was suffering from debilitating chronic disease, and the expected white school teacher from the East decided not to come. In the East there was resistance to fundraising because of the continuing barrage of slander originating in Washington and suspicion that Hopkins might reappear and abscond again with contributions. Yet Sarah's school had the wholehearted support of a large number of women, and supporters did send seeds, clothes, and sewing goods. In the spring of 1886 the citizens of Lovelock inspected the school and wrote an enthusiastic letter of commendation to Elizabeth Peabody. Having once pledged ten dollars a week, she now pledged a hundred dollars a month to make it possible for Sarah to board the children through the summer while their parents went away to gather their traditional foods.

But because of the prevailing philosophy in favor of the boarding schools, attempts to get government support were hopeless. Just a few years later E. Jane Gay wrote concerning the Nez Perces and the Carlisle School: "Mr. McConville, the school superintendent, would be very glad to send all his little brown children away while they are yet clean and pure in heart so they could grow up white inside, if they did have to be darker in skin than their little brothers and sisters."[81]

This philosophy, marching on deep into the twentieth century, caused immense pain for countless Indian children, as we now know from the many autobiographies of people who attended the boarding schools. Sarah's was one of the few challenges to the basic assumptions on which the philosophy rested, that children had to be rescued from the pernicious influences of their homes, parents, and native language.

When Sarah's school was a year old, an official from Washington came to see Sarah and Natchez and explained that the only way for the school to receive federal funds was for Sarah to give up the directorship and for Natchez to turn over ownership of the land to the United States government.

Alice Chapin, the veteran white teacher who had earlier decided against coming to the school, changed her mind and arrived after all. She found Sarah in poor health, administered quinine to her, and took over doing the reports to Elizabeth Peabody. She wrote approvingly of Sarah's methods and the students' progress. Sarah was treating all the students as potential teachers, having each child learn something and then teach it to another child. Academic work was supplemented by instruction in practical skills. Alice Chapin also noted the continuing troubles about water and tried to straighten things out, but at the end of the summer she returned East.

In late September Sarah telegraphed an urgent request for cash. Elizabeth Peabody was unable to come up with it, and a potential donor refused to make a loan, believing that Sarah was not managing her finances well and that she and Natchez should not get into the habit of borrowing money. The issue of Hopkins was again brought up, together with the rumors about Sarah drinking and gambling.

What had happened, according to Sarah, was that the Paiutes helping Natchez with his grain harvest had been told that the hundred dollars a month Sarah received for her school was intended for their payment and that Sarah was keeping it for herself. They refused payment in grain for their labor and demanded cash. Without cash on hand to pay them, Natchez had to sell the grain at a disadvantageous price rather than withholding it from the market and waiting for the price to rise. Natchez only received about half the price he anticipated, and when the workers had been paid off in cash, there was nothing left over. Penniless, Sarah and Natchez had to leave Lovelock to seek work to raise some money yet again, Natchez as a cowboy and Sarah as a housekeeper.

When she understood the situation, Elizabeth Peabody started another round of fundraising and put out another printing of Sarah's autobiography. She also had a pamphlet on Sarah's educational philosophy printed and sent to congressmen. The school reopened. There were forty-five students, and some of the Pyramid Lake Paiute children wanted to transfer. Expenses were met by pledges from friends of the school, and when Mary Mann died that year, she left her small estate as an endowment.

But early in 1887 the passage of the Dawes Act rendered all this effort futile. This piece of legislation was named for Senator Henry L. Dawes, a man who had consulted with Sarah when she was in Washington and who shared with her the view that the hope for Indians in the future was land allotment and eventual citizenship. This was a course supported by many humanitarian groups, by Sarah, and by Charles Eastman too. Everyone hoped that it would bring an end to the abuse of Indians and their quick assimilation into American society. But a clause in the Dawes Act intended to implement this assimilation compelled all Indian children to be educated in white-run, English-speaking boarding schools, with the children isolated from their families and forbidden to speak their own languages. And this was to be effected whether parents gave their permission or not. This was totally unacceptable to Sarah and to Elizabeth Peabody, who shared Sarah's educational philosophy.

Sarah made one more fundraising trip to the East to promote the idea of educating Indian children at home, but she could not compete with the enthusiasm for the Carlisle School and Hampton Institute. On the trip she located Hopkins and brought him back with her to Nevada. Her Paiute relatives and white supporters were of one mind that he would exploit her again, and they were right. He absconded with the money from Natchez's grain harvest that year. Then he returned to her, having spent every cent of it, and died of tuberculosis.

During 1888 Sarah struggled on with twenty-four students and not much income. Elizabeth Peabody continued lobbying congressmen for a federal appropriation for the school, and General Howard came by to say he hoped he could influence the government to support it. But when the Peabody School recessed in 1888, Sarah knew she could not keep it going. She closed it four years after its founding and went to Elma's home in Idaho. Elma's husband, a man held in much respect by the Bannocks, died soon after, and the two women went on living together as Sarah's health continued its relentless decline.

Sarah died suddenly on October 17, 1891. The sisters had shared some homemade wine with their dinner, and the coroner put down alcohol poisoning as cause of death. Sarah was about forty-seven years old when she died, more likely of cardiovascular collapse than of chokecherry wine. Even in death she was between worlds. The *New York Times* carried her obituary. The Bannock Indians buried her.

THESE THREE WOMEN

I have lived a long time with the white people and I know what they do.
They are people who are very kind to any one who is ready to do
whatever they wish.

—*SARAH WINNEMUCCA* [82]

Before we pass on to the next group of people who lived between worlds, let us pause and contemplate the three "Indian princesses" whose careers we have just examined. What did they have in common, and what can we learn from them? One commonality is that exploitation of their special talents helped them to survive in a pervasive atmosphere of sexual violence.

It has been important to non-Indians to picture Doña Marina, Sacajawea, and Sarah Winnemucca as the beautiful daughters of hereditary rulers. This has set them apart in the popular imagination from Indians in general, who have been perceived and treated as inferior beings. But if we think of royalty in terms of command, they were poor princesses indeed. Despite their influential relatives (Doña Marina's mother and half-brother, Sacajawea's brother, three generations of Winnemucca men), they themselves had little room to maneuver.

Doña Marina and Sacajawea were, for all intents and purposes, enslaved. Only Sarah Winnemucca had any degree of autonomy, and her freedom was circumscribed. By race and by gender she was doubly disenfranchised. She might lobby Congress, but she could not vote. In Nevada she could not marry a white man. Sharing the life of the Paiutes on the reservations, she was exposed to hunger and lack of medical care in situations where Paiute traditional medicine was ineffective. Without income from her interpreting jobs and her public lectures, she would have been unable to help herself or anyone else. In this sense, she had hardly more choice about her service in the camps of the United States Army and on the reservations than Doña Marina or Sacajawea had. For all of these women, survival was a prime driving motive.

What made these women singularly useful to the men they served was neither their beauty nor their family connections. It was their uncommon intelligence—remarked upon by everyone who met them—coupled with their multilingualism. Doña Marina was able to deal with several distinct dialects of Nahuatl and of Maya, and she acquired Spanish. Sacajawea spoke Shoshone, Minnetaree, and some French, and in the course of her year with the Lewis and Clark expedition, she must have learned some English as well. Sarah Winnemucca knew some Spanish and was bilingual in English and Paiute. Moreover, the Bannocks shared a common language with the Northern Paiutes, a language that was in turn related to Shoshone, and from her employment record it seems that she was competent to interpret for all these people.

In their work they provided more than translation of words and sentences. They served as both linguistic and cultural interpreters, providing both sides with information about motivations and context. But one of many woman given to Cortés, Doña Marina uniquely became a working partner in the enterprise of conquest. She was obviously special among the women, not simply multilingual but also skilled in her ability to deal with people. Both sides reportedly preferred her as interpreter over others who could do the job. A witness testifying in court proceedings related that during the seige of Tenochtitlan a Spanish soldier who had learned to speak Nahuatl was interpreting, but the Aztecs insisted on having Doña

Marina instead, and Cortés had to send a boat to the city of Texcoco to fetch her before the negotiations could go forward.[83] As we have seen, the Spanish chroniclers also credit Doña Marina with repeatedly saving Cortés from entrapment.

In a similar vein, Sacajawea not only translated between the captains of the expedition and her brother, but she warned Lewis and Clark of her brother's plans to depart and abandon them. Less conspicuously, she carried on the daily business of procuring food for the men, and when the expedition needed horses, she negotiated for them. The old woman on the Wind River reservation who may have been Sacajawea had become skilled in making the white government's case in Shoshone councils, and she carried documents and a Jefferson medal in recognition of her services.

Sarah Winnemucca tells in her autobiography of assuring soldiers that they had less to fear than they imagined. On one occasion she interpreted a signal fire to be that of a single individual rather than a threatening group, and on another she showed a company of soldiers that what they took to be Indians ranged on a distant hillside were rock decoys set up to conceal a withdrawal. In her writing, she seeks to put some Paiute beliefs and practices in a sympathetic light for her readers. As for interpreting whites to the Paiutes, an incident Sarah relates from her childhood connects to another many years later. Paiutes destroyed all the belongings of their dead. The white woman who helped care for Sarah during her bout with poison ivy gave her several dresses, but when the Paiutes discovered that they had belonged to the woman's own daughter who had died, they burned them. Many years later as Agent Parrish was about to leave the Malheur reservation, he sought to make a gift to Chief Winnemucca, who—treating Parrish's departure as a symbolic death—would not co-operate until Sarah explained to her father that white people give each other keepsakes when parting, and he should accept in order not to hurt the agent's feelings. Like Doña Marina and Bazil's mother, Sarah also knew how to speak persuasively in council, extracting meaningful information from English bureaucratese and recasting it in terms that made sense to the Paiutes.

Sarah Winnemucca's exceptional talent for persuasive rhetoric is obvious from her speaking career and her autobiography. Other Paiutes, including many of her cousins and sisters-in-law, spoke English and could interpret for agents and officers, but Sarah was preferred by both sides for negotiations. Both the Paiutes and the Bannocks asked her to speak for them in their struggles against reservation agents, and the government asked her to get the Paiutes to accommodate themselves to reservation life. None of her cousins took to the lecture podium, much less addressed

Congress. By her own account and from reports of people who met her while she was still an adolescent, Sarah had been vehemently outspoken from childhood. A newspaper columnist who attended one of her lectures in San Francisco remarked on her "easy, unembarrassed manner" before an audience, striking on the same term Bernal Díaz had used in describing Doña Marina.[84]

Had these guides been mothers of large families, they would not have been able to do their jobs. Bernal Díaz wrote that during the battles leading up to the defeat of Tenochtitlan, Doña Marina made herself available at any hour of the day or night to interpret for Cortés. In such circumstances, barrenness was an advantage, and we should recall that she gave birth to her son only after the fall of the city. Then little Martín was left behind in the care of others so she could once again give her undivided attention to her tasks as she accompanied Cortés to Honduras.

Despite her several marriages, Sarah Winnemucca remained childless. Had things been otherwise, she could not have served as army scout and courier, for unlike Sacajawea, she could not go about her work with an infant strapped to her back.

And finally there was the matter of sheer physical endurance. These women traveled with mounted men. To serve as guide (or "pilot" as Clark characterized Sacajawea), they had to keep up. It was not a life for sheltered princesses. We have seen what Doña Marina endured, especially on the last overland trek. When Lewis and Clark paid off Charbonneau, Lewis wrote of Sacajawea, "She has borne with a patience truly remarkable the fatigues of so long a route,"[85] and Clark wrote to her husband, "Your woman, who accompanied you that long and dangerous and fatiguing route to the Pacific Ocian and back, deserved a greater reward for her attention and service on that route than we had in our power to give her."[86] As for Sarah and her sister-in-law Mattie, even when the women were not involved in battles, flights, or pursuits, they often covered thirty to forty miles a day on horseback in the closing days of the Bannock War. On the occasion of bringing her father and his band out of the Bannock camp, Sarah made a round trip of over 200 miles in two days.[87]

These were uncommon individuals living in extraordinary times. Circumstances put them at the centers of immense clashes of cultures, and their horizons, both geographical and intellectual, exploded. But did these special circumstances also provide an opening for talents that would otherwise have been stifled? Margaret Caffrey, in her biography of the anthropologist Ruth Benedict, speaks of "the struggle between the individual and her culture, and the attempt to remain an individual when one is a misfit in a repressive culture with whose values one cannot agree."[88]

Did the intruders perhaps offer these women the opportunity to escape traditional roles to which they were unsuited?

If their worlds had remained undisturbed, they would have lived much narrower lives. For a young noblewoman like Doña Marina, this meant close confinement to her parents' home as a child, to a religious institution for womanly education as an adolescent, and to her husband's home as a married woman. Recall the speech that Bernal Díaz ascribes to Doña Marina. According to him, she said she was grateful to have been freed from idolatry, glad to serve Cortés and to have borne him a son, and happy to be married to Jaramillo. Moreover, she would not exchange what she had even for a kingdom all her own. We might dismiss this as wishful thinking on the part of the old chronicler, but suppose there had been a core of truth to what he reports. Her own world was generally characterized by stringently defined social roles that were taught in childhood and enforced throughout life. Deviation from the ideal brought dreadful punishments. According to their own literature, the Aztecs pricked recalcitrant children with thorns, beat them with nettles, and held them face-down in the smoke of burning chile peppers, while adults who gave even the appearance of impropriety were put to death.[89] This was a dangerous society for exceptional people.

Here is what Alonso de Zorita, a veteran of many years' experience in Mexico and Guatemala during the sixteenth century, wrote about the life of young noblewomen:

> A ruler's daughter was reared with much discipline and propriety, with great solicitude and care on the part of her mother, nurse, and elder brothers. When she reached the age of four, they impressed on her the need for being very discreet in speech and conduct, in appearance and bearing. Many daughters of rulers never left home until the day of their wedding. . . . A ruler's daughter went about in the company of many elderly women, and she walked so modestly that she never raised her eyes from the ground. . . . She never spoke in the temple, save to say the prayers she had been taught; she must not speak while eating, but must keep absolute silence. . . . The maidens could not go out to the gardens without guards. If they took a single step out the door, they were harshly punished, especially if they had reached the age of ten or twelve. Maidens who raised their eyes from the ground or looked behind them were also punished cruelly. . . . They were taught how to speak to the ruler's wives and to other persons, and were punished if they showed themselves negligent in this. They were constantly admonished to heed the good counsel they received.[90]

Is it imaginable that well before Cortés came on the scene Doña Marina had been given away by her own family to the people of Xicalango because it was already evident that she would not or could not conform to the role to which she was born? Is it possible that they feared that with an ungovernable tongue she would bring shame and disaster to her lineage?

All, too, is conjecture about the young Sacajawea. The old woman on the Wind River reservation was bright, outgoing, and robust even in advanced age, and the Shoshone tradition relates the adventures of an uncommonly self-possessed woman who would travel where she pleased, present her credentials to white people and Indians alike, and take an active part in community deliberations. Could the sister of Cameahwait have become this sort of person had she never been snatched from the Shoshones?

Unlike the city-dwelling peoples to the south, the Shoshones and Paiutes, men and women alike, roamed over large areas, but their migrations followed the annual cycles of the game and plants they ate, and they moved year after year over much the same routes. When Doña Marina was enslaved by the Maya and Sacajawea by the Minnetaree, they were taken to places they would not otherwise have known, but still to communities that had their own predictable patterns.

It was white men who took the women off on routes they constructed as they went along. Such was the high adventure of discovery. In retrospect the native peoples of the Americas might say there had been nothing to discover; they had known their lands forever. But few individuals had traveled the distances covered by the expeditions of Cortés and of Lewis and Clark, and certainly not young women. Who ever before had walked from the coast of the Gulf of Mexico to the high central valleys of Mexico and then through the rain forests to Honduras before Doña Marina did it at the side of Cortés? Nor did Shoshones go all the way to the Pacific coast and return home to tell of it, and as a result, the Wind River Shoshones dismissed stories of seals and whales as sheer fantasy.

As for Sarah Winnemucca, she not only found herself far out of the range of the Northern Paiutes' migrations, first over the Sierra Nevada to California, then north of the Columbia River, but ultimately, thanks to the transcontinental railroad, she made her way to one of the most exotic spots on the North American continent, the United States Capitol.

Once experienced, mobility is not easy to give up. Writing of a woman he identified as Sacajawea, a man said of her, "She was not a woman that was satisfied anywhere . . . and the stage companies helped to make her this way, for they gave her free rides."[91]

These women came to know things that set them apart. They had learned firsthand that beyond their own people and their people's immediate allies and enemies there were many other human communities in the world, some of them very strange indeed. Among the most alien of people were those who employed them as interpreters and guides. In the course of their employment they had learned the languages of these strangers, and they had some understanding of what the men believed and how they behaved.

This knowledge made the women powerful brokers between their employers and their peoples, but it located them out on the periphery of their home communities, where they were regarded with suspicion. We have seen that popular imagination over time invested Doña Marina with most of the characteristics associated with European witches: unbridled sexuality, beauty masking ugliness, the power to lure people to their deaths. According to the chroniclers, residents of Mexico City reported visions of her burning in hellfire with Cortés while the two of them were still alive. The grandson of the old Shoshone woman living on the Wind River reservation wrote that she had been "very careful to keep the early part of her life to herself."[92] And her great-grandson wrote, "Even though it was realized that Sacagawea had done an unusual thing and that the white men were under obligation to her . . . the Indian men did not like to see a woman go ahead of them. . . . It was a natural thing that the men should not rejoice in a woman's being a chief."[93] As for Sarah Winnemucca, she acknowledges more than once in her autobiography that the Paiutes suspected she was not working for their best interests, and at times no one would speak to her. In the end she gave up on them and spent the few remaining years of her life with her sister, who had withdrawn from Paiute society thirty years earlier.

It probably was somewhere between difficult and impossible for these women to return to any sort of conventional life within their communities after performing the work they did. Traditional society as they had known it was disappearing underfoot like snow in May. Indian communities could no longer afford protection to those at their very core, much less to those on the edge.

Need we even ask why these intelligent, multilingual, robust women cast their lot with foreign men—to work for them, protect them and seek protection from them, and to form sexual unions with them? Consider this passage from a letter written by a man who accompanied Christopher Columbus on his second voyage and had been given a young Carib woman by the Admiral:

> Having taken her into my cabin, she being naked according to their custom, I conceived desire to take pleasure. I wanted to put my desire into execution but she did not want it and treated me with her finger nails in such a manner that I wished I had never begun. But seeing that,

· (to tell you the end of it all), I took a rope and thrashed her well, for which she raised such unheard of screams that you would not have believed your ears. Finally we came to an agreement in such manner that I can tell you that she seemed to have been brought up in a school of harlots.[94]

So wrote Michele de Cuneo in 1495 of a woman he found "very beautiful." Most men who have written about Indian women seem unable to admit the fact of rape. Time and again Bernal Díaz speaks of "good-looking women," women the Spanish soldiers found so pretty that they hid them away whenever their superiors took to branding Indians on the face. But he doesn't say a word about what the Spanish men did with them and what happened to the women afterwards. Somonte weaves a cloak of romanticism to shroud the sexual use of Doña Marina, and Howard is something of an apologist for Charbonneau, remarking, "It was the pinnacle of many Indian girls' ambition to marry a fur trader."[95] In the company of Cortés and his companions Doña Marina had no more opportunity for resistance or escape than had the Carib woman who fell into the hands of Columbus. Nor did Sacajawea chose to be the wife of Charbonneau, who acquired her from her kidnappers before she reached puberty and impregnated her and her Shoshone co-wife when they were still hardly more than children. One of the rare people to be completely candid about what men did with Indian women was Michele de Cuneo.

Sarah Winnemucca enjoyed a modicum of protection thanks to her male relatives and various commanding officers, but we see how vulnerable she was when that protection lapsed. During her estrangement from her father and brother over her first failed marriage, she left the Paiutes and the army to work in a railroad town, where she took to carrying a knife to defend herself. From this period, when she was a woman alone, came the rumors of Sarah as street brawler and prostitute.

She is frank about the stress of constant sexual threat, ascribing the root of more than one deadly conflict between Indians and white settlers to the kidnap and rape of young women. Concluding a section about an Indian woman's chances of defending herself, she refers obliquely to personal experience: "It is something an Indian woman dare not say till she has been overcome by one man. . . . My dear reader, I have not lived in this world for over thirty or forty years for nothing, and I know what I am talking about."[96]

Doña Marina, Sacajawea, and Sarah Winnemucca were not women with stable positions in their struggling communities. Given their circumstances, had they any chance at all of unions with anyone but white men? The answer seems to be at most a tentative maybe. Doña Marina, it is said, was offered marriage in Cholula and chose to remain with Cortés. If the Shoshone tradition is to be believed, Sacajawea left the abusive Charbonneau and lived happily with a Comanche husband until she was widowed. Records suggest that the oft-married Sarah Winnemucca may have lived for a while with an Indian husband too. But what sort of lives could they have had within their own societies? If the tradition that the Wind River woman was Sacajawea is accurate, she only returned to her people as an elderly widow. And if Sarah Winnemucca really did have an Indian husband at one time, that marriage failed like her others.

Sarah's marriages were so unsuccessful that it is hard to imagine what she hoped for from them. But she must have had some expectations, especially for the marriage she made in the home of the Parrish family, witnessed by her cherished friends and their children. And in Hopkins she did find a husband who would accompany her, introduce her, conduct research for her, and handle her mail. Had he not also been a pathological gambler and tubercular besides, it could have been an advantageous match, but Sarah could not have been blind to his poor health and his addiction. Perhaps she had no clear idea of what might be normal in the world of white men, or perhaps she thought she could do no better. Had she been willing to settle for an early marriage and a life of profound retirement, as her sister Elma had, she might have been able to avoid destitution, vilification, and day-to-day incidents of racism, but it would have been a suffocating life for a woman of such incandescent intelligence.

In any case, given that they were especially gifted individuals living in times of social upheaval, perhaps all three women at crucial moments in their lives knew that their best chances lay with non-Indian men.

But while unions with men from outside might have been an escape route from enslavement or the strictures of traditional society, they were not safe passage to better lives. Doña Marina's life was short indeed, and although her name is known to us for her role in the conquest, she also shared the fate of many anonymous or near-anonymous Indian women who were given to Cortés and his men. Though some were daughters of high nobility and others were not, their common fate was to to receive Christian names in baptism and to be turned over to Spanish men. Bernal Díaz personally asked Montezuma to give him a pretty woman, and Montezuma obliged. The Aztec noblewoman was baptized Doña Francisca, and that is the last we hear of her. His biographer says that he had two daughters by another Indian woman and that he took good care of these children on into their adulthood, but what happened to their mother when he went off to Guatemala, married a Spanish woman, and had nine children by her? And what about the Guatemalan Indian woman by whom he had a son? Some women given to Spanish soldiers undoubtedly died of European diseases, and some Indian women were killed outright. The fate of most—including Doña Marina and the daughters of Montezuma and Xicotencatl—was to be impregnated by Spaniards and to give birth to mestizos. The fathers sometimes legitimized their children, but for the most part the mothers vanished without a trace after living long enough to produce daughters who became mothers of yet more mestizos and so on for the better part of five centuries.

Meriwether Lewis remarked on the role of sexual hospitality among the Indian groups he met. Men and older women offered the sexual use of young female relatives to visitors in exchange for goods and favors, and Charbonneau and many other white traders like him were happy to accept very young Indian women. As Howard says, some of these men might have been kind husbands and fathers, but the term "squaw-man" was contemptuous, and their wives and children were not welcome in white society.

Sarah Winnemucca may well have been grateful for her childless state. She wrote, "My people have been so unhappy for a long time they wish now to *disincrease*, instead of to multiply. The mothers are afraid to have more children, for fear they shall have daughters, who are not safe even in their mother's presence."[97]

Of the three women, it is only Sarah Winnemucca who speaks to us directly about her own feelings and perceptions. The tone of her autobiography is one of overwrought emotion. She repeatedly describes herself as fatigued, incapacitated by weeping. Tears of frustration, outrage, exhaustion, and pity flood her life story.

This contrasts markedly with the general stoicism in portrayals of Doña Marina and Sacajawea. But they are known to us through the perceptions of others, whereas Sarah Winnemucca tells us about herself. Even if we are cautious about taking everything she says at face value, there are things we can learn about her from her autobiography that we cannot know about Doña Marina and Sacajawea.

All three women had conveyed many promises: Christian salvation, deliverance from error and idolatry, government by just rulers. If Doña Marina and Sacajawea had left their own statements, would they have condemned the hypocrisy? There was much to rage against: the promises of the Christian evangelists both Catholic and Protestant; the glorification of the Spanish monarchs and the presidents of the United States of America; use, abuse, and nonpayment for services. Can we generalize from what Sarah says to what they might have said? Is Sarah spokesperson for them all? We simply cannot know.

Her editor writes in the preface, "I am confident that no one would desire that her own original words should be altered. . . . It is of the utmost importance to hear what only an Indian and an Indian woman can tell." Toward the end of her book, this is what Sarah says:

> You who are educated by a Christian government in the art of war; the practice of whose profession makes you natural enemies of the savages, so called by you. Yes, you, who call yourselves the great civilization; you who have knelt upon Plymouth Rock, covenanting with God to make this land the home of the free and the brave. Ah, then you rise from your bended knees . . . and your so-called civilization sweeps inland from the ocean wave; but, oh, my God! leaving its pathway marked by crimson lines of blood, and strewed by the bones of two races, the inheritor and the invader.[98]

C h a p t e r   T w o

Three
Civil Servants

FOR BISHOPS AND REIGNING MONARCH:
Gaspar Antonio Chi (ca. 1532–1610)

*Due to his royal Indian lineage, Gaspar Antonio was respected by the
Indians, who sought his aid when they became entangled in the newfan-
gled Spanish methods of law. Due to his mastery, not only of the Spanish
language but also of Latin and Nahoatl [sic], or Aztec, languages, he
was trusted and esteemed by the Spaniards. Through him went the
grievances of both sides, and, as he was astute and wily, he gained great
power. He took the same place in the final conquest of Yucatan as that
taken by Doña Marina in the conquest of Mexico.*

—*FRANS BLOM*[1]

The story of Gaspar Antonio Chi is the story of the conquest of the Maya
of Yucatan and of how one man survived an evangelist's love and hatred
for the Maya.

The Maya of the Yucatan peninsula were the first mainland people
contacted and the last subjugated by the Spaniards. Off a nearby coast in
1502 Christopher Columbus encountered a trading canoe plying the
coastal commercial route of the Maya, but when he parted company with
the craft and its crew, he sailed directly away without ever setting foot on
the Mayas' land of dense jungle, limestone caves, and beaches of white
sand finer than ground salt or the most refined sugar imaginable.

But other Spaniards did fetch up on those beaches. A small group survived a shipwreck in 1511 and were carried onto the shore. Some were sacrificed and consumed by the first Maya who found them, and a few others died before that fate could befall them, but two men found protection with a Maya nobleman who was inclined to keep them alive. One of these was Jerónimo de Aguilar, later to be rescued by Hernán Cortés and to become Doña Marina's interpreter colleague in the conquest of the Aztecs.

From Aguilar and his companion Gonzalo Guerrero, the Maya learned firsthand of the Spaniards who had been occupying islands of the Caribbean for close to twenty years. They had, no doubt, already heard of the Spaniards from Caribbean peoples affected by the occupation. It was only a matter of time until Spaniards found the Yucatecan coast.

While they waited, the Maya were attacked by a deadly disease that covered the bodies of its victims with pustules, a disease that sounds like smallpox.[2] Its horror did nothing to help unite them in anticipation of the Spanish threat.

The Maya of Yucatan were a divided people. Although just one language was spoken over the whole peninsula, the people who spoke what they all called "the Maya language" belonged to more than a dozen rival factions. According to their histories, a union of the different Maya groups had fallen apart in the middle of the preceding century. The breakup had been occasioned by the slaughter of Cocom noblemen by members of the Xiu faction. (*Xiu* is pronounced approximately like "shoe.") After the bloodshed, the various groups had packed up as many of their hieroglyphic books as possible and carried them off to their own provincial centers, leaving the old capital city of Mayapan in ruins.

During the rest of the century each Maya province had built up its own main town with its own temples and its own priesthood, to say nothing of its own loyalties and allies. And each watched its neighbors warily.

In 1511 the Maya were living in smaller communities than they once had. In the forest lay the remains of great cities no longer inhabited. Chichen Itza was deserted and overgrown, although people still made pilgrimages to its large *cenote,* a water-filled sinkhole in the limestone shelf of Yucatan. Into the waters of the cenote they cast ornaments and sometimes men and women, in the belief that the water covered an opening into another world where lived the deities who gave or withheld the life-giving rain and who knew the secrets of the times to come.

Waterholes are of crucial importance to Maya communities. Yucatan is a land without rivers and lakes. During the rainy season, water stands in puddles everywhere, because the thin soil on top of limestone cannot absorb it. Soon after the rain ceases, the water disappears. Months go by before it rains again, months in which there is no surface water at all. Yet crystalline water lies below, where it has trickled through cracks in the limestone to caves large and small. Where a cave ceiling has worn thin and collapsed there is a hole open to the sky, and in the bottom of the hole lies the precious water. Only where there is access to underground water can people live. The Maya had learned to fearlessly wedge themselves through the smallest cave entrances and to descend hundreds of feet in darkness to reach water. They might pitch men and women into the depths of Chichen Itza's cenote of sacrifice to consult with the gods on the other side, but it was unthinkable to foul their own water with corpses.

Another asset of each Maya town was its books. Written in hieroglyphs on pages of fine deerskin or of bark paper, these books kept the count of days and astronomical events, which told when to plant and when to harvest. Consulting them, the Maya priests foretold the fates of newborn children and prescribed treatments for illnesses. The books also preserved a record of Maya history. Each town had professional interpreters of its books, who kept them up to date and periodically read them to the assembled citizens. Their books were the heart and soul of Maya communities, and in some places they still are, although they have long since ceased to be written in glyphs.

The books kept alive the memory of each Maya faction's origins. They preserved the recollection of Mayapan and of the slaughter of the Cocoms by the Xius. They recorded the disasters of invasions and hurricanes and epidemics and famines. They even seemed to prophesy the coming of strangers like the Spaniards.

When Spanish ships first began nosing along their shores, the Maya went out in their own boats and invited the Spaniards ashore. It was an invitation to an ambush, but the Maya had not reckoned with swords, crossbows, and muskets. The Spanish escaped wiser in the ways of the Maya. With them they carried off two Maya men, whom they baptized Julián and Melchor.

More conflicts with the Maya took place wherever the Spaniards put ashore for fresh water. Finally the Spaniards departed back to Cuba, taking Julián and Melchor with them. The two captive Maya were to learn Spanish so they could serve as interpreters in later dealings between the Spaniards and the Maya.

To the Maya it must have seemed no time at all before another Spanish fleet arrived. Everyone who lived on the coast withdrew to the protection of the jungle, so there was hardly anyone around to talk with Melchor.

(Julián had died in captivity.) Once again the Spaniards tried putting in here and there, only to be met by Maya stones and arrows. But the visitors were persistent, and so the Maya tried to buy them off. They gave the Spaniards a sampling of ornaments and indicated they could find more of the same if they would just keep going west, west to Montezuma's realm.

And now it was Hernán Cortés who came to the Yucatecan coast. On the island of Cozumel he smashed Maya incense burners and set up an altar and cross in a Maya temple. Then he recovered Aguilar from the mainland and sailed away to the Tabasco coast, where he engaged the Maya in furious battle. Melchor, whose rudimentary Spanish had not served the Spaniards well in any case, took advantage of the moment to escape. But now Cortés had Aguilar, fluent in Maya, a bit rusty in his native Spanish, but nonetheless a master interpreter.

Once again the Maya, having given combat a try, switched to bribes. They gave Cortés and his men twenty women and urged the company to keep on going west. Cortés did as they suggested and discovered that in bilingual Doña Marina the Maya had given him a key to Montezuma's empire. The conquest of the Aztecs and their neighbors kept the Spaniards busy for years. Perhaps the Maya imagined they would not come back.

Yet news reached Yucatan of the disasters visited upon the peoples of Central Mexico. Maya coastal trade fell off as markets collapsed and Spanish ships came and went from the Veracruz coast. When a brother of Montezuma, garrisoned in Xicalango, heard of the Spaniards' successes against the Aztecs, he reportedly died of apoplexy, leaving his wife and infant daughter stranded in that Maya borderland. The Maya identified the smallpox epidemic that ravaged Montezuma's land with the dreadful pustular "Maya Death" they had so recently experienced.[3]

After a while Cortés, with Doña Marina still at his side and the young Aztec ruler Cuauhtemoc as his prisoner, visited the Chontal Maya on his way to Honduras. The Chontals recorded that it was in their territory that Cortés executed Cuauhtemoc. Then Cortés passed through the Itza Maya city of Tayasal, where he had Doña Marina give testimony about his military successes and left behind his lame horse before pressing on. By then his lieutenant Pedro de Alvarado was carrying the Spanish conquest to Guatemala, and the Tabasco and Honduras coasts were swarming with Spanish soldiers and settlers. Only Yucatan remained unoccupied.

What happened next is confusing in retrospect and must have been at least as confusing to the Maya who lived through it. Groups of Spaniards continued intruding onto the peninsula, now from the east, now from the west, mostly from offshore, but sometimes overland from the south. They came and then they withdrew. A few years would go by, and then they would be back. To add to the confusion, three different men with the same name led the intrusions. There was Francisco de Montejo, who had skirted along the Yucatecan shores even before Cortés. There was his son, also Francisco de Montejo, who accompanied Cortés on his visits to the Chontal Maya and the hidden city of the Itza Maya. And there was a nephew as well, yet another Francisco de Montejo. Just as the Indians of central Mexico merged Cortés and Doña Marina into one "Malintzin," so the Maya tended to think of anyone who led an invasion of their land as one and the same "Adelantado."

It was the eldest Francisco de Montejo, veteran of early exploration, who successfully petitioned the king for permission to pacify the Maya and claim Yucatan. To him the king granted the role of *adelantado* (a person with official license to engage in conquest), since Montejo had previous experience with the Maya and had traveled to Spain with the first shipment of treasure Cortés sent from Veracruz. (His companion on that voyage had been Alonso Hernández de Puertocarrero, the man to whom Cortés had briefly given Doña Marina before he realized her potential and took her back.)

In 1527, with all papers in order and ships provisioned, Montejo and his party set out to subjugate the Maya. As he explored the Caribbean coast of Yucatan, he became aware of the presence of Gonzalo Guerrero, the other Spanish shipwreck victim, who had now lived as a Maya among the Maya for more than fifteen years. The interpreting services of Guerrero would have been of inestimable value to Montejo, but Guerrero declined to be rescued. Throughout the next several years he advised the Maya about how to outwit the Spanish forces until finally he died fighting at their side against Spaniards in Honduras.

Leaving the coast he had come to know painfully and with little profit, Montejo sailed away. Next, on the Tabasco coast, he joined with his son, Francisco de Montejo, who had learned much about the base of the peninsula by accompanying Cortés on his overland expedition to Honduras. By 1534 men working for Montejo had explored most of the north and central areas and had cut straight across the peninsula from west to east. They had visited the Xius and found them somewhat well-disposed towards the Spaniards as potential allies against the Cocoms.

The Montejos now knew that the interior of the peninsula held no great living cities. Ruins of cities there were, their time long past. The Maya were expert at living in their jungle, growing corn and conserving water, and they supported a class of noblemen and noblewomen of considerable refinement, but there was nothing to be found that had much

appeal for Spaniards. After occupying Chichen Itza for awhile, the Spaniards beat a retreat and abandoned the peninsula again.

During the years when the Spanish forces had been ashore in Yucatan,
a Maya child was born in the Xiu town of Mani, a child of fine lineage and,
as later became apparent, great intellectual gifts. His mother was a daughter of the Xiu ruler, and his father was a Maya priest. Soon after the boy's
birth, his father was among the Xius who met with Montejo's forces as
they explored the interior in the early 1530s.

The child was born into difficult times. Subsistence in Yucatan was
delicately balanced. It was necessary to plant and harvest at exactly the
right moments, and the presence of Spanish explorers moving about in
the countryside had upset the rhythm of crop cultivation and wasted corn
that should have been stored. A drought exacerbated by grasshoppers set
in and went on and on. Starvation beset the Maya, and their suffering
approached the magnitude of the days of the Maya Death.

According to the Xius, a delegation of more than forty of their
noblemen set out in 1536 to make offerings at Chichen Itza to alleviate
the famine or at least to seek to learn what would next befall the Maya.
The way from Xiu territory to Chichen Itza led across enemy Cocom
territory. The Xius asked for safe passage and were invited through by the
ruler Nachi Cocom, but it was a ruse. When the Xiu delegation's guard
was down, the Cocoms slaughtered them. The Cocoms had their revenge
for the previous century's massacre, and they also dealt a punishing blow
to neighbors who had recently accepted a visit from Montejo's Spaniards.
The little Xiu boy lost his father and many of his relatives. Growing up in
Mani he learned the story of the massacre well, and as a man he retold it
many times.

When Montejo's soldiers left Yucatan in 1535, five Franciscan friars
arrived. They came from central Mexico, where the Franciscans had been
learning Nahuatl in order to preach to the Indians there. But evangelism
could not wait. The name of Jacobo de Testera, the leader of the little
group that came to Yucatan, is associated with picture-book catechisms
that look very much like comic strips without words. With paintings and
perhaps with books of this sort they made their first efforts to convey
something of Christianity to the Maya.

Still, it was not the aim of the Franciscans to simply teach new
converts to cross themselves and recite the Creed and some Latin prayers
by rote. They wanted to obliterate the Indians' own religion and make of
them true converts, people who understood sin and salvation and were
responsible for their own souls. This required the Indians to master more
than the outward forms of Catholicism, and so it was that wherever the

Franciscans went, they set themselves to language-learning. In central Mexico they had found many other Indian languages beside Nahuatl. Testera and his colleagues must have been pleased to learn that the Maya of Yucatan had just one.

In and around what had been Montezuma's capital the friars had established schools for teaching well-born Indian boys Latin and how to use the same Roman alphabet to write and read their native language. The boys the Franciscans took into their schools were already familiar with their own painted books, and they showed talent for learning how to use the new Roman alphabet. Juan de Tecto had begun to write a catechism in Nahuatl for them before he left for Honduras with Cortés, and others carried on. By 1535 the Franciscans were anxious to extend their attention to the spiritual state of the Maya in similar ways.

Jacobo de Testera had not wished the conversion of the Maya to be linked to military conquest. The withdrawal of Montejo's soldiers offered the Franciscans the opportunity to go among the Maya as a men of peace. He was assured that they would have the peninsula to themselves, and so they went. The Maya offered them no harm, and the friars believed that they accomplished much good, but Spanish assurances proved false. Soldiers arrived, and Testera stood by his principles and departed.

Now the Maya had been acquainted with the two forces that were to reshape their lives and their society: the Spanish conquerors and settlers who came to take possession of Maya land and goods, and the Franciscans who came to take possession of Maya hearts and minds. Each group would later claim they were the patrons and protectors of the Maya, while portraying their rivals as murderers. The little Xiu boy growing up in Mani would in the course of his life serve both sides.

When Montejo's forces came back for yet another stab at conquest, they hardly recognized the peninsula they had abandoned. They returned to a place devastated by imbalances: too little rain, too many insects, too many blood feuds, a population decimated by famine. It seemed a ruined land.

It was 1540 when the old Adelantado's son struck out to finish up the job begun so many years before. In the course of a year he established himself in one of Yucatan's long-abandoned cities and there founded the Spanish city of Mérida at the very beginning of 1542.

Nachi Cocom, great-grandson of the Nachi Cocom who had slaughtered the Xius, immediately attacked the new capital of the foreigners, but Montejo turned back the assault and then used Mérida as a base for bringing the northern and eastern Maya provinces under his control. The Xius, given a chance to wreak havoc on the Cocoms, allied themselves with the Spaniards. The last area to be pacified, with great ferocity, was the extreme southeast. Toward the end, the Maya in desperation were not only abandoning their towns, but also destroying their crops and ruining their precious water holes so the Spaniards could not benefit from them.

Three groups were spared the devastation wrought by Montejo's lieutenants. The Xius escaped because of their collaboration; the Chontal Maya were under other Spanish authority; and aside from Maya refugees with terrible stories to tell, nobody found the way back to the Itza town of Tayasal for nearly a hundred years.

The last paroxysm of Maya resistance took place in 1546 in the recently pacified eastern provinces of Yucatan. Spanish settlers were already living on the land with their wives and children, and the Maya slaughtered them—some quickly, others by slow torture. When troops from Mérida reached the scene of the massacre, they reported that the Maya had crucified some Spaniards; other victims had their hearts cut out; and two Spanish children had been roasted in the smoke and fumes of burning incense. These reports planted the seed of fear that the Maya, instead of giving up their religion for Christianity, were incorporating features of Christianity into their own religion. It was a suspicion that would have horrific consequences for the Maya sixteen years later.

Not only had settlers come to Yucatan, but Franciscan friars had also returned in force. They built a monastery in Mérida and set up a school there, and then they fanned out to the provincial towns establishing churches and regional schools. This is how the Franciscan Diego de Landa described their enterprise:

> The way the friars used to teach religious doctrine to the Indians was to take the children of the lords and chieftains and to send them to live in houses which each town had constructed for its own people to the monasteries; here all the people from the same place lived together and their parents brought them food. With these children they placed only those who came to learn the doctrine and, because of their attendance, many became devout and asked for baptism. Once they had been instructed, the children were diligent in informing the friars about cases of idolatry and drunkenness and in destroying the idols, even if they belonged to their parents. . . . Although they were threatened by their own people, they did not stop because of this, but on the contrary replied that they were doing them an honor because it was for the good of their souls. . . . At first the lords were reluctant to give over their children, thinking that the friars wanted to make slaves of them . . . but when they understood the business, they handed them over willingly.
>
> In this manner the young people made so much progress in the school and the other people in the catechism that it was a wonderful thing. The friars learned to read and write in the language of the Indians,

which was so successfully reduced to a grammatical art that it could be studied like Latin.[4]

The Franciscan said to have mastered the Maya language best was Luis de Villalpando. In 1547 he and a fellow Franciscan set out from Mérida to Christianize the Xius. On their first visit they were treated with courtesy in spite of their demands that the Xiu nobleman free their slaves and receive Christian baptism. On a return visit, things did not go so well. The Xiu had constructed a church building for them not in Mani, under the eye of the ruler, but off in a neighboring town. When irritated local Maya decided to burn the church, a Maya boy informed on the plotters, and the two Franciscans spent the night in the church, daring the Maya to burn it down. When the Xiu ruler came from Mani to deal with the disturbance, he turned over to the Spanish civil authorities those of his subjects who had threatened the friars.

In Mérida the Adelantado sentenced the prisoners to be burned alive, as they might have burned the Franciscans in the church, but Villalpando made a dramatic plea for their pardon, and by this act established himself and the Franciscan order as compassionate protectors of the Maya. Many Xius, their ruler among them, then accepted baptism, and the Franciscans wisely moved their church to Mani.

The Maya boy of noble Xiu lineage, the boy who had lost his father to the treachery of Nachi Cocom, was baptized at age fifteen as Gaspar Antonio de Herrera Chi. Beatriz de Herrera, wife of the Adelantado Montejo, stood as his godmother. The Adelantado himself was godfather for the ruler of Mani, who took the name of his sponsor in baptism. Now there were four Francisco de Montejos, this newest of them being Francisco de Montejo Xiu.

Gaspar Antonio was given to the Franciscans for education and proved such a brilliant student that we learn of his accomplishments from Spanish settlers and administrators, people with no love in their hearts for the friars. Testimonies to his skill and competence came from *encomenderos,* men who, in recognition of their services in the conquest, had been granted the service of Indians in Maya towns. About forty years after the final phase of the conquest began, Pedro de Santillana, an ancient veteran and encomendero, described Gaspar Antonio as a man of about fifty, fluent in Spanish, Nahuatl, and Maya, a man wise in the ways of the Maya and at the same time trusted by the bishops of Yucatan. The old man not only gave Gaspar Antonio credit for assisting him but had Gaspar Antonio place his signature beside his own in the report they had drafted together for the king of Spain. Pedro Sánchez de Aguilar, a churchman, recalled in

1613 that Gaspar Antonio had "placed the grammar book in my hands when I was a child." At the time Gaspar Antonio was chapel master of the church in the town of Tizimin, where he served as organist. Sánchez de Aguilar says, "He was as learned as any Spaniard, sang plain song (canto llano), and sang to the organ with great skill."[5]

The Spaniards used the word *nahuatlato* 'one who speaks Nahuatl' to mean an interpreter of any Indian language. In keeping accounts, they often referred to payments made to Maya "nahuatlatos" who spoke only Maya and Spanish. But others besides Santillana asserted that Gaspar Antonio really spoke Nahuatl, and Gaspar Antonio did not contradict them. Under instruction from the friars he had learned three languages in addition to his native Maya, for Santillana neglected to mention Gaspar Antonio's mastery of Latin, for which he was famous.

Gaspar Antonio came late to learning foreign languages and European music; he was already a teenager when the Franciscans established their schools in Mérida and then Mani. But the Maya imposed a rigorous education of their own on the children of their noblemen, and the discipline and habit of study were not new to the boy. Learning to read books written in Maya glyphs took years of study. Diego de Landa wrote, "These people also used certain glyphs or letters in which they wrote down their ancient history and sciences in their books; and by means of these letters and figures and by certain marks contained in them, they could write about their affairs and taught others to read about them too."[6]

Reading and writing were among the main responsibilities of the Maya priests, who "also taught the children of other priests and the second sons of the lords, who were reared for the office from infancy if they showed any inclination to it."[7] Gaspar Antonio's father had been such a priest, and the boy had an aptitude for learning. And so, just as the Franciscans built churches on the foundations of Maya temples, they lay down their Christian training of Gaspar Antonio on a foundation of Maya education. As an adult, when called upon to relate the history and customs of the Maya, he was pleased to do so at length and in great detail.

The Franciscans were frank about the roles the Indian boys in their schools were to assume in the evangelization effort. They were educated to be interpreters and agents for the friars. Since there were few Franciscans and many Indians, the boys were to prepare sermons under the supervision of the friars and then go among their own people to preach to them. When they had completed their studies in the friars' schools, they were to become resident teachers in Maya communities. There they would teach the catechism, instruct people in the Catholic prayers, and direct sacred music in the churches. In Spanish documents from Yucatan, Maya men who assumed these duties are called "chapel masters" rather than "schoolmasters," but the Maya always called them "song masters." Nor is it surprising that church music caught the imagination of the Maya more than the catechism or recitation of Latin prayers.

Young Gaspar Antonio did not disappoint his teachers. In applying for a pension late in his career, he described his early service to the Franciscans in this way: "I aided and served . . . as the first native who learned the Spanish and Latin languages, interpreting to them (the natives) the things concerning their conversion to the Holy Catholic Faith. . . . (I) have taught the said friars . . . the language of these natives, which I interpret to them. . . . I have made . . . a grammar for this, and I have written sermons for them in the language to preach to the said natives. . . . They have commanded and made use of me for the said language, to interpret to the natives the sermons which they preach to them in Spanish."[8]

What the friars did not count on was that their school boys would appropriate what they learned to Maya uses. When they engaged boys like Gaspar Antonio as assistants in compiling grammars and dictionaries of Maya and adapting the Roman alphabet for writing the language, they had catechisms and sermons in mind. But after the graduates of the Franciscan schools left the friars to serve as chapel masters, some of them used their skills in the new kind of writing to transcribe what was written in the Mayas' own hieroglyphic books. They also taught others to read and write in the new way, and Maya leaders took to communicating with each other by letter.

Among the Franciscans in Mérida the great linguist, according to tradition, was Villalpando, the hero of the Mani incident and the man who had evangelized the Xius. In the scant ten years before his death in Yucatan, he produced a grammar of Maya, translated a Christian doctrine into Maya, and worked on a Spanish-Maya dictionary. But there is no way of judging the quality of his description of the Maya language or comparing it with the one Gaspar Antonio claimed he wrote, for—like all the Mayas' own books—both grammars have long since been lost.

The next Spaniard to become a real master of the language was Diego de Landa, who was born in Spain in 1524 and entered the Franciscan order at age seventeen. In the year he became a friar, Montejo's soldiers were just launching their final assault on Yucatan, and Mérida had not yet been founded. In 1549, when Landa arrived in a group of Franciscan recruits, Villalpando was still alive, and Gaspar Antonio was still receiving his education. But Sánchez de Aguilar, the Spaniard who had Gaspar Antonio as his grammar teacher in Tizimin, is mistaken when he says that

Landa personally raised Gaspar Antonio from childhood, since Landa was but seven years older than Gaspar Antonio. Gaspar Antonio was around eighteen years old and Landa around twenty-five when Landa came to Yucatan.

At the time Landa knew no Maya at all, and he was sent to the town of Izamal for total immersion in the language and culture. Izamal was an intimidating place, full of tall pyramids and strange stone carvings. Not satisfied with even that degree of alienation, Landa asked for and received permission to go out alone to the Maya villages of the east, among the people who were alleged to have crucified Christians and roasted their children in 1546. Soon he gained a reputation for disrupting Maya community gatherings and leading the Maya in smashing anything and everything he took to be an idol.

To the Maya Landa must have seemed yet another inexplicable Spanish phenomenon. He was fearless and seemed to offer no physical threat. He appealed to them by working hard to speak their language, and they permitted him a kind of intimacy. At some time, by his own account, he befriended the Spaniards' implacable enemy Nachi Cocom and learned a great deal from him. The leader of resistance against the Spanish submitted to baptism and became Juan Cocom. Landa characterized him as "a man of great repute and very learned in Indian affairs and very wise and versed in their physical world." According to Landa, his dear friend showed him how one of the Cocoms' hieroglyphic books seemed to predict the coming of horses to Yucatan.[9]

If Landa was sometimes disruptive among the Maya, he was even more a gadfly to the Spanish colonists, unsparingly critical of the encomenderos to whom the defeated Maya now owed service. His indignation on this matter was shared by Villapando and his brother Franciscans, who had already denounced the servitude imposed on the Maya and asked for protective regulations in letters they wrote to Spain in 1548 and 1549.

During the 1550s there ensued a mighty struggle between the encomenderos and the friars. The friars condemned the encomenderos for working the Maya so hard that there was no time for religious instruction. They also made up lists of sensational crimes Spaniards had committed against the Maya. The encomenderos, who thought not in terms of the service of Indians they had been granted, but of "their towns," countered that the friars kept moving people around and destroying their houses. They said the Maya were dying off from homesickness and that the friars overworked them by requiring them to build churches and monasteries.

Both sides were right. The Maya were suffering unbearably under the double demands of the encomenderos and the friars. They were being assaulted, exploited, exhausted, and punished. The Franciscans did put Maya towns to the torch to force their residents to resettle closer to monasteries. Epidemics were taking their toll, the population was declining, and all the Spaniards were to blame. The world Gaspar Antonio knew from childhood and that Landa glimpsed on his foot travels was already splintered, and the Maya were trying to survive and find a way to live under hard new circumstances. The Franciscans did not want the Maya to rebuild their own culture; they wanted to replace it with their vision of Christianity.

Since there were so few Franciscans in Yucatan, probably less than three dozen, no one had to wait long for promotion. As soon as he arrived, Landa was named assistant to the *guardián* (superior) of the monastery at Izamal. The local Maya had conceded one of the pyramids to the friars, and the little group lived there in thatched houses like the Mayas' own. By 1553 Landa had taken over as guardián of Izamal. Now, with a fellow Franciscan serving as architect, he undertook to build a permanent monastery.

Their vision has been described as megalomaniac, and no one who visits Izamal even four centuries later can fail to be impressed. They had Maya laborers level the pyramid that had been given to the Franciscans, creating a vast platform. At the rear the workers raised a large church and cloister, and before it they laid out a court comparable in size to the court of St. Peter's Basilica in Rome. They paved the walkway around the edges of the court with cut stone from the demolished Maya temple, so as one walks, one treads on fragments of Maya culture.

The work began in 1553 and ended in 1561. Before it was finished Landa personally brought on donkeyback from Guatemala a statue of the Virgin Mary that would be venerated as the Patroness of Yucatan. The whole establishment was so contrary to Franciscan principles of humility and self-denial that when another Franciscan, Francisco de Toral, newly appointed as Bishop of Yucatan, went to inspect it, he wrote, "It is a fine thing to see it, and a scandal to permit it, for surely Saint Francis condemns it in his rule."[10]

During the eight years the church and monastery were under construction, Landa also engaged in another piece of un-Franciscan behavior. In 1556 an encomendero named Francisco Hernández was jailed for slandering the Franciscans. The Franciscan court found Hernández guilty, sequestered all his property in Yucatan, and sentenced him to exile and a fine. Hernández appealed to civil authorities and succeeded in getting a new trial but now came up against Landa himself. In the course of their three-year legal battle Landa asserted that his jurisdiction was not only independent of the civil court of appeals, but also of the authority of the archbishop in Mexico City. Landa claimed that he was subject directly to the pope. Hernández fought these outrageous assertions but eventually broke under the strain of repeated incarcerations. Finally he confessed, submitted to Landa's authority, was immediately released from prison, and died within days.

It was November 1561. The year had seen the completion of the monastery at Izamal and the obliteration of Hernández. In the first of these accomplishments, Landa had imposed his will on untold tons of stone and earth. In the second, he had broken a powerful member of the landed gentry. Within a few months he would begin an assertion of his authority over the Maya that was yet more megalomaniac.

While Landa was involved in empire building, Gaspar Antonio had, for the first time on record, contracted out his skills to the Maya and the Spanish civil government. Divided as they had been for a long time, the Maya were meticulous about boundary lines. They marked them with piles of stones and periodically walked their borders to warn off intruders. Disputes were inevitable, and the chaos of the Spanish conquest gave rise to even more contention than usual.

Now that the Maya were required to provide labor and goods to the Spanish conquerors, it was all the more important for each province and town to claim every last bit of its land. In the mid-1550s the Spanish civil government appointed a special judge to oversee the reestablishment of the borders of the towns within Gaspar Antonio's home province of Mani, and Gaspar Antonio served the judge as "commissioned interpreter." Together they went to the ancient Maya city of Uxmal to meet officials of other towns who would take part in the deliberations. Some of these representatives came from Cocom towns, but Nachi Cocom wisely stayed away. According to one copy of the Mani land treaty, "Don Juan Cocom, governor of Sotuta, was sick, having fallen ill, and did not come."[11]

Once the party had assembled at Uxmal, the judge, his interpreter, and at least a dozen Maya noblemen proceeded back over the hills to Mani to meet with the ruler, Francisco de Montejo Xiu. On the back of a map dated 1557 there is a description of their arrival and how the officials of all the towns under the the jurisdiction of Mani and also the officials from the distant towns certified Mani's internal divisions. Upon agreement, twenty-two stone crosses were planted to mark the boundaries. A second document also relates the arrival of the judge with Gaspar Antonio as his interpreter.[12]

Gaspar Antonio's and Diego de Landa's lives now began to converge. In 1561, as his contest of wills with Francisco Hernández drew to its conclusion, Landa was elected by the Franciscan friars of Yucatan and Guatemala as their supreme authority, their *provincial*. Taking up his new post in Mérida, he was for the first time in a position to work on a regular basis with Gaspar Antonio, who was by now thirty years old and married. Through the fall and winter and on into the early spring, neither man could have foreseen what lay just ahead.

Outside the city, both Spanish settlers and Spanish friars were troubled by the suspicion that the Maya continued to hold secret meetings. The settlers feared another uprising like the one of 1546. The Franciscans were obsessed with the notion that the Maya continued to practice idolatry, in other words that the Maya were trying to reconcile their own way of life with the new situation in which they found themselves.

Neither of these fears was baseless, since there were many more Maya than Spaniards on the peninsula, and the Maya were driven to desperation by the prohibition of their familiar traditions and by the demands of colonists and friars. Should that desperation lead to united action, the Spanish settlers were extremely vulnerable.

As for idolatry, there were so few friars and Maya assistants to carry on instruction that even if the Maya had all been willing to become the most doctrinally pure of Christians, there was seldom anyone around to show them how. Under the circumstances they had to find a way to avoid the wrath of the encomenderos, the wrath of the Franciscans, and the wrath of their old gods as well, in order to keep the corn growing and the rain returning every year. The Maya tried to make compromises so at least some of them might survive. The Franciscans would tolerate no compromise.

In May of 1562 two young Maya men reported to Pedro de Ciudad Rodrigo, the friar in charge of the monastery at Mani, that they had found idols and human skulls in a nearby cave.[13] Ciudad Rodrigo had the contents of the cave brought to the patio of the monastery and arrested all the Maya men who lived near the cave. Upon interrogation the men acknowledged that the idols were theirs and said they depended on them for rain, good crops, and success in hunting deer. They implicated other neighbors, and soon the Mani jail was filled to overflowing.

It came as a shock to Ciudad Rodrigo and the half dozen Franciscans studying the Maya language at his monastery to have tangible proof of the continuance of the Mayas' old ways right in Mani of all places, among the Xius, the oldest and best friends of the Spaniards. If Catholicism was not solid in Mani, how could the Maya be trusted anywhere? And if the Maya were still making offerings to idols, might not some of these offerings be human blood? Ciudad Rodrigo could not but remember the corpse of a baby he had examined the previous summer that seemed to bear signs of crucifixion.

Back then, upon receiving a letter from Juan Xiu notifying him of a dead Maya baby with marks on its body like the stigmata, Ciudad Rodrigo had notified Landa and dismissed the matter as certainly not a miracle. The body had been brought to him in an advanced state of putrification, and his examination had been cursory and unrevealing. He and his fellow friars were not at that time looking for evidence of human sacrifice.

In the aftermath of the events of the summer of 1562, Ciudad Rodrigo still maintained that the strangely marked baby was probably stillborn. But at the moment when the idols and skulls were discovered in Mani, accumulated stress reached a tip-point. In a flash the senior friar was convinced that all the Spaniards' darkest suspicions had been realized, and he was consumed with ungovernable anger.

Instead of trying to protect the Maya from his rage, his fellow Franciscans joined in. In the past, Franciscans had been restrained in punishing Maya. Now they strung their prisoners up by the wrists, hung weights from their feet, and whipped them to make them confess their transgressions. Some days following, the offenders had to stand through a wrathful sermon while holding their idols in their hands and wearing dunce caps on their heads, after which they were whipped some more. The Franciscans also required them to pay cash fines.

Landa received notice of the matter and after obtaining authorization from Diego Quijada, the head of the civil government, he came to Mani to conduct an inquiry. With him he brought Gaspar Antonio as interpreter, not so much for himself, since Landa spoke fluent Maya, but as a mouthpiece for Quijada, for Landa intended that the force of civil, not religious, authority would fall on the Maya. It was to be a reprise of the legendary moment in 1547 when the Adelantado pronounced sentence on the would-be Maya arsonists, while the friars pleaded for their forgiveness. But as events unfolded in 1562, civil authority and religious authority this time did not successfully play the manipulative game that we today call "good cop, bad cop."

For weeks Landa carried out his investigation, continuing the same bloody procedures Ciudad Rodrigo had begun. Maya in Mani and then in Nachi Cocom's Sotuta were arrested en masse and subjected to torture. First they were tortured to make them admit to possession of large numbers of idols. Later they were tortured to make them admit to much worse crimes. After their bodies were so broken that they readily confessed to anything the Franciscans suggested, they were sentenced to further whipping, one or two hundred lashes each on their already shredded backs and shoulders. Maya women were not spared. Responsibility for the torture deaths of María Che and Isabel Mo of Panabchen and María Xiu of Sotuta were later attributed to individual friars.

Some weeks into the proceedings the Franciscans were ready to hold an auto-da-fé in Mani. In preparation, they brought in cloth and set women to making *sambenitos*, yellow robes painted with red crosses. The Franciscans kept accounts of how much they spent on having these made, and according to their accounts they also paid for new shirts, pants, and hats for the young men who had first reported the idols in the cave and new huipil blouses for their wives.

On July 12 Gaspar Antonio waited in front of the Mani church to do the Franciscans' bidding. Before they were brought out of jail, some of the Maya who had been forced to confess to idolatry were made to don the sambenitos, and others were given candles to carry. Then they were paraded in the presence of the friars, Quijada, a crowd of intimidating Spaniards on horseback, the two young Maya couples in their fine new clothes, and a throng of distraught Maya relatives. The Franciscans told Quijada to pronounce sentence on the convicted men, and Quijada in turn commanded Gaspar Antonio to declare their punishments to them in Maya.

There in the center of his hometown Gaspar Antonio told each in turn whether he was condemned to continue to wear the sambenito, to have his head shaved, to be bound in personal service to a Spaniard for a number of years, or to receive yet one or two hundred more lashes.

Judgments, like the torture that had preceded them, fell on the highest and the humblest members of Mani society, but it would have been out of the question publicly to humiliate or whip the ruler, Francisco de Montejo Xiu, or his closest associates, so the civil authorities would deal with them in Mérida. The Xiu noblemen heard their fate from the lips of their kinsman, Gaspar Antonio. According to the Franciscans' meticulous financial records, Gaspar Antonio was well paid for his services, and his wife also received a gift.

Maya who had admitted to owning idols were required to surrender them to the Franciscans. The friars feared that the Maya would compromise again, bringing in some idols and holding back others, and so by torture they forced the Maya to admit to possessing ever larger numbers and then producing them. To meet their demands, the accused and their relatives combed the province for every article that could possibly satisfy the friars, whether idol or ancestral relic, contemporary or ancient, real or completely inauthentic, their own or someone else's. They searched the ruins of the ancient cities and sent out calls for help through the other

Maya provinces. Before the eyes of Landa and his interpreter, all the clay figures, incense burners, skulls, and bones that could be found were smashed and burned. It is a wonder that anything was left for nineteenth- and twentieth-century archaeologists to uncover.

And at some time, too, although we do not know whether it was at the auto-da-fé in Mani, Landa made a bonfire of the Mayas' books. Writing not specifically of the events at Mani but of the Maya writing system, he later remarked, almost offhandedly, "We found a great number of these books in Indian characters and because they contained nothing but super- stition and the Devil's falsehoods we burned them all; and this they felt most bitterly and it caused them great grief."[14]

Of all the Maya, the Xius had enjoyed special treatment from the Spaniards. Finally they too had been brought down, and of them just Gaspar Antonio had been spared. But when the fire consumed the paper and deerhide books, Gaspar Antonio was no better off than they. Half- blinded by tears they all watched their patrimony spiraling to the heavens in smoke and ash. Now they were completely at the mercy of madmen.

The Maya were not the only ones to mourn the destruction of their recorded history. Antonio de Ciudad Real, the next great scholar of Maya among the Franciscans, lamented in 1588, "Thus was lost the knowledge of many ancient matters of that land which by them could have been known." His contemporary José de Acosta wrote that "afterwards not only the Indians but many eager-minded Spaniards who desired to know the secrets of that land felt badly." Fifty years later the church historian Bernardo de Lizana shared their sentiments: "They burned many historical books of the ancient Yucatan which told of its beginning and history, which were of much value if, in our writing, they had been translated because today there would be something original."[15] Some of the books had already been secretly translated into alphabetic writing, and a few did survive, to be confiscated later by other churchmen. But the loss to the Maya and to humanity was irreparable.

In August Landa moved his investigation to Sotuta. His old friend Nachi Cocom, the ruler of Sotuta who had excused himself from the Mani land treaty meeting a few years earlier because of illness, had since died and received Christian burial. Now his brother and successor Lorenzo Cocom committed suicide while awaiting interrogation. As Landa un- loosed torture on other Cocoms, he extracted shocking confessions from them. They said that at about the time Nachi Cocom became ill, human sacrifices were reinstituted in Sotuta, under the old ruler's personal super- vision. Perhaps he and his people were hoping to extend his life yet a little longer, but even after he died, his brother Lorenzo continued them.

According to the confessions, the sacrificial victims were children who were crucified, and then their hearts were cut out and their bodies thrown into cenotes.

Franciscan interrogators, assisted by Quijada's civil officials, made mass arrests, focusing their interrogation on Maya chapel masters and their students. As in Mani, they hoisted prisoners by the wrists, stretched their suspended bodies with weights, and beat them to extract information. Not all the Maya survived. Those who did described more and more instances of child sacrifice, more and more bodies dumped into more and more community waterholes. They implicated more and more Maya chapel masters for encouraging the preservation of the Mayas' own traditions. And the more they obliged the friars with confessions, the more the fury of the friars grew.

As the Sotuta investigation got underway, the head of the Homun monastery instituted a similar one in his town and in neighboring Hocaba with even more gruesome tortures. The Maya were not only subjected to "hoisting," but tight cords were twisted around their arms and legs, and they were forced to swallow gallons of water after which the Spanish constable stood on their stomachs to force the water up again.

At last authority stepped in. Francisco de Toral, a Franciscan who had seen long service in central Mexico, had just been named Bishop of Yucatan and arrived at the height of the bloody business. From Mérida he summoned Landa back to explain to him what was going on. Landa stalled and finally returned late in August to lay before the bishop his appalling story of the secret life of the Maya.

With him he brought the sensational confessions he had obtained at a terrible price. During the three summer months of 1562 over 150 Maya had died under torture, and more than a dozen had committed suicide. Juan Xiu, who had written to Ciudad Rodrigo about the baby with the stigmata and whose letter had been turned over to Gaspar Antonio, was one of those who had died. Pedro Xiu also succumbed to ill treatment; he had been confined to a narrow damp cell after being hung up, beaten, and sprinkled with drops of burning wax. Like the encomendero Francisco Hernández, who had suffered at Landa's hands the year before, he died soon after release. In the final accounting it was established that the Franciscans had put to torture over four and a half thousand Maya.

If Landa expected unconditional support from the bishop, he was disappointed. Toral himself had spent years carrying out the Franciscan agenda among the Mexican Indians. He had learned to speak Nahuatl and then had personally written a grammar and a dictionary of another language known as Popoloca. As head of the order in Mexico City, he had provided encouragement and support to Bernardino de Sahagún, who was working with a staff of Nahua assistants to produce an encyclopedia of Aztec history and culture. Toral was also aware that the Franciscans' early optimism about their Indian converts was changing to bitter disappointment. Yet granted that Indians everywhere persisted infuriatingly in their old ways while acting as though they had been converted, still Toral knew the difference between discipline and abuse, and in Yucatan he saw abuse approaching genocide.

To Landa's dismay, Toral began an independent investigation, sending agents of his own choosing to Hocaba and Sotuta to inquire about missing children and whether any corpses had actually been found in cenotes or anywhere else. In Mérida he consulted with the several Franciscos de Montejo. He asked advice from Francisco de Montejo the Son and Francisco de Montejo the Nephew, and after privately interviewing the imprisoned Francisco de Montejo Xiu, he released him and sent him home.

Rumor flew among the Maya that Toral had come to vindicate them, that he sympathized with them, and that he would personally punish Landa for his wicked deeds. They also thought that Toral had imprisoned Gaspar Antonio for his role in aiding Landa, but to the contrary, the bishop had asked Gaspar Antonio for his assistance. Toral spoke no Maya, and he needed a competent and trustworthy interpreter.

For Gaspar Antonio the bishop's request was fraught with peril. If he went to work for the bishop, Landa might become his implacable enemy. The example of what Landa had done to Francisco Hernández had proved sufficient to keep Diego Quijada in line, and that was as nothing compared to what Landa had done to the Xius and the Cocoms. Gaspar Antonio had a wife, and after what he had been forced to do in Mani, there was little chance his relatives would look after her if anything happened to him. In the face of all these considerations, Gaspar Antonio accepted the risk and agreed to become Bishop Toral's interpreter.

One of the documents Gaspar Antonio wrote for Toral was a summons to Landa to present evidence before his bishop about why certain Indians had been forced to wear sambenitos and to render personal service to Spaniards. At the conclusion of the document he identified himself as "notary and translator and interpreter general" in service to the bishop. When he wrote a document freeing the last of the detained Maya, he signed it "Executed before me, Gaspar Antonio, notary."[16]

Matters moved along as depositions were taken from all sides. Friars described the interrogations and detailed the confessions, while minimizing the extent of the torture. In private interviews, Maya told Toral through Gaspar Antonio that their confessions had been forced from them and that they wished to retract them. The bishop consulted with the encomenderos, who were distressed that the summer's fiasco had interrupted planting, and feared that everyone, Maya and Spaniard alike, would soon go hungry. Although they dreaded the specter of a Maya uprising, they feared the destruction of the Maya people even more, since "their Indians" in "their villages" were the source of their income. Hardly anyone was anxious for the investigation to continue. The truth, however that might be defined, would never be established.

From his vantage point as interpreter general, Gaspar Antonio witnessed at close range a titanic power struggle between the Franciscan friars who had once trained him and the Franciscan bishop who now employed him. As notary, he certified document after document pertaining to the controversy. At about the same time that Toral released the last of the Maya, Landa announced that he was departing for Spain due to ill health.

Gaspar Antonio, in making his choice, had put himself on the winning side, but Landa's absence did not bring peace. The friars resisted their bishop's authority by withdrawing from Maya towns to their urban monasteries and leaving the rural Maya they had striven so hard to convert abandoned without anyone to administer the sacraments.

Another act of subversion that followed was the drafting of a letter in Maya in seven nearly identical copies putatively signed by Maya noblemen and sent with Spanish translations directly to the king of Spain. The letters praised the Franciscans and especially Landa and begged the king to send him back with more friars:

> Because we, your majesty's vassals, all understand the desire your majesty has that we shall be saved . . . and that it is your pleasure and care that we be told what is most truly needed, according to our inferiority and capacity, and our poverty in temporal goods; Wherefore we make known before your majesty that from the beginning of our conversion to Christianity we have been taught the doctrine by the Franciscan friars, and they have preached and in their poverty do preach and teach us the law of God. We love them as true fathers, and they love us as true sons. . . .
>
> And for this cause we beg that you will have compassion on our souls, and will send us Franciscan friars . . . and especially those of them who have been in this country, and went back from here to Castile, those who know well our language . . . especially fray Diego de Landa for he is great, sufficient, worthy, and good in the eyes of our Father God.[17]

Undercutting the letters' claim to authenticity, however, is that each letter and all the Maya "signatures" at the end are written in the selfsame handwriting. Another partially similar letter with the names of some of the same Maya officials was sent a month later.

The following month Francisco de Montejo Xiu and three other Maya officials sent a furious rebuttal to the king, denouncing the Maya letters as a Franciscan hoax:

> The religious of San Francisco of this province have written certain letters to your majesty and to the general of the order, in praise of fray Diego de Landa and his other companions, who were those who tortured, killed and put us to scandal; and they gave certain letters written in the Castilian language to certain Indians of their familiars, and thus they signed them and sent them to your majesty. May your majesty understand that they are not ours, we who are chiefs of this land, and who did not have to write lies nor falsehoods nor contradictions. May fray Diego de Landa and his companions suffer penance for the evils they have done to us, and may our descendants to the fourth generation be recompensed the great persecution that came on us.[18]

While all this was going on, the encomenderos and other colonists were at work unseating Quijada for his collaboration with Landa, and a battle-weary Toral was growing more and more anxious to return to Mexico City. It must have been through an act of kindness on the bishop's part that Gaspar Antonio left the chaos behind and moved his family to the town of Tizimin, where he played the church organ and taught Latin to the little brother of the encomendero Sánchez de Aguilar.

Tizimin is in the northeast corner of the peninsula. It is far from Mani and Sotuta, far from Mérida and Izamal. After the uprising of 1546, the Franciscans had been especially active in "congregating" the Maya of the area and making sure they stayed congregated close to churches. But that activity was in the past, and now the local Maya had only to deal with the encomenderos. One of them was Giraldo Díaz de Alpuche.

One of the original conquerors, Díaz de Alpuche was a bachelor when he received his reward for service. Some time after that, the king required that all unmarried encomenderos take wives on pain of losing their grants if they did not. Since there was a shortage of marriageable Spanish women in Yucatan and especially in the Tizimin backwater, Díaz married Montezuma's niece, the very girl whose father had died of anger in the Tabasco garrison twenty or so years before. Perhaps because of his high-born Indian wife, the encomendero took an interest in the history of his encomienda Indians and made some effort to learn what Maya culture had been like before the arrival of people like himself.

Díaz de Alpuche had the typical encomendero's hatred for the Franciscans, whom he accused of sexually corrupting Maya women, and unfortunately for Gaspar Antonio, his intolerance carried over to the young Maya men educated by the friars. These young men he considered impudent, sly, and deceitful. The bookish Gaspar Antonio, so admired by Sánchez de Aguilar, did not likely find congenial intellectual companionship with this old encomendero and his Nahuatl-speaking wife.

Otherwise, it is pleasant to imagine Gaspar Antonio's life in Tizimin in the mid-to-late 1560s as an idyllic retreat into music, teaching, and the pleasure of watching his family grow. It was a life far from the resentful Xius with their tragic eyes and the permanent marks of torture on their bodies, far from Spanish political jockeying and slander.

Back in Mérida he was sorely missed. Bishop Toral, who had long been accustomed to speaking with Indians in their own languages, was utterly frustrated by his inability to speak Maya. From time to time he would forget himself and burst forth to them in Nahuatl. He repeatedly sent off letters requesting that he be relieved of his post in Yucatan and allowed to retire, but his requests were ignored, as were his requests for additional personnel to help him attend to the needs of the Maya. More and more he became obsessed with the injustice done to these people whose minds and hearts and souls were rendered inaccessible to him by an impenetrable language barrier. In a last bitter letter to the king, written in December 1570, he recalled the talent God had given him for Nahuatl and Popoloca and characterized himself as deaf and mute among the Maya. Despite his deteriorating health and intolerance of the hot climate, he wrote, he had traveled the length and breadth of Yucatan consecrating churches and personally administering sacraments to the Indians, ever suffering from bad conscience, because "as I am old, I have not learned the language of this country, for which reason I have been most unhappy, since I have not been able to preach to my flock."[19] In the end he abandoned his post without permission and fled back to Mexico City to die.

Mortality was taking its toll all around. Quijada, too, had died, and when, in 1572, his widow was ordered to make payments from his estate to Maya for uncompensated services, it seems Francisco de Montejo Xiu was no longer living either; the last we see of him is his indignant letter of 1567. On March 3, 1572, Gaspar Antonio himself, no longer at Tizimin, signed a receipt for payment from the Quijada estate characterizing himself as "governor of Mani and lieutenant of the governor of this province." Jorge Xiu, his fellow interpreter under Landa, was cosigner.[20] For the moment Gaspar Antonio had risen to the very top of Maya society, but it was not to last.

In Spain Landa occupied himself by composing a celebration of the

Maya. In his *Relación de Yucatán* ('Account of Yucatan') he painted an almost lyrical word-picture of beautiful, hard-working Maya women and plump, happy Maya babies. He wrote of the fine buildings and wonderful fruits and charming animals of Yucatan. He told of how the Maya, before their conversion, held coming-of-age rites for boys and girls, of how young couples entered into marriage, and of Maya feasts where women modestly turned away as the men drank their intoxicating honey drink called *balche*.

He wrote of Maya history and science and bloody rituals, of Mayapan and of Aguilar and Guerrero, and even, briefly, of the Franciscans' auto-da-fé at Mani. Nachi Cocom he described with affection, omitting entirely the old man's apostasy, the error of interring his body in sacred ground, and the grim satisfaction of having his bones exhumed and burned.

Of Gaspar Antonio, now ruler of Mani, Landa wrote not a word. Just as Cortés barely acknowledged Doña Marina in his letters about Mexico, so Landa remained silent about the best and the brightest of the Franciscans' protégés.

Yet Landa dealt in detail with matters he could not have known firsthand: of religious rites already suppressed when he arrived in Yucatan in 1549; of the legal system the Maya rulers administered before the encomenderos and friars took over; of the Maya Death, the Maya calendar, and the Maya writing system. This information came from someone else; most scholars agree Landa had gotten it from his two pet Maya, old Nachi Cocom and young Gaspar Antonio. Betrayed by both of them, Landa withdrew to Spain with the notes he had taken and composed a book as though nothing particularly bad had happened.

Many a scholar has sought to explain Landa's *Relación*. Since it exists only in a copied manuscript, some have suggested that copyists edited out part of Landa's original text. Or perhaps Landa glossed over the hardships and the disappointments and ultimately the bloody horrors of Yucatan because he intended to use his writings to recruit new Franciscans to go to the peninsula. Or perhaps, just perhaps, Landa was not entirely sane and never had been, and the compelling logic of his madness, like Rasputin's or Hitler's or Stalin's, had swept up men of lesser will. How else to explain his selective amnesia? How else to explain Izamal? How else to explain Franciscan friars laying lash after lash into the backs and shoulders of Maya for whom they expressed such sweet paternal love? Or should we blame the victims and their alien land? In the end, didn't Yucatan break Bishop Toral too?

When news of Toral's death reached Spain, the unthinkable became the obvious. The only man who truly knew the Maya, as so ably demonstrated in his writings, was Diego de Landa. He was named the new

Bishop of Yucatan and returned in triumph from Spain with thirty Franciscan recruits.

But things could never be the same. Soon after he arrived in the fall of 1573, he attempted to reassert his power over the Maya only to discover that many of them had learned to speak in that same voice of outrage to be found in Francisco de Montejo Xiu's letter to the king. When Franciscans sought to punish Maya now, the Maya filed legal briefs against them, for there was a new regulation that friars were forbidden to imprison or whip Indians or even to cut their hair.

Within the year Gaspar Antonio no longer held office as governor of Mani, but the bishop found he could no longer manipulate the Spanish civil government; he tried excommunicating the Spanish governor, but the governor refused to be intimidated. The stalemate did not last very long. At age fifty-four Diego de Landa died, and after a while his bones were sent back to Spain.

Gaspar Antonio was approaching fifty. Just as Landa may not have guessed when he returned to Mérida that he had only six years left to live, so Gaspar Antonio probably did not anticipate that thirty more years of life lay ahead for him. Who would have imagined that he would outlive two bishops? Or that one of the brightest periods of his professional career was about to begin?

In the year Landa died, the encomenderos of Yucatan received a fifty-item questionnaire from the king of Spain. The information requested was encyclopedic; for each of their encomiendas they were to describe the climate; the physical features of the land; its mineral resources, flora, and fauna; modes of transportation and ports; details of civil and religious organization; its system of taxation; and the history of conquest. Among the questions were specific ones about the languages spoken, the meaning of Indian place names, the former rituals and customs of the local Indians, whether there were more or fewer Indians living in each town than previously, and whether Indian health had improved or declined recently and why.

When the encomenderos of Yucatan were called to Mérida to receive their copies of the questionnaire, old Díaz de Alpuche from Tizimin settled down with gusto to writing the story of Montezuma's brother, of his thirty-year marriage to Montezuma's niece, and of their children and grandchildren. He even told about his blind son, born to another woman, and about that son's children. Blaming the unhealthful influence of shallow lagoons in the region, he claimed that Spaniards and Maya were equally afflicted by epidemic disease. He described the 1546 massacre and its aftermath in the eastern provinces and claimed that the practice of idolatry continued down to the present. His report was a tour de force.[21]

Few of the encomenderos responded so expansively. They simply could not provide answers to the questions. Some responded briefly without taking up the questions one by one. Others unabashedly wrote, "I don't know." One crotchety Spaniard expressed to the king his intense dislike for literate Maya "who have been reared by the friars, because they think that knowing how to read and write, they are equal to Spaniards."[22] But other encomenderos were of a more generous and practical turn of mind and turned to Maya assistants for help.

Between 1579 and 1581 Gaspar Antonio participated in the preparation of a dozen reports. Along with the encomenderos he personally signed the reports from the city of Mérida and the town of Muxupip. Others conclude with a credit line that varies so little from document to document that it appears he formulated it himself. It says that Gaspar Antonio, Indian native of the town of Mani, resident of the city of Mérida, a competent and educated man, fluent in Spanish, assisted in the preparation of the report. That, in a nutshell, seems to be his vision of himself: able, bilingual, bicultural. The encomenderos readily put their signatures to these testimonials.

The reports from all quarters of Yucatan recorded a sharp drop in Maya population. This was serious business for the encomenderos, for they had been granted not land but the service of Indians on that land. Fewer Indians meant less income. The encomenderos were quick to blame the Franciscans for their practice of relocating Indians near monasteries, and many of the reports from the eastern half of the peninsula contain descriptions of how the friars had burned houses so the Maya could not go back home. From western Yucatan came fewer complaints about people being displaced from their homes, but the population seemed to be falling at the same worrisome rate. Some encomenderos mentioned epidemics, bad water, crop failures, and the like, but the theme that plays again and again through these reports is that the Maya, with all their former pleasures prohibited, had given up on life.

Díaz de Alpuche, writing from Tizimin, said he had personally consulted with elderly Indians about the problem, and they told him that before the Spaniards came, they had led a contented life, always going to celebrations, dances, and weddings where they drank balche. Now they were required to wear clothes and practice monogamy. Everyone was so sad they had just decided to die. Díaz de Alpuche wrote approvingly of balche and provided a recipe.

Gaspar Antonio concurred with the many encomenderos who reported that the vitality of the Maya population had been damaged by the prohibition of balche. It was a healthier drink than the Spanish wine the Maya had taken up in its place, because wine, he wrote perceptively, burned the liver and killed people.[23]

Gaspar Antonio enriched the reports with pieces of historical information about the Xius, related the founding of Chichen Itza, and expressed a commonly held opinion about the better moral tone of Yucatan before the coming of the Spaniards. Blom put together this composite statement from several of Gaspar Antonio's answers to the king's question about the "customs, good and bad," which the Indians had in times past: "In olden times all lands were communal and there were no property marks, except between provinces, for which reason hunger was rare as they planted in different places, so that if the weather was bad in one place, it was good in another. Since the Spaniards have arrived in this country, this good custom is being lost, as well as the other good customs which the natives had, because in this land there are more vices to-day (1581) than fifty years ago."[24]

The towns for which Gaspar Antonio assisted in writing reports are spread across much of northwestern Yucatan, from the northern coastal town of Dzidzantun to Tabi in the extreme south of Mani province, from Mérida eastward to a cluster of towns around Izamal. After the Mérida report was filed promptly in 1579, more than a year passed before the other reports were all dated and submitted within a few days of each other in February of 1581.

One could hardly collect and translate local place names long-distance from Mérida, so Gaspar Antonio may have spent the intervening year visiting the encomienda towns, riding out as he had done with Judge Felipe Manriques when they made their trip to Uxmal and Mani years before, and then turning over his notes to the encomenderos at the turn of the year.

In the meantime he had also written an account of his lifelong services to the religious and civil government in order to request a pension from Spain. Such a *probanza* required supporting statements by witnesses. When Doña Marina's daughter, for instance, submitted one concerning her mother's contribution to the conquest of Mexico, several veterans served as firsthand witnesses. In Gaspar Antonio's case, the only relative who gave a deposition on his behalf was Jorge Xiu, who, like Gaspar Antonio, had served Landa as an interpreter at Mani.

Ralph Roys, a distinguished scholar of the Maya, studied this probanza and a subsequent one and concluded that like many a Spanish conquistador Gaspar Antonio resorted to misstatement in order to further his personal interests. Roys points to instances in which he misrepresented the power of the Xiu lords, but even in smaller matters we see the exaggeration so characteristic of the time and the genre. Gaspar Antonio wrote, "I have not been remunerated in any way for more than forty and some years that I have aided and served in all the aforesaid. Nor have I any other employ or benefaction with which to earn a living, to support myself, my wife, home, children and family, as well as a horse with saddle and bridle. . . . Also I am poor, in need, and burdened with debt without being able to avoid it or pay it for this reason." [25]

If Gaspar Antonio did travel the great distances between towns where he helped with the king's questionnaire, he needed a horse, although horses had a hard time of it on the stony tracks through the close and thorny Yucatecan jungle. But a horse was also a status symbol permitted to only a few Indians. By maintaining a horse, just as by demonstrating his perfectly fluent spoken and written Spanish, Gaspar Antonio could keep up appearances and advertise that he was as good as any Spaniard.

As for having already served forty and some years in 1580, he was playing fast and loose with numbers. Forty years before, he had been a child and the Spaniards had been planning the final assault of Yucatan. And when he claimed not to have been remunerated at all, he was conveniently forgetting that he had at least been paid for the agonizing summer of 1562.

But considering the limited resources of Yucatan and that even most Spanish families lived much on the edge, it is easy to imagine that Gaspar Antonio, despite his industrious nature, was hard put to make a living and pay his debts. Fortunately the probanza met with approval, and he was awarded a grant of eighty pesos a year, not only on his own merits but on those of his grandfather, father, and two uncles.

With the encomenderos' reports filed, Gaspar Antonio at the behest of the Governor of Yucatan wrote his own. Although it does not proceed by the numbers, it covers the social questions posed by the king's questionnaire. Beginning with the statement that there is but one language, and the inhabitants of Yucatan call it Maya-than ('the Maya language'), Gaspar Antonio then tells the history of Mayapan. He describes what people paid in taxes, how land use was governed, people's freedom to move around and live where they pleased, and the hospitality accorded to travelers (certainly a sore point between the Xius and the Cocoms).

A section deals with the conduct of lawsuits and what sort of punishments were meted out for various crimes (none for debt; imprisonment for theft; death for murder, rape, or proven adultery). Interspersed among the descriptions of crimes and punishments are flat statements that the Maya did not eat human flesh and that flogging had been unknown to them; the remark that although they wrote and understood hieroglyphic characters, they did not use them for writing letters; and the assertion that things like little copper bells, shells, and cacao beans had been used as money in the markets. There are also brief references to slavery and human sacrifice.

The disorder of these statements gives the document the appearance of a first draft. Moreover, it is briefer and less detailed than the composite account that can be made from the answers in the dozen reports he wrote for encomenderos.[26] In his own report the emphasis is on Maya justice, characterized as stern but consistent and compassionate, with the implied criticism of Spanish justice left unsaid. Yet Gaspar Antonio had been more outspoken about even this in one of the reports he wrote over an encomendero's signature, where he stated that the Maya rules had been strict, but otherwise people were allowed to lead their own lives.[27]

Gaspar Antonio signed and dated this last report on March 20, 1582, but either it was not sent to the king, or a copy remained behind, because the historian Diego López de Cogolludo quoted it almost verbatim in the history of Yucatan he published three-quarters of a century after Gaspar Antonio's death. He wrote, "I have in my possession a manuscript written by Gaspar Antonio, descendant of the rulers of the city of Mayapan, who was a Xiu before he was baptized as an adult by the friars who first evangelized this province, who taught him not only how to read and write but also Latin grammar which he mastered very well."[28]

For three and a half centuries Gaspar Antonio's report was known only through López de Cogolludo. Then the original was discovered in the Archive of the Indies in Seville, and it was translated into English and published in 1941.[29]

Three years after it began, Gaspar Antonio's royal pension stopped. He waited nearly ten years before filing another probanza in which he indulged in yet more glorification of the Xiu lineage and its loyal service to the Spanish king. Despite apparent misstatement of his place in the Xiu ruling lineage, Gaspar Antonio's writing proved once more persuasive, and the pension started up again, with a grant of a hundred pesos added on. Yet another grant of two hundred pesos was made in 1599. Apparently this was to be paid to Gaspar Antonio's daughter in case he were no longer living, but Gaspar Antonio was still very much alive and involved in yet another civil project.

On August 8, 1600, grandly identifying himself as "I, Gaspar Antonio, interpreter of the reigning King," he certified his Maya translation of a decree concerning a land dispute. It involved Sotuta, where his family's enemy Nachi Cocom had come to such a bad end thirty years before. In September he translated and signed two related land agreements. At seventy he was still working at his profession.

In January of 1609 he witnessed the wedding of his granddaughter to a Spaniard in the Mérida cathedral, and the following year their first child received his great-grandfather's name in baptism: Gaspar Antonio del Castillo.

Old Gaspar Antonio at the age of nearly eighty served one last time as interpreter at a trial held in Mérida of men accused of assaulting yet another Xiu governor of Mani. His signatures on the documents of this trial are his last. When he died, he had outlived just about everyone who had employed him. He had even survived by a decade the tumultuous sixteenth century.

Blom seems mistaken about Gaspar Antonio. Unlike Doña Marina, Gaspar Antonio's association with the Spaniards did not begin until the combat was over and done. And unlike her, he did not stay loyally beside the first masters he served. When Diego de Landa and his fellow Franciscans had gone too far in their dealings with the Maya, Gaspar Antonio switched sides. Eventually he slipped away from the church altogether to work as a civil servant and became, however briefly, governor of his native province.

As time went by and both Landa and Toral receded in memory, Gaspar Antonio promoted himself as the friend and protégé of bishops. (No matter that the bishops in question were antagonists.) And he was fond of ever grander titles, moving himself along from humble notary and translator to interpreter general, lieutenant of the Spanish governor, interpreter of the reigning King, and Indian governor of Mani. Doña Marina, by contrast, remained just "Doña Marina, the interpreter" (la lengua) until she was recast centuries later as "Malinche, the traitor."

Yet Gaspar Antonio appears more of a traitor to his own people than Doña Marina was, for while the butchered people of Cholula were strangers to her, his uncles and cousins were among the broken, bleeding, and dying Xiu in Mani. And as a survivor, Gaspar Antonio was more successful than Doña Marina. From the day she was given to Hernán Cortés, Doña Marina lived less than a decade, and she never knew her children. On the day he met Diego de Landa, more than three score years of life, replete with children and grandchildren, lay before Gaspar Antonio.

Yet there are ways in which Gaspar Antonio and Doña Marina truly were alike. Both fatherless, both unusually gifted with a talent for learning languages, they had passed while very young into the power of Spanish men of boundless ambition, ferocious energy, and more than a whiff of madness. Both were on intimate terms with terrorists. After the Cholula massacre, Doña Marina stood face-to-face with Montezuma and translated to him the terrible demands of Cortés. At Mani Gaspar Antonio stood by Diego de Landa and his puppet Quijada and declared the punishments to be executed upon his fellow Maya.

Both surely knew as they were doing it that the damage could never be repaired, the old order never regained. If they stopped to reflect on the meaning of it all, they were lost. They did what they had to do to survive, looked to the alliances they needed, and apparently made their peace with themselves. Unlike the sullen Indians who frustrated their Spanish masters by running off or dying of willful discontent, these two hard-working interpreters actively negotiated the seams between Indian and Spanish worlds, she for a little while and he for a very long time indeed.

BETWEEN PRINCE AND KING:
Guaman Poma de Ayala (ca. 1535?–after 1615)

Your Majesty may wish to ask the author of this book some questions with the object of discovering the true state of affairs in Peru, so that the country can be properly and justly governed and the lot of the poor improved. I, the author, will listen attentively to Your Majesty's questions and do my best to answer them for the edification of my readers and Your Majesty's greater glory. . . .

In my capacity as a grandson of the Inca of Peru I would like to speak to Your Majesty face to face, but I cannot achieve this because I am now 80 years old and in frail health. I cannot take the risk of the long journey to Spain. However, I am ready to pass on the observations which I have made in the last 30 years, since I left my home and family to live the life of a poor traveller on the roads of my country. We can communicate with one another by letter, with Your Majesty asking for information and myself replying.

—*DON FELIPE GUAMAN POMA DE AYALA*[30]

On St. Valentine's Day, 1615, an angry man signed and dated a letter announcing completion of his 1,200-page report to King Philip III of Spain. Then he took the manuscript to Lima, bid it a reluctant farewell, and sent it off to Madrid. He said in various places in those pages that he had been working on the report for twenty or thirty years. Around 1612 he began making a clean copy from beginning to end, illustrating it with four hundred drawings. It is a wonder that anyone, much less an eighty-year-old, could complete the final work in three years, yet the handwriting is firm and clear, and the drawings, too, are done with a steady hand.

This immense production was driven by rage. The author had lost hope that the Spanish administrators in Peru would take any steps to protect him and his people. Yet the words and pictures in his head would not let him rest. Night and day Guaman Poma wrote and drew his vision of what Peru had been and what it had become since the Spaniards had overthrown its Inca rulers. Today his illustrations are widely reproduced, the only visual record of their kind of Inca society and the conquest of Peru.

The author signed his Quechua name as "Guaman Poma," but it is also to be seen spelled Waman Puma. In the language of the Incas, "waman" means 'hawk' and "puma" means 'mountain lion', just as in English, for English has borrowed the word from Quechua.

Although Guaman Poma the Hawk-Lion introduced himself to Philip III as grandson of the tenth Inca ruler and thereby a prince on equal footing with European royalty, he was by no means a friend of the Incas. He claimed Inca heritage through his mother—a relationship that did not count for much in his society, which paid attention to father-to-son and mother-to-daughter descent. He said that his father, Martín Guaman Malqui de Ayala, was of a different noble lineage known as Yarovilca, and that his ancestors had been rulers of the city of Huanuco before the Incas came to power in Peru. One of the many grudges Guaman Poma held was against people who wrote about the Andes without acknowledging that there had been rulers other than the Incas, realms that had existed before they rose to power. And yet, living in the chaos of post-conquest Peru, he also yearned for the orderly existence the Andean peoples had known before the coming of Francisco Pizarro and his soldiers, even as it was under the Inca usurpers.

In the course of something over a century the lives of the peoples of the Andes had been reordered twice, once by the rise of the Incas and then by the arrival of the Spaniards. Or, to put a finer point on it, their lives had been ordered by the Inca dynasty and disordered by Spanish conquest. Guaman Poma had been born into the aftermath and was obsessed with trying to straighten matters out.

The Andes, South America's spine, run down the west side of the continent through what are now the countries of Ecuador, Peru, Bolivia, and Chile, all once united under Inca rule. The mountains separate the brown desert coast of the Pacific Ocean from the green tropical forest of the Amazon Basin. Melt water from their snowy summits has cut river valleys down to the ocean, bringing fertility to a land where rain does not fall. Up in these valleys Andean civilization took shape.

In the course of five thousand years, towns grew into cities and periodically a city would extend its influence over a region and then lose

its influence and subside again. Throughout all this expansion and con-
traction, with immense investment of human labor, the Andean peoples
built terraced fields up the steep sides of their valleys. To carry water to
them, they laid irrigation systems. At lower elevations they grew corn,
and up above potatoes. Beyond the potato fields they tended herds of
llamas. Down in the hot desertlands where the west-flowing rivers run to
the sea, yet other crops were cultivated: lima beans, tomatoes, sweet
potatoes, avocados, and cotton among them. It was impossible to live self-
sufficiently at one altitude in the Andes; people had to trade up and down,
and the flow of commerce had everything to do with the passion for
organization and reciprocity that became the foundation stone of Andean
society.

Organization not only moved food and goods from where they were
produced to where they were needed, it also made possible grand civic
projects. Andeans, for reasons unknown, cut into the dry earth outlines of
huge birds, animals, and plants that have endured for over a thousand
years. With only stone and bronze implements, they became master stone
cutters and builders, moving immense blocks long distances and fitting
them together so perfectly that their walls stand to this day, despite the
forces of earthquakes and human destroyers. In the city of Cuzco the
Spaniards simply built the church of Santo Domingo atop the eternal walls
of the Incas' Temple of the Sun. Bernabé Cobo, a Jesuit scholar of the
seventeenth century, wrote an encyclopedia of Andean civilization and
natural history, and in it he says of such buildings as the temples at
Tiahuanaco:

> I find two things about these constructions that should not be passed
> over lightly without giving some thought to them. The first is the
> amazing size of the stones and of the whole complex. And the second
> is the extraordinary antiquity of the site. Who would not be astonished
> to see the unusually large stones that I have described? Who would not
> wonder how human strength would suffice to carve such huge stones
> out from quarries and bring them to where we see them now? This is
> all the more amazing since it is a known fact that no stones or quarries
> are found within several leagues of this site; moreover none of the
> people of this New World have ever made use of the invention of
> machines, wheels, or winches for the purpose of pulling such stones,
> nor did they have any animals that could pull them.[31]

He goes on to say that the site was so ancient that no living Indians
could tell him anything more about the structures than that they had
existed before the Incas came to power. Guaman Poma, who did not live
to know of Cobo's conclusions, would have been gratified by the Jesuit's

perceptive remarks. Today archaeologists have confirmed that Tiahuanaco's time of glory had come to an end hundreds of years before the rise of the Incas.

On a smaller scale, the peoples of the Andes became expert in ceramic work, weaving, and goldsmithery, leaving behind exquisite pots, fabrics, and jewelry for us to wonder at. Yet perhaps it is only to us that these artifacts seem more humanly expressive than the vast stone walls and hundreds of thousands of terraces built by people working like ants. For the fabrics, too, were the product of innumerable people working endlessly to gather the fibers, spin the thread, and weave countless miles of cloth. Everywhere every day Andeans spun and spun, wove and wove, just as others pecked and pecked with stone on stone to shape the building blocks of palaces and temples.

Yet the Andeans found security in cooperation and complementarity. Apart from the disruptions of war and natural disaster, life before the conquest held few surprises. Social class and gender determined what a person would do in life, and the annual agricultural cycle, punctuated by religious rites, governed everyone's year. There were few choices to make. So long as an individual fit his or her assigned role in the community, life ran a fairly smooth course. On the other hand, as among the Nahua and Maya peoples to the north, if one did not acquiesce to one's role, or if one were constitutionally unfit for it, there was little margin for accommodation. Like most human societies, Andean society enforced conformity.

Today we tend to think of the Maya, the Aztecs, and the Incas as the three high civilizations of the Americas, but there is a difference. "Maya" and "Aztec" are ethnic terms that refer to whole peoples. In the Andes, "Inca" referred to the ruler and his lineage. His subjects, whether they spoke Quechua as their ruler did or some other Andean language, were not Incas. The people the Inca ruled in the years before the Spanish conquerors came to Peru spoke many different languages and had their own traditions and their own rulers. They would have been unmanageable if the Inca had not taken strong measures to control them. And in the twilight years, as the state crumbled into civil war, those controls were no longer working as well as they once had.

But they had worked for a century. In their capital city of Cuzco a succession of more than half a dozen Inca rulers had led to one known as Pachacuti Inca Yupanqui, who, beginning in the late 1430s, transformed raids against his neighbors into grand military conquest. He and his son Topa Inca managed to extend their power north into what is now Ecuador and south into what is now Chile. By the time Topa Inca died in the closing years of the fifteenth century, his lineage was governing a huge social and economic machine they called *Tahuantinsuyu,* the 'World of the Four Quarters'.

To make the Inca state function, local rulers' children were taken away to Cuzco for language training and indoctrination, then sent out to be teachers and administrators. Ordinary working people's local allegiances were broken by moving them away from their ancestral homes to new places where their only connections were to their small group of fellow deportees and to the central government. Everyone had to learn Quechua in order to have a common language with all the other relocated groups. Everyone had to participate in the state religion imposed by the Incas. And to support the Inca state and the Inca religion people had to work incessantly, for one-third of their produce and labor went to the Inca and one-third to the state religion.

Dislocation and fatigue kept the Incas' subjects from organized rebellion. United under the Inca dynasty, the Andean region became a totalitarian state. Every six months every man, woman, and child lined up and was counted, and the Inca's administrators always had a current census recorded on knotted strings known as *quipus.* Inca law imposed severe punishments on the peoples of Tahuantinsuyu, and the worst punishments of all were for disobedience and rebellion.

Under their system the Incas' subjects provided llamas and bales of fabrics to the state for the personal use of the ruler and for consumption in sacrificial fires. They also surrendered some of their children, both boys and girls, but many more girls. The boys and some of the girls were sacrificed as part of the state religion. Other girls were given by the Inca to his administrators as rewards for good service. Some became concubines of the Inca himself, and many lived out their lives in closely guarded seclusion as "chosen women," spinning and weaving the finest of cloth for the Inca's clothing.

Garcilaso de la Vega "el Inca," a half-Inca contemporary of Guaman Poma, wrote that Andean mothers "never took the babies into their arms or in their laps when giving suck or at any other time." He said the mother leaned over the baby's cradle three times a day to give her infant her breast and otherwise did not respond to crying. When the child was able to crawl, she knelt on the floor, and the child had to crawl around her from one side to the other in order to suckle. "Mothers pampered themselves even less than they pampered their children," he wrote, "for on giving birth they went to a stream or washed themselves in the house with cold water and resumed their household duties as if nothing had happened."[32] If what Garcilaso reports is anything like the truth, there was little opportunity for parents and infants to bond, which perhaps made it easier for parents to give up their children to Inca officials who carried them off to Cuzco for the Inca's disposal.

There were rewards for cooperation with the Incas. Parents whose children were chosen and taken away were afforded honor and prestige. Local rulers who yielded to diplomacy and submitted to Inca rule were spared military subjugation. Under central government, cities no longer suffered from raiding and looting by their neighbors. Warfare was generally carried on at the edge of the Inca realm, away from most subjects' daily lives. Moreover, the swift and severe justice meted out by the state not only held down civil strife, but also kept ordinary crime to a minimum.

Work levies built thousands of storehouses to hold the produce delivered to the state, and they built a system of roads on which information and goods could be conveyed rapidly from any part of the realm to any other. Located along the road were inns for traveling administrators and huts for relay runners who could carry a message fifty miles in a day. According to Guaman Poma, "It was said that a snail picked off a leaf at Tumi in the north of the Empire could be delivered to the Inca in Cuzco still alive."[33] And Bernabé Cobo remarked, "If, while he was in Cuzco, the Inca felt a desire for some fresh fish from the sea, his order was acted upon with such speed that, although that city is over seventy leagues [more than two hundred miles] from the sea, the fish was brought to him very fresh in less than two days."[34] The roads served more than just the Inca's whims. When a shortage arose in one part of Tahuantinsuyu, it was quickly relieved by transfer of goods from warehouses elsewhere, minimizing suffering and starvation from crop failure.

During this time people throughout the Andes were able to feed and clothe themselves as well as to set aside impressive surpluses for the state. People did not go hungry or suffer from lack of clothing or shelter.[35] They worked so efficiently that despite all the road work and construction of public buildings, the Inca, according to tradition, sometimes had to resort to make-work to keep people occupied. John H. Rowe, a modern historian of Inca culture, wrote, "Huayna Capac is said to have ordered a hill moved from one place to another merely for want of a more useful project. Whether the story is true or not, the Indians who remembered *Inca* times evidently regarded it as perfectly plausible."[36]

As for the state's administrators and military leaders, if they served the Inca well, they received from their ruler gifts of beautiful clothes and lovely young wives. In principle the Incas were the embodiment of generosity, and they carried on grand feasting and gift-giving. In the same spirit of spectacular consumption, they led monthly religious rites in which precious goods were burned to ashes as an offering to their sustaining deities.

The privileged inner circle of the Inca dynasty also engaged in the sharing of coca. In 1615 a disapproving Guaman Poma said of coca, "Inca Roca [the sixth Inca] and his son introduced coca leaf into their empire and were the first to adopt the custom of chewing it. Until then it was unknown in the high Andes, but the use of it became established as a habit or vice. Like tobacco it is only held in the mouth, not swallowed, and serves no useful physical purpose." He goes on to say, "Our rulers were undoubtedly responsible for the widespread custom of chewing coca. This was supposed to be nourishing, but in my view it is a bad habit, comparable with the Spanish one of taking tobacco, and leads to craving and addiction." He claimed that the wife of the seventh Inca was so addicted to chewing coca leaves that she would fall asleep with a quid in her mouth and that she was a melancholy, unsociable person "likely to burst into tears at the slightest excuse."[37] Of a later Inca Guaman Poma said that he was so parsimonious that his wife had to still her hunger pains by chewing coca leaf.

Inca unity fell apart when the son of one of the ruler's secondary wives challenged his half-brother for control of the realm. Pachacuti Inca Yupanqui and his son Topa Inca were followed in turn by Topa Inca's son Huayna Capac. Guaman Poma describes him as "white-skinned," amiable, and married to a woman who knew well how to live the role of royal consort, putting on lavish entertainments, sponsoring the arts, and engaging in public relief work for the needy.[38] Unfortunately, she bore her royal husband only two children, according to Guaman Poma, while his concubines provided him with many others, and therein lay seeds of destruction.

Huayna Capac came to power in Cuzco at the same time that Christopher Columbus reached Hispaniola. As the Inca continued the exploits of his father and grandfather, extending the realm north and putting down brewing internal revolts, Spanish explorers reached the mainland, crossed the Isthmus of Panama and began exploring along the coasts. Meanwhile the Aztecs and the Maya came under attack, and Pedro de Alvarado moved on to establish his authority over Guatemala, but Huayna Capac was unaware of the threat.

In the 1520s, when Huayna Capac had been in power for more than thirty years, Spanish explorers first reached his realm. One apparently made his way from the Brazilian coast, and others came down the Pacific coast and began seizing some of his subjects to serve as interpreters for

Francisco Pizarro. Of the several they carried off to learn Spanish, one was baptized Felipe and another Martín, and these young men came back with Pizarro after Huayna Capac's death to take their place in the events of the conquest of Peru. In one of Guaman Poma's drawings Felipe appears with the label "Felipe, Indian interpreter" written on his arm.

By the time Pizarro arrived with his soldiers and interpreters, the Inca empire was coming apart. Huayna Capac was an old man when he died, but his death was anything but natural. In the 1520s, out ahead of Pizarro, the Spaniards' diseases had arrived in Tahuantinsuyu, and the Inca's subjects were dying in an epidemic of what was probably smallpox. The royal Incas themselves were not immune. On a campaign in the far north the elderly Huayna Capac was stricken and died trying to get home to Cuzco. One of his two legitimate sons was named heir to the realm, but that son died almost simultaneously with his father, and the succession passed on to the Inca's other son, Huascar, the last person who could become a true Inca ruler according to the rules that had governed Inca succession until then. But Atahuallpa, one of Huascar's half-brothers, challenged him for the rulership, and fighting broke out to compound the disaster of the deadly epidemic. In 1532, with Huascar defeated, Atahuallpa not yet securely established, and Tahuantinsuyu brought to its knees by disease and war, Pizarro and his forces arrived.

They landed at a coastal city that had seemed appealing four years earlier. Now they found it ravaged, and searched along the coast for a better place. In their explorations they came upon the Inca roads and warehouses, and learning of Atahuallpa's presence in the Andean highlands, they went up looking for him. They found him at the city of Cajamarca and in the course of two days, they seized him and made him their prisoner. So ended the Inca empire.

Atahuallpa offered a kingly ransom for his life and liberty, a room completely filled with gold and silver. The Spaniards took it, and half a year later, they put him to death anyhow, even as Cortés had ultimately executed Cuauhtemoc. In Guaman Poma's illustration of the execution, the youthful Atahuallpa lies on a block with a cross in his bound hands. Three bearded Spaniards hold the young ruler down, as a fourth beheads him by holding a knife across his throat and hammering it with a mallet.

The conquerors scoured the realm for treasure, took the king's share back to Spain, and set off a rush of Spaniards for Peru. A year after seizing Atahuallpa at Cajamarca, Spanish forces took permanent control of Cuzco and set up Spanish civil government there. The next year a new capital, Lima, was established on the coast. From this time forward, Cuzco would represent the old Inca order in Peru and Lima the new Spanish one.

Yet the Spanish and Indian worlds did not stay apart. Within a year Andean women began giving birth to children fathered by Spaniards. Few of these unions involved marriage, and generally the Spanish conquistadors put aside the Indian mothers of their children later in order to marry Spanish ladies. This fate befell women of the Inca lineage as well as their humbler sisters, and a whole generation of mestizos began to grow up, despised by the Indians and without legitimate claims as their Spanish fathers' heirs. Such was the fate of Guaman Poma's contemporary, Garcilaso, who wrote his own vast history of Peru entitled *The Royal Commentaries of the Incas*.

Into this time Guaman Poma was born. He was not, he made it clear, a mestizo. "My father was no Spaniard," he wrote, "but an Indian like other Indians, and my mother was an Indian and no lady from Castile."[39] Nor was he born in Huanuco, the region he claimed as his patrimony. In the service of the Inca, he explained, his parents had relocated to the south in the province of Lucanas.

From sections of his report to the king that he wrote in Quechua (without providing the monarch with a Spanish translation!) it can be seen that the variety of Quechua he had learned as a child was southern but different from the Quechua of Cuzco, the Inca capital city off to the east.[40] In other words, by the way he spoke he would not have been identified with either the Yarovilcas, the lineage he claimed for his father, nor with the Incas, the lineage he claimed for his mother. Yet there was nothing wrong with Guaman Poma's Quechua. He wrote in it with style and subtlety, even making up wicked parodies of Spaniards who did not speak it well. He also poked fun at one Spanish evangelist, Cristóbal de Molina, who did speak beautiful Quechua, by putting into his mouth phrases even more florid than Molina might have thought up for himself.

On the other hand, Guaman Poma's Spanish, though fluent (over a thousand written pages of it), is distinctly the Spanish of an individual whose first language was Quechua.[41] It would be easy to dismiss Guaman Poma's Spanish as poor, with its sometimes quaint spelling, mistranslations, and frequent failure of number agreement between subjects and verbs, adjectives and nouns, but that would be to overlook the writer's powerful accomplishment.

Guaman Poma was an impressively literate man. He said that his older half-brother, his mother's child by a Spaniard, had entered the priesthood as Father Martín de Ayala. This mestizo priest had taught his little brother his letters and, whether by intent or not, made a voracious reader of him. Guaman Poma's magnum opus is studded with literary references to scripture and to Spanish historical, legal, and religious writings. Although he obviously did not have the kind of schooling that Gaspar Antonio Chi received from the Franciscans, Guaman Poma was nonetheless a scholar, albeit a self-made one. His intellect shines forth in his writing the more brightly because it is so original. But he inclines to the sort of self-advertisement characteristic of people who have had to make their own way. This is what he says about himself:

> I, the author, Huaman Poma, declare that every Christian reader will be amazed and astounded to read the various chapters of my book and will ask himself who taught me and how I ever learned so much. So I say that it has cost me thirty years of work, if I am not mistaken, or at least twenty years of toil and poverty. Leaving my family, my house and property, I have mixed among the poor and learnt the various dialects which they speak. I have studied with the wise and the unwise and served in the palaces of government. I have acted as interpreter to Viceroys, royal administrators and Bishops. I have spoken with indigent Spaniards as well as Indians and negroes. I have seen the Visitors of the Holy Church come and go and been present when our Indian lands were divided up.[42]

There is question, however, about whether Guaman Poma was who he claimed to be. Doubt was raised in his lifetime and continues to this day.

He said that his ancestor, Guaman Chahua Yarovilca, of whom he provides several portraits in his report, had served Topa Inca as viceroy, dining with the ruler and going to the far ends of Tahuantinsuyu on his business. Throughout his report, Guaman Poma can hardly mention Topa Inca without mentioning the ruler's second-in-command Guaman Chahua. Guaman Poma refers to him as an "emperor" set above all the great lords and ladies of the realm and provides a genealogy of the Yarovilca lineage, asserting that they were all kings and emperors above all other local rulers and had been so before the rise of the Incas. For Philip III's benefit he compares Guaman Chahua Yarovilca to the Spanish Duke of Alva.

The end of the story is tragic, for Guaman Poma's last portrait of the elderly Guaman Chahua shows him staring helplessly out over a barricade of rocks that traps him in his house as a Spaniard demanding silver and gold sets fire to the roof. Still, the reader of the report is not to imagine that the Inca's viceroy was forgotten in death, for Guaman Poma provides the text of a Quechua song in which the names of Guaman Chahua and of the Yarovilca lineage are woven together with that of the Inca and with Guaman Poma's own, implying that the fame of the Yarovilcas continued to live among the populace. And toward the end of his report, he tells of responding to the challenge of an overbearing Spaniard by stating that he, the author, is a man of substance, the heir of Guaman Chahua as well as grandson of Topa Inca, in full confidence that such a dual pedigree should impress everyone in Peru eighty years or more after the conquest.

Of his father, Guaman Malqui, Guaman Poma wrote that he had also served the Inca ruler as second-in-command and that he headed a group of emissaries sent by Huascar Inca to meet Pizarro and his soldiers and that the Spaniards and the emissaries knelt together and embraced, after which they dined together. Having pledged the loyalty of Peru to the Spanish sovereign, asserts Guaman Poma, his father served the Spanish crown ever thereafter, always doing battle on the side of the king in all the rebellions that sprang up like wildfire in Peru.[43]

As pointed out by Rolena Adorno, who has devoted herself to understanding and explaining Guaman Poma's sprawling report to the king, the author asserts that there was no conquest of Peru. The emissaries of Huascar Inca welcomed the representatives of the Spanish monarch, and all the fighting and disorder that took place afterward had to do with Spanish rebellion, incompetence, and mismanagement. The Andeans immediately became good Christians who loyally served their good Spanish monarch, but the world was turned upside down by people who pretended to be Christians and were in fact evil men.[44]

His father he portrays as particularly saintly. Fighting alongside a Spanish captain named Luis de Avalos de Ayala against the forces of the rebellious Gonzalo Pizarro, Guaman Malqui saved the Spaniard's life and in return received a crown grant of land and the name of Don Martín Guaman Malqui de Ayala. Or so says his son. And Guaman Malqui took on more than land and a Christian name from Avalos de Ayala, according to his son's account. Doña Juana Curi Ocllo, the legitimate younger sister of Topa Inca, had borne a son to the Spanish captain, and the generous Guaman Malqui married her and adopted the boy. So it was that Guaman Poma had a half-Spanish older brother.

The mestizo boy was a pious child, and at age twelve, says Guaman Poma, he took the habit and began to lead a life of rigorous Christian observance. One of the drawings shows the boy now grown and ordained as Father Martín de Ayala, holding up a book and instructing young Guaman Poma and his parents as they hold rosaries. According to Guaman Poma, Martín taught his younger siblings to write and led his mother and stepfather into selfless Christian service.

As a priest Father Martín continued his self-punishing ways. Another of Guaman Poma's drawings shows him scourging himself before an altar as an angel flies down with a crown for his head.

Father Martín sought a martyr's death and finally found it tending to the dying at a hospital in Huamanga, a city whose founding Guaman Poma credits to their father Guaman Malqui. Thereafter his mother and step-father carried on his work. Guaman Poma writes, "A good example in the way of service to the poor was set by my father, who in spite of his high rank worked for thirty years in the hospitals of Cuzco and Huamanga, and by my mother with her direct descent from the Inca dynasty. They both preferred to die in God's service rather than live selfish lives."[45]

As for himself, Guaman Poma says he worked as interpreter for the Spanish civil and religious hierarchy and had been present at the division of land, and indeed documents do show that he interpreted at a land distribution in 1594.[46] He does not hesitate to drop names, saying that a former viceroy of Peru, Luis de Velasco, would vouch for him, and he includes a portrait of the viceroy wearing wire-rimmed spectacles. He also says he interpreted for Cristóbal de Albornoz, a priest who dedicated himself to stamping out idolatry in the Andes, and he speaks admiringly of the man's godliness. On the other hand, he denounces Francisco de Avila, another zealous extirpator of Indian religion, providing examples of cruel behavior that bring to mind Diego de Landa in Yucatan.

Guaman Poma's thorough familiarity with the works of such controversial churchmen as Bartolomé de las Casas, and also with the writings of the archbishop of Lima, shows that he had access to a religious library. But Guaman Poma, unlike his half-brother Martín, was no ascetic. He married and had a family, and at some time he went to court to recover land he felt was his birthright. Then at midlife, he tells us, he left his family and spent decades wandering incognito to gather material for his great report.

Guaman Poma gives some hints about crisis and disillusionment in his life at that time. Certainly the uproar of the Spanish factions fighting it out among themselves while exploiting the Andean peoples to extract and send away everything that could be squeezed out of Peru would have been reason enough for despair. But the author hints at more personal reasons. Of his suit, he writes:

> I had to go to court in order to defend my right to some lands which had belonged to my family since the Incas and indeed since the foundation of our country, long before the Spaniards ever came here as conquerors. Our title to the property was duly established and formally confirmed by the court after a review of the evidence; and was later upheld by the Viceroy. . . . At this stage the deputy of the royal administrator, a certain Pedro de Rivera who lived at Huamanga and who was unable to read or write, sent two of his clerks to stir up trouble and oppose the judgement pronounced in your majesty's name.[47]

After that, he says, he lost faith in the Spaniards and began to ally himself with Indian leaders, although he soon found them unreliable as well. It was when he put on commoners' clothes that he discovered how very badly ordinary people were being treated. Like them he was endlessly robbed and abused, cheated and insulted.

And why did he abandon his family, for decades as he tells it? One of the great villains in Guaman Poma's report is a priest-historian named Martín de Murúa, who published in 1590 a chronicle of Andean culture under the title *History of the Origin and Royal Genealogy of the Inca Kings of Peru*. There are strong parallels between the two men's works that are not very well accounted for, and professional jealousy may have been an issue. Guaman Poma says of Murúa's work that he set to writing and neither began nor ended but got everything into a hopeless muddle. He simply loathed Murúa and parodies him in a fake Quechua sermon as well as drawing a picture of the friar kicking an elderly woman working at her loom while at the same time beating her on the head with a stick.

But most devastating of all, Guaman Poma accuses Murúa of trying to take his wife away from him. He was obsessed by the idea of Spanish men, especially priests, commandeering all the Andean women, begetting mestizos by the thousands, and leaving Indian men without a hope of ever having wives and children of their own. "Some Indian men, as I know from my own experience," he writes, "feel a sort of pure shame at the way in which their wives behave like whores and have children by other men, and they leave their villages never to return. Otherwise they would have to kill the women or become their accomplices."[48] Is this why Guaman Poma abandoned his home?

Included at the beginning of the report is the text of a dated letter to the king from Don Martín de Ayala which implies that Guaman Poma's elderly father was still alive in 1587 and that the author had completed part of his report. Don Martín putatively states that his son has composed some accounts of their ancestors from the time before the Incas. He hopes the work will be published and that the king will look with favor upon his son Don Felipe de Ayala. If his father really did write such a letter, it remained with Guaman Poma for a quarter of a century until he finally dispatched his manuscript to Spain in 1615. At the last moment, when he had finished the clean copy of the whole report, the author went back and altered the wording at the very beginning to state that his father was not just a member of the nobility and an Indian governor, but an Andean prince.[49]

So it would seem that Guaman Poma had not disappeared completely into a hobo existence, but that he remained in touch with his father and had the paper, ink, and other necessary supplies to write manuscripts, to say nothing of having a safe place to store them. Still, he says it was a long time before he returned home to find his patrimony irrevocably lost and his land occupied by others. When he identified himself and sought restitution, those who had taken over expelled him from the province. Then, he says, he set out over the mountains to Lima, accompanied by his oldest son, Don Francisco de Ayala, his horse, and his two dogs. In the accompanying illustration he draws himself not as the gray-haired ancient he professes himself to be, but as a vigorous man in Spanish dress, striding through the mountains with a walking stick in one hand and a rosary in the other. His son Don Francisco, walking ahead of him, appears to be a little boy.

Guaman Poma narrates more acrimonious debates with Spaniards along the way and a run of bad luck that begins with a robbery and continues with Don Francisco abandoning him. Then, with snow falling in the mountain passes, even his dogs leave him to run back the way they came. After many adventures, he says, he reached Lima, where he found no hospitality or comfort. There was nothing but disorder in the Spaniards' capital city, which was full of displaced Indian men fleeing from taxation and forced labor and Indian women trying to survive by prostitution. It was, he said, not for the first time, a world turned upside down.

The pages in which Guaman Poma describes his journey to Lima during the snowy Lenten season of 1615 were composed after he wrote his Valentine's Day letter announcing that his report was done. Having declared himself finished, he still could not let up on his relentless documentation of wrongs and injustices. In Lima he continued to write and stick pages into the back of his report before letting it go, and so it is that the author's most ringing conclusion is separated in the manuscript from the illustration that would best accompany it. In the drawing Guaman Poma, richly dressed in seventeenth-century Spanish court attire, kneels before Philip III, holding his report open before him and conversing with the monarch. In the half-incorporated pages written afterward in Lima, he states grandly:

> It was to remedy these ills of my country that I had changed myself into a poor man, endured many hardships, and given up all that I had in the way of family and property. Among the Indians I was born as a great lord and it was indispensable that someone of my rank should communicate personally with Your Majesty, whose dominions are illuminated in turn by the Sun. Who but I, the author, could dare to write and talk to you, or even approach so high a personage? It was this consideration which made me venture upon my long letter. I have written as your humble vassal in the New World but also as a prince, or *auqui* as we say in our language, the grandson of our tenth King,

Tupac Inca Yupanqui, and the legitimate son of Curi Ocllo Coya, a Queen of Peru.[50]

And yet, there is considerable doubt that Guaman Poma was all that. Rolena Adorno, seeking to authenticate his claims, has come upon many a mystery. "The perplexing fact about the wonderful name of Waman Puma," she writes, "is that it does not appear in any of the provincial historical records that catalogue the prominent clans of the late sixteenth century. . . . There is no trace of the Waman Puma clan in Lucanas during the time they were allegedly there."[51]

Although the author portrays himself as born into a family where all took Christian baptismal names, there are no baptismal records. His story of how his father Guaman Malqui saved the life of Luis de Avalos de Ayala and received as a reward his name and a grant of land from the Spanish crown cannot have happened as he describes it, for the dates and battles do not coincide, and the author claims that in the rescue his father killed a man who was in fact alive and the mayor of Cuzco in 1573.

The author says he was raised in the court of the viceroy and that he had abandoned a privileged career as an administrator of an Indian municipal district and interpreter for the civil government and the church. Yet there is only evidence of his being employed once to interpret during a land distribution, and that was during the years when he said he was wandering in disguise among the common people. This is very sparse indeed compared to the documentation that exists for the career of Gaspar Antonio Chi, whose life spanned the same time period as Guaman Poma's.

Concerning Guaman Poma's attempt to regain the land he claimed, it is a matter of record that he did file suit, but his description of the outcome, according to which his family's title was confirmed and upheld by the viceroy, is contradicted by a document found in the local archives. The court judgment states that Guaman Poma's claim was denied, and it labels him a troublemaker of humble birth always trying to pass himself off as a nobleman.

Having left his family and his comfortable living, Guaman Poma says he walked all over the former realm of Tahuantinsuyu interviewing people and collecting evidence for the king. Yet his report shows that he had firsthand knowledge of a much smaller area, namely his native province of Lucanas and the city of Huamanga; Cuzco to the east; a mining area to the west; and the road to Lima.[52]

At the end of his labor, when the 1,200 pages and 400 drawings were done, he stated that he was a prince and the son of a queen of Peru. Then he went back through the whole vast manuscript, writing in that he and his father were princes, going so far as to alter the letter dated 1587 and signed with his father's name.

Was Guaman Poma an imposter? From available records it is hard to say. While the lineage he claims for himself seems fabricated, the other Andean noble families he mentions are authentic. Likewise, the Spaniards he names in his detailed account of post-conquest Peru were real people who were there and engaged in the activities he describes. In other words, he was well-informed, and, as we have seen, he was also well-read. A conniving Indian of humble status, as he was described by the damning court document, would hardly have had access to the sort of books he had read.

Perhaps Guaman Poma was brilliant and privileged and pathological all at the same time, but the times themselves were pathological. Perhaps, realistically, he had to style himself a prince in order to talk directly to a king, but what monarch was likely to be willing to make his way through 1,200 pages of what is at times sheer rant? Looking long and hard at the report, Adorno concludes that ultimately Guaman Poma was defeated by his own project. His obsession to write down everything destroyed its coherence and made it virtually unreadable, especially in the seventeenth-century Spanish court to which he directed it.

His material about Andean agriculture and the annual calendar with its festivals, as well as detailed descriptions of social organization and characteristic dress, is generally accepted as accurate. Andean scholars today consider the drawings covering these topics very important illustrations of precontact dress and behavior, and the spatial organization of the pictures is thought to be governed by subtle Andean principles that scholars have been slow to appreciate. The report also contains a wealth of Quechua song lyrics as well as Guaman Poma's satires of Spanish clerics speaking Quechua. On the other hand, Guaman Poma's history of the Incas, especially the last several generations, is self-serving, as is his claim of family service to the Spanish king. In this respect, his report is akin to the probanzas of Doña Marina's daughter and the aging Gaspar Antonio.

Guaman Poma is doing something else again in his effort to show that Indians were not racially or morally inferior to Europeans, in part by recasting biblical history to include the Andes. Moreover, by his denial that the Andeans resisted the coming of the Catholic faith and Spanish sovereignty, he asserts that his people were being persecuted unlawfully by corrupt churchmen and administrators. In preparing his report he is going over their heads to the Spanish king himself to plead the just case of the Andean people.

And a strong case was to be made for those he sought to represent.

Long before the Spaniards arrived, the Andean peoples themselves had learned how to carry out large-scale projects through the coordinated efforts of many people. They had not devised a writing system, but they recorded a great deal of complicated information in their quipus. By means of these records they maintained a functioning welfare state, albeit one that was short on personal freedom.

Once the Spaniards had established themselves over the Incas' former subjects, they drew off the fruits of their labor and interfered with the system of mutual support that had been a positive feature of Andean life. The Inca rulers had been exploiters, but the Spaniards were plunderers, especially with respect to the mines where they extracted silver with forced Indian labor. Nor were Indian women more gently treated under Spanish rule. They continued to produce woven cloth in huge quantities, no longer the exquisite cloth for Inca garments and burnt offerings, but coarse cloth for the Spaniards to export to markets elsewhere. Now all the Andeans' products were flowing out of Peru, and nothing much was being set aside for social welfare or disaster relief, although there were disasters on all sides. Not surprisingly, demographic collapse was under-way. Guaman Poma warned the king:

> As matters stand at present, the Indians are in the process of dying out. In twenty years' time there will be none of them left. . . . It is possible that Peru will lose all its value and your Indian subjects will no longer exist. Where once there were 1,000 souls, now there are hardly 100 left. Those who remain are many of them old and incapable of having children. The young men cannot find young brides to bear them sons. The girls and women, whether single or married, are all removed into the Spaniards' homes. . . . If by any chance one of our girls bears a child to an Indian man, the parish priest and the other authorities treat her like a criminal.[53]

This, the author pointed out, was not in the best interest of the monarch, for with the disappearance of Indian labor the king's income would disappear as well.

In offering a plan for reformation, he—in his guise as prince—offers his son directly to the king's service: "My grandfather serves as the model of a great King reigning over the Four Quarters. In a similar manner Your Majesty ought to preside over the four parts of the World, with four lesser Kings under your sway. As one of these I offer my son, who is a true prince of Peru." As for himself, he would have a special advisory role distinguishing between individuals with genuine claim to authority and low-class people making illegitimate claims: "The proper procedure is for me, as a writer and a prince of the Indian race, to give evidence upon all claims to titles and send it to Your Majesty, duly signed. When I am gone, my descendants would be empowered to continue in the same office for all time to come."[54]

In other words, Guaman Poma is asking to be made what he said Guaman Chahua once was, second in command to the supreme ruler. In the restored order of a new Peru, the Spaniards and the Andeans would lead separate lives. Spanish men would keep to their Spanish wives, and Indian women would bear children to Indian husbands. Priests would live godly lives on limited incomes, and land would be returned to the rightful Andean lords and their descendants. But it appears that the author had little faith in his plan for fixing Peru and gave himself over to passionately documenting wrongs. In the end, by piling up case after case of injustice, illustrated by drawing after drawing of physical abuse, he gives up entirely on a program for justice and restitution and simply becomes an outraged, eloquent witness.

To look at the drawings of Spaniards—soldiers, civilians, and priests alike—kicking, beating, whipping, degrading, and killing Andeans is painful. It is unlikely the Spanish king would have inspected them unless he had been forced to by an extraordinary social conscience or by a powerful advocate for the Indians standing before him, as Guaman Poma admitted that he could not do. Moreover, as Adorno points out, the pictures are restrained compared to the accompanying text, as though Guaman Poma's intuitions warned him that at some point looking at these scenes would prove unbearable. But while the author could temper his visual representation of what was happening in Peru, he could not restrain his words about the catastrophe that had been brought upon its peoples.

He raged on and on, repeating himself and revealing himself for what he was, a vociferous champion of the oppressed, but a not altogether sympathetic figure and certainly a contradictory one. Here let some of his words speak for themselves as he intended that they should.

First of all, he believed in strict racial segregation and loathed miscegenation to the same degree that he loathed Martín de Murúa. Even among different groups of Andeans, he advocated separation. Back in the days of the Incas, he said, the general census and accounting "had the effect of grouping the Indians in their own villages, where they bred with one another. It was possible to avoid the multiplication of half-castes, which is such a feature of the present time. The result is as unfortunate as the mixture of the vicuña and taruga, two kinds of Peruvian sheep, which produces an offspring resembling neither the mother nor the father. Thus a degenerate race is created."[55]

"Creoles," he went on, "are the children born of unions between our native Indians and Spanish settlers. . . . Unfortunately, many of them are . . . always ready to commit some act of treachery with the aid of a knife or dagger, a noose for strangling, or a stone. . . . Picking a pocket is more in their line than herding cattle. They . . . go about in the manner of gipsies in Spain. Looking for new adventures, they are always moving on to the next place." [56]

He concludes, "Your Majesty would do better not to employ half-castes at all, since they only cause uproar, dissension, crime, and scandal. They are the sworn enemies of their own uncles, the Spaniards. Moreover, those who have been ordained as priests are the worst of all." [57]

Guaman Poma could hardly have known any Jews, but he had absorbed anti-Semitism nonetheless. He complains, "At present the Spanish administrators and Indians of noble family sit at the same table, eat and drink and gamble with every sort of buffoon, thief and drunkard. Jews and half-breeds are allowed to join in as well; and of course they pretend to be just as good as the rest." But it was not just Jews he despised; of the Spaniards putting on airs in Peru, he opines, "Often they have the further blemish of Jewish, Moorish, Turkish, or even English blood." [58] His depiction of Africans tends to be sympathetic in some parts of his report, but in other places he says they are prone to running away and committing theft.

Guaman Poma was also a misogynist. He speaks forcefully against the Spaniards' appropriation of Indian women, often telling heart-rending stories of families unable to protect their daughters, and of girls heart-brokenly pleading for help, but he is also adept at blaming the victims: "If by chance one of our girls bears a child to an Indian man, the parish priest and other authorities treat her like a criminal. Then the priest takes her into his kitchen so that he can sleep with her whenever he likes. She starts to bear him children and finds this style of life much to her taste. Other Indian girls, too, notice the privileges which she enjoys and want to share them." Elsewhere he writes, "It is impossible to accept some Indian women as witnesses in any sort of legal proceedings, for the reason that they are lazy, deceitful trollops, seditious and hostile to men. They easily resort to tears and think nothing of giving false evidence." [59]

For Indian noblewomen in unions with Spanish men, he reserves special contempt: "They usually call themselves by names such as Doña Juana or Doña Maria, but if when they are widowed they marry a Spaniard, or if they marry their daughters to Spaniards, they lose the right to any such appellation and to the special style of dress, for they have chosen to abandon their high caste and become members of a mixed race." [60]

Overall Guaman Poma's concern for Indian women is proprietary.

Indian women should not be carried off by Spanish men because they are the rightful property of Indian men. Once, it seems, Andean men and women had functioned more as complements to one another, each with specific skills and roles to play, so that only a married couple formed a whole social entity. But under the Inca rulers, women had become something of a commodity, belonging as children not to their parents but to the ruler, who directly or by proxy decreed all the marriages throughout his realm. Thus he gave the women to their husbands, and from the Inca's consort to the humblest agricultural worker, women were subordinate to their husbands.[61] Guaman Poma shows himself possessed of this mindset, which exposure to then-current European ideas about the proper relationship of women to men could only reinforce. So it was that he wrote of women debasing themselves and their descendants by marrying down:

> It is the man who determines caste in marriage. A woman, even if she is able to call herself Doña Francisca or Doña Juana, takes the caste of any husband who is beneath her rank. Her title of Doña . . . is thereby cast into the river, carried away, drowned and lost in the sea, and it may never come back again. If she dies, she dies forever and sinks in the sea without a trace. Her close relations such as her father and mother, are as responsible as she is. From that moment . . . the honor which she possessed has become virtually irrecoverable. Not only she, but all who come after her, will be disappointed. She and her children and still more her grandchildren will have come down very low in the world.[62]

Given these opinions expressed by Guaman Poma, it is difficult to imagine his attitude toward his half-brother Martín and his mother Doña Juana Curi Ocllo. Could his mother, besmirched by bearing Don Martín, have regained the worthiness that the author imputes to her throughout his report? Could Don Martín have transcended his half-caste nature? How is it that they escape his blanket condemnation? Consistency is not one of Guaman Poma's strong points.

We have seen how disapproving the author was of coca. He also condemns gambling, drunkenness, promiscuity, laziness, and nonconformity. In Inca Peru, he reports, there were severe punishments such as a hundred lashes for wearing inappropriate clothes. He exhibits a continuing concern for conformity in dress: "It is only proper that everyone should be dressed according to his or her station in life so as to be easily recognized and greeted. Indian chiefs who wear beards resemble boiled prawns and are indistinguishable from half-castes."[63] Yet Guaman Poma deliberately violated his own principles if he did dress as a poor man and travel incognito. Moreover, in his self-portraits, he depicts himself in Spanish clothing.

All in all the author was a man of many "shoulds," from the list of royal Inca ordinances he lists early in his report, to the analogous list of answers to the king's rhetorical questions that he includes toward the end. In his vision of the new and better-governed Spanish Peru, everything should be regulated with the same rigor as in the days of the Inca rulers right down to dress, hair length, and seating in church.

We also see the author's Andean mindset expressed in his readiness to sort and type things and people. The principle of a place for everyone and everyone in his or her place extends in his work to a set of character-istics for each category and all its members. Not only did Guaman Poma have stereotypes for mestizos, priests, and women, but for just about every human group he could think of, even for ones about whom, like Jews, he could have little or no firsthand information. Grouping people by physical type, he says that thin, narrow-chested ones have a high energy level and become influential, but tall men and women "with no calves to their legs" are given to lechery and jealousy. Well-proportioned men with sparse beards and their female counterparts with "waists like ants" are generally trustworthy, but dark-skinned, curly haired ones are untrustworthy, and fat ones are worst of all.[64]

On the other hand, Guaman Poma did make objective observations and came up with hypotheses in agreement with those of Bernabé Cobo, who was a great natural historian and thinker. For instance, while to most Spaniards an Indian was an Indian, both Guaman Poma and Cobo observed the diversity of languages and cultures in the Americas and sought to understand how the continents had been peopled. By extended reasoning, Cobo concluded that the Indians had come into the Americas from Asia via a land route in the far north and then spread south through both continents, diversifying over a long period of time. Without going into his own reasoning, Guaman Poma simply states, "Each country has its own race of Indians, who may have come from China in the first instance."[65]

He also noticed the pronounced effects of language contact in Spanish Peru: "At first there was almost no mutual comprehension between the conquerors and the Indians. If a Spaniard asked for water he was likely to be brought wood. Then as a new race of half-castes grew up, a mixture of the Quechua and Spanish languages became usual but was still not fully understood by either race."[66] In a drawing of a purely imaginary encoun-ter, the Inca Huayna Capac inquires in Quechua of a conqueror, "Is it gold you eat?" and the bearded soldier labeled "Candia, Spaniard" confirms in Spanish (although Pedro de Candia was actually a Greek), "We eat that gold."[67]

There is little enough to smile at in Guaman Poma's report to which he ultimately gave the awkward title of *The New Chronicle and Good Govern-*

ment, so these rare moments of intended or unintended humor come as a relief. Much of what he wrote is a sustained cry of pain edging toward madness. What if this happened in Spain, he asked the king bluntly. "Just imagine that our people were to arrive in Spain and start confiscating property, sleeping with the women and girls, chastising the men and treating everybody like pigs! What would the Spaniards do then?"[68] This is hardly the way to speak to one's sovereign, but in any case Philip III was not listening.

Guaman Poma wrote, "In this book I have set down both the good and the evil of life in my country, so that the next Government may be correspondingly improved. My hope is that my work will be preserved in the archives of the Cathedral of Rome."[69] This is not what happened. His manuscript did reach the royal court, but in view of how utterly uninterested the King of Spain had already shown himself to be in Garcilaso's *Royal Commentaries*, it is unlikely he ever examined Guaman Poma's work.

Somehow, instead, the great illustrated manuscript passed into Danish hands and was deposited in the royal library in Copenhagen, where it was listed among the holdings when the library was catalogued in the 1780s. And there it lay, beautifully bound and gilded but unread until 1908, when it was discovered by a German scholar. Since then it has been published, translated, and made famous in Peru, Spain, Denmark, and many other countries as well. At last, after more than three centuries, it has given its author the audience he sought as he wrote, "Now it is my honor to dedicate the record of this long and painful labor to Your Majesty and indeed the whole world."[70]

FROM DEEP WOODS TO DARTMOUTH:
Charles Eastman (1858–1939)

I felt as if I were dead and traveling to the Spirit Land; for now all my old ideas were to give place to new ones, and my life was to be entirely different from that of the past.
—OHIYESA AT AGE FIFTEEN[71]

Had Sarah Winnemucca lived a while longer and continued her work, she and Charles Eastman might have met on the East Coast lecture circuit. He was born in 1858, about fourteen years after Sarah, and he was completing his senior year at Dartmouth College when she made her last fundraising trip east in 1887. By then he had already begun his own career of speaking in public about Indian culture and Indian claims.

Yet until he was fifteen years old, he had spoken Sioux and had never been to school to learn to read and write. He had not been Charles Eastman then, but Ohiyesa. What route had led him, as he put it, "from the deep woods to civilization," from life with refugee Santee Sioux in Manitoba to the Dartmouth football field and the Phi Delta Theta fraternity, from training for the hunt and warfare to the study of Latin and Greek, chemistry and physics, political science and history?

Like Sarah Winnemucca, Eastman was born into a world already much altered by the burgeoning population of North America. The Santee had grown crops, tapped sugar maples, and harvested wild rice in the forest and lake land of Minnesota. During the colonial period the French in Canada had provided firearms to their traditional enemies, the Chippewa, who had used this advantage to drive the Santee out of the forests onto the Great Plains, where they quickly took up the aggressive culture of horsemanship, buffalo hunting, and warfare of their western kinsmen, the Yankton and Teton Sioux.

During the American Revolution and again during the War of 1812, the Santee sided with the English. Their first treaty with the government of the United States was negotiated just when Sacajawea was accompanying Lewis and Clark westward to the Pacific coast. New treaties were needed in 1815, and from that time forward the government of the United States tried one strategy after another to wean them from their wild ways. Ironically, the goal, hardly ever achieved, was to make these formerly agricultural people into citizen farmers.

From 1819 onward the Santee had a military post in their midst. Heavily fortified Fort Snelling was located at the joining of the Minnesota and Mississippi Rivers. In its shadow Santee and Chippewa held uneasy meetings, and its soldiers frequently served as a peacekeeping force between them. Missionaries came and devised a writing system for their language, then a grammar and a dictionary to the end that Christian converts should be literate in their own language, the better to carry forward evangelization among their people. They even had a printing press and a Sioux newspaper.

One of the early converts was Charles Eastman's great-grandfather Cloud Man, who accepted Christianity in 1829. Despite severe trials, he retained his adopted faith until his death in 1863, five years after the birth of his great-grandson. By then the white world had long since touched his family in another way.

In 1831, soon after Cloud Man's conversion, Seth Eastman, a young officer recently graduated from West Point, was assigned to Fort Snelling. An otherwise unremarkable student at the military academy, Eastman had demonstrated talent for drawing and was sent out to make maps. He was also a daring horseman and an enthusiastic hunter who soon found himself in trouble for sharing these enthusiasms with the Sioux. The Indian agent at Fort Snelling felt called upon to remind him that army officers could not command respectful behavior from the Santee if they came to "identify themselves with Indians and become as it were allied with their families."[72]

To what extent Seth Eastman had already allied himself with Cloud Man's family was soon to become apparent. Within the year, one of Cloud Man's daughters bore Eastman a daughter. In the meantime he had applied for a position in the topographical service and was assigned to a new post in Louisiana. And so the little girl, Mary Nancy Eastman, became a ward of the Indian agent, one of nine "half-blood" children under his guardianship who owed their existence to the men of Fort Snelling.

Seth Eastman did not stay away forever. When Mary Nancy was ten years old, he was reassigned to Fort Snelling, bringing with him a Virginian bride also named Mary. By Mary Eastman's own report, the Santee were delighted to have her husband back and to meet his white wife. Seth Eastman spoke fluent Sioux, and Mary Eastman learned it to the point that she could heartily enjoy the telling of traditional stories and easily render them in English. They stayed at Fort Snelling for seven years, he as a skillful negotiator among the area's Indians, and she caring for their home and children.

In addition to their primary duties the Eastmans both carried out ethnographic work of enduring value, he documenting the culture of the Sioux, Chippewa, and Winnebagos in paintings that earned him honor as a peer of the artists George Catlin and Karl Bodmer. Mary Eastman, for her part, took notes about dances, folklore, and family life, and published a best-selling book, *Dahcotah: Or, Life and Legends of the Sioux around Fort Snelling*. To this day her book is a valuable source of information about Santee culture in the mid-nineteenth century. In it she never mentions her husband's daughter Mary Nancy.

But Mary Nancy had not disappeared from the face of the earth. During the seven years the Eastmans were at Fort Snelling, she grew from childhood to young womanhood, acquired a Sioux name meaning 'Goddess', and married a Sioux leader. In 1851, two years after her father and his wife moved on, another artist, Frank Blackwell Mayer, came through and sketched two studies of her, depicting her as a very beautiful young woman with European features. She bore her husband five children, the last of them a son, and did not survive the last birth, dying at about age twenty-eight. Her life had not been long, but neither, apparently, had it been blighted by Seth Eastman's departure at the time of her birth nor by his return with a new wife. His professional stature as military officer and as documentary painter seems to have enhanced the standing of her Sioux family, and she also had claim to five hundred dollars in a fund for children born to Indian women and white soldiers.

The son she left behind could not, however, survive on good social standing alone. According to Charles Eastman's memoirs, he narrowly escaped infanticide. Mary Nancy's mother was certain that deprived of nursing he would soon die, and she wished to bury him in the same grave with his mother. His other grandmother, Uncheedah, disagreed and kept him alive with boiled rice water and maize gruel until he teethed and was able to take solid food. Although he lived, he was burdened with the name Hakadah 'the last', until later on in childhood he received a better one, Ohiyesa 'winner', which he proudly kept all his life, placing it in parentheses on the title pages of his books and passing it on to his only son.

Born into a Santee family with a committed Christian patriarch and having a distinguished white grandfather, Ohiyesa might have been prime material for the assimilationist programs of the missionaries and educators working with the Sioux, but circumstances drove him far from white society. First, the death of his mother placed him in the hands of Uncheedah, who was a deep traditionalist. Then an event known as the "Minnesota Massacre" separated him from his father and swept him off to the forests of Manitoba.

The Minnesota Massacre of August 1862 apparently took place against the inclination of the Santee chief Little Crow, who sought to carry on negotiations with representatives of the United States government despite simmering resentment among his people over their continuing victimization by that government and by newcomers hungry for their land. Young men led the initial action against white settlers. Farms and trading posts were the first targets, but a detachment of volunteer infantry was also decimated. Once the uprising was under way, Little Crow stood by his people. The killing on both sides continued into September, but by the end of the month the army had overwhelmed the Santee, and those who could fled to the Dakota Territory or Canada. Among those who escaped were Ohiyesa, his grandmother, and his uncle Mysterious Medicine.

Ohiyesa's personal memories of childhood began just at the time of total break with white society. The rest of his life would be shaped by his need to integrate life as he led it from age four to fifteen with all that came afterward. Decades later, as Charles Eastman, he would publish a short story, "The Chief Soldier," about the Minnesota Massacre and the conflicting loyalties of individual Santee.

Of the Santee who stayed behind, 303 men were tried and sentenced to be hanged, but President Lincoln personally reviewed the sentences and commuted 265 of them. The remaining thirty-eight Santee Sioux were hanged on the day after Christmas, 1862. Word reached Ohiyesa's family in Canada that his father was one of them. Mysterious Medicine immediately adopted the boy and set about training him to take revenge for his father's death.

As a man Eastman idealized his boyhood experiences in the Manitoba woods as the way Indians had lived before their world had been ruined by contact with the white man. Its poignant memory sustained him through hard times and gave him absolute moral assurance. Yet it had not been a return to the life the Santee had once lived in the Minnesota woods. Despite his idyllic recall of sugaring and rice harvesting and game hunting, once they were in Canada the Santee refugees did not revert to their old lifeways. They hunted with steel knives and guns as well as arrows, and they had to engage in trading to get ammunition. What could not be traded for was stolen. For their flight north Ohiyesa's group had helped themselves to a settler's wagon and yoke of oxen.

Little Crow, who had also managed to escape to Canada, led a horse-stealing expedition back over the border and was shot to death by settlers defending their property. Mysterious Medicine habitually went south in the summer to raid whites. He brought back scalps, and he once returned with a soldier's white horse, a pack train of mules, and several loaves of yeast-raised bread. Nor was Santee violence always directed outward; for offending the community by hunting buffalo alone (a charge his nephew claimed was baseless), Mysterious Medicine's home was destroyed by other Santee men who broke its supports to pieces and tore up its coverings while Ohiyesa and his grandmother cowered beneath flying bullets and flashing blades.

Ohiyesa underwent hard training in this rough world. His uncle startled him from sleep with loud, threatening yells or with gunfire. He would send the boy to draw water in the dark, then pour out the water and send him back for more. He would blacken the boy's face and make him go all day without eating while other boys tried to get him to take food.

Ridicule was a principal means of social control. Sioux children became exquisitely sensitive to it and would plunge into all sorts of hazardous or painful behavior to avoid being mocked. In fact, the Minnesota Massacre had been set off by dares issued among young Santee men. Boys being prepared for adult exploits were set to attacking hornet nests and were disgraced if they cried when stung. Around age eight they were expected to unflinchingly give up something very dear to them; in Ohiyesa's case, his grandmother directed him to surrender his beloved pet dog to be killed, which he did with heartache but no protest.

Having survived this brutalization in the name of character building, Ohiyesa was convinced that it was a positive good and was necessary to achieving manhood. Long after he left the Canadian forests, he continued to discipline his body with stringent diets and prolonged hard exercise. At Dartmouth he became a star athlete and a fraternity man. A few years out of college he would feel disappointed with himself that he minded getting soaked to the skin, when in his younger days he would have been oblivious.

By the age of fifteen Ohiyesa had behind him years of hard swimming, wild riding, and sharp shooting, all in preparation for the day he would take blood revenge for his father's death. And then in 1873 his father appeared in Manitoba to take him back to the United States.

His father had not, after all, been among the Santee men hanged a decade before. Spared by Abraham Lincoln, he had instead served three years in a federal penitentiary, where he had been converted to Christianity. He gave up his Sioux name, Many Lightnings, for the name Jacob. As a surname, he adopted that of his dead wife, Eastman. His eldest son, who was with him, took the name John Eastman and began training as a Presbyterian minister. Finding reservation life intolerable, they set out with a group of Sioux families for South Dakota, where they received homesteads and established the farming community of Flandreau. Once all this was accomplished, Jacob Eastman went to Canada to retrieve his youngest son from the care and training of Uncheedah and Mysterious Medicine.

Ohiyesa had been well trained to face alarming situations with self-mastery. Without expression he submitted to being dressed in white man's clothes and taken away from his life in the forest by a father transformed beyond recognition, a father who sang hymns and quoted the Bible chapter and verse all the way to South Dakota, where Ohiyesa acquiesced to baptism and became Charles Alexander Eastman.

His account of the trip to Flandreau is comparable to Sarah Winnemucca's description of her passage into the white world. Firearms he knew firsthand, but he had only heard of steamboats and railroads. He had no personal memory of them, and on the way to South Dakota his first encounter with a train put him to flight.

School, too, sent him running at first. Tall, long-haired, and unable to speak or understand English, he was the laughingstock of the younger Sioux boys at the mission school at Flandreau. At home, a battle of wills erupted between Jacob and Uncheedah over his future, but he submitted to his father, let his hair be cut short, and endured the mission school for another year. Then he walked 150 miles to the Santee Normal Training School in Nebraska where his brother John was working as an assistant teacher.

The purpose of normal schools was to train students to be teachers of basic skills, not scholars. In the case of Santee Normal School, founded by Stephen Riggs, a Presbyterian missionary who had written a grammar and dictionary of Sioux, the practical curriculum was designed to produce Sioux teachers, preachers, entrepreneurs, and translators. Controversy swirled around its policy of carrying on instruction in the Sioux's own language and teaching them to read and write it, but the school stuck to its principles. It was a fostering place for Charles Eastman, who was sustained by the presence of his older brother, letters from his father, and the mentorship of Alfred Riggs, the son of the school's founder.[73]

Coming to schooling as late as Gaspar Antonio had, Eastman brought to the enterprise the same sharp intelligence and aptitude for languages. As Alfred Riggs observed his new student's progress in mastering English, interpreting between Sioux and English, and acquiring the elements of arithmetic, he perceived that Eastman was unusually gifted.[74] Here was an individual who, with additional training, could make an outstanding contribution to the future well-being of his people. Riggs saw to it that Eastman was accepted from Santee Normal into the preparatory department of Beloit College in Wisconsin and that he received a scholarship to go there.

At this juncture, word came from Flandreau that Jacob Eastman had died. John Eastman impressed upon his younger brother that he could best honor their father by continuing his education, and Charles, no longer terrorized by trains, boarded one for the trip to Wisconsin. He arrived at Beloit just three months after Custer's defeat at the hands of Sitting Bull and Crazy Horse. It was a hard time to be a Sioux in white society, and he insulated himself from taunts and racial slurs by withdrawing into his studies, ending up at the top of his class in some of his subjects.

Riggs then sent him on to his own alma mater, Knox College in Illinois. Now it was time to choose a career of service to the Sioux. Eastman contemplated law and medicine and inclined to medicine.

Riggs, who had orchestrated his progression from Santee Normal to Beloit to Knox, indicated to Eastman that Dartmouth College in Hanover, New Hampshire, had been founded as an Indian school. In fact, Eleazar Wheelock had founded Moor's Charity School for Indians in Connecticut in 1754. It was an institution that took Indian boys away from their families and sought to civilize and Christianize them. The school had some distinguished alumni, but by its own account it also had a dismal record of failure, for most Indian students returned to their peoples' own ways after they left the school. Nonetheless, active campaigning in England raised funds for the school to move to New Hampshire in 1770, where it changed its name to recognize the man in charge of the English funds, the Earl of Dartmouth. In New Hampshire the school continued to have indifferent success with Indian students and turned to educating whites. In principle the white students were to go forth as missionaries to the Indians, but the school evolved into a college that prepared its graduates for careers in law, medicine, business, and politics as well as for the pulpit.

Since Charles Eastman had decided to direct his studies to the practice of medicine or law, Dartmouth was an appropriate, albeit ambitious choice. Riggs could certainly appeal on behalf of his protégé to Dartmouth's self-image as a school with a founding mission to Indians, but New Hampshire may have held another, personal attraction for Eastman. Although Seth Eastman had been born in Maine, he was from colonial New Hampshireman stock. Charles Eastman may have seen an opportunity to explore his white grandfather's roots when he acquiesced to Riggs's latest plan for him.

When Eastman arrived by train in Boston in January 1882, he was met by Mr. and Mrs. Frank Wood, trustees of Wellesley College and members of the circle of reform-minded northeasterners who worked on political, educational, and religious fronts for what they perceived to be the advancement of the Indian. Friends of Alfred Riggs, the Woods pledged themselves to Eastman's success, and they never ceased to be his supporters. They immediately arranged for him to give a lecture at Wellesley, for which he received an honorarium, and so was launched his public career in a manner rather more decorous than Sarah Winnemucca's debut eighteen years before at Sutcliff's Music Hall in Virginia City, Nevada.

Eastman did not feel ready to take on Dartmouth immediately but continued his preparation at Kimball Union Academy in New Hampshire for three semesters, acclimating himself to yet another world where there were deep woods and sugar maples but also European languages, higher mathematics, history and science, baseball and tennis and card games. When he matriculated at Hanover in the fall of 1883, he was twenty-five years old.

Colleges then as now depend on the largesse of their alumni, and so they seek to build solidarity among their undergraduates through competitive sports, student organizations, and identification with one's class. After graduation, class reunions carry on the tradition. Dartmouth was successful with Eastman. An ardent sportsman as well as an honors student, he became a loyal Dartmouth man and leader of reunion processions. At age fifteen he had spoken only Sioux. By the time he received his Bachelor of Science degree from Dartmouth in 1887, at age twenty-nine, he had become a powerful speaker and writer of English and had studied Greek, Latin, French, and German as well.

He was already considered an expert on Indians to be consulted on such matters as the Dawes Act of 1887, which allotted land to Indian heads of households in yet another attempt to transform them into yeoman farmers. But he had been away from the Sioux for quite a while, and it seemed time to return and begin to serve their immediate needs. Nonetheless, his mentors were not yet done with him. They once again raised money and saw him through Boston University Medical School. Finally in 1890, after sixteen years in six educational institutions, at age thirty-two he was a Doctor of Medicine and ready to take on the world.

In all this time, he had moved among the same circles of people who supported Sarah Winnemucca's efforts to maintain her school for Paiute children. They were idealistic people who believed in the educability of Indians, people who had faith that education and enlightened legislation would bring Indians into full participation in American society. Charles Eastman was their shining example, and he had absorbed their idealism. He would never be able to admit failure to the people who had done so much for him and expected so much in return.

Just as Sarah Winnemucca and Alfred Riggs believed that effective education could only be delivered to students in their native language, so Eastman was certain that effective medical care could only be delivered to people by a physician who spoke their language. With Frank Wood putting in a good word for him with the Commissioner of Indian Affairs, he submitted an application for government employment with the Indian bureau, expecting to be sent to a Sioux agency. Instead, he was stunned to find himself assigned to the Gros Ventres of North Dakota, who, like the Chippewa, were traditional enemies of his people and not likely to welcome him. They were a people whose language he would have to learn from scratch.[75]

Though he had learned five languages since he was fifteen, still Eastman wanted to get on with practicing medicine, not conducting linguistic fieldwork. He and Wood protested the assignment. To their relief it was changed to the Sioux agency at Standing Rock, but the difficulties were not yet over. The agent there insisted on keeping his current physician and suggested that Eastman might serve as the physician's assistant or be assigned to a smaller agency somewhere else. And so Eastman, with his tickets already purchased and his belongings already shipped to Standing Rock, found himself reassigned once again to the Gros Ventres. After more eloquent protests on Wood's part, Eastman was finally appointed physician to the Sioux at Pine Ridge Agency in South Dakota. He arrived there two months before the massacre of Wounded Knee.

Those two months leading from fall into winter of 1890 were filled with frantic work. He had to furnish quarters for himself and set up a dispensary, examine and diagnose patients at all hours of the day and night, and make long trips on horseback to settlements scattered over the reservation. Everywhere he turned he found debilitating disease and problems with sanitation. Children in boarding schools were especially at risk, and Sioux returning from European tours in Wild West shows brought back with them the threat of cholera. The agency needed a hospital with staff and equipment. There was no such thing.

What the suffering Sioux had for comfort was the Ghost Dance. It had begun among the Paiutes, and for many years had simmered among the peoples of the Great Basin and the Northwest. Then, in the late 1880s, it swept onto the Great Plains. In its early form it had been pacifist; its adherents kept the faith and waited for the coming miracle when the whites would disappear, the game would return, and all the dead Indians would be restored to life. The Sioux took a more active view of how the whites might be made to disappear, and they danced in Ghost Dance shirts they believed would protect them from bullets. A ban on the Ghost Dance on Sioux reservations in November 1890 was ineffective, and white settlers were frightened. As Eastman was setting up his practice at Pine Ridge that month, Ghost Dancers were gathering in one corner of the reservation. By mid-November the agent called in troops, a move Eastman thought dangerously provocative. In his opinion the Ghost Dance would have run its course without incident if left to itself.

In the midst of all the hard work and rising tension, the Reverend Charles Cook, the Sioux Episcopal missionary at Pine Ridge, introduced Eastman to a person unlike anyone he had ever known before. Elaine Goodale was at the time government supervisor of education for the Sioux. She spoke their language as fluently as Seth Eastman had, was an enthusiastic player of Indian stickball, and went about in moccasins and sometimes Sioux dresses as well. At age twenty-seven she had been living among the Sioux for four years, first teaching in their schools, then serving as school inspector.

When she was free from her duties, she roved with Sioux families as they hunted and visited across the reservations. Out on one of these trips she had first heard the story of the coming savior who would let down the sky on the whites and bring back the buffalo. Later she would observe firsthand the dance in which people fell into trances and saw their departed relatives living in happiness. Recovering their senses, the dancers called upon converts to discard everything manufactured by white society and to return to traditional dress and customs. The genuineness of the ceremony commanded her respect, yet she observed how nearly impossible it was in practice to return to the old ways. She, like Eastman, felt unthreatened by the movement and was appalled by the arrival of troops. "We who really knew and loved the Sioux," Goodale wrote, "were convinced that, with patience and redress of their grievances, the sane and loyal majority might safely be counted upon to bring a fanatical few to their senses. It cannot be too clearly understood that the clash was between two cultures—not two races. The cause of the pretended Messiah was already lost and time was on our side."[76]

Eastman was fascinated by this Sioux-speaking white woman with sunbleached hair and skin deeply tanned from life outdoors. Just as he was one of a kind among the Santee, so she was unique among young women from New England. Who was she, and how had she come to Pine Ridge in November 1890?

Born in western Massachusetts of Yankee stock like Seth Eastman's forebears, she had been educated at home with her sisters. She and her sister Dora, both precocious children, wrote poetry, which their parents encouraged and circulated. At fifteen Ohiyesa had completed his training in Sioux manhood and emerged from the Manitoba woods. At fifteen Elaine Goodale was a published poet with her first book on the market. She and Dora attended a boarding school in New York and would have been welcome at Radcliffe College. Instead at twenty, Elaine, rather boastful of her social ineptitude and unconventionality, went off to teach at Hampton Institute in Virginia.

Hampton Normal and Agricultural Institute had been founded after the Civil War by General Samuel Armstrong for the training of freedmen. During the Indian wars of the 1870s, reformers began to perceive the problems of American Indians as similar to those of former slaves and their families, and Hampton opened an Indian division. It was one of those institutions Sarah Winnemucca found so unacceptable, taking young Indians far from their families and trying to teach them exclusively in English.

General Armstrong himself, who had once visited the Goodale home, offered Elaine a position in the Indian department. She started out in the sewing room but soon was standing up in front of a classroom full of adult Indian men, trying to impose her authority and teach them basic English. Armstrong also set her to writing articles to bring Hampton's work to the attention of the public, a job she found especially congenial. After a year of teaching at the Institute, she requested and received permission to visit the Sioux agencies.

Upon return, she successfully solicited support from the Commissioner of Indian Affairs to carry education to the Sioux on their own land through community day schools. To her credit she did not seek to remove children from their families, and she endeavored from the first to learn their language. In the course of four years among the Sioux she felt free to go where she wanted, unarmed, unhindered, unprotected. As she traveled, she recorded her observations about living conditions, school standards, Sioux legal claims, and agency problems not only for her superiors but for newspapers and magazines with national circulation.

When they met at Pine Ridge, Charles Eastman and Elaine Goodale must have felt that no one else in the world understood and loved the Sioux as they did. Under ordinary circumstances, their initial acquaintance would have been brief, with Goodale continuing on her circuit of school inspections. But all government employees were under military order to remain at the agency. Unwillingly confined, she occupied herself with decorating the church for Christmas, preparing gift boxes for distribution, and visiting sick children under Eastman's care. Eastman, in turn, found time to visit her at the rectory. Together with the Reverend Cook and his family they waited and hoped that disaster might be averted. During this month of barely endurable tension he asked her to be his wife, and she accepted his proposal.

Disaster was not averted, not by the engagement announcement under the Christmas tree, not by the bags of candy for the Sioux children, not by time that was supposed to be on the side of the righteous. The Ghost Dancers at Pine Ridge sent for Sitting Bull to join them, but before he could set out from Standing Rock, he was killed in a fight with Indian police who had been sent to arrest him. It was December 15. Frightened Sioux fled southward, bringing word to Pine Ridge.

One group traveling south with their leader Big Foot had been invited by Pine Ridge Sioux who were trying to keep the peace. The infantry, perceiving them as yet more reinforcements for the Ghost Dancers, met them and instructed them to camp for the night of December 28 at Wounded Knee Creek, eighteen miles from the agency. The majority of people with Big Foot were women and children. Many were sick. Big Foot himself was incapacitated with pneumonia. As they made camp, the soldiers trained four Howitzers on them.

In the morning, the soldiers insisted that the Sioux turn in their firearms. After some debate, they reluctantly began to do so, but, by some reports, a deaf Indian failed to understand what was going on. As a soldier forcibly took away his rifle, it discharged. Shooting began on every side, the heavy artillery opened fire, and the soldiers began chasing the fleeing Sioux. Goodale wrote that women's and children's bodies were found as far as two miles away from where the shooting began, and Eastman wrote that he found a woman's body three miles from the scene. Estimates of how many Sioux died range from a conservative 150 to a Sioux claim of four hundred. Twenty-five infantrymen were killed, and thirty-nine wounded. They were taken to an army field hospital. Wounded Sioux were brought to Charles Eastman.[77]

Eastman, Goodale, and the Reverend Cook, and Mrs. Cook hauled out the Christmas tree and the church pews, spread hay and quilts on the floor, and converted the church into a makeshift infirmary. There they did their best to treat Sioux suffering from gunshot wounds. As they worked to comfort those they had little hope of saving, winter brought down a two-day blizzard on South Dakota.

When the snow finally stopped falling on January 1, 1891, Eastman led a party the eighteen miles out to Wounded Knee. Amazingly they found a few more living. Eastman himself found two; others found five more. Armed Sioux nearby refrained from firing on Eastman as he rode back alone to the agency to bring in soldiers who dug a mass grave for the dead. Sioux memory of that burial is long and bitter. Some today are convinced that the soldiers buried helpless Sioux alive.

Eastman, Goodale, and the Cooks worked around the clock caring for the survivors lodged in the church. They lost most of them, and the Reverend Cook collapsed from the strain. Eastman did not, but he emerged from the experience embittered. Later both he and Goodale wrote accounts of the action that are substantially in agreement. Here is his version:

> At Pine Ridge, in December of 1890, the ghost dancers had come in to the agency and the situation was apparently under control when the attempted arrest of Sitting Bull in his cabin by Indian police led to his death and the stampeding of his people. Several of the stampeded bands came down to Pine Ridge, where they were met by United States troops, disarmed, and shot down after one man had resisted disarmament by firing off his weapon. This was the massacre of Wounded Knee, where about 300 Indians, two thirds of them women and children, were mown down with machine-guns within a few minutes.

Then Eastman's dispassion gave way to outrage echoing that of Sarah Winnemucca. Writing of the sufferings inflicted indiscriminately on traditional and Christian Indians alike, he continued, "Many Indians now believe in Christ's teachings as explained to them by their missionaries, but they find it impossible to believe that this Government is Christian, or the average official an honest man." Warming to the topic of incompetence and corruption at Indian agencies, he lamented, "Alas! the skirts of the Goddess of Liberty have never been quite clean!" Looking back to the years after the Minnesota Massacre, he remarked, "It was estimated at this time [during President Grant's administration] that every warrior killed in battle had cost the Government twenty-three lives and a round million of dollars. At this rate, the race would not be 'wiped out' for generations. Kindness would be infinitely cheaper, as well as more pleasing, doubtless, to the white man's God!"[78]

Goodale's report of the massacre was sent on to eastern newspapers and appeared under the headline, "Miss Goodale Blames the Troops for the Killing of Women and Children." She and her fiancé were launched on a joint career as whistle-blowers even before their wedding. Like Sarah Winnemucca before them, they would soon be made to suffer for their outspokenness.

They were married in New York in mid-June 1891, six months after Wounded Knee. Following the church wedding, the Woods gave them a large reception, and the popular press made much of the union of a white woman with an Indian man, no matter that he was a Dartmouth graduate and physician.

They went into marriage loaded with freight few mortals could hope to bear. Wood had promoted Charles Eastman endlessly as an object lesson of what education could do for an Indian, a shining example for the rest of his race to emulate. Goodale, who had behind her most of a decade of independent life, resolved to give it all up to be a proper wife and mother and to serve the Sioux through her husband. They imagined they would be happy and successful.

Trying to save the survivors of Wounded Knee had called upon all of Eastman's medical training and skill, but trauma management had not been the goal of his long preparation. He had intended to serve the Sioux in positive ways, especially in the field of public health. Little did he know as he and his bride returned to Pine Ridge that the heroics of the past winter marked the culmination of his medical career so soon after it had begun. From this point on he periodically tried to practice, but his efforts came to little, the investment in his medical education was largely lost, and in the end he might better have studied law.

Troubles arose because both Eastman and Goodale did not hesitate to tell the truth as they saw it. Moreover, for Goodale, a veteran free-lance writer for magazines and newspapers, sending out press releases was second nature. Both addressed the injustices they saw all around them with minimal diplomacy. In no time at all they were embroiled in contro-versy at Pine Ridge, and the agent there was doing everything in his power to rid himself of them. The Eastmans saw what he was up to and fought back. More and more people were drawn into the fight on both sides. Letters flew, and verbal attacks were made left and right. Goodale was portrayed as ambitious to drive out the rightful agent and install her husband in his place, and quite incredibly, Eastman's professional integrity and command of English were called into question. Eastman refused reassignment to another agency and resigned. He had served as a physician to the Sioux for barely over two years.

The couple now had their first child and needed some security and income. Eastman moved the family to St. Paul, Minnesota, where he took the state medical board examinations and for a year tried to establish a practice. But his dedication to his people would not let him settle into private life, and he soon was trying, without success, to get rehired and assigned as a physician to one of the other Sioux agencies.

At this point another route opened before him. The Young Men's Christian Association, which had been growing in strength throughout the last quarter of the nineteenth century, had met with success among the Indians at boarding schools and even on some reservations. They offered Eastman a salaried position as supervisor and developer of their Indian programs, and he willingly took it. Three years after their June wedding, the Eastmans found themselves parting ways, for his job was one of constant travel, while his wife remained at home with their growing family. Whereas Goodale had risen to one professional challenge after another while unmarried, she was now a spectator to her husband's success. She did not cease her own lecturing and fund-raising, but she found herself much in the shadow of her Indian-celebrity husband.

Eastman worked for the YMCA for four years, and during this time he had a chance to visit not only most of the Sioux, but the Crow in Montana and the Sac and Fox in Iowa. His work among the non-Sioux was less than successful, and even among the Sioux he encountered serious rifts. Yet during these years habits of thought, seeded during his boyhood days and shaped during his first isolated years in white colleges, hardened into a set of beliefs about "Indian" virtues and philosophy. But "the Indian" was very much a construct of Eastman's own experience and imagination. No ethnographer, he did not question his intensely personal philosophy or test it against any sort of objective observations. In a few years he would begin to publish books for children and for adults in which he laid forth his ideas and his ideals. The more he worked them out, the more difficult it must have been to live with him.

Before he left the YMCA, Eastman had joined with his brother John to lobby Congress for Santee claims. After his resignation, he moved his family to Washington, and Goodale sometimes joined him in his lobbying activities. But their joint efforts were undercut by their enemies in the Indian bureau and by dissenting factions among the Santee. Eastman fell into debt in Washington and within a year had taken a job at Carlisle Indian School in Pennsylvania. From there he quickly moved on to another try at being a physician for the Sioux, this time on the Crow Creek Reservation in South Dakota. His debts pursued him from place to place, and it took him a long time to settle them. The Santee claims were in court until 1922, and when they were finally settled, Eastman, who had devoted time to them through all the intervening years, did not receive the large commission he felt he had earned. On the contrary, he had incurred many uncompensated expenses and been accused of trying to make a profit on Santee misfortune.

By 1900, when Eastman was offered the position at Crow Creek, he had been out of medical school ten years, and he and his wife had four children. They all moved to the agency and settled in. Unhindered this time by military operations, he engaged in public health work, fighting smallpox and measles with vaccination programs. To begin with all was well.

Then a new agent took over, and soon he was accusing Eastman of being a troublemaker and an agitator. Eastman tried to keep out of the way, but once again he found himself serving under an agent who was trying to get his physician transferred elsewhere. This time, to the list of complaints about Eastman speaking with the Sioux in their native language and being uppity were added complaints about negligence and sexual misconduct. Eastman did what he could to hang on and continue to treat patients, but again he was forced to resign. Once more his service as physician to the Sioux had lasted just over two years.

Fortunately for the Eastman family, the Commissioner of Indian Affairs had another position available. It was the Sioux names project, and Eastman worked at it for six years. In the long run, this endeavor—unanticipated by Eastman or his mentors—probably served more Sioux in a direct and positive way than any of his other accomplishments.

Sioux naming practices were utterly different from the Anglo-American ones upon which United States law depended for tracing family relationships. Sioux children received at birth names that indicated their sex and birth order. All first daughters shared the same name, all third sons, and so forth. In the course of life individuals received other, more personal names. Some were positive, as for instance Ohiyesa 'winner'. Others were descriptive, such as Crooked Foot and Sullen Face, and many were nature names such as Smoky Day, Checkered Cloud, and White Dog. Some Sioux carried as names phrases such as Chasing Crane (the man from whom Goodale first heard of the Ghost Dance vision), Let Them Have Enough, or The Man That Walks with Women. Some were derisive; the Indians at Pine Ridge named their agent Young Man Afraid of His Indians.

In the course of a lifetime, a Sioux usually went by several different names, and they rarely gave a clue to family affiliation in the way English surnames do. The exception was that sons might carry their fathers' names, as Eastman's son Ohiyesa II did.

The names given here in English are, of course, translations of Sioux ones, which English-speaking officials found hard to pronounce and spell and impossible to remember. Sioux names were simply not going to serve Eastman's people in the American legal system as they tried to assert their claims to land allotments and cash settlements. Eastman's job was to provide families with surnames that were acceptable to them and to the United States legal system.

The project took years of travel, research, and interviews to make sure that relatives were consistently grouped together under surnames they were willing to have. The Sioux appreciated Eastman's sensitivity to their esthetics and sense of self, and in recognition of his work they bestowed on him a new sobriquet. Having once called him The Pitiful Last and then Winner, they now called him Name Giver.

During the long period in which he established the family relation-ships of the entire Sioux nation, Eastman's family, whom he had moved to Amherst, Massachusetts, did not see him for weeks or months at a time. Altogether there were six children—five daughters, Dora, Irene, Virginia, Eleanor, and Florence; and one son, Ohiyesa II. Feeding, clothing, and educating six children was expensive, and the Eastmans were ever short of money. Eastman explained to his superior that his wife and children had gone back east because adequate housing for them all in Minnesota was beyond their means.

To augment their income, the Eastmans marketed their writing. Goodale, who admitted to having written some potboilers for cash as well as countless magazine and newspaper articles, used her connections to get her husband's childhood memoirs serialized in a magazine. From these pieces grew his first book, *Indian Boyhood,* which was published in 1902 just before he began work on the names project. Ten more books followed during the years when the family was based in Amherst. Goodale appeared as co-author of two of them, but the rest were published under her husband's name alone, she serving as his editor.

Some of the books were for children and were issued as school editions. *Indian Boyhood,* dedicated to Ohiyesa II, and *Old Indian Days,* dedicated to the Eastman daughters, sought to demonstrate through example what sort of people Eastman hoped his children would become. Others were directed to adult audiences and dealt with the history of contact between whites and Indians. They are all deeply personal books, invested with Eastman's own philosophy and life experiences. Editing them, Goodale may have come to know her much-absent husband better than when they had lived more together and to see how irreconcilably different were some of their views. Her revisions of his work seem to have been a sore point between them, and in their published form it is hard to tell what sort of compromise the books represent between the author-husband and the editor-wife.

Fortunately Goodale's own memoirs have been published and provide a base for comparison between her views and those of her husband. In fact, a three-way comparison of the writings of Mary Eastman, Elaine Goodale, and Charles Eastman is illuminating.

Mary Eastman and Elaine Goodale, women observing Sioux life from up close over a long period of time, were sympathetic in a way that few whites of the nineteenth century were. But the Sioux world they portray is nonetheless one in which hardship, domestic violence, and untimely death were part of everyday life. In 1849 Mary Eastman wrote that it would be well if the Sioux stuck to killing their enemies. "But," she wrote, "they are wasting in numbers far more by their internal dissentions than from other causes. Murder is so common among them, that it is even less than a nine days' wonder; all that is thought necessary is to bury the dead, and some relative must avenge his quarrel."[79]

She reported that female children were less valued than male children, that young Sioux men were ardent suitors but careless, often abusive husbands, and that women were so powerless within the family that they often had no other avenue of expression than threats of suicide, which they carried through with alarming frequency. Chastity was prized in unmarried women, and there was a ceremony in which men could shame young women by accusing them of sexual experience.[80] But life went on; in one of her stories, a young woman so exposed to public scandal does not take her own life or waste away in humiliation, but moves to another Sioux community where she supports herself and her fatherless child by telling fortunes and tending the sick.

Mary Eastman found young Sioux of both sexes physically attractive. She was impressed by their dignified carriage. It was a race, she wrote, of "tall, fine-looking men." Describing a young woman she did not think pretty, she nonetheless writes that she is "tall and well made, and her hands and feet (as is always the case with the Dahcotah women) are small. She has a quantity of jet-black hair, that she braids with a great deal of care. . . . Her teeth are very fine, as everybody knows—for she is always laughing, and her laugh is perfect music." Yet the hard life of the Sioux and their custom of slashing their arms and legs as a sign of mourning made their attractiveness short-lived. Of the older Sioux woman she says, "Her bent form was once light and graceful. Labor and privations are not preservative of beauty."[81] Aged Sioux she perceived as ugly and often dirty. She described old grandmothers as closely attached to their grandchildren, but quarrelsome, officious, and superstition-ridden.

Elaine Goodale, writing of the Sioux as she knew them a half-century later, paints a different picture, partly because defeat and dislocation subsequent to the Minnesota Massacre had profoundly changed Sioux society; partly because she lived among Sioux who were trying to be Christian farmers and who were sending their children to school; and probably partly because Goodale was writing to a different audience. Mary Eastman had regarded the Sioux as an archaic race soon to be gone, and sought to acquaint the curious reader with a culture on the brink of extinction. Elaine Goodale, on the contrary, saw them as an enduring part of the American population and much in need of assimilation. Her writing aims to engage the reader's sympathy with both the Sioux and her efforts on their behalf. The cumulative effect of these considerations is a gentler depiction of Sioux daily life, against which the massacre at Wounded Knee stands as all the more shocking.

Goodale, too, found the Sioux people and their language attractive. She described them as "a gifted, lovable, self-reliant people," and wrote of the "the musical ripple and purr of the vernacular." She ignored advice not to learn the language, and habitually wore at least some articles of Sioux clothing, which she found as beautiful as the "intensely feminine Sioux women" themselves. She frankly admitted, "It was possible to become sincerely attached to these young Sioux" (the men at Hampton who regarded her with "timidly respectful devotion"), albeit only "in an elder-sisterly fashion."[82] Concerning her decision to marry Charles Eastman—making a gift of herself to a Sioux, as she put it—she wrote that she had observed with interest unions between whites and Sioux, in particular that of a Santee clergyman and his German wife. Their harmony created for her the expectation that such bicultural marriage was possible. Violence, discord, and neglect seem to have had little place in her view of Sioux domesticity.

As for women's position in Sioux society, she wrote, "I have never seen them treated as 'slaves' or 'beasts of burden,' but always as equals and companions. They laughed and chatted freely with husbands and near relatives—especially brothers-in-law, with whom a certain jesting familiarity was permitted—advised and scolded them much as womenfolk do their menfolk all over the world." Here and elsewhere Goodale emphasized the universal human qualities common to Sioux and white alike. "The better we came to know our new neighbors," she recalled, "the more unreal appeared the popular emphasis on racial traits."[83]

But Goodale did find things to improve, and unlike Mary Eastman, who sometimes hesitated to intrude,[84] she assumed an activist role in transforming Sioux behavior. In the name of civilization, she taught them to knock at her door before entering, to live by the clock, to sit down at her table as dinner guests, and to celebrate Christmas with an evergreen tree and presents. Although she admitted that she "found the Dakotas far more cleanly under primitive conditions than most of us habitual house-dwellers when camping out," the Sioux's flea-ridden dogs were a trial for her, and she could not countenance life without soap.[85] Nor did she question the utility of teaching young Sioux women to sew dresses in the fashion of the time, wear hats, and bake leavened bread. With unintended poignancy she noted in her memoirs that whenever she did not keep them busy at lessons, the Sioux boys drew pictures of horses, and the girls created new beadwork patterns. Yet while she insisted on white etiquette in her quarters and in the classroom and spoke only English in school, she understood and observed Sioux etiquette when she visited Sioux in their homes and took pleasure in understanding and speaking their language.

She was, nonetheless, more than willing to obliterate Sioux cultural heritage. In a public address four years after her marriage, she said of Sioux grandmothers that they stood in the way of progress, prophesying death for children who attended school (not so unrealistic in a time of rampant tuberculosis) and keeping alive the traditional Sioux songs. She smugly related how a Christianized man had driven the other bathers from a sweat lodge by countering their songs with "Jesus, Lover of My Soul." And she also strove to supplant the Sioux dances with "Community suppers, magic-lantern shows, and other wholesome diversions," since "these not only involve paint and Dakota dress, but revival of war games, late hours, and a general relaxation of rules." It is hard to reconcile this with her lyrical description of the Grass Dance "performed by young men attired mainly in paint of gorgeous hues with elaborate feather headdresses and ornaments of shells, bells, and bear's claws."[86]

Goodale perceived herself as "Sister to the Sioux" (the title she gave to her memoirs), and kinfolk have the obligation to speak up about matters affecting the well-being of the family. But she directed the sharpest of her criticism at her birth family rather than her adopted one, arguing against white racism and publicly detailing the ways in which white society had wronged and dispossessed the Sioux.

All this is not to say that Mary Eastman and Elaine Goodale were diametrically opposed in their views. Mary Eastman wrote with a passion equal to Goodale's about white injustice: "Here, in a country endowed with every advantage that God can bestow, are perishing body and soul, our own countrymen. . . . White men, Christian men, are driving them back; rooting out their very names from the face of the earth. Ah! these men seek the country of the Sioux when money is to be gained: but how few care for the suffering of the Dahcotahs! how few would give a piece of money, a prayer, or even a thought, towards their present and eternal good." "No intelligent citizen of these United States," she wrote, "can without blame forget the aborigines of his country. Their wrongs cry to heaven; their souls will be required of us. To view them as brutes is an insult to Him who made them and us."[87]

On the negative side of the ledger, Mary Eastman and Elaine Goodale were both ethnocentric white women, secure in their sense of superiority, and given to making fun of aspects of Sioux culture with which they did not identify.

Charles Eastman wrote from an entirely different stance, as a man formed within traditional Sioux culture and deeply committed to it, yet with an acquired overlay of nineteenth-century white gentility. Like Goodale, he was anxious to engage the sympathy of mainstream readers, but the main thrust of his writings was to convince them as he had convinced himself that Indian culture was as good as white culture, in some ways better, and that it had much to contribute to American civilization as a whole.

In describing "the Indian," he drew upon his personal memories from childhood and adolescence. Hence, when he asserts in *The Soul of the Indian* that there were "no temples or shrines among us save those of nature," he was not only ignoring the city-dwelling Aztecs and Maya and Inca beyond the borders of the United States, but the North American mound builders whose impressive earthworks occupy an area from the Gulf of Mexico up the Mississippi valley to the southern tip of Lake Michigan.[88]

The heart of Indian religion as he perceived it was a nature mysticism akin to the New England transcendentalism of Henry David Thoreau. Spiritual power derived from withdrawal into untouched wilderness and contemplation of natural beauty. In Eastman's view, oneness with nature was the highest good. Animals were more in touch with nature's primal truths than people, so it was important for individuals to periodically seek solitude from human society and learn moral and rational behavior by careful observation of animals. By virtue of their hunting life, Indians—at least those not completely ruined by contact with white society—were superior to members of urban societies. "Being a natural man," Eastman wrote, "the Indian was intensely poetical."[89]

Not only was nature sustaining and uplifting, but close human contact was degrading: "To the untutored sage, the concentration of population was the prolific mother of all evils, moral no less than physical . . . and not less dreaded than the pestilence following upon crowded and unsanitary dwellings was the loss of spiritual power inseparable from too close contact with one's fellow-men." The Indian, he said, was "careful to avoid a centralized population, wherein lies civilization's devil."[90]

At the core of Indian religion as Eastman conceived it lay the "Great Mystery." Human acknowledgment of a greater, awe-inspiring force manifested in the natural world, he argued, was the common base of Indian and Christian religion. Conflict, as he saw it, arose from Christians not practicing their religion truly and honestly. They preached one thing, but practiced another, thereby inspiring contempt among Indians. He held up a mirror to his white readers' paternalism:

> "You are a child," said the white man in effect to the simple and credulous native. "You cannot make or invent anything. We have the only God, and he has given us authority to teach and govern all the peoples of the earth. In proof of this we have His Book, a supernatural guide, every word of which is true and binding. We are a superior race—a chosen people. We have a heaven fenced in with golden gates from all pagans and unbelievers, and a hell where the souls of such are tortured eternally. We are honorable, truthful, refined, religious, peaceful; we hate cruelty and injustice; our business is to educate, Christianize, and protect the rights of the weak and the uncivilized."[91]

Indians, on the other hand, Eastman portrayed as consistently reverent in their solitary communion with nature, in secret group rites such as the Medicine Lodge (which he compared to Free Mason ritual), and in public ceremonies such as the Maidens' Feast. Many of the Sioux songs—praise songs, sacred songs, victory songs, peace songs, the "fearless heart song," gratitude songs, death dirges—that Goodale found so objectionable are present in the collected stories of *Old Indian Days*. Hardly anything in his prolific writings is as openly emotional as his recollection of the sacrifice of his beloved dog, carried out with the greatest ceremony and honor.

That the Sioux honored fallen enemies there is no doubt. While Sioux women danced with the stretched and decorated scalps, the Sioux men blackened their faces and attired themselves in mourning for the people they had killed. Mary Eastman described in graphic terms a Sioux attack on a group of Chippewa men, women, and children and the scalp dance that followed and found it not more barbarous than "civilized" warfare. But Charles Eastman, whose uncle brought back scalps to Uncheedah from his summer raids, held back from full acknowledgment of the nature of Indian warfare. He described it as a sort of tournament and compared it to college football, in which a few young men happened to die through ineptitude. The killing of women and children he represented as an act of mercy, so they would not suffer or grieve. And ultimately he blamed white society and its alcohol for encouraging Indians to take scalps indiscriminately. He claimed that the Sioux originally took just a small lock of hair from an enemy, but Mary Eastman had written earlier, "In Indian warfare, the victor takes the scalp of his enemy. If he has time, he takes the entire scalp, including the ears; but if hurried, a smaller scalp-piece is taken."[92]

The Sun Dance is a feature of Great Plains culture perennially fascinating and repellant to non-Indians. Artists and reporters acquainted the general public with the dance through sensational paintings and descriptions that reinforced the view that Indians were a bloody-minded lot. Men participating in the Sioux version of the dance may perforate their chests or shoulders in order to insert wooden skewers behind muscles. Lines attached to these skewers tether the men to a pole, around which they dance leaning their body weight against their bonds. Sometimes the dancers hang suspended from the pole until the skin tears and the skewers pull loose. Eastman denounced the Sun Dance in its extreme form as a perversion from an earlier, more benign one, and as with the practice of taking scalps, he blamed contact with white society for exaggeration of traditional Indian behavior.

In general he lay the falling off of Indian virtues to bad white influence. Reacting to the stereotype of his people as "lazy, dirty, good-for-nothing Sioux," he retorted that before the coming of the white man Indians were "God-fearing, clean, and honorable." It was white society, after all, which had brought the "two great civilizers," whiskey and gunpowder, to the Indians, to say nothing of smallpox, venereal disease, cholera, and politics. Politics, in Eastman's view, was by its very nature as polluting as urban life, and yet Indians became adept politicians by necessity in order to defend themselves, and once they attained full citizenship, he insisted, their experiences made them especially well-informed voters.[93]

Quite aside from the matter of gender and despite Eastman's claim that they had once practiced "broad democracy and pure idealism," traditional Sioux society had been by no means egalitarian. Class sentiments reveal themselves in Eastman's own view of bicultural unions such as his white grandfather's and his own. He looked with approval upon children born of Indians and "the higher class of Europeans: officers, nobles, etc." But unions of the "lower classes of both races" produced half-breeds, whom the Sioux would not admit into their communities. Half-breeds figure in a number of Eastman's stories. One is Antoine, a brave, competent, and admirable man who is a devout Catholic and who talks to his horse, "after the manner of an Indian." But in general Eastman describes them as drunken and riotous in their behavior and says, "Some of the half-breeds loved money better than the blood of their Indian mothers."[94]

Eastman was not without criticism of the Sioux. He thought them improvident: "Such was the Indian's wild life! When game was to be had and the sun shone, they easily forgot the bitter experiences of the winter before. Little preparation was made for the future. They were children of nature, and occasionally she whips them with the lashes of experience, yet they are forgetful and careless. Much of their suffering might have been prevented by a little calculation."[95]

He also criticized them for extreme individualism that kept them distracted by internecine conflict and unable to unite against the white threat. And then there was his disdain for people who provided the public with what he considered inauthentic Indian lore. "Give a reservation Indian a present," he wrote, "and he will possibly provide you with sacred songs, a mythology, and folk-lore to order!"[96] Throughout all Eastman's writings there runs a thread of distaste for what had become of the Sioux, and a profound nostalgia for a purer life in bygone times.

With the Ghost Dancers' dream shattered and the golden age of the Indian irretrievable, why did Eastman offer his writings to the public? For one thing the Eastman family needed income, and there was a market for his books. With the closing of the American frontier and the spread of urbanization, Americans had developed an avid interest in the old days. But beyond the economic attraction of this ready market, writing for a mass audience gave Eastman an opportunity to memorialize the Indian past and to rescue it from misrepresentation. The books for adult readers served to explain how Indian/white relations had evolved and even at such a late date to appeal for justice for the surviving Indians. The books for Eastman's children and for non-Indian children encouraged them to internalize Indian virtues. Thus the Indian heritage would become part of every American's heritage and not be lost through Indians' complete assimilation to white culture.

A primary Indian virtue that Eastman stressed was reticence. In *Indian*

Boyhood he portrayed children, himself included, as impulsive talkers who had to learn not to interrupt. (Yet it is young Ohiyesa's questions that move the stories along.) Courage, endurance, sharp attention, and fast reflexes are other characteristics that should be cultivated in young males. Violent exercise and ardent competition serve to subdue adolescent sexual energy.

In Eastman's ideal world, boy children and girl children were soon separated and set on different paths. Two stories in *Old Indian Days,* "Winona the Woman-Child" and "Winona the Child-Woman," describe the education of a first-born daughter by her mother and her grandmother. From the two of them she receives constant instruction in womanliness. She is to become competent, generous, nearly silent, and unassertive. In particular, she is to avoid contact with young men, just as young men are to avoid contact with her. For proper young women the averted, down-turned gaze is requisite. The product of this training was the inevitably beautiful and good-hearted Sioux woman.[97]

The time for choosing partners, in Eastman's ideal world, came suddenly and took young people by surprise. After brief and furtive conversations, abrupt decisions were made by people previously unacquainted with each other. In several of his stories, the man and woman begin marriage sharing no common language, without hindrance to their happiness. "She simply responded with a childlike smile. Although she did not understand his words, she read in the tones of his voice only happy and loving thoughts."[98]

After marriage the ideal woman continued in her silent ways, instructing her children as much by gesture as by words. But this silence, according to Eastman, did not amount to powerlessness, for the Sioux woman was the linchpin of Sioux society: "She has always been the silent but telling power behind life's activities, and at the same time shared equally with her mate the arduous duties of primitive society. Possessed of true feminine dignity and modesty, she was expected to be his equal in physical endurance and skill, but his superior in spiritual insight . . . and no woman of any race has ever come closer to universal motherhood." Moreover, women were the owners of all the gear of daily living: "She preserved man from soul-killing materialism by herself owning what few possessions they had, and thus branding possession as feminine. . . . She was, in fact, the moral salvation of the race."[99]

Mary Eastman had written that the measure of a society is how well it treats its women. By her observation, Sioux women were unvalued, ill-treated, and openly compared to dogs by Sioux men. This is all very different from Charles Eastman's emphasis on the moral superiority of women and the sacredness of motherhood, a view strikingly similar to white middle-class thought in the second half of the nineteenth century, which held that it was women's natural role to control and civilize men's aggressive impulses. Whether held by a Sioux or a Victorian male this philosophy readily makes scapegoats of women. Describing the Sioux woman as a "tower of moral and spiritual strength," Eastman asserted that "when she fell, the whole race fell with her,"[100] yet another Eden lost through woman's weakness.

For one of his books Eastman composed a roster of distinguished Indian women. It includes Pocahontas, Oneida and Stockbridge Indian women who opposed King Philip in the seventeenth-century uprising in New England, and Catherine, a Chippewa woman who warned Fort Detroit during Pontiac's conspiracy. Considering their shared irony about white society and its treatment of Indians, one might have expected Eastman to recognize Sarah Winnemucca and her years of effort on behalf of the Paiutes, but Eastman does not mention her. Surely he knew of her, since they had traveled the same lecture circuits and fought their battles with the same Bureau of Indian Affairs. Was he perhaps embarrassed by her public life? Sarah was not silent or modest or self-effacing. Her marriages fell apart, and she was not a mother. She did not and could not wait for old age to speak her mind. Eastman's approval went to Indian women who made their contributions in "feminine" ways. Of Catherine the Chippewa he wrote, "She stood between two races, and in her love and bravery cut short a struggle that might have proved too full of caprice and cruelty on both sides. She was civilization's angel, and should have a niche in history beside Pocahontas."[101] This was not the sort of thing he could say about Sarah. By his standards, her life was scandalous.

Although a physician, Charles Eastman was remarkably prudish. In his instructive writings for his daughters all is a wordless mystery. The adolescent girl undergoes a period of seclusion, but Eastman does not say, as Seth Eastman had, that this marks her first menstruation. Instead, he writes, "Thus she is expected to develop fully her womanly qualities." Of a young couple he said, "These two had yielded to a simple and natural impulse." The pregnant woman seeks no assistance in childbirth, which seems to take place practically without labor; the newborn baby just appears. He describes childraising as though every mother has just one child, and he does not describe unions in which Sioux men took on additional wives, although polygamy was still practiced when Elaine Goodale lived among the Sioux.[102]

As a grandmother the Sioux woman was finally permitted a voice. In Eastman's view, the grandmother was the repository of Sioux knowledge and ethics. Not only did she instruct the young and reprove the full-grown, "a woman who had attained to ripeness of years and wisdom, or who had displayed notable courage in some emergency, was sometimes invited to sit in the council." (One is reminded of the role played by the aged Sacajawea or her impersonator in the Shoshone council at Fort Bridger.)[103]

Ultimately death comes to people and to animals, and in Eastman's writing it too was remarkably without pain or disfigurement or putrification. Both animals and people in death appear to be sleeping.

Editing her husband's manuscripts, Goodale must have felt personally repudiated. In 1911 he had dedicated *The Soul of the Indian* to her "in grateful recognition of her ever-inspiring companionship in thought and work and in love of her most Indian-like virtues." But in his books Eastman's ideal women were all real Indians, not just Indian-like. They blushed and hung their heads in a way that Goodale also found charming, but from which she had considered herself exempt. On the contrary, she had prided herself from an early age on looking men straight in the eye and speaking her mind, whether to Indian men at Hampton, bureaucrats in the Bureau of Indian Affairs, or representatives sent out from Washington to negotiate with the Sioux. She certainly did not wait to become a grandmother to express her opinion.

When Eastman said that he thought the Sioux custom of couples secretly going away together first and celebrating their union with the community later to be superior to beginning marriage with a public wedding, Goodale must have taken it as criticism of their own wedding with its large reception and newspaper reporters. Writing of Indian family planning, her husband stated that women should have three years between births and that no woman should bear more than five children, but despite his frequent and protracted absences, she had borne him six, and it is unlikely that they just appeared without the discomforts of late pregnancy and labor. She had raised the children very much by herself, providing home instruction to them when they lived in places without access to appropriate schools, and she had worked hard to supplement the family income. Eastman appears to have taken her efforts for granted.

And then there was the philosophical gulf between them about whether Indian culture should be valued and maintained (his view) or put aside as something that inevitably held Indians back (her view). As Eastman's vision began to gain political support in the 1930s, Goodale opposed it bitterly.

Goodale's resentment showed itself in her memoirs. She had never stopped writing, but being denied recognition comparable to her husband's, she did not value her own publications. "I can't remember a time," she wrote, "when I wouldn't 'rather write than eat,' and while literary ambition was for many years entirely subordinated to 'the cause' (and later to my family), the notion still stayed unreasonably in the back of my head that some day I might write a book that would live." She took some comfort in recalling her son's assurance: "You've always been a poet . . . whether you put words on paper or not." It also bothered her that when Eastman went on the lecture circuit and traveled abroad, she was housebound and starved for the chance to meet interesting people. Having set aside her independence to work for and through him, she saw too late the isolation she had brought upon herself: "Whether or not this was wise is perhaps an open question," she observed. "Obviously it was far from modern."[104]

When Eastman completed the Sioux names project, he became associated with the nascent Boy Scouts of America and the Campfire Girls. Founded in 1910, the American Boy Scout movement was an outgrowth not only of Sir Robert Baden-Powell's Boy Scout organization in England, but also of two boys' organizations in the United States, Daniel Beard's Sons of Daniel Boone and Ernest Seton's Woodcraft Indians. Beard's group sought to teach boys to be "ideal pioneers," while Seton's stressed life in the wild and the emulation of Indians. Both Beard and Seton, like Eastman, had enjoyed a boyhood of free roaming in the woods, boyhoods that had been brought abruptly to a close in their mid-teens. Their organizations, like Baden-Powell's, appealed to turn-of-the-century adult concerns about boys: that growing up sedentary in cities, they might not become strong and manly like frontiersmen, and that they were certain prey to such bad habits as smoking and masturbation. Going to the woods to play outdoor games was a wholesome antidote to enervating urban life. This fit perfectly with Eastman's own views, and not surprisingly, Seton was a reader and admirer of Eastman's books. Seton soon had a falling out with Baden-Powell and was marginalized from the Boy Scout movement. Eastman, however, with his past experience as a YMCA executive, found a niche in the Boy Scouts and the Campfire Girls, writing a book for them, promoting membership, and serving in their national organizations.

This work led the Eastmans to open a summer camp in New Hampshire in 1915. Its special appeal was that its Indian activities were certified authentic by Eastman's own presence. During the summers the whole family worked at the camp, and Eastman promoted it on his travels during the rest of the year. Goodale complained that it was hard to start such a demanding new enterprise when she was past fifty, but the camp was a great success during the years of World War I. Then, just as the war drew to a close, tragedy struck the Eastman family. Their daughter Irene, endowed with a fine soprano voice and already developing a concert career, was serving as a counselor at the camp in the summers. In August 1918, a wave of deadly influenza struck military bases in Massachusetts and spread to wherever there were concentrations of people, engulfing office buildings and hospitals and summer camps. One of its victims was Irene.

It could be no comfort to the Eastmans that their daughter was but one of thirty million people worldwide who died in the 1918 flu pandemic. Charles Eastman's iron mastery of his emotions denied Elaine Goodale his support in their common grief. Their strained marriage eroded further, and within two years of Irene's death, Eastman simply left his family and went away by himself, never to return.

For one last time he entered the service of the Bureau of Indian Affairs, this time as an inspector. Formerly condemned as a troublemaker, he now was sent to look into situations where trouble had already been made. One of his investigations was the controversy about whether Saca-jawea had died in 1812 at Fort Manuel on the Missouri River or as an old woman on the Wind River reservation in Wyoming in 1884. It was his last piece of work for the Indian bureau, and he went about it with characteristic thoroughness and sensitivity. He was now in his mid-sixties, and when this project was completed, he retired.

It was a busy retirement. Still in demand as a speaker, he traveled and lectured, and he attended Dartmouth functions. He even practiced a little medicine. He also continued to write, but without Goodale's copyediting, nothing came of his efforts, and he never saw another book into print. Still, he kept at his manuscripts and helped others with theirs. Assisting a Minneapolis newspaperman in some research on the Santee, he came across Mayer's drawings of Mary Nancy Eastman and confirmed with his own eyes the family tradition that his mother "had every feature of a Caucasian descent with the exception of her luxuriant black hair and deep black eyes."[105]

After he left his family, Eastman built a spartan cabin on an island on the Canadian side of Lake Huron, and there he would retreat from his public life. To his disappointment, his son did not share his devotion to the outdoors. Living in Detroit, he provided a home for his father during the cold winter months, and over the years tried to get him to let up a bit on his rigorous rejection of creature comforts, but Eastman simply became more reclusive. An illness in 1934 temporarily laid him low, but he returned to alternating his cabin life with travel and lectures. Then, when Eastman was eighty years old, he suffered a heart attack and died almost immediately, undoubtedly just as he would have wished.

His unfinished manuscripts were shipped to Goodale, and his body was buried in an unmarked grave in Detroit. The son who had turned out so different from what his father had intended survived him by only a year and lies buried beside him. Elaine Goodale completed her memoirs and saw one last manuscript of her husband's into print. When she died in her ninetieth year, she was buried in Northampton, Massachusetts.

Like Sarah Winnemucca's, Charles Eastman's fame was not enduring. During his lifetime, he was much sought after as a speaker because he was attractive and well-spoken and accessible to people who might have felt threatened by less acculturated Indians. But with his death he was quickly forgotten. He had tirelessly promoted the idea of the American Indian and helped to embed it in American Boy Scout and Campfire Girl lore, but it is Ernest Seton who receives the credit. Eastman's name does not appear in the index of the American Heritage popular history of the movement, *The Boy Scouts: An American Adventure,* nor in David Macleod's scholarly study, *Building Character in the American Boy: The Boy Scouts, YMCA, and Their Forerunners, 1870–1920.* As for his own writings, the children's stories seem overly sentimental now, the highly subjective adult works perhaps outdated as well. Only *From the Deep Woods to Civilization,* with its eyewitness account of the events leading up to and through the massacre at Wounded Knee, retains its power.

Eastman was too much of two worlds and far too self-conscious for his writings to have immediate appeal to anthropologists, and what he had to say about the injustice done to Native Americans (a term he used before it came into general use) is too uncomfortable for the American public to retain in memory. His nature philosophy, like Seton's "woodcraft," was anachronistic for urban Americans even at the beginning of this century. Not even his wife and children could live by it, yet he could not live without it.

The ultimate dichotomy in Charles Eastman's thought was not between good Indian society and bad white society but between the good natural world and the perverse human world. It was not that Indians were better than white people but that their contact with nature made them somewhat less bad. His pessimism about human nature is captured in "The Laugh-Maker," a moral tale he included in a book for children. A human being lives among the bears. He has a bear for a wife, and they have a half-bear, half-human son. Periodically the bears all go off to the shore to share a good laugh together. The man is curious, so he takes his son along, and they watch the assembled bears from hiding. The bears' spokesman calls for the Laugh-Maker, perhaps an otter, that comes swimming to a rock near the shore and delights the bears with its antics. When the bears are helpless with mirth, they dismiss the Laugh-Maker. The man watches all this unamused. After the bears disperse, his bear-son calls the Laugh-Maker back, and when the man sees his own child overcome with laughter, he shoots the animal dead. Long before the bears are aware of their loss, the man has made the Laugh-Maker's skin into a container for his weapons.[106]

THESE THREE PROFESSIONALS

It is my personal belief, after thirty-five years' experience of it, that there is no such thing as "Christian Civilization."
—*CHARLES EASTMAN*[107]

Gaspar Antonio Chi, Guaman Poma de Ayala, and Charles Eastman could all be accused of biting the hand that fed them. They owed their bilingualism and literacy to education provided by missionaries: Gaspar Antonio to Luis de Villalpando and the Franciscan educators; Guaman Poma perhaps first to his half-brother, the Spanish-speaking priest who taught him his letters, and then to some sort of religious establishment where he read his way through the library; and Charles Eastman to the Riggs family and all the other godly folk who moved him on from school to school. Yet their experiences failed to convince these men that the arrival of Christianity had rescued their peoples from savagery and established civilization among them for the first time. Although they earned their livings at least in part by opportunities that came their way via the evangelists, they insisted on detailing what had been lost when their own civilizations had been smashed: their recorded histories, their consistent systems of justice, the sustaining power of their own religions, their well-ordered daily lives. They all of them criticized the disorder that had been introduced, the chaos and exploitation, degradation and brutality they witnessed on all sides.

Their mentors themselves provided models for this frank criticism. The Franciscans complained bitterly about the encomenderos' misuse of Indians; the thundering denunciations of Spanish abuses by Bartolomé de las Casas were well-known all the way to Peru;[108] and it was mainly churchmen and churchwomen who decried the ruination of North American Indians as the frontier swept westward to the Pacific. Yet in their writings, these three men do not exempt the missionary enterprise itself from criticism. None of them express the sentiments that Bernal Díaz attributes to Doña Marina; they do not say that they are grateful to have been snatched from the darkness of paganism, that they are delighted to work for white men, and that they would not give up the positions they had attained for kingdoms of their own. On the contrary, they unhesitatingly condemn Christianity as they saw it practiced, and they pour their energies into describing how things had been better once and making their own bold recommendations for improvement in the future.

For their trouble they all became objects of intense animosity. White society at large—whether Spanish or Anglo-American—detested uppity Indians; the more cultivated and articulate, the more they were resented, and in this Sarah Winnemucca was a sister in suffering to the men of this chapter. The hatred such individuals evoked was quite impersonal. Old Díaz de Alpuche, who considered himself a champion and protector of the Maya, dismissed Maya graduates of the Franciscan schools across the board as debauchees and rascals, and centuries later an inspector who had just been assigned to investigate charges against Eastman described him as "crafty and adroit." [109] According to Guaman Poma, he was usually called a troublemaker as soon as he fell into conversation with strangers at country inns. (Recall that parents' pressure on the convent school led the nuns to send Sarah and her sister away before anyone could possibly have become acquainted with them.)

Attacks on them as individuals were yet more vitriolic and sometimes hardly rational. We know nothing of Guaman Poma's background beyond what he claims for himself. The lack of corroborating documentation may not be damning, for almost nothing in the way of Quechua written records has survived. If he was who he said he was, it must have been maddening to be accused of being an imposter and to have no way of proving otherwise. As for Charles Eastman, how could anyone seriously suggest that a Dartmouth honors graduate had an inadequate command of English? And when he, like Sarah Winnemucca before him, was accused of sexual improprieties and misuse of funds entrusted to him, what defense could possibly be raised? Innuendo played on popular stereotypes of the sneaky, incompetent, childlike Indian; of the lascivious male physician; in the case of Sarah, of the dirty, alcoholic army-camp whore. As public figures, they were vulnerable, and the character references they presented in their own defense could not shield them from the mudslinging.

Racism and unremitting slander led to an appalling waste of their talents. Having acquired a level of education well in advance of everyone around them, these people struggled day to day to meet the basic needs of themselves and their families, and they did not do well. A great deal of their energy was absorbed in patching together paid employment, trying to meet expenses, going to court, appealing to high officials for redress. It was an exhausting, endlessly humiliating business, and it is a wonder they managed to get any of their own writing done. It is no wonder, on the other hand, that what they wrote about was injustice. If their potential had been fostered rather than bludgeoned, things might have been otherwise.

As it was, unrelieved frustration manifested itself in an ascending spiral of self-promotion. To make themselves heard, they beat their own drums, and when that proved ineffective, they raised the volume. And so it was that Gaspar Antonio elevated himself from notary public to interpreter general of the reigning monarch and in his probanzas moved himself closer to the direct line of succession of the rulers of Mani. So it was, too, that at the end Guaman Poma styled himself a prince in order to talk man-to-man with the Spanish king. When Charles Eastman attended Dartmouth reunions in ceremonial robes, his bonnet of trailing eagle feathers proclaimed coups he had never counted in battle. The same process had been at work when Sarah Winnemucca posed for publicity photos in princess costumes such as no Paiute woman had ever worn and proclaimed herself the daughter of the supreme leader of her people.

Despite the barriers thrown up before them, Gaspar Antonio, Guaman Poma, and Charles Eastman managed to work and support themselves throughout their long lives, unlike Doña Marina and Sarah Winnemucca, who died young, and Sacajawea, who may have. It was not that Indian men in general were employable and Indian women were not. Whether it was Sacajawea or an impersonator at Wind River, some old woman worked alongside her sons as an interpreter there until her death. Nor was it that in these times and places Indian men generally had a better chance at longevity than women. Indian women bore the special burden of sexual violence, but there was violence and deadly illness enough to go around. Most Indians, men and women, died before their time, and while they still lived, most were—regardless of gender—sunk in destitution.

Women without income and living under threat of violence are inevitably sexualized, if not in fact, then in others' imagination. We see this in the universal characterization of Doña Marina as Malinche, the mistress of Cortés; in Clark's description of Sacajawea as Charbonneau's squaw; and in the affidavits that circulated in Washington claiming that Sarah Winnmucca was a prostitute who would sell her body for a bottle of whiskey. That sexual commerce might be an avenue open to men as well is seldom admitted as a possibility. No one, to my knowledge, has yet suggested that Gaspar Antonio might have been the sexual plaything of Diego de Landa, that Guaman Poma's bitter obsession with the sexual behavior of priests might have proceeded from being discarded by Martín de Murúa, or that any of Charles Eastman's promoters were ever infatuated with his undeniable physical beauty—that Sioux masculine grace and hauteur Mary Eastman and Elaine Goodale found so attractive. A woman, so goes conventional wisdom, can trade her body to a man for support and protection, but a man has to go out and get an honest job.

Be that as it may, for some gifted, hardworking Indian men there was a niche, the profession of civil servant. They could find employment drawing up legal documents, making certified translations, carrying out investigations, and writing reports. Among the Aztecs, Maya, and Andeans, such a profession existed prior to the arrival of the Spaniards, a secure position open only to men. Until very recently there has been nothing equivalent available for these men's female counterparts in most indigenous societies or in white society either, for that matter. To be a civil servant has required schooling unavailable to women. A woman's language skills might be called on in a parley out in the field, but in an institutional setting, lack of qualifications would exclude her from employment, a job title, and a dependable salary.

Sarah Winnemucca's engagement as an army scout was odd for a woman and not an occupation anyone could expect to grow old in. She tried to make the transition to the acceptable female profession of school mistress, but blocked from appointment on the reservations and lacking sufficient capital to maintain her own school, she was unsuccessful. Uncomfortable though their lives were, Gaspar Antonio, Guaman Poma, and Charles Eastman survived professionally much longer than she did.

In their long lives they found time, place, and means to write, and they were all driven by internal compulsion to do so. Defining themselves as self-appointed cultural interpreters/historians, they untiringly detailed what their cultures had been, what ruin had been brought upon them, and how things might yet be salvaged or how at least a positive memory might be preserved. Once the Maya books had been burned, Gaspar Antonio sought to perpetuate a history of the Xius and their neighbors by addressing himself to the king's questionnaire. Likewise, Guaman Poma, the unsolicited informant, told the king about the Andean past, suggested a mighty reform, and requested that his report be archived for future reference. Charles Eastman devoted himself in book after book to elaborating his vision of the Indian and how the adoption of Indian values could ennoble the lives of all Americans.

They were men in love with their ideas. Each of them constructed an elaborate context for himself. For Gaspar Antonio it was the glory days of the Xius, for Guaman Poma the Inca and, even more, the pre-Inca world of the Andes. Charles Eastman remade all Indians in the image of the Sioux. Living in the wreckage of a way of life so recently torn asunder, gripped with nostalgia, reconstructing what had been in light of their own self-interest, making heros of themselves along the way, they all tried to teach their visions to the world at large.

It is sometimes said that everything we know about the Maya we owe to Diego de Landa. Perhaps Gaspar Antonio's own fragmentary report together with all the encomenderos' reports he drafted do not equal in luster Landa's *Relación*, but he surely was an unacknowledged source for Landa's work as well. The terrifying priest has receded in history; not only were his bones sent back to Spain, but in recent years his statue in Izamal has been relegated to a traffic island. Gaspar Antonio has not correspondingly come forward to take his master's place, however much of what we know of the Maya we may really owe to him.

Guaman Poma could hardly have guessed how well he would succeed at his project in the very long run. Better than being available for consultation in Rome, his report has worldwide distribution, and rare is the publication about Inca times and the conquest of Peru that does not use some of his drawings as illustrations.

Charles Eastman tucked Indian values as he perceived them into Boy Scout and Campfire Girl ceremonials to live on in American culture even if all the Indians passed away. After his own death, he was forgotten, but his Indian lore was not. Buried in an unmarked grave, he has his real monument in edition after edition of the Boy Scout handbook.

Three Native Informants

VERSES OUT OF SERFDOM: *Larin Paraske*
(ca. 1834—1904)

Come death across the swamp,
pestilence along the winter road.
Take away this apple,
bear away this berry,
lure away this little lily.

—*PARASKE'S CRADLE SONG* [1]

The maidens walked along . . .
with full breasts, with aching nipples.
They milked their milk onto the ground, let their breasts spurt;
they milked onto the ground, milked onto the fens, milked onto gentle
    waters.
One, the oldest of the maidens, milked out black milk;
the second, middle one of the maidens, spilled white milk;
the third, the youngest of the maidens, spurted red milk.

—*THE KALEVALA* [2]

Her breasts hurt as she walked along the forest track toward the Russian city of St. Petersburg. Milk began to soak through her shirt, warm at first but cold against her skin as it spread and cooled in the air. There was more wetness and misery under her skirt; her baby had not outlived the bleeding after childbirth. Now she was hurrying to the Petersburg foundling hospital to collect an infant some other mother needed to be rid of. She would present herself as a lactating woman from the border villages licensed for wet nursing, and they would hand over a baby and the payment. They knew this gaunt long-boned woman with the overflowing breasts who replaced her own lost babies with Russian foundlings.

She would sit down to nurse right away, to keep the milk coming and to rest her legs. As soon as the authorities would permit, she would board a cart heading out of the city, now that she had a baby to carry.

Then came a jouncing ride back toward home with an infant sucking at her breast and she herself sucking on a hard crust of rye bread she had begged on the way to the city and kept knotted up in her handkerchief for the return trip. Sooner or later, and usually sooner, the nursling died, and Paraske went back for another.

By her own account, she relieved the foundling hospital of fifty children over the years. Paraske was what was known in the nineteenth century as an angel maker.

St. Petersburg in the nineteenth century was a magnet drawing in people from the lands all around the east end of the Baltic Sea. It had been built by order of Czar Peter the Great at the mouth of the Neva River, in a land peopled by Ingrians and Vots and Vepses and Karelians, relatives of the Finns. It had taken czarist inducements to get Russians to move to the new city, but the people who were already there became its street sweepers and hod carriers, coachmen and scullery maids. In neighboring Finland a new railroad line threading down through the west of the country to a Baltic embarkation point would funnel off the landless unemployed to jobs in North America.[3] But for people in eastern Finland, nowhere near a railhead, the job market was in Petersburg.

A great many young women, Finnish and Russian, came to Petersburg to work. Separated from their families, dependent on their jobs, they were preyed upon by the men of the households that employed them. With no means of contraception and with abortion difficult and dangerous, these women found themselves with babies they did not want, could not keep, must not kill. To their ranks were joined women of gentler circumstances but pregnant out of wedlock nonetheless, whose condition would shame their families, undermine their futures, and muddy lines of inheritance. Their conditions had to be concealed at all costs, the human product of their pregnancies tucked into some sort of revolving door that would come back around again empty.

This was not a problem peculiar to Petersburg. It was and still remains the problem of big cities on the make throughout the world. At the end of the eighteenth century and on into the nineteenth century, it was

Europe's time to suffer with it. As the countryside began to empty into the new industrial cities, civil authorities everywhere were taxed to the limit by the scourge of abandoned babies—infants left on trash heaps, drowned nurslings strewn on river banks, newborns dropped down out-house holes. If a newly delivered woman were caught with no baby to show for it, she could be tried for murder and her fate held up as a public deterrent, but this only served to double the number of victims. The baby was already dead, and the woman who had been sexually used was now executed for her misfortune. Such is the theme of the ballad about the lady-in-waiting, Mary Hamilton, with its tragic refrain, "Last night there were four Marys, tonight there'll be but three."

The foundling hospital was an institution that offered women an alternative to infanticide. The mother gave birth in an adjacent lying-in hospital or elsewhere, and the infant was brought to the foundling hospital. The woman recovered and went on with her life, making her peace with her conscience and the few people who knew of her predicament: guilty of fornication but not of murder.

But this seemingly humane solution to the tragic social problem of unwanted pregnancy simply passed on the act of infanticide from the woman who bore the child to someone else. For the babies did die, most of them, but by the time they died they had usually been handed on again—to the angel makers.

Wealthy families had always employed wet nurses. They chose lactating women carefully for health and abundance of milk, brought them into their households to nurse their offspring, and fed them as well as they fed prize livestock. In humbler households women were called to nurse other women's babies if the mother died or was very ill, for the loss of mother's milk was a death sentence for infants until very recently and still is where nursing bottles, infant formula, and means of sterilization are not available. And increasingly in European cities, especially in Paris, another practice became entrenched in the nineteenth century. Urban parents sent their newborn children off to wet nurses in country villages for the first year of their lives and posted monthly payments for their upkeep and clothing.

When one woman nurses another woman's child, there is another child somewhere. The women with full, leaking breasts who presented themselves for inspection, hoping to capitalize on healthy looks and the newness of their milk, had recently given birth. Where were their babies, and how were they being fed? Not all these lactating women had just lost babies of their own. What a Parisian woman feared was that a wet nurse engaged to take her baby off to the country had another baby at home waiting with open mouth to compete with the urban baby for her milk.

And this was often true. But to receive the monthly payments the wet nurse had to keep the commercial baby alive, so it was usually her own child that did with less or was handed on to yet another woman to nurse or was fed bread-and-water pap from a spoon or given a rag soaked with cow's milk to suck. The fate of wet nurses' own children troubled authorities, but their attempts to regulate the profession were aimed mainly at preventing the spread of syphilis and smallpox from wet nurses via infants to their healthy parents.

Such was the situation with wet nurses who were paid to return babies after weaning. When a woman received a subsidy for taking one away and had complete freedom to return for replacements, there was no incentive for keeping any particular child alive. Whenever an infant succumbed, she could put her milk on the wet nurse market again before lactation ceased. Although the situations were theoretically different, the end result was appallingly the same. If a wet nurse joined a household, the baby she was hired to nurse usually did well, but her own child, if not dead before she took the position, was likely to die in someone else's care. Babies taken off to be wet nursed in the country, whether monthly payments were made or not, died at a terrible rate, as did wet nurses' own children. Europe was awash in infant death.[4]

Striving to emulate the grandest aspects of western Europe, Petersburg was a progressive city, a city of plans and bureaucrats and institutions. To relieve women of the products of unwanted pregnancies it built a foundling hospital. Unable to provide enough wet nurses for the rising tide of unwanted infants, it took to exporting some of them to Finland.[5]

For centuries neighboring Finland had been a province of Sweden, but where Finland ended and Russia began was a matter of considerable fluidity. Depending on the fortunes of war and the art of negotiation, the border was sometimes well to the west of where it lies today and sometimes well to the east, only about twenty miles from the mouth of the Neva. The Vots and Vepses lived outside the Finnish border, although their languages were like Finnish. The Karelians and the Ingrians on the north side of the Gulf of Finland, whose speech was even more like Finnish, had only to sit still to find themselves in the course of generations sometimes on one side of the border, sometimes on the other. Once, when Finnish Lutheranism swept eastward with the border, many Orthodox Karelians packed up and headed off deeper into Russia to avoid Lutheran evangelism.

In the nineteenth century, Sweden lost all of Finland to the Russian czar, who kept it apart for himself as a grand duchy. Since Finland now posed no threat, it was not important to the czar/grand duke where the border lay, so for this period it zigzagged from the shores of the Baltic just west of Petersburg up to the shores of Lake Ladoga in the northeast.

Although it did not make much difference to the czar which of his villages lay on the Russian side of this border and which on the Finnish side, it made a tremendous difference to the people who lived in them. Although the villagers understood each other across the border far better than they understood the Russian spoken in Petersburg, religious differences separated them. There were Lutheran churches and pastors on the Finnish side, while the Orthodox faith was unchallenged on the Russian side. And until Alexander II abolished the institution in 1861, serfdom bound people to masters and estates on the Russian side, while the villagers on the Finnish side, impoverished and landless though they might be, were free men and women.

In 1840 five villages on the Finnish side of the border were granted a license for providing wet nursing and fostering services to the Petersburg foundling hospital. Women from these villages could fetch from the hospital nursing infants or foster children, "the crown's children," as they were called. In principle the women were to raise them in their own homes for six or seven years before returning them to the Petersburg workhouses, where they would be set to the sort of Dickensian child labor common to nineteenth-century cities. For taking the children away, the women received a payment in rubles. In practice, no one expected or wanted to see the children again, and they rarely did.[6]

Lactating women could also remain in the Petersburg hospital to wet nurse infants awaiting placement. In this service they generally suckled several different babies a day, spreading ever-present infection from baby to baby. [7]

In the early days, the border villages absorbed about three hundred Petersburg foundlings. As the end of the second decade of their monopoly approached, they were looking after about two thousand of the crown's children. Finally, the Governor General of the Grand Duchy of Finland had their license revoked on the grounds that this way of siphoning off illegitimate children was encouraging immorality, spreading venereal disease from the congenitally infected, and causing neglect of the foster mothers' own children.[8]

Paraske was born in Russian Ingria around 1834 of an across-the-border marriage. Her father's family had been bound to the Kusova estate for generations, but her mother was from Sakkola, just a few miles away in Finland.[9]

Although they were from Ingrian border villages, members of Paraske's family knew Petersburg well. Her father, Nikitta, had learned blacksmithery in the city and afterwards constructed a forge on the Kusova estate. According to family history, Paraske's maternal grandmother, though from the Finnish side, had been packed off to serve a master in Petersburg, only to be rescued by her brother when he found her drawing water barefoot on the ice of the frozen Neva. Although there is a legal distinction between serfs and slaves, Ingrians then and ever after bitterly referred to their condition in those days as *orjuus* 'slavery'.

Suffering from tuberculosis, Nikitta's Finnish wife Tatjana nonetheless gave birth to eight children, of whom Paraske was the fourth. At some time Tatjana managed to take Paraske back over the border to visit her relatives, but from the age of ten Paraske spent most of her summer days in a pack of Ingrian children herding animals in the estate's forest. To pass time and to distract themselves from hunger and bad weather, the children tried to outdo each other with songs that they had learned—cradle songs, dance songs, wedding songs, laments.

What the children were doing there in the woods on the Finnish/ Russian border was going on in villages from the shores of the Gulf of Finland all the way to the edge of the White Sea. In nineteenth-century Karelia and Ingria, for men, women, and children alike, singing was the undisputed arena for competition. Where survival dictated that under-nourished people not expend unnecessary physical energy, and where people could acquire or display few material goods, virtuoso feats of memorization and improvisation were a way for individuals to measure themselves against one another.

On the Kusova estate the two children with the biggest stock of songs were Paraske and a boy named Ontropo Melnikov. According to Ontropo, telling his life story many years later, he and Paraske were a good match for a while, but Paraske finally got the edge on him and eventually knew all the songs there were to know.

The songs the children sang belonged to a body of folk poetry shared by Finns, Karelians, Ingrians, and their linguistic relatives, poetry recognizable by its alliterative verse structure and by a company of heroes who appear in various exploits. Scholars had already taken notice of these heroes and their adventures in the eighteenth century, and by the time of Paraske's birth in the first half of the nineteenth century, a physician named Elias Lönnrot had written down thousands of lines of the poetry and begun publishing it. While Paraske and her companions were competing to outsing each other in the woods near the shores of Lake Ladoga, Lönnrot was polishing his expanded second edition of *Kalevala,* an immense poetic construction he had woven together from songs like theirs.

Lönnrot had gone by foot on long poetry-collecting trips through northern and eastern Finland and that part of Karelia that lay north of Lake Ladoga stretching to the White Sea. In the course of his career he even went by boat to Archangel and thence south through the country east of Lake Onega and to the northern shores of Ladoga. Everywhere he found men and women who sang to him of Väinämöinen the singing magician, Ilmarinen the smith, Lemminkäinen the womanizer, Kullervo the strongman, and Jokahainen the upstart challenger of Väinämöinen. Narratives about these men provided the substance of Lönnrot's Kalevala, a framework which he adorned with charms, prayers, wedding songs, lullabies, songs of grief and sorrow.

A connecting theme was the *sampo,* a magical engine that perpetually ground out prosperity. A powerful woman commissioned it; Väinämöinen promised to deliver it; Ilmarinen forged it; and then Väinämöinen, Ilmarinen, and Lemminkäinen set out to steal it back from its owner. During a battle for its possession, it was broken and its fragments scattered on the bottom of the sea, and so it is that since then prosperity has been so rare and arbitrary.

The father of the Kalevala did not collect folk poems in Ingria, but he inspired a younger generation to set off on their own collecting trips. As they brought back ever more poems, a difference became apparent. In the dense forests north of Ladoga, where the Russian estate system was weak, Karelian men sang the long accounts of the Kalevala heroes, but in Paraske's Ingria the singers were mostly women, and what they sang were short, lyrical poems of profound emotion while tears flowed freely down their cheeks. Finnish folklorists attributed the difference to the long hours of exhausting work the estate serfs performed, but there was more reason. The Russian masters suspected the poems, sung in a language they did not understand, to be subversive. When a Finnish sculptor named Alpo Sailo interviewed a former serf from an estate in Ingria, the old man explained: "'When times were very hard in the village, we came together, all the neighbors, and talked about our sorrows and kept singing the rest of the night. We got power from singing, it made a serf feel easier.' Sailo asked him what happened if the master knew that they had come together to sing. The man bared his back to the visitor, which was covered in scars from lashes. 'Well, they whipped us. And if you did not leave, they called the cossacks, and then the whole village was whipped.'"[10]

According to a Finnish folklorist, Ontropo Melnikov had received lashes for singing. When asked how it was that Paraske bested him at singing, Ontropo remarked that whipping made one's memory go to pieces.[11] Women might snivel their laments at weddings and funerals, but men in slavery robustly singing of voyages, warfare, and magic were not

1. *The Sacajawea statue in Washington Park, Portland, Oregon. (Oregon Historical Society, Or Hi 27715)*

2. Doña Marina (center) interprets at the presentation of the daughters of the lords of Tlaxcala to Hernán Cortés and his men in token of their alliance. The man standing behind Doña Marina and making the same gesture may be her interpreter colleague Jerónimo de Aguilar. From the anonymous Lienzo de Tlaxcala Manuscript. (Archer M. Huntington Art Gallery, The University of Texas at Austin, Archer M. Huntington Museum Fund, 1964. Photograph by George Holmes.)

~PREGVNTA·EL·AVTOR
MAVILLAVAI·ACHAMITAMA

pregunta   autor   y muestra

3. "The author inquires," one of Guaman Poma's depictions of himself in his report to the King of Spain. Here he conducts an investigation, hearing complaints of Andeans abused by Spanish colonists. (Nueva Corónica y Buen Gobierno [Codex péruvien illustré], 364. Paris: Institut d'Ethnologie, 1936)

4. *Charles Eastman and his daughter Dora in 1892. (Courtesy of James W. Dayton, Jr.)*

5. *Doña Luz Jiménez and her daughter Concha in 1926. (Tina Modotti gelatin-silver print, 7 1/4 × 7 1/2″. Museum of Modern Art, New York, anonymous gift)*

6. Flower Seller, *painting of Doña Luz and Concha by Diego Rivera, 1926. (Honolulu Academy of Arts, gift of Mr. and Mrs. Philip Spalding, 1932. Photograph by Tibor Franyo.)*

7. Larin Paraske, *painting by Albert Edelfelt, 1893. (Hämeenlinna Art Museum, Finland).*

8. *Photograph of Paraske at the time Edelfelt painted her portrait. She was about fifty-nine years old at the time and does not appear as aged in the photograph as in his painting. (Porvoo Museum, Finland. Photograph by Natalia Linsén.)*

9. *Dersu Uzala, carrying his pack and his father's rifle, and V. K. Arsenjev contemplate a map during the 1906 cartographic expedition.*

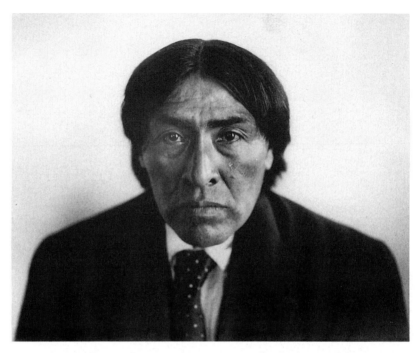

10. Ishi dressed in suit and tie. (Phoebe Hearst Museum of Anthropology, The University of California at Berkeley.)

11. *"Your loving sister Sarah Winnemucca," autographed photo from Sarah to her brother Natchez. (Nevada Historical Society, Reno. Photograph from the studio of Bradley and Rulofson, San Francisco.)*

12. *María Sabina in 1960, seven years after R. Gordon Wasson paid her his first visit. She wears a distinctive Huautla huipil. Photo © 1993 by Frederick A. Usher.*

13. *A Huao man declares kinship with Dayuma as other Huaorani look on. (Used by permission of Wycliffe Bible Translators, Huntington Beach, California.)*

14. *Chloe Grant at her home in Queensland, Australia. (Courtesy of R. M. W. Dixon.)*

15. *George Watson on Palm Island, Australia. (Courtesy of R. M. W. Dixon.)*

16. *Laurinda Andrade on the occasion of her retirement from teaching. (Library of the* Standard-Times, *New Bedford, Massachusetts. Photograph by Ron Rolo.)*

tolerated. Yet although they were constrained from singing the long narrative songs, the Ingrians had not forgotten their heroes. When Paraske was an old woman, she had Lönnrot's Kalevala read aloud to her from beginning to end. After some thought she announced, "That's all mixed up," and began to set it right.[12]

Though Paraske and Ontropo and the other Ingrian children knew of Väinämöinen and his companions and their exploits, the *kantele*, a stringed instrument as important in the Kalevala as the sampo, was as much a thing of mystery to them as the sampo itself. They knew it only by name. On the estates of Ingria no one had such a musical instrument; when Ingrians danced, it was just to the voices of singers. Among the herdschildren, one would stand up on a stump and sing while the others danced the figures they had seen at weddings. A half century was to pass before Paraske would hold a kantele in her hands.

Paraske's days of singing in the forest were numbered. Tatjana finally succumbed to tuberculosis when Paraske was in her mid-teens, and Nikitta died soon after. Upon his death, the master of the Kusova estate confiscated the forge Nikitta had built. Paraske's brother Vasle, the estate's coachman, objected and was punished by such a severe lashing with the knout that he never recovered, but died after weeks of suffering. Paraske herself had a taste of the same punishment.

An orphan at seventeen, Paraske longed for a life over the border in Finland, but she was bound to the estate. She was already in demand as a public singer, and as she went from village to village singing at other people's weddings, she advertised herself as a bride for the man who would buy her out of serfdom. The news carried to the other side, and an offer came from Kauril Stepanova, who lived in her mother's old home village.

Kauril was twice her age, forty years old to her twenty. He was poor and in bad health. Paraske was no beauty. She was tall and angular with a prominent nose and deep-set eyes. He needed a strong woman to do the heavy labor he could not do. Her price, it is said, was twenty-four rubles.[13] Kauril paid it to the Kusova estate, took her back to Sakkola, and married her in the Orthodox chapel in mid-July 1853.

As the mistress of Kauril's tiny Larila homestead, Paraske dropped the patronymic from after her given name and acquired her new home's name in front of it. Before her marriage she had been Paraske Nikittina; for the rest of her life she would be known as Larin Paraske.

Much has been made of Kauril Stepanova's physical debilitation, but whatever it was that ailed him did not prevent the couple from conceiving children. Paraske gave birth at two- to three-year intervals beginning in

1854. Her last child was a daughter who died without baptism in 1878 when Paraske was in her mid-forties and Kauril was in his mid-sixties. Altogether Paraske gave birth to nine children, of whom only three survived: Nadeschda, their third child; Tatjana, their fourth; and Vasle, their sixth.

Throughout her pregnancies Paraske plowed and dug, planted and harvested Larila's fields. When the land lay under snow and ice, she spun wool and flax, wove cloth, and embroidered it. In the early years she was able to supplement their income by taking nurslings from the Petersburg foundling hospital. With the wet nursing operation closed down by the authorities, she joined work crews hauling freight barges along nearby waterways.

The Russian painter Ilya Repin's painting "The Volga Bargemen" shows what the work was like. Haulers worked with broad leather bands across their chests. The bands pinned their arms to their sides as they leaned forward so far that only the harness kept them from falling on their faces. They used their whole body weight to move the vessel behind them as they trudged through sand and water. It was work for mule teams, but in that time and place it was human beings, not mules, that did it. Among the dark, hardened bargemen in Repin's painting is a young blond boy with a cross on a chain around his neck and a face as pretty as a girl's. He stands upright with one hand under the chest band, holding it away from his flesh. Imagine that boy as a young woman with tender, milk-engorged breasts. That was Paraske.

She was tall, she was strong, and work made her tough. She was still a singer, and hard times deepened her art. In that corner of the world life transitions called for dramatic weeping. When a young woman was to be married, she engaged in a round of tearful farewells to her mother who had raised her; to her sisters and brothers from whom she was parting; to her home where she had lived until then. As she imagined living in a strange house among people she did not know, at the beck and call of a mother-in-law, she went into a frenzy of lamentation. And of course, her family reciprocated with their own weeping. Talented singers were engaged to lead all this crying. Professionals needed only to concentrate for a few moments, handkerchief pressed to cheek, and then the tears would begin to flow, inspiring tears in all beholders. And so a wedding would be off to a proper start.

Likewise, on certain feast days of the Orthodox calendar people went to the burial grounds to weep for their deceased relatives. The graves resembled miniature chapels. Each was covered by boards, and marked by a cross with its own little roof. The woman who led the weeping would rest her cheek against a grave marker, ready her handkerchief, begin to speak to the ancestors, and then the tears would come.

Mrs. Alec Tweedie, an English women traveler who visited eastern Finland in the 1890s, witnessed lament-singing and published her impressions:

> First she sang a cradle song, and, as she moaned out the strange music, she patted her foot up and down and swayed her body to and fro, as though she were nursing a baby.
>
> Abundant tears shed for no sufficient cause—for no cause at all, indeed—would seem to be a characteristic of these lady vocalists.
>
> During one of the most mournful of her songs, she sat so close to me that her elbow rested in my lap, while real tears coursed down her cheeks. It was quite shocking to witness the emotion of the woman; she rocked herself to and fro, and mopped her eyes with a neatly folded white cotton handkerchief, the while she seemed totally oblivious of our presence and enwrapped (*sic*) in her music.[14]

Mrs. Tweedie may have perceived no reason for the rocking and weeping, but then she hadn't buried the crown's children or leaned her chest into a barge harness in the shallows of Taipale River.

Paraske became adept at weeping on cue. When she was an old woman and living in the home of Adolf Neovius, the composer Jean Sibelius and a friend came to hear her sing. Neovius, who knew her songs by heart, stood behind her and silently signaled to her little audience whenever she was about to break into tears, and he was right every time.

Scholarly investigators were not impervious to the power of her art. Another Larila woman recalled that once Neovius asked Paraske to sing about the bride leaving her childhood home. Paraske warned Neovius that he wouldn't be able to endure it, and he replied that he would make his heart as hard as a stone. But as they sat side by side, she engrossed in her lament, he too began to weep, as did everyone present. Everyone who saw and heard her sing was struck by the intensity and volatility of her emotions during her performances.

In her cradle songs, Paraske invoked death as the sandman that came to put children to sleep for eternity. She sang of the boys and girls beneath the sod, the child with hands full of flowers borne to the land of the dead. This conspiracy with death, this willingness to let children go, was common to the people of the border lands, where epidemics and famine were everyday fare and subsistence was always just beyond reach.

Katri Peräläinen, born in Ingria at the end of the nineteenth century, told this story of her family. Her mother Maria was seventeen when she entered an arranged marriage with a man she had never met. Her mother-in-law, a woman of Paraske's generation, was pleased with the bride's industriousness but appalled by her fertility. In fifteen years of marriage Maria gave birth to twelve children. Five of the babies died, but that still left a larger family than her mother-in-law felt they could support. Then disaster struck. Three months after the twelfth baby was born, Maria fell ill and became permanently disabled. She lived on eleven more years as an invalid, and Katri took on all the work of looking after her little brothers and sisters. Some time thereafter when smallpox visited the village, her grandmother picked up the littlest brother, who was already sick with some sort of infection, and carried him off to a house where a boy had just died. She did this, as Katri explained, "because there was too much work for a fourteen-year-old girl like me, and if the boy would die, it would free me. But this brother of mine is alive to this very day in Estonia. He didn't die or even get infected." Her grandmother, Katri said, openly offered the family's children to death, calling, "Death, bear one away." Katri observed that her grandmother spoke of death by its Finnish name but directly addressed it in the estate owners' language, as though death itself were a Russian master.[15]

In a world so devoid of sentimentality, emotion was of a fabric tougher than we can imagine. Devout Orthodox Ingrians thanked God for the few years or days of life that had been granted, commemorated the fleeting beauty and goodness of those gone on ahead, and wept bitterly for themselves that they had to continue in the hard world, bereft of the loving mother, the faithful spouse, the baby starved to death during summer haymaking.

After Paraske's ninth child died at birth, there were no more. In his mid-sixties Kauril had become a total invalid. Neglect would have ended his life then and there, but Paraske did not neglect him. Like Katri Peräläinen's disabled mother, Kauril lived on for years, fed and tended like yet another household infant. When he died in 1888, he was nearly seventy-five years old.

Paraske's biographers have emphasized Kauril's unproductivity and Paraske's and Kauril's mutual exploitation: she using the marriage to escape serfdom, he using his mysterious condition (which did not affect his potency or his life span) to force her into doing all the work the two should have shared. Yet Paraske, whose sharp tongue seldom spared other relatives and neighbors, never let fall a critical word about her husband, and her poems about marriage express deep gratitude and even deeper grief at the loss of his companionship.

I was doomed to wander wretched,
travel troubled
along a sorrowful shore
. . . .
A thousand thanks to my bridegroom,
upon his beloved inclined brow,
for he salvaged me from slavery,
from the sorrowful shore,
from the burden of village bondage![16]

At age fifty Paraske found herself in an increasingly precarious situation. Larila did not exactly belong to Kauril. Although it had been his family home, technically it belonged to the government of Finland. So long as Kauril and Paraske paid a nominal annual rent or tax on it, they had the right to live there and farm the land. They had the option of buying the land outright, but it was out of the question that Kauril would ever accumulate purchase money. As he declined into old age, Paraske found it difficult to get together the annual payment that would keep them on the land with a roof over their heads.

As their surviving children matured, they became less help rather than more. Tatjana married a Lutheran and moved away. Nadeschda, having inherited her father's delicate constitution and her mother's great jib of a nose, remained unsought in marriage, unhelpful with the heavy work at home. Vasle went courting and married a girl from a neighboring village the summer after his father's death. But something was wrong with Vasle too. A.M.C. Clive-Bayley, another traveling Englishwoman, visited Paraske at home and described Vasle as "a nice-looking, blue-eyed fair man, with a troubled expression on his brow."[17] Observing the undisguised hostility between Paraske and her daughter-in-law, Clive-Bayley felt that what Vasle needed was independence from his mother. But what Paraske had every reason to expect was the support of a hard-working son and daughter-in-law, and that was not what she found herself with. Like his father before him, Vasle was somehow unable to work much at all. Something had to be done. Salvation appeared in the guise of a Lutheran pastor.

Adolf Neovius was a quarter-century younger than Paraske, born the same year as her daughter Nadeschda and brought up on Lönnrot's Kalevala. At age twenty-seven and just married, he had been sent out on his first assignment as assistant pastor in Sakkola. It was a difficult position on the frontier of Finnish Lutheranism, the parsonage and church surrounded on every side by Orthodox chapels. Many of the residents of Sakkola parish felt threatened by Lutheranism, and rightly so. Lutherans, for their part, considered the Orthodox no better than pagans and felt compelled to free them not only from their religion, but from their whole superstition-laden culture.

Not only was there a pervasive atmosphere of competition and distrust, but living conditions in Sakkola were spartan, to put it mildly. The parish's population had burgeoned during the nineteenth century, and its villages had become densely built with cottages and outbuildings practically wall to wall and gable to gable. Because everyone had to work all the time for the bare necessities of life, there was no time for upkeep. Houses were ramshackle, and among them Paraske's was particularly so. There was mud everywhere when the ground wasn't frozen and excrement everywhere as well.

In Sakkola, Neovius and his bride were very far from city lights, orchestral music, theater, painting and sculpture, libraries, grand buildings, and modern medicine—all characteristic of Finland's rapidly growing cities. For some young couples the assignment would have seemed a misfortune. Adolf Neovius perceived it as the opportunity of a lifetime.

In the 1880s Finns were still seeking their national and cultural identity on the very edge of their own country or out beyond its borders. Within Finland, foreign investment had fueled development of textile mills, granite quarries, glass and ceramic factories, steamship lines, railroads, and the like. Traditional culture seemed on the retreat before internationalism. Young Kaarle Krohn, son of a Finnish folklorist and destined to become a more famous folklorist himself, theorized that the folk poetry from which Lönnrot had constructed the Kalevala had originated in western Finland and spread out to the east and north. Now it had been obliterated at the core and only survived on the fringe, where it was soon to expire. Collectors went to the eastern border areas to salvage it from the lips of aged singers.

Neovius was of this generation, and his parish assignment took him right where he wanted to go. In Sakkola he was the soul of responsibility in his spiritual and administrative roles, aiding poverty-stricken parishioners from his own limited personal funds. But he also took advantage of his four-year stint in Sakkola to hear the songs of every old lady he could find. Word went out that rubles were to be earned for singing at the Lutheran parsonage.

In the spring of 1887 Larila was about to be auctioned off for back payments. One day late in May Paraske appeared at Neovius's door to inquire about a Lutheran church matter on behalf of a friend of hers. Neovius politely inquired about his visitor's home village and remarked that he had heard that in that village there lived a famous singer. Paraske identified herself and on the spot began to reel off verses. Thus appearances were preserved. As an Orthodox woman she had not gone seeking help at the Lutheran parsonage. On the contrary, the young pastor had discovered her.

It was not the first time she had been discovered nor the first time she had earned money from Finnish collectors. As early as 1847 they had been through the area, and in 1854, right at the time of her own wedding, she had sung for a collector named August Ahlqvist. But Ahlqvist hadn't given Paraske her due when he wrote down over fifty poems from her village without troubling to indicate which women sang which ones. In 1876 Theodor Schvindt, a representative from the Finnish national museum, had come buying embroidery from the local women and met Paraske for the first time.

The following year, when her next-to-last child was born, Neovius's best friend Aksel Borenius had visited her village, heard Paraske sing, and written down a brief life history for her. When he learned that Neovius had received the Sakkola assignment, Borenius wrote congratulating him and directing him to Paraske's village for the excellence of its singers. Paraske well understood when she set out to meet Neovius that he was a potential source of income for her. In the words of Paraske's most recent and acute biographer, Senni Timonen: "Obviously prior to May 1887 they had traveled separately along a ready-made road and now were consciously seeking one another. Their encounter was no longer by chance but an inevitability."[18]

Neovius paid singers at the rate of one ruble per hour to let him write down their verses line-by-line. Paraske assured him that she could sing without repeating herself for days on end. Sometimes she came to him, and other days her neighbors observed him visiting in her cottage. Toward the end of the summer she stayed at the parsonage for five days during which she provided Neovius with a hundred different songs. That year and the following year as well she met her land payments with money she had earned by singing.

In 1888 Paraske followed Kauril's coffin to the Orthodox burial ground and sang him into his grave. In front of the villagers gathered in the cemetery she wept over the desolation of widowhood, silent evenings, lonely mornings, the cold bed, alienation even from God's comfort. More privately she sang:

> All the others lie by twos,
> it's just me passing the night alone,
> all the others two-by-two,
> me alone in solitude.

Pairs of mosquitoes in the air,
pairs of birds are flying,
pairs of fish are in the sea—
me alone in solitude.[19]

She had the rest of 1888 to mourn Kauril and half of 1889 to prepare for another loss. Neovius had proved himself at his hardship post and was now called to his next assignment, his own comfortable hometown of Porvoo. At the end of the summer he and his family packed up for the trip home.

The young pastor left Sakkola, but Sakkola never relinquished its hold on him. His former parishioners remembered him ever after as the man with a pocketful of rubles who helped them through hard times. He was now too far away to hear them, but in moments of crisis he was the one they wrote or dictated letters to, asking him for help, for loans, for cash.

Neovius had a need too. Other collectors of folk poetry sought to visit as many different villages as possible, to hear the largest number of singers, collect the record number of lines, the most variants of the same song. Neovius did not concern himself with breadth or variation. He sought completeness in another way; he wanted every single one of Paraske's songs. Other people in Sakkola he could help a little bit by sending money. Paraske he brought to Porvoo to live with him and his family, to sing for him until the wellspring of her verses ran dry. She came in January of 1891 and stayed through the spring of 1894, only going back to Sakkola for one summer visit.

Such a life it was away from Sakkola! Paraske was living in a house where the roof didn't leak and cold wind didn't blow through the walls. In the corners of the rooms tile stoves radiated warmth day and night. Outdoors were paved streets, a market square, rows of shops, a waterfront, and a steamboat dock. Mrs. Neovius managed a staff who took care of the shopping and cleaning and laundry and childcare. Almost everyone in Porvoo spoke Swedish, and that was the language the pastor and his wife spoke with each other and to their children. Petersburg and the Russian language were far away.

When Neovius was ready to "sing" Paraske, he got out his notebooks, and they sat down together. She sang a song from beginning to end, dictated the words line by line, and explained the meanings of the many words he did not know. When Neovius was busy with parish duties, Paraske did embroidery and tried to free herself, a woman in her mid-fifties, from a lifetime of illiteracy.

Aid came from two quarters: spectacles to sharpen her fading vision and the help of a veteran teacher, seventy-two-year-old Charlotta Molin, a retired deaconess. Together they turned the pages of books as Paraske tried to learn to read. When she went home for a summer visit in 1892, and again after she had moved back permanently, Paraske sent greetings to her elderly Lutheran mentor in letters from Sakkola directed to "Miss Mulina." But to the end of her life Paraske needed the assistance of others to get such letters written.[20]

In March Paraske visited Helsinki for the first time. She went to sing at a meeting of the Finnish Literature Society in its ornate new building that had just recently been completed. Neovius wrote ahead to Kaarle Krohn, the folklorist, asking him to put Paraske up in his home for the duration of the meeting, and received an unexpected rebuff. Krohn replied that his wife had just given birth, and his mother-in-law and a nurse were in residence at their house, so there was no room.[21] Fair enough, but Krohn went on to suggest, by way of being helpful, that some poor family would take Paraske in for cash. Neovius had hoped that Krohn would have Paraske to sing for him privately while she was in Helsinki, but he didn't, not that year or ever.

Why this coolness on the part of a scholar who Neovius had every reason to expect would be fascinated with Paraske and her art? There were probably two different reasons. Krohn and his colleagues were collectors. Like their contemporaries who collected material artifacts—textiles, householdware, tools, weapons—they were somewhat fixated on things and careless about how and from whom they had gotten them. As in the case of Ahlqvist in Sakkola, they sometimes failed to write down with the verses they collected the name and life history of the person who sang them. Krohn might be interested in Paraske's songs but perhaps not in her as a person. And as for her songs, Neovius already had them, so what was there for Krohn to gain by spending time with her?

The other factor was class. In Sakkola, Neovius and Paraske had freely visited back and forth between his home and hers, and in Porvoo she was a member of his household. But this was exceptional. At the end of the nineteenth century Finns were acutely aware of the social distance between employer and employee. Masters and mistresses might use the same informal pronoun to their servants that they used with children, but employees always spoke as formally as possible to their employers, even avoiding saying "you" to them by speaking in an indirect third-person style.

In small Finnish towns that could only afford one school, children of the gentry found themselves in classrooms with children of the working class. Mrs. Tweedie reports that a mother said this to her about the situation: "I dislike it very much; my son is in such a school, and he sits next to one of our soldier's daughters, and according to school etiquette, every one uses *thou*. This is all very well in school hours; but if I go to see the girl's mother, and take her a little soup or something, my boy and her girl naturally continue to address each other in the familiar form. I find it very awkward, and as I will not let my daughter, at all events, mix upon such intimate terms with the children of my servants all day long for years, I have a governess for her at home."[22]

Little girls were taught to drop curtsies to their parents, older relatives, and all their betters. Girls who grew up to be cooks and maids and nannies went on curtsying for the rest of their lives. Paraske was the type of woman who would be curtsying to people until her knees would no longer bend, not the sort of person one had as a house guest. Probably in Kaarle Krohn's opinion she would have been much more comfortable boarding with people of her own kind.

Back in Porvoo the snows of that first winter melted away, the lilacs bloomed, and Sibelius came to hear from Paraske's lips how Kalevala verses were truly sung. He listened intently, made notes, and in the next year completed his Kullervo symphony about the most tragic of the Kalevala heroes.

Paraske and Theodor Schvindt renewed their acquaintance. He was working on a book about the embroidery patterns and woven ribbons he had collected in and around Sakkola, and he sought her assistence. Like the collectors of folk poetry, Schvindt was searching for things he could feel were genuinely Finnish. He rightly perceived that along the west coast folk art was constantly being modeled on foreign objects that seafaring men had seen or brought home from abroad. He imagined that the embroidery patterns and the decorative ribbons had been invented centuries earlier and maintained without outside influence. For his book he painstakingly drew the basic patterns and showed how women combined them into much more complex ones. Paraske provided the traditional names for stitches and patterns and explained how one could tell what village a woman was from and whether she was in mourning by the embroidery she wore. When the book was published, Schvindt described Paraske in the foreword as not only a famous singer from Sakkola but also one of her area's finest needlewomen.[23]

By now Paraske was a celebrity, and she made her public appearances in a handsome folk costume. With a dark skirt she wore a long white overgarment embroidered at the wrists and neck and tied at the waist with a woven woolen ribbon. A heavily embroidered Ingrian headcloth concealed her hair. The dress was not hers. Women in Sakkola no longer wore such clothes, and in any case Paraske had always been too poor to have anything so fine. In 1887 Neovius had bought it in mint condition from a woman in Sakkola who had made it thirty years before and never worn it. But he did not give the costume to Paraske. According to a note written by Neovius's daughter, Paraske got to wear it, but the dress belonged to Mrs. Neovius.[24]

Dressed in it, Paraske sat for portraits and photographs in Porvoo and Helsinki. A half dozen or more artists drew and painted her likeness. The most famous of them were the celebrated Helsinki painters Eero Järnefelt and Albert Edelfelt, for whom she sat as a model in January 1893. Edelfelt painted her seated on a rock in a field, elbows on her knees, large work-hardened hands clasped, eyes set on something far away or deep within. He painted her again with her hands playing across the strings of a kantele, her face lined with the emotion of her song. In Järnefelt's painting, she appears even more tragic as she leans her cheek against a black cross, her hands folded on its arm, eyes welling with tears, mouth drawn in grief. But in a sketch Järnefelt also caught another characteristic mood of Paraske's; in it she leans forward, eyes bright, a wry smile on her strong face, with the air of pride and pleasure she always took in showing off her accomplishments.

While she was in Helsinki on this visit, Paraske shared a room with Hetta Kauppinen, the nanny for Järnefelt's family. Hetta was from a rural district in the heart of Finland, far from the Russian border and its Orthodox villages, and she belonged to a religious movement that condemned all ornament, color, and frivolity. Oddly matched roommates though Hetta and Paraske were, yet they became friends, and Paraske managed to coax Hetta into accompanying her to Orthodox services at Uspensky Cathedral. Paraske, who knew St. Isaac's Cathedral in Petersburg, may not have been overwhelmed by the scarlet and gold, flicker and boom of divine liturgy at Helsinki's Russian church, but poor Hetta's pietist sensibilities must have been severely taxed. For her part, Paraske had made a remarkable passage from a childhood hemmed in by the strictures of life on the Kusova estate to this time of easy familiarity with people like Sibelius, Neovius, Charlotta Molin, Hetta Kauppinen, Schvindt, Järnefelt, and Edelfelt.

Albert Edelfelt assumed a place at the right hand of Neovius in Paraske's personal pantheon. She affectionately compressed his names together into "Albertfelt," and as he painted, she observed him as intently as he observed her. From time to time they would interrupt their concentration to be served coffee in gold-rimmed cups. Later Paraske's reminiscences of the rich dark coffee, the delicate coffee cups, and Albertfelt's beautiful hands would irritate the people of Sakkola who had never had the chance to know such things.

In Porvoo Neovius had completed the first volume of Paraske's poems, and it too was published in 1893, a golden year for Paraske in what Finns then and to this day consider their golden age of painting, music, architecture, and literature. Three portraits of her hung in the Helsinki Exhibition. Within Finland and beyond, Paraske was featured in newspaper and magazine articles. Mrs. Clive-Bayley, spending the year in Finland and writing notes for a travel book, decided to go see her.

But Clive-Bayley waited several months before presenting herself at the parsonage in Porvoo, and when she finally did in the spring of 1894, Paraske had departed. In the introduction to the first volume of her poems, Neovius reported that together they had set down 32,676 lines of verse. They had gone through *Kanteletar,* a collection of lyric poems published by Lönnrot; they had read through the original Kalevala and through its expanded later edition, with Paraske explaining and annotating all the way. She had recalled the songs she had learned from her mother and from all the older women on both sides of the border. She had sung to him all the songs she had made up herself about joy and sorrow, birth and marriage and death. It was phenomenal that one person could hold so much in memory. For Paraske there had been no other way but to learn by ear, to compose, and to remember. There had to be an end to it, and as 1893 drew to a close, she was exhausted.

Back in Sakkola she had a new grandson, born to Vasle and his wife. But Vasle hadn't kept up payments on Larila. When the winter lifted and travel was possible, Paraske had thanked the Neovius family and set out eastward for home. She had hoped to realize a profit by selling her embroidery to Helsinki ladies and perhaps engaging in some other small commerce, but it hadn't worked out. She had been well housed and fed during her time in Porvoo, but she was returning almost as poor as she had set out.

In June when Clive-Bayley found to her disappointment that Paraske was no longer in Porvoo, Mrs. Neovius proposed that the two of them go to visit her in Sakkola. Paraske was delighted to welcome them, and all the neighbors rushed to see the visitors. Schvindt had written of his visit in 1876 that within an hour of his arrival, the house he was visiting was teeming like an anthill with women offering embroidery for sale. So it was with Mrs. Neovius and Clive-Bayley. Thirty or forty neighbors managed to crowd into Paraske's little cottage to see them. Everywhere they stopped on this summer visit news spread like wildfire, and "poor folk," as Clive-Bayley described them, came offering "odds and ends of quaint things," "embroideries, silver brooches, magic stones, and flint instruments," and "dresses just off the loom."[25] The locals danced and sang for the ladies, and the ladies dispensed tea to them. Paraske presided with considerable self-importance over all the excitement, and Clive-Bayley noticed resentment and contention in the air.

Her visitors had come at a bad time, and Paraske was putting on a brave face for them. Larila, which she had saved repeatedly with her singing, was on the point of auction again. In fact, Clive-Bayley says it was sold off to a neighbor while they were still in Sakkola.

The seven fat years from 1887 to 1894 gave way to cold and hungry years. The publisher of the first volume of her poems discontinued the series for lack of public support. In Sakkola Paraske had no livelihood, no income at all. Her health began to give way, and as winter loomed, she sent letters to Neovius, and he sent money. He promised to get the Finnish Literature Society to help, and he succeeded. Paraske was awarded 1,500 marks compensation for her contribution to the nation's cultural treasury.[26] Vasle was able to recover their cottage, and there was enough left over for Paraske to get a pair of shoes and have her winter coat refurbished. And so she made it through that winter.

In her travel book Clive-Bayley recommended to her English readers that they make a summer trip to Sakkola for the quaintness of it all. Members of the Finnish middle class, having drunk deep at the fount of national romanticism, were already taking their summer vacations in the eastern villages. In the summer of 1895 a teacher named Edla Hiilos rented a cottage near Paraske's. Soon after she arrived, she was stopped on the road by a familiar-looking woman with a little boy in tow. The woman identified herself as Paraske, introduced her grandson, and explained that she was on her way to the teacher's cottage to beg. Hiilos, whom Paraske undoubtedly knew all along to be the teacher, identified herself in turn, and Paraske began her appeal on the spot. Hiilos found it hard to believe that such a famous person should be destitute, but she gave Paraske some money in any case. To the teacher's chagrin Paraske fell to her knees and kissed the hem of her skirt in gratitude.

Unsupported by children or community, confined to bed for days at a time, without money, Paraske was in deeper trouble than Hiilos could imagine. Neovius appealed to Krohn for the Finnish Literature Society to take over some ongoing responsibility for Paraske's welfare, writing forcefully about the injustice of letting the nation's leading singer of folk poetry suffer in poverty and hunger. Hoping to arouse the public about Paraske's precarious situation, Neovius wrote an entry for Paraske in a biographical dictionary of Finnish women and included the fact that her home was in danger of being auctioned. But nothing came of either effort. As another summer drew to a close and winter came again, Paraske moved in with a neighbor, because she was unable to heat her own cottage. She was no longer up to cutting and splitting her own firewood, and no one did it for her.

Schvindt sent money for Paraske to come to Helsinki to do more consultation about embroidery. In November she was back in the capital, where Schvindt introduced her to other members of the literary establishment and tried to engage the government in providing for her. From Helsinki she went to spend Christmas with the Neovius family, arriving very weak and ill. They kept her through the winter and spring, and once again she returned home to Sakkola.

During the summer she did some repairs and apparently felt some optimism, but fall and winter again brought crises. She coughed all the time and didn't have the means to pay for medicine. She wrote to both Neovius and Edelfelt asking for money. At some point she also began seeking and receiving help from the wife of a Finnish senator she had met in Helsinki. Neovius was beginning to suffer from the drain on his family income. To raise money, he sent some of his manuscripts to the Finnish Literature Society, asking that compensation for them be directed to Paraske rather than to him. This raised another hundred marks, which were sent at the very end of 1897.

In 1899, Paraske wrote that the hundred marks were all gone. She was bedridden, and her daughter Nadeschda had to stay by her side and so was unable to go out begging. She was once again about to lose Larila. The Finnish Literature Society got up another hundred marks, but Paraske owed twice that much, and in the summer her house was once again sold out from under her. This time she moved into her neighbor's sauna for the summer. The current pastor in Sakkola applied pressure to the Finnish Literature Society, and they sent yet another hundred marks but too late to recover the house. As cold weather set in, Paraske went to Porvoo to seek shelter with the Neovius family once again. She was appallingly aged and ill, and she yearned to be in Sakkola, close to her Orthodox faith and Kauril's grave. She feared dying far from home, but she was now homeless.

Since the 1880s the Finnish Literature Society had been providing a pension to a member of the Perttunen family who had provided Lönnrot with many narrative poems in the 1830s. Miihkali Perttunen had died in 1889, and after making one more hundred-mark contribution to Paraske in 1900, the Society finally decided to settle a pension on her. In Sakkola too, people relented a bit. The purchaser of her house let her move back into it. Neovius was no longer in Porvoo; he had received a new assignment to a parish west of Helsinki. But he continued to send Paraske money, and she continued to post him letters. In January 1903 she wrote to him that a payment she was supposed to receive from the Finnish Literature Society had not arrived.

By Eastertime she could no longer leave her bed. She spent her days in earnest prayer that God would bless and reward her benefactors and finally deliver her from life. Through the summer days and through the darkening autumn she prayed. God only relented in January when the ground was frozen solid against the gravedigger's shovel. Her daughter wrote to Neovius that her last words had been, "Now I want to be alone. I have my own work to do."[27]

The battles were not yet over. Nadeschda wrote that a large crowd of local people had followed Paraske to the burial ground. The coffin was donated, and they had marked her grave with a plain black cross like the one Paraske embraced in Järnefelt's portrait. There was no money for anything more.

Neovius wrote back pledging a stone marker for Paraske's grave, but he was in debt and his finances were in shambles. Years went by as Nadeschda waited patiently, but there came a day when Neovius knew he could not purchase the stone himself. He asked Krohn if the Finnish Literature Society would do so. Krohn replied that the Society could pay sixty or seventy marks for a stone but claimed that Paraske's family did not want one. Neovius must have pushed ahead anyhow, because some months later a memorial company wrote to him apologizing that they were unable to do the job, because they hadn't the right size in stock.[28] One can only surmise that the order was too small for them to trouble with.

In 1909 the Society placed a marker on Miihkali Perttunen's burial place. Nadeschda could contain herself no longer; six years after her mother's death she wrote to say that the promised gravestone had not arrived. Neovius took it up with the Society again. A year later the Society said it could come up with 150 marks.

Finally in 1911, the South Karelian Youth Society under the leadership of a young local poet named Mikko Uotinen stepped in and raised 550 marks. Correspondence was opened with Neovius seeking his advice and keeping him abreast of the details. There was to be a likeness of Paraske in relief on the stone, done from photographs taken in Porvoo and from Edelfelt's painting. There would be no kantele, since Paraske had never really played one.

On a day in high summer seven and a half years after her dark January burial, several thousand people gathered for the unveiling of Paraske's memorial. Uotinen related her life story as he had received it from Neovius and drew the ceremony to a close with his own verses for her.

> You grew up as a fettered flower
> There in weeping Ingria-land,

With a song within your soul,
Favored flower of the gods.[29]

For Paraske Finland had held the promise of freedom, yet there she had lived in poverty almost beyond comprehension. She had known devotion in marriage, disappointment in her children. She had inspired the greatest creative minds in Finland, but for her contribution to the national patrimony the Finnish Literature Society had always offered her too little and too late. In her Orthodox community where she had sung so many into marriage and into eternity she was left cold and hungry in her old age, yet she had been cherished and supported by a circle of Lutheran friends. Ontropo Melnikov, with his back ruined and spirit broken by the knout, outlived Paraske by more than a decade; Neovius, young enough to be her son, had joined her in death long before their complete collection of her poems was finally published in 1931.

In the 1940s the border moved again, and Paraske no longer sleeps in Finland.

IMAGES IN PAINT, PICTURES IN WORDS:
Doña Luz Jiménez (ca. 1895–1965)

They paid me for my time, no? And if I want to look at what they made of me, why there I am, all over the walls of the National Palace. Why should I need to own a picture of me, when it's there for me and anyone else to see, free?

—LUCIANA[30]

Luz was a young girl selling tamales in the town square when the revolutionary forces of Emiliano Zapata swept into town. She took cover behind a column of the market building as bullets cut down the soldiers breakfasting on the square. Almost as soon as the shooting had begun, the Zapatistas wheeled and rode out of town, leaving the plaza once again piled with dead men. It was not the first time. Luz said that earlier the Zapatistas had killed so many federal soldiers that "their corpses were like pebbles scattered on the ground."[31]

The town of Milpa Alta ('High Field') is situated south of Mexico City, up on the lip of the ridge that looks down into Morelos, the heartland of the Zapatista rebellion. The people of Milpa Alta followed footpaths through the mountains to trade with the people of the town of Tepoztlan on the other side, and Zapata and his followers had come by the same routes up out of Morelos to their town to denounce President Porfirio Díaz and declare a new social order, with land for the landless and freedom from oppression.

Zapata had received a sympathetic welcome in this largely Indian town that was already in the process of breaking with its traditions. In her autobiography Luz relates that men and women greeted him with flowers, fireworks, and band music, much as they had recently been coached to celebrate the hundredth anniversary of Mexico's independence from Spain. Education in Milpa Alta had been making rapid advances. There were handsome new public schools. Girls were being educated in them as well as boys, and the townspeople had been encouraged to leave behind their traditions and look toward a bright future in which their children would enter professions. It was Luz's ambition to become a schoolteacher herself. She did not want to be a house servant, grinding corn, patting out tortillas, and doing other people's laundry.

Zapata spoke of class struggle and inequality to a community that was well aware of the gulf between landholders and landless workers. He spoke to the *macehualtin,* the ordinary folks, and according to Luz, he spoke to them in their own language, Nahuatl.

There is a line in a Nahuatl song that says, "I long for flowers. Let them come lie in my arms, for I . . . am discontent."[32] The flowers the people of Milpa Alta gathered in their arms for Emiliano Zapata left them torn and bleeding and worse than discontent. According to Luz, here is what followed that flowery welcome.

A garrison was set up and one of Zapata's lieutenants was left in charge of Milpa Alta. He required the people of the town to provision the revolutionaries and their horses and mules. Prominent local men began to disappear. The Zapatistas extorted money, burned buildings, and destroyed property. Girls were carried off, raped, and abandoned, never to be seen again. Federal troops came in, and in the fighting between the two forces the schools were blown up, Luz's home was burned, and children were cut down in the crossfire.

Zapata's men were driven out, to be replaced by the forces of Venustiano Carranza, who turned out to be just as rapacious. After suffering repeated raids by the Zapatistas, the Carrancistas turned on the town's people, punishing them as collaborators. In 1916 they rounded up all the men and boys—five less than two hundred, as Luz put it—and machine-gunned them. After the women and children had buried their dead, they were driven from the town, and Milpa Alta lay deserted for four years.

The Mexican Revolution had broken Luz's life in two. She would not be a schoolteacher. She would not convey to the children of Milpa Alta the virtues of literacy, cleanliness, punctuality, and patriotism. When her town was repeopled after the Revolution, it would no longer be her home.

Many years later, as she composed her autobiography with Fernando Horcasitas at the National University, they constructed her life story in two parts. In the first, she describes life in Milpa Alta in the waning days of the thirty-four-year reign of President Díaz, the distant "little father" who sought to transform Indian communities like Milpa Alta into modern un-Indian towns. She tells of the campaigns against Indian clothing and against the old ways of doing things, how parents were threatened with fines and jail if they did not wash and brush their children and send them to school in clean clothes and underwear and with shoes on their feet.

Little Luz did not need to be coerced. According to her memoirs, she wept and begged and demanded education for herself, and once in school, she won prizes for her diligence. In 1908 she was enrolled in the new free Concepción Arenal public school where girls were taught not only lessons from school books, but also drawing, dressmaking, embroidery, and how to bake wheat bread—skills to set them apart from their Indian mothers. As September 16, 1910, approached, they practiced singing to the flag in Nahuatl and Spanish and marching onto a platform four-by-four to receive diplomas. On Independence Day, the regimented white-clad children with red, white, and green sashes and arm-bands represented a triumph for the policies of President Díaz and his minister of education, Justo Sierra.

As she carried off her Centennial medal, Luz gave all her heart to Díaz, Sierra, and their vision of "the proper way of life." But as things later turned out, it was fortunate for her that the process designed to mold a new kind of citizen did not succeed in obliterating who she had been or where she had come from. An observant child, she knew how her father cultivated century plants to draw their sap for pulque. She was knowledgeable about mushroom gathering and water hauling, woodcutting and hunting in the forests around Milpa Alta. She knew when to expect pilgrims passing through on their way to the shrine at Chalma, and what dances were done for each holiday. The stories people told about the surrounding mountains, about ghosts, and about miracles took firm root in her memory.

Luz's depiction of life in Milpa Alta in the first decade of the twentieth century is bathed in the nostalgia that so tenaciously clings to childhoods abruptly cut off and irrecoverably lost.

The second half of her autobiography recounts the terror years: townspeople stepping over dead bodies in the streets, armed men displaying severed heads, a priest brutalized, churches desecrated. She recalls, "Bombs and machine guns burst, and our two schools were destroyed. When these two buildings collapsed, many federal soldiers were buried in their ruins. One of the schools was called Concepción Arenal, and I do not remember the name of the boys' school. The federal soldiers were crushed to death, together with their camp followers, in my school—in the same classroom where I had learned so many things."[33]

In the 1916 massacre she lost her father and uncles. Ever the clear-eyed observer, she tells of finding one uncle lying in front of the church, eviscerated by dogs that had found the body first. The warring factions held their fire while the women and children struggled to dig mass graves for their husbands and fathers. Then the Carrancistas went house to house robbing the widows before herding them off to a walled cemetery in Xochimilco where they left them.

Luz's history of Milpa Alta is almost told. The refugees made do as best they could in Xochimilco and in Mexico City. Girls became house-maids. Vendors learned how to call their wares in Spanish. Zapata was assassinated. Four years after the massacre, people began to return to their town only to find it overgrown and taken over by snakes and ghosts. Gradually more people came to live there. The next generation produced professionals—the lawyers and teachers and priests her generation had aspired to become. Almost at the end she says, "Yoixtlapouhque. / Their eyes are wide open now. Nican yotlan notlatol ipan Momochco Malaca-teticpac, altepetl tepetzalan. / Here ends my story about Milpa Alta, the village between the mountains." [34]

And so the account concludes in the 1920s, without a word about the thirty and more years that passed before she began to tell it. And so it is that although Luz is ever present in the chapters, her autobiography nonetheless seems more a history of a community than of a person. It ends just when her adult life begins.

Luz's mother went back to Milpa Alta and lived out her long wid-owhood there. Luz did not. Nor did she become a housemaid. Instead, in an extraordinary act of resistance, she became a life model for Mexico City's many art schools and the muse of the radical artists of the 1920s. But like many an ordinary housemaid on her own in the city, she eventu-ally found herself pregnant out of wedlock. One of the painters, Jean Charlot, drew her sitting on a bed in a tiny room looking pensive and large with child. To one version of the drawing he added a couplet about her internal musing on the life taking shape within her. Later he com-mented on a 1927 print of her nude: "This is Luciana, or Luz. . . . I thought of her as a sort of earth mother." [35]

To the artists Fernando Leal, Diego Rivera, Charlot; to the photog-raphers Tina Modotti and Edward Weston; to Anita Brenner the author and journalist, she was Luciana, their muse, the eternal Indian woman. Some people took her to be Anita Brenner's housemaid. Brenner herself seems to refer to Luz as her cook from time to time. The baby, Concha, was everyone's pet, always dressed up in little bonnets, handed from lap to lap, and drawn, painted, and photographed again and again. For the artists and their friends Luz organized trips to the countryside, visits with her mother in Milpa Alta, pilgrimages to Chalma, and they in turn poured their impressions of these excursions into their art.

Charlot wrote in his diary that he, Anita Brenner, and Frances Toor, a folklorist, went to Milpa Alta on January 2, 1925, and joined Luz's family setting out on horseback at 2 A.M. on January 3 for Chalma. After seventeen hours in the saddle the party reached the village of Santa Marta, where they camped with Luz's family, rising again before dawn in order to arrive in Chalma before noon. There the priest offered them a room apart from the crowd. They stayed until January 8, observing the dance dramas of the pilgrims and participating in their activities—ritual bathing in the river and the High Mass—before pushing on to Tenango, where they could board a train and make their way back to Mexico City. Commenting on a drawing of the dancers, Charlot wrote, "This was a memory of the pilgrimage to Chalma, which I mentioned. I went with the family of Luz. It is a very long trek—three days more or less, from Milpa Alta, with two nights on the way. There were all kinds of pilgrims. Some had horses; some had burros; others just went on foot. We had a horse and a donkey, but there were many of us." [36]

Within the year Frances Toor had founded a journal called *Mexican Folkways* illustrated by the artists and carrying advertisements for Edward Weston's and Tina Modotti's photography studio. As for Charlot, he was deeply impressed by the visit to Chalma and made many drawings and lithographs based on themes from the pilgrims' dances.

Fernando Leal, who shared a studio with Charlot at the Coyoacan open-air art school, had already painted a mural of the Chalma dancers. He had begun painting with the theme all worked out in 1922. About his first wall painting, he wrote, "To document myself on the costumes and steps, I made friends with a leader of dancers who let me witness the rehearsals of the brotherhood. Also Luciana, an Indian girl who had posed for many of my pictures, took me to her village to gather further data." [37] In the fresco he painted Luz in the right foreground, young and beautiful.

For Luz herself Chalma is a recurring theme. In the folktales she dictated to Horcasitas there are stories of the strange fates that befell pilgims, and a chapter of her autobiography is devoted to Chalma stories and her family's annual pilgrimage to give thanks for her mother's recovery from illness.

In December of 1925 Weston wrote in his diary, "*December 25. Christmas day. . . . La Buena Noche was spent with the Salas, Carleton and friends. Gayety forced with habanero and vino rioja, an immense guajalote*—turkey, dancing and games until 4:00. Up at 9:00 to keep a date with Anita. Luziana cooked a tasty meal—real Mexican. ¡Qué bravo la chile! I sweat while eating. Conchita in her inevitable pink bonnet was the important guest. She was handed in turn to each, down the table's length, always bright and cooing. Charlot swears she said '¡Ay Mama!' at two months."[38]

Charlot spoke from a position of special privilege; although young, unmarried, and barely scraping out a living for himself, he had become Concha's godfather. In Mexico, especially in Indian communities, the responsibilities of godparents are serious and enduring. Entering into the relationship of *compadrazgo* 'coparenthood' with a child's parents, the godparent promises to support the child in case the parents cannot. In return, the parents of the child promise the godparent a lifetime of unstinting courtesy, correctness, and gratitude. Becoming the *compadre* of an unmarried mother inevitably drains one's own resources, and neighbors and relatives may try to avoid such a commitment. Luz could hardly look to Milpa Alta for godparents for her baby, and instead Charlot and Anita Brenner accepted the burden, providing cash and employment to Luz, to Concha, and ultimately to Concha's children for decades.

Concha had appeared as though by immaculate conception. Horcasitas, writing the preface to Luz's autobiography, assumed that as a young woman, she had married. In "Luz: Her Legend," an unsigned memorial column that appeared in *Mexico This Month,* the writer—probably Anita Brenner—wrote that Luz had "met a man of her kind and conceived a daughter. She refused to marry him. The days of being locked in and ordered about were over, she said."[39]

Charlot, having observed Luz's attachment to Fernando Leal, speculated that he might have been Concha's father,[40] but Leal, an urbanite born in Mexico City, was scarcely one of Luz's "kind" in any obvious sense. Charlot and Leal had shared studio space when Luz was modeling for Leal, not only for his fresco commission but also for a large painting of "Zapatistas at Rest" that Leal claimed caused quite a scandal and got him the commission in the first place.[41] It was at this time that Charlot, too, had begun employing Luz, his earliest dated drawings of her being from 1922. Within the year, however, an angry rift—not to be healed for several decades—had occurred between Charlot and Leal, and by the time Concha was born, Charlot could only surmise the nature of Leal's relationship with Luz. From her letters to Charlot at the time of Concha's wedding, it is clear that Luz maintained some minimal contact with Concha's father, and that her cool attitude toward him contrasted with her warm feelings for Leal, whom she also referred to as a compadre—like Charlot, a godfather to her daughter.[42]

At least publicly, Luz's affection for Leal seems to have been unreciprocated. Writing in 1946, he mentions "Luciana" somewhat offhandedly as "an Indian girl" who modeled for him those many years ago. Yet in 1964, Luz wrote to Charlot of the shock she felt when she was told of Leal's death,[43] and according to Concha, upon his passing the light went out of her mother's life. From that day on to her own death the following year, she said, Luz went through the motions of daily life, but her heart was no longer in it.[44]

Whoever was the father of her baby, Luz did not marry him or anyone else, and she never bore another child.

How had Luz gotten from the walled cemetery of Xochimilco to the artists' studios? Although it was a stupendous cultural leap, it was a short trip through space. The National School of Fine Arts, founded in 1785 as the Royal Academy of Fine Arts of San Carlos, had by the end of the Porfirian regime become so stultifying that to many young artists it seemed more to crush than nurture their talent. In the first heady days of the Revolution, the students began to demand improvement and soon found themselves locked out of their school's studios. In response, they took their notebooks to the city parks and began drawing what they saw around them outdoors on the streets. A couple of years later, in 1913, a new director of San Carlos made open-air drawing a part of the curriculum and established the first of several open-air art schools in Santa Anita, a town south of the city among the canals and *chinampas* (Mexico's renowned "floating gardens") where produce was raised for the city market. There the director provided the students with live Indian models, posed in natural outdoor light. Leal began his art studies in this new milieu and later wrote, "My models had always been Indians."[45]

Santa Anita was the site of a flower festival, celebrated, as Charlot described it, "by the weaving and wearing of crowns of poppies."[46] The writer of Luz's memorial column describes the coming of Luz to Santa Anita in the following terms: "The spring festivities that brought gondolas and dugout canoes loaded with lilies and red carnations, radishes and corn and squash blossoms down the ancient network of canals to the old produce market of Santa Anita, also brought many pretty girls who competed for costume, produce, gondola and other prizes. Luz won first prize as 'the loveliest flower of the field' and, in that spring when the artists of Mexico were rediscovering their heritage, she was persuaded to go and sit for the art classes at the National Academy."[47]

It was at such a spring festival soon after, continues the columnist, that Luz met the father of her child. In fact several years had passed, many drawings and paintings were finished, and numbers of field trips made between the time Rivera, Leal, and Charlot began portraying Luz in their work and the 1925 Christmas dinner when baby Concha was handed around to be admired. By his own account Leal had already drawn and painted her many times when he received his fresco commission in 1922, and Edward Weston writes that Charlot offered him a choice from among thirty or so drawings of her in 1922. Luz must have begun working as a model by 1920 or 1921, staying behind in the Xochimilco/Santa Anita area when the Milpa Alta refugees began going back home.

As they had left their town in 1916, Luz said, the refugees "had but one thought—that of keeping their children and parents alive without starving for need of money."[48] In her autobiography Luz does not specifically say how she and her mother survived from 1916 to 1920; she only speaks in generalities about how some refugees made tortillas, atole, and tamales to sell in the Xochimilco market and that some girls took jobs as servants in very exploitive situations. In one of her letters to Charlot, however, she is more explicit, writing that in some households young women were "dishonored" as a matter of course, as had happened to one of her own sisters.[49] Some people had simply become beggars on the streets, and for everyone without a home, life was terribly hard.

Anyone as intelligent as Luz would capitalize on whatever assets she had to avoid the poverty and exploitation she saw on every side. Porfirio Díaz and Justo Sierra had imagined that progress for the Indians of Mexico was tied to their becoming as un-Indian as possible. But her school drawing lessons were not of much use, and reliance on her ability to do sewing-machine embroidery and to bake wheat bread would have guaranteed Luz a lifetime of ill-paid drudgery. Contrary to the expectations of Díaz and Sierra, her best hope lay in maintenance of her Indianness. As the embodiment of all that non-Indians perceived as eternal, primordial, ancient, and mysterious, she had a chance to earn a living by simply *being*. People at the art schools paid her by the hour just to look at her, and later linguists and anthropologists would pay her by the hour to listen to her. According to the account in *Mexico This Month,* she got their attention to begin with by winning yet another prize.

Her earlier prizes had been for schoolwork well done, neatness, attendance, and decorum. To earn the prize that brought her employment, she decorated herself and maybe one of the chinampa canoes and won by virtue of her own "earthly-unearthly beauty."[50] Perhaps Luz, who in her autobiography never refers to herself by any other name than "Luz," created "Luciana" for the competition. And "Luciana" she remained for the artists and their friends. She also had to create herself as an "Indian," for while the painters and folklorists and anthropologists had an idea of "Indians," the people they thought of as Indians did not.

In the Nahuatl text of her autobiography, Luz never uses any word that corresponds to "Indian." The people of Milpa Alta were just people. As for how they spoke, she does not say that her parents (and Emiliano Zapata and his men) spoke "Nahuatl"; she says they spoke *macehualcopa* 'in the manner of ordinary folk'. In Nahuatl *macehualli* means someone who gets on by the sweat of his or her brow, someone without leisure or resources or power. Such were her parents. In the beginning her parents could manage on the proceeds from her father's pulque business, but as the family grew to eight people, he had to become an agricultural day laborer. They were so poor that Luz was a recipient of free clothes and shoes for the 1910 Centennial celebrations at her school.

Something Luz does not mention directly in her autobiography is that there were two kinds of people in Milpa Alta. There were hard-working subsistence farmers like her own family. And there were wealthy land-owning families, also Nahuatl-speaking, who had their children educated in Mexico City. Writing in 1913, Isabel Ramírez Castañeda, a teacher and native of the town, described Milpa Alta's population as divided into two classes. The children of the wealthy upper class, a group that considered themselves to be direct descendants of Aztec nobility, received their education outside and thereafter devoted themselves to managing their family property. These people had little in common with the parents of the children in the Milpa Alta schools. It is remarkable that Doña Luz doesn't so much as acknowledge their existence. Yet a Dutch anthropologist who went to Milpa Alta in the 1950s to do fieldwork described a similar situation still enduring there, having survived the Mexican Revolution. Remarking on the Mexico City education and conservatism of the local upper class, he asserted that although they continued to speak Nahuatl, their speech was so different from that of working-class Nahuatl speakers that the two groups had difficulty understanding one another.[51]

When one looks through Luz's autobiography seeking this other class of people, they emerge. There was, for example, the physician Basurto, who resented competition from the priest Father Polo and, it was ru-mored, betrayed the priest to the Carrancistas. There was the rich man Luis Sevilla, whose house and stored grain and domestic animals were all put to the torch by the Zapatistas. There were Malintzin and Mauro Melo, who kept a private school before the public school was opened in Milpa Alta. And there were the busy cobblers of the *barrio* neighborhood of San Mateo whose fine products included high-button shoes and laced boots.

In day-to-day life within Milpa Alta before the Revolution, the dis-tinction was not between Spaniard and Indian. It was between the people with resources and those without. When people who spoke Otomí and

Zapotec arrived with the Zapatistas, Luz remarked upon the unintelligibility of their languages and their sharp mercantile skills, not on their Indianness.

In Mexico City things were quite otherwise. There the distinction among Nahua, Otomí, and Zapotec was hazy. City people had an idea of "Indian," and among the intellectuals of the 1920s, struggling to define a new postrevolutionary national identity, it was an idea that Luz could capitalize on.

Posing for the painters and photographers, Luz allowed herself to be a screen on which the painters projected their own concepts of the Indian woman. Leal painted her sitting down to a picnic with Zapatistas, an unlikely scene, far from her personal experience of the revolutionaries. In the lower right corner of Diego Rivera's mural "The Liberation of the Peasant" in the building of the Secretariat of Public Education, a woman, "The Rural School Teacher," perhaps modeled by Luz, sits outdoors with a circle of students around her, teaching them from a book. Such a scene was closer to Luz's dream, if not her real experience. But just beyond the circle of rapt students is the ubiquitous revolutionary wearing cartridge belts. The irony of it all is that those among the painters who had seen military action had served under Carranza. Rivera himself had passed the revolutionary years in Europe, only returning when the shooting was over. Yet in no time he was dressing up in cartridge belts and pistols and implying that he had ridden with Zapata.[52]

Charlot depicted Luz pregnant, nude, in the pinafore of a servant, bent over grinding corn on a stone with her baby tied on her back. She disrobed for Weston's camera. Rivera used her for the allegorial figure of "Comedy." A sculptor had her model for a statue "To Motherhood." They portrayed her as huge, maternal. They drew her vacant-eyed and gaping-mouthed. They had her down on her knees at the sort of labor she wanted to avoid at all costs. Looking at her, they portrayed not Luz but "Indian womanhood." As Leal wrote about his Indian models, Luz included, "I aimed at giving their racial types a monumentality undiluted by occidental standards."[53] One of the most human representations of this period is Tina Modotti's direct, unwavering photograph of Luz and baby Concha gazing straight into the camera. And among the many stylized, abstracted studies by Charlot, there is one drawing of his—used to illustrate the memorial column in *Mexico This Month*—that is a stunning likeness of the same woman and child of Modotti's portrait.

Luz had modeled for Rivera as he produced his first mural in the auditorium of the National Preparatory School. Then he used her as he covered the walls of the Secretariat of Public Education. In 1929 she was the model for some of the Indian women in his murals in the National Palace. Where her presence is most felt is in the Tlatelolco market scene, surely drawn from Rivera's personal observation of the Santa Anita produce market from whence Luz had come into the company of the painters. From left to right at several levels are women in indigenous dress and jewelry, with their hair bound into the distinctive little horns that women wore when Europeans first came to Central Mexico. Some of the women are young, some older, and one has deep wrinkles, but all have something of Luz about them. "There I am," she said, "all over the walls of the National Palace."

By 1929, the great communal fever for mural painting was past. Rivera had edged the other painters out to become the official Mexican muralist, and the winds of politics had changed. Leal assumed the directorship of the Coyoacan open-air art school. Chalot moved to New York, where he immersed himself in making lithographs of pictures of Luz. One version of her, wrapped in a shawl, carries the caption, "Wisdom. Her feet busy not to move, her hands not to do and her eyes not to see." For Charlot she was still the woman of deep, compelling mystery.

The apolitical Weston had long since returned to California. After his departure, Tina Modotti acted on her own convictions, and in 1930, after arrests and a trial and more arrests, she was expelled from Mexico, having been present at a murder and being suspected (probably baselessly) of involvement in an attempted presidential assassination.

Frances Toor remained, eking out funds issue by issue for *Mexican Folkways*, and Anita Brenner, having just published her book *Idols Behind Altars* (a theme for which Leal claimed credit), continued to live and work in a Mexico that had turned in a new direction.

No one had given Luz paintings or drawings, which would have become a valuable legacy for her family. Her daughter excuses the artists, explaining that their paintings were not theirs to give but belonged to the art schools or to whoever commissioned them. Yet Charlot had felt free to offer Weston his choice from a sheaf of drawings of Luz, and surely they all had preliminary studies for which she had modeled. Perhaps Luz herself colluded in what appears to be an act of ungenerosity. The columnist in *Mexico This Month* wrote on the occasion of her death: "None of the great art that Doña Luz inspired is owned by her family. Queried once why she had not asked Rivera, Charlot, any of the painters, for at least a water-color or line drawing, she replied as if explaining smilingly to a child, '. . . if I want to look at what they made of me, why there I am. . . . Why should I need to own a picture of me?' "[54]

Perhaps this was not simplicity. Perhaps she did not wish to live with what they had made of her. What was important was the salary they had paid her. Since they had paid her, they could look at her, but what they had made of her was theirs, not hers.

Now Luz was a single mother in her mid-thirties and always in need of work. Anita Brenner recommended her to the American linguist Benjamin Lee Whorf, who went to study Nahuatl in Milpa Alta in 1930. So began a second career as Luciana became Doña Luz, native informant.

Modern anthropology had just been getting underway in Mexico when the storm of revolution broke upon the country. The International School of American Archaeology and Ethnology had been founded in Mexico City in 1910, a cooperative venture of the Mexican and German governments, the Hispanic Society of America, and several universities, including Columbia. A Columbia University–trained Mexican protégé of the anthropological superstar Franz Boas served on the board of directors. Another Mexican, Pablo González Casanova, German-trained in philology, had come home for a brief visit, intending to return to Europe right away. But World War I and the Mexican Revolution intervened, and he stayed to carry out fieldwork on Nahuatl as it survived in the villages surrounding the pyramids of Teotihuacan and in the Tepoztlan / Milpa Alta area.

Boas himself arrived at the beginning of 1912. He spent January and February traveling in rural Mexico, and he also acquired some Milpa Alta texts, which he published years later. The first group of Boas's Milpa Alta texts appeared in 1920 with no indication of who had been the informant or how Boas had gotten them, but the introduction to the second group of Milpa Alta stories states that two natives of Milpa Alta, a teacher named Isabel Ramírez Castañeda and a young man identified only as "Lucio," had written the texts for Boas in Mexico City in the winter of 1912. Following the Boas texts in the 1926 issue of *The Journal of American Folk-Lore* is another Milpa Alta text, transcribed at some unspecified time by González Casanova from an otherwise unidentified "individual of Milpa Alta."[55]

By the time these publications appeared, the International School of American Archaeology and Ethnology was no more. Unable to function in the chaos of revolution, it had closed in 1920, just as the artists and political philosophers were beginning to try to draw on Indian sources to define a new national identity.

But while Luz was still a schoolgirl, the long fingers of anthropology had already reached out and touched Milpa Alta. Isabel Ramírez Castañeda had beaten Boas to publication. She had presented her own paper on Milpa Alta folklore at the Eighteenth International Congress of Americanists, which met in London in 1912, and it appeared in the proceedings the following year.

And what of Boas's other informant, Lucio? A free federal primary

school had opened in Milpa Alta in 1905. When Luz entered the Concepción Arenal School in 1908, the principal was Lucio Tapia. He lived
upstairs over his classrooms and worked with the local prefect to get all
the children of Milpa Alta into school. Together they used coercion and
punishment, promises and reason. He insisted that parents get up at dawn
to fetch water from a distance to bathe their children before sending them
to classes and reminded them that they had already enjoyed a century of
freedom from the Spaniards who had once branded their ancestors with
red-hot irons. Luz puts the following speech in his mouth in Nahuatl:

> I beg you to listen to what I am telling you. We are going to turn out
> children who will become teachers or priests or lawyers. Others may
> have to find work far away from the village. When they grow to be
> young people, the girls who have gone to school will not have to become
> servants—grinding corn, kneading dough for tortillas, slaves of the
> washboard.
>
> Are you not ashamed at the way in which you are spending your
> lives? Are you not sorry for yourselves? If you knew how to read and
> write, you would have a much better position in life. I insist that you
> look out for your children. You will grow old, and your children will
> turn their backs on you because you did not give them an education.
>
> . . . They will learn other useful things [in school] as the years go
> by. Then they will remember everything they have learned, and if their
> parents die tomorrow or the day after, the children will know how to
> make a living. I beg you to follow my advice.[56]

This progressive voice was not the one folklorists were seeking.
Although they were literate people, what Isabel Ramírez Castañeda and
Lucio provided to Boas were charming *zazanilli* 'folktales'.

It is not known whether Lucio was, in fact, Lucio Tapia or whether
Maestra Isabel knew and influenced young Luz. But back when Luz and
her classmates were in school practicing to celebrate the Centennial, this
woman older than she, a native of Milpa Alta—a woman who spoke both
Nahuatl and Spanish—was already a schoolteacher. And Maestra Isabel
came to know Franz Boas and to write out Nahuatl texts for him. If they
were acquainted, how Luz would have longed to emulate her!

Maestra Isabel and Lucio were among the first contributors to the
Nahuatl folktale market, and later Doña Luz would bring many zazanilli
to that market as well, artifacts of the time and culture from which Lucio
Tapia had tried to lead the children of Milpa Alta away.

Benjamin Lee Whorf came to Mexico with a research grant in 1930.
Perhaps he was attracted to Milpa Alta because of the Nahuatl texts
already published. Or perhaps he went there because Luz, by taking the

artists to visit, had made it a well-known and convenient place to go. In an article published after his death, he wrote that his principal informant in Milpa Alta had been a man named Milesio Gonsales, but he also acknowledged contributions from Luz and praised all his informants as excellent.[57]

What Whorf was after was not folklore. He was a linguist listening for fine details of pronunciation and the way Nahuatl uses its myriad prefixes and suffixes. He asked for stories in order to hear the language itself. He valued a description of what his informant had seen while out on a long walk as much as he valued a folktale. In fact, he undoubtedly preferred the naturalness of such a narrative, because, unlike a folktale, it was constructed for the first time as it was being told. It is this sort of text that he included as a sample of Milpa Alta Nahuatl in his report on his 1930 fieldwork.

Working with Whorf, Luz would have learned a new kind of patience. Instead of holding a pose while artists worked to capture their vision on paper, on canvas, or in clay, she now dictated while her speech was written down. Speaker and transcriber had to work together in rhythm, proceeding phrase-by-phrase, each of a length Whorf could hold in mind long enough to get it down in phonetic symbols. It was necessary for fieldworker and informant to sit close together communicating with nods and gestures so as not to interrupt the flow of speech. They had to work at understanding each other. Being a linguistic informant is at least as intimate and exhausting as modeling, and Luz's experience with the artists would have helped prepare her for this new line of work.

After Whorf moved on, Lázaro Cárdenas was elected president of Mexico in 1934, and the following year a disaster befell the villages around Milpa Alta. At the beginning of June, as pilgrims from Tlaxcala passed through on their pilgrimage to Chalma, they were caught in a flash flood in the villages of San Pedro Atocpan and San Gregorio. People from Milpa Alta and Tepoztlan died with them. Whole families died together. Red Cross ambulances came from Mexico City, but there were few survivors. The following day President Cárdenas himself came to San Pedro to oversee the relief effort. All of this Luz observed and stored away in memory along with the sights and sounds of the revolution twenty-five years before.

Nineteen-forty initiated a decade in which Luz entered a new circle of acquaintances as activist as the 1920s artists had been. In August an extraordinary event took place in Milpa Alta; the town hosted the "First Aztec Congress." The linguistic section of the congress made a policy decision on how Nahuatl should be written, rejecting the traditional

Spanish-based orthography in favor of one that used k's and w's, giving the written language a more un-Spanish appearance. They also issued a statement encouraging the writing of poems, folklore, and literature in Nahuatl. Other sections called for the use of Nahuatl in official Mexican publications; better mail service, better roads, and street lighting for Indian towns; encouragement of authentic handicrafts; and other such improvements. Strong concern was expressed about indigenous women being taken into the city to work as domestic servants and being forced into hard manual labor. Recognizing Mexico as one nation containing many peoples with their own languages and cultures, the congress issued a statement against assimilation and called for recognition of Mexico's many different Indian groups. Finally, the delegates called for an international congress to which not only Mexico's Nahuatl speakers but those from Central American countries would be invited.[58] (This spirit of pan-Indianism reached new heights at the Oaxaca Indian State Fair in December 1941, with delegates from many ethnic and language groups demonstrating their communities' indigenous dress, crafts, and dances.)

That summer a young American arrived in Mexico to study Nahuatl. Robert Barlow was twenty-two years old, about the age a beginning graduate student might be, but he had not yet been to college. As a precocious, somewhat rootless army brat, he had begun a correspondence with the author H. P. Lovecraft. Before Lovecraft died six years later, he appointed the nineteen-year-old boy his literary executor. Instead of pursuing an education Barlow had spent those six years corresponding with Lovecraft enthusiasts and writing his own fantasy fiction purportedly found in ancient books written in an archaic language. The year after Lovecraft's death, as he cast about for a way to make a living, Barlow made his first trip to Mexico. Back in California, he was encouraged to take courses toward a degree in anthropology, and so it was that he returned to Mexico two years later to take the Nahuatl course offered at the National University Summer School.

Pre-Columbian civilizations and their languages replaced fantasy worlds and made-up languages in Barlow's imagination, and he threw himself into learning about them. Nahuatl as it was taught at the National University was a book-language, rather like Classical Latin. In fact, it was and still is referred to as Classical Nahuatl. It was taught according to sixteenth- and seventeenth-century grammar books and later exegeses of these grammars by scholars who did not always fully understand them. It is clear from some of the writings of nineteenth- and early twentieth-century Nahuatl academic authorities that they had never consulted a living speaker of the language. Even teachers who did come from a

Nahuatl-speaking background distinguished between Classical Nahuatl and the language spoken in the twentieth century, feeling that the modern language was a ruined version of the language of the Aztecs, an attitude prevalent among Nahuatl-speakers to this day.

But there were people who sought to learn Nahuatl from Indians rather than from books. The members of a Mexico City hiking club had decided in 1926 to start taking private Nahuatl lessons. For most, enthusiasm quickly waned, leaving a core group including Byron McAfee, who continued taking lessons with a native of Tepoztlan twice each week for ten years. They typed up each lesson, over six hundred of them by the spring of 1936. Barlow fell in with McAfee's little group and brought along a friend from his university Nahuatl class. They all worked together throughout the 1940s, writing articles about hieroglyphs, codices, mythology, and the like. All were associated at one time or another with the Benjamin Franklin Library in Mexico City, and they shared an interest in the physical side of bookmaking—printing and bookbinding—as well as scholarship and writing. With their own limited funds and using their own production skills, they founded *Tlalocan: A Journal of Source Materials on the Native Cultures of Mexico.*

They also set out to serve Nahuatl-speaking readers, providing a venue for the literary efforts called for by the Aztec Congress. In 1943 the first issue of *Mexihcayotl: Lo Mexicano,* a Nahuatl-language newspaper, appeared with McAfee as an editor. It continued for several years and then was succeeded in 1950 by *Mexihcatl Itonalama,* edited by Barlow, among others. Nahuatl speakers from many towns sent in poetry, the lyrics for songs, and brief essays. A few native speakers of Nahuatl began to write prolifically, and the name of one of them topped *Mexihcatl Itonalama*'s masthead.

Barlow had moved permanently to Mexico and along with all his writing and editing work also learned to speak Nahuatl so fluently that the Mexican government appointed him in 1945 as director of a Nahuatl literacy project in the state of Morelos. Throughout the 1940s he held grants from universities and foundations to support his work. Toward the end of the 1940s, with only a bachelor's degree, he became chairman of the anthropology department at Mexico City College.

During the 1940s Luz began working for Barlow. In a folder of Barlow's unpublished papers there are a dozen texts identified with her name, including a song about the Aztec god Huitzilopochtli that Luz claimed her mother always sang while sweeping the house. (Barlow was skeptical about this.) Another text, a ghost story, that Luz and Barlow worked together on in 1949 was eventually published eleven years later. A new element had been introduced since Luz's time with Whorf. As she mentions in a letter to Charlot, Barlow and his associates were recording their work sessions.[59]

Transcribing her speech, they used the spelling approved by the Aztec Congress, and Barlow wrote down more detail about her pronunciation than the older orthography would have shown, although less than what is to be found in Whorf's detailed phonetic transcription. When *Mexihcatl Itonalama* came into being, Luz contributed essays written with the same Aztec Congress–style spelling.

Around 1948 or 1949 Fernando Horcasitas met Luz at Barlow's house. Horcasitas, Los Angeles–born of Mexican parents, had returned to Mexico in the mid-1940s and was just beginning studies at the National School of Anthropology. About the same age as Barlow had been when he began to study Nahuatl in 1940, he also had the same teacher, and despite his youth, he soon found himself not only a member of Barlow's group but on the editorial board of *Tlalocan*. Barlow had Horcasitas join in the sessions with Luz (always respectfully referred to by Horcasitas and his associates as "Doña Luz"), including their work on the ghost story.

In Barlow's house was recreated something like the intellectual ferment Luz had known among the artists in the 1920s. Money was always short, but enthusiasm ran high. People came and went and met and typed copy for the newspaper. Charlot returned to Mexico on a Guggenheim Fellowship and wrote a puppet play about Chalma for Barlow's Nahuatl class. They gave it a performance in May 1946 in San Pedro Atocpan, the village Luz had witnessed devasted by the 1935 flood.

Barlow worked with manic energy and swept everyone else along with him, even the slow and deliberate McAfee. During the decade he wrote a book and about a hundred and fifty articles about Mexican history, its antiquities and Indian languages. Having acquired a firm grasp of Nahuatl, he was teaching himself Yucatec Maya and studying Maya hieroglyphic writing. Amidst all this, the people at his house managed to bring the newspaper out weekly from May through the end of 1950. The December 8 issue included an essay by a contributor relating a dark dream about Barlow, a fatal woman, bones, and death.

After the guests left his New Year's party ushering in 1951, Barlow hung a do-not-disturb message in glyphs on the door of his room, shut himself inside, and swallowed a lethal dose of sleeping pills.

Barlow's suicide staggered his associates. Luz had recently gone to Milpa Alta to look after her ailing mother and only learned upon her return to the capital that she had lost an employer and colleague. The newspaper died on the spot; the December 29, 1950, issue was its last. Barlow had left a letter directing that Horcasitas and a colleague should continue editing *Tlalocan*, which they managed to do despite daunting funding problems. Things came back together slowly. Horcasitas earned a master's degree, and in 1957 he and Doña Luz began teaching Nahuatl together to students at Mexico City College.

In the meantime, two more anthropologists had gone to do fieldwork in Milpa Alta. William Madsen was directed there by Barlow's and Horcasitas's Nahuatl teacher. Madsen, supported by a research grant, spent 1952–53 in the outlying village of Tecospa, where the mayor assured him that he wanted the Tecospa children to become literate in Nahuatl as well as Spanish. The ideal of universal literacy instigated by Lucio Tapia, yoked by the Aztec Congress to retention of Nahuatl, and helped along by McAfee's and Barlow's support of Nahuatl-language newspapers, was still on the minds of some of Milpa Alta's residents.

Rudolf van Zantwijk, a Dutch anthropologist, spent the spring and summer of 1957 living in Milpa Alta's barrio of La Concepción Xaxahuenco. At the time he went there, van Zantwijk spoke Nahuatl with a very classical flavor, and he fell in with a group of local people who styled themselves the "Teomexica" (which might be translated as the 'super Aztecs'). These residents of Milpa Alta strove to free their speech from Spanish influence, to speak as they imagined the nobility of Montezuma's court once had, and they did not think well of the everyday Nahuatl of people like Doña Luz. They dictated to van Zantwijk lists of invented Nahuatl words for things that had not existed in the time of the Aztecs, such as buses, trains, telephones, and television, and took pains to demonstrate to him refinements of language and culture. According to van Zantwijk, he interviewed 130 people, among them poets and writers, and after he left he exchanged letters in Nahuatl with several people he had come to know during his fieldwork.

Van Zantwijk's observations of the social structure of Milpa Alta in the 1950s illuminates the incompleteness of the Mexican Revolution. As in Isabel Ramírez Castañeda's time, there was still a conservative Nahuatl-speaking upper class, and there was still the day-laboring macehualli class Doña Luz had been born into. The classes were still separated by resources, values, and ways of speaking. But there was now more potential for social mobility. Children educated in Milpa Alta were finally growing up to enter professions, as Lucio Tapia had predicted back in 1908. And after suffering poverty they would never forget, Doña Luz and Concha were enjoying the satisfaction of seeing Concha's children off to a good start too. Later it was recalled, "She laughed at her eldest grandson who was treasuring only English and French, but helped him buy the books and records he wanted in those languages."[60]

Madsen's and van Zantwijk's Milpa Alta books were both published in 1960, and so was the ghost story Doña Luz had done with Barlow. It was during a period of transition for the family as Doña Luz aged and her grandchildren grew up. In 1958 she notified Charlot of her mother's death at 102. Nearly thirty years before Charlot had described her mother as around ninety.[61] Charlot had been mistaken, but friends of the family were given to misjudging ages. In the introduction to the ghost story recorded and transcribed by Barlow in 1949, Doña Luz herself is described as seventy years of age. She was in fact in her mid-fifties when Barlow recorded her and was still well short of seventy when the article was published. These misperceptions seem to have to do with non-Indians' stake in seeing Indians as part and parcel of the past, survivors from a remote time.

Around the time of her mother's death, Doña Luz—in addition to her joint teaching duties with Horcasitas—began working with him and two graduates of Mexico City College, dictating folktales and other texts for them to transcribe. They wrote the texts down in phonetic transcription, forty or more of them in the course of a year, paying Doña Luz thirty pesos per session.[62] In 1963 Horcasitas moved to the National University's Institute of Historical Research. Once more he asked Doña Luz to provide him with texts, this time the story of her own life. What she told him was the history of Milpa Alta from her earliest childhood memories of it until 1920.

Advancing age, exhaustion, and personal loss were wearing her out. While engaged in her informant work, she had gone on modeling for art classes in schools all around Mexico City while also living in with Concha's large family and helping with an endless round of family illnesses and accidents. In 1963 she wrote to Charlot that her vision was failing and that she had nearly been run down by a car she didn't see coming.[63] The next year she learned of Leal's death while at her sister's funeral. Grief piled on grief. Concha described her mother in these times as being as fragile as a soap bubble drifting in the wind.

On a January morning in 1965, she set out for yet another new job, and in the evening she failed to return home. Concha and her family waited, going out to the street corner to look for her and returning to the house in anxiety. In the morning they began telephoning people who might have seen her. They learned that when she had reported for work, to her disappointment she had been told to come back the next day. Then she had paid a visit at Anita Brenner's house, and no one had seen her since. Finally they located her in a hospital. A few blocks from Anita Brenner's, she had been struck by a car and gravely injured. The hospital staff let Concha see her mother long enough to identify her and then said her condition was too critical to permit visitors. Anita Brenner's daughter, however, managed to make her way to her bedside and was with her when she died.[64]

The family's old friends rallied to their support. It was probably Anita Brenner in her capacity as editor who wrote the unsigned memorial column that appeared in *Mexico This Month*. Jean Charlot contributed the drawing of Doña Luz as a madonna-like young mother with Concha on her lap to accompany the column. Flanking the column's other side, facing Charlot's drawing, was printed an excerpt from "The Broken Water Jug," by the Mexican poet Octavio Paz. The three elements—the drawing, the intimate portrayal of her life, and the poem—constituted a touching, sentimental farewell.

Horcasitas took time to create another sort of memorial. From the texts Doña Luz had dictated in Nahuatl and in Spanish versions, he put together her story, the history of Milpa Alta in the first twenty years of the twentieth century. Turning aside from the guidelines of the Aztec Congress, he rewrote the transcription of her Nahuatl in the traditional spelling that scholars trained in Classical Nahuatl would read, and he provided an introduction and chapter headings. Alberto Beltrán, a noted Mexican artist of about the same age as Concha, provided illustrations for Doña Luz's story of life in Milpa Alta. It was published in Nahuatl and Spanish in 1968 and in Nahuatl and English in 1972. The Nahuatl/Spanish version was so successful that a second edition was issued in 1974 and a third in 1989.

And still Horcasitas worked with Doña Luz's texts, now aware that cancer would soon claim his life. In 1979 a second volume was published, forty-four of her stories as she told them in Nahuatl and again in Spanish. Horcasitas died the following year.

In both *Life and Death in Milpa Alta* and in the *Cuentos* ('Stories') there are two kinds of narrative. One kind is the folktales that Indians were expected to know—animal stories and legends of the sort Boas and González Casanova collected from their informants. Doña Luz was able to retell these stories just about word-for-word whenever the occasion arose, whenever an anthropologist or folklorist wanted that sort of thing.

Her other kind of narrative is vivid eyewitness reporting. When she relates how the Zapatistas rode into town, she names the street they came down, and what they were shouting, and how she and other girls in the plaza took cover behind the columns of an arcade. As a witness to the 1935 flood, she describes the scene from a ridge above the stricken villages, telling how the floodwater glittered like shards of mirror in the sunshine that followed the deluge. She reports extensive speeches verbatim. In other words, she had the instincts of a fine journalist.

For anything like this sort of narrative in Nahuatl, one must go back to the Indian historians and annalists of the sixteenth to eighteenth centuries who wrote accounts of earthquakes and floods and eclipses, bread riots, English pirates, and many other catastrophes. These Nahuatl writers of the colonial period were known to some scholars at the National University, but their works had not been available for Doña Luz to model her craft on them.[65] And this sophisticated type of narrative was not what people who sought to get in touch with the pre-Columbian Aztec past were looking for. Perhaps, however, Doña Luz had been encouraged by Whorf, who had been only too happy in 1930 to write down from one of his informants all the sights observed and conversations shared during a long ramble through the villages around Milpa Alta. In these posthumous publications Doña Luz emerges as her own person, not the reflection of others' fantasies about her. She comes across as a woman with her "eyes wide open."[66]

Two circumstances stood like a wall shutting her out of postrevolutionary Milpa Alta. One was that she was a mother but not a wife. Without a husband she would have no support and no protection there, no means to meet her responsibilities to her aging mother and growing daughter. Here is what Madsen writes about an unwed mother and her child in one of Milpa Alta's villages:

> Tecospa has only one illegitimate baby. A young girl named Alicia had a baby by a boy who broke his promise to marry her. People feel sorry for her because she is completely disgraced. If her father and brother were alive they probably would force the boy to marry Alicia. Her baby girl is called "ixtacaconetl" (bastard).
>
> "The little girl will always be a bastard, even if Alicia marries another man," Doña Manuela said. "When she grows up and becomes engaged, people will say, '_____ is going to marry a bastard.' But someday the child will go to heaven, because this is not her fault. I think Alicia will get to heaven too, but the boy who deceived her will go to hell."[67]

Concha sometimes lived with her grandmother while her mother worked in Mexico City, and people probably did call her a bastard. Despite periods of residence in Milpa Alta, Concha resolutely did not learn to speak Nahuatl, perhaps to keep a defensive screen about herself. Whether people meant ill by it or not, *ichtacaconetl* was a hurtful word. One of Doña Luz's stories is about three mysterious strangers who offered to solve Milpa Alta's chronic water shortage but demanded in return the lives of four children, two boys and two girls. In the Nahuatl version Luz uses the word *ichtacaconetl,* but in her Spanish version, she delicately refers to the would-be victims not as "bastards" but as "orphans." Without father, brother, or husband to defend her, she herself stayed away from Milpa Alta and refused to live with the label "mother of the bastard."

The other obstacle to life in Milpa Alta was her commitment to modernism. The intellectual life of Milpa Alta was in the hands of the arch-conservative Teomexica. Even had they been open to a woman from the macehualli class, joining them would have meant dressing up in costume and playing at Old Aztec Days. In the time of Porfirio Díaz, Milpa Alta's traditional ways of dressing had been condemned as Indian and backward, and their folk beliefs as superstition. As the local elite sought to reclaim their Indian identity in the reconstituted Milpa Alta, they turned back not to the days of Luz's cherished childhood memories, but tried instead to reach back to a time untouched by European influence. For municipal celebrations in the 1950s men dressed in full pre-Columbian regalia: loincloths, diadems, feathered capes, gilded high-backed sandals, arm and neck ornaments.[68] Doña Luz had authentic roots in the nineteenth century, but hardly in the sixteenth, and her commitment was to the twentieth.

She had adopted the passionately expressed principles of the 1920s about equality of the sexes and the dignity of labor, and more than some of the artists and intellectuals, she lived by these principles. She apparently had two loves: One was Fernando Leal, who did not, in his essay on the work of the muralists in the early 1920s, return the compliment. According to her daughter, Doña Luz took his death very hard: "For her it was a terrible blow." Her other love was the life of the mind. When asked whether her mother seemed to prefer the company of the artists or the anthropologists/linguists, Concha replied that what she liked was being with people from whom she could learn, whether they were anthropologists, painters, sculptors—people of any sort who were in contact with modern civilization. That was the delight of her life.[69] This resonates with the memorial column in *Mexico This Month:* "She was discovering a fascinating heritage of her own: books, music, ideas, people, and the marvelous world of learning. . . . On the block and up and down the street, other families were pursuing the same objective; aware with deep respect, however, that Doña Luz was already at home in the world of the intellect and the arts."[70]

A cynic might protest that she uncritically bought into everything: the "proper life," Sierra's vision of assimilation via education, Zapata's revolutionary rhetoric, the radicals' ideas about labor and class and the didactic role of public art, the politics of Lázaro Cárdenas, Barlow's literacy campaign. Did she ever meet an idea she didn't like? Could she ever slake a thirst for like-minded people, an enchantment with ideas and plans and principles?

It must often have been a lonely life, yet she acknowledged little disappointment with people or circumstances. Her published autobiography shares none of the bitterness of Sarah Winnemucca's about promises made and broken. Apparently unscarred by the horrors she had witnessed, her capacity to see good on every side—from Díaz to Zapata—is striking. She does say that the people of Milpa Alta could never forgive Zapata for abandoning them to the Carrancistas, and she is direct about the wickedness of the Carrancistas. Yet in these accounts, she maintains a certain distance, rather like the professional detachment of a journalist.[71]

It is in the letters she wrote to Charlot, two decades' worth preserved among his papers at the University of Hawaii, that we see how hard life continued to be after her official autobiography concludes in the early 1920s. Being an artist's model and a native informant did not provide dependable income, nor did her high principles and love of grand ideas protect her from being robbed and cheated as defenseless poor people usually are. People disappointed her and insulted her and failed to pay her for her work, and poverty did not afford her the luxury of pride. Concha had married very young, and she and her husband had a larger family than they could support; thus far from being looked after in her last years, Doña Luz continued to work to help raise and educate her grandchildren. She had to ask Charlot for money time and again. He was her confidant, but both she and Concha at times feared that their endless neediness would wear out his patience.[72] But such was their loyalty to the bonds of compadrazgo that Doña Luz and Charlot never faltered in their social contract. He sent money, and she responded with all the formalities and elaborate expressions of respect that the relationship required. To the end of her life, she never addressed him by name or the informal Spanish pronoun *tu*.

It is sobering to reflect that Luz was the same age as Leal, Charlot, Brenner, Modotti, and most of their circle. Yet her compelling attraction for many twentieth-century intellectuals was as a means by which they could connect with the distant past. They did not seem to regard her as their peer. So anxious to use her as a direct line back to ancient times, they missed the obvious, that she was a startlingly modern woman. By intelligence and will, in the face of tremendous obstacles, she managed to live her entire adult life in daily contact with the intellectuals whose company she cherished.

MUSHROOM VISIONS, MUSHROOM VOICES:
María Sabina (ca. 1900–1985)

After having eaten the mushrooms, we felt dizzy, as if we were drunk,
and we began to cry; but this dizziness passed and then we became very
content. Later we felt good. It was like a new hope in our life.
          —A MEMORY FROM MARÍA SABINA'S CHILDHOOD[73]

About the time the men of Milpa Alta were rounded up, the soldiers of Carranza also came for María Sabina's young husband in the high mountains of Oaxaca. Serapio offered no resistance when they took him to the nearby town of Huautla de Jiménez and from there off to their campaigns. He played the bugle for them, and when they learned that he was brave and agile, they made a soldier of him. He sent money home for his wife and infant son when he could, and just as their little boy was beginning to walk, Serapio came home from the revolution.[74]

Unhappily for María Sabina, her man had changed. Following local custom, at age fourteen she had been sent by her family to live with a man she had not met.[75] There was no ceremony, only an agreement negotiated between her family and his. Yet she had learned to like and respect him because he did not drink much and worked hard at long-distance trading. Somehow in that place without schools Serapio had learned to read and write Spanish, and she was proud of that.

Before the soldiers took him away, he comforted her, and although she was illiterate and knew no Spanish, he once sent back a note to her from the field, assuring her that he was well. A neighbor told her what it said. But when he came home with his soldier's cap and rifle and cartridge belt, he was no longer the devoted husband; his army days had given him a taste for women. While his wife was pregnant, he brought other women to their house, and he went off to yet others on his trade route. In her autobiography María Sabina said he was away with one of these women when he died, and his pack animals and inventory never came back.[76] At twenty, she was a widow with three children and a mother to support.

It was hunger time again, something she knew all too well. Her mother, María Concepción, had also been widowed at twenty and left with two daughters, María Sabina and her sister María Ana. With no man to support the little family, María Concepción had taken her children home to her own mother, María Estefanía. (If there were six women in a family or even twelve, still they would all share the same first name. For generations the custom had been to baptize all baby girls María.)

María Sabina's grandparents, mother, and aunt lived together and got by raising silkworms and spinning and weaving. Like everyone else, they grew corn, squash, and beans and raised chickens and a goat or two. Bit by bit the little girls were drawn into the subsistence labor of the household. They cleaned silk, learned to garden, and were sent into the woods with the chickens to protect them from foxes and hawks.

In the woods grew handsome mushrooms, but they were not the sort to be taken home for dinner. They were mushrooms treated with elaborate respect by the Mazatecs, treated in fact as though they were people. They were so sensitive to contamination that people even avoided looking directly at them. The only time María Sabina had seen them picked was when her uncle had fallen ill and a "Wise One" had been called to cure him. The man brought some of the mushrooms with him, ate them in the course of his treatment of her sick uncle, and then sang curing songs.

Back in the woods with the chickens, suffering gnawing hunger, little María Sabina ate a raw mushroom and then another. She and María Ana ate them until they were dizzy and scared. But then the dizziness cleared, and they didn't feel hungry any more. Under their influence María Sabina had a comforting vision of her dead father. Having discovered that the mushrooms made their lives more endurable, the children ate them often, and so it was that one day the adults of the family found the girls in the woods dazed and disoriented. They carried them home, being gentle with them, as María Sabina explained, "because they knew that it isn't good to scold a person who has eaten the *little things* because it might cause contrary emotions and it's possible that one might feel one was going crazy."[77]

From the day María Concepción bundled up her daughter's clothes and told her that she was henceforth to live with a man and be a little woman to him, María Sabina gave up eating the forest mushrooms. The Mazatecs believed that if one did not abstain from sexual contact for four or five days before and after eating them, one would go insane or die, and she had no confidence that her husband would leave her alone so many days at a time. Nor did she resume eating them immediately after she was widowed. But when María Ana fell ill and no one else in the community could help her, María Sabina gathered a basketful. Six she gave to her sister, and the rest she ate herself. Her visions were immense. She heard herself singing as the Wise One who had cured her uncle had sung. She received an absolute sense of her own destiny as a Wise One who cured people through the mushrooms' authority. And María Ana recovered.

As news of María Ana's cure spread through the mountains around Huautla, people began to seek María Sabina's help. They came long distances and brought their sick. By local etiquette a Wise One could accept only small gifts, but her clients paid her for her services in ways that were a welcome supplement to the meager income she derived from picking coffee beans and digging ditches.

The forest mushrooms were *Psilocybe* mushrooms, hallucinogens that along with peyote, tobacco, and morning glory seeds have had a traditional part in the religious practices of Mexican Indians. People used these psychotropic agents, as well as fasting, sleep deprivation, and bloodletting, to get into otherworldly states of mind while searching for information hidden from ordinary people. After the conquest of Mexico, European evangelists sought to wipe out even the memory of Indian religious practices, but the consultation of fate through the mushrooms survived in some communities for centuries. During all that time it absorbed more and more outward trappings of Christianity, because the people who asked the mushrooms about the course and treatment of illness, the location of lost objects, and the fate of missing persons were also practicing Catholics.

Members of María Sabina's community had every reason to respect the mushrooms and to watch over people who had eaten them. The visions they inspired were often beautiful, but they could also be terrifying. To the Mazatecs their use was perilous. They believed that "if a man takes them and three or four days afterwards he uses a woman, his testicles will rot. If a woman does the same, she goes crazy." [78] Using the mushrooms was, they said in Spanish, *muy delicada* 'a very sensitive matter'.

When she had grown old and was urged to teach her ritual chants to members of the next generation of Mazatecs so that they would not be lost, María Sabina insisted that the mushroom ceremonies and the songs that poured forth during them were not something that could be taught or memorized. They came from the mushrooms themselves, just tumbling through her body on earth. Her chants were like the chants of other Wise Ones, as María Sabina took for granted, since it was always the same mushrooms speaking, now through one person, now through another. Yet they did not talk through just anyone who ate them, and on the other hand, they had talked through members of her own family for several generations.

The Mazatecs recognized three types of people who worked through supernatural channels. There were sorcerers who could turn themselves into animals at night and range far and wide. These people were inclined to mischief, and the Mazatecs were always worried about who among their neighbors and acquaintances might use such powers to bring them misfortune. Then there were curers (called in Spanish *curanderos* and *curanderas*) who aided the ill with massages and medicinal herbs. The curers also had the skill of drawing illness and misfortune into unbroken eggs to be carried away and buried. But most rigorous and most respected of all were the Wise Ones, the people who ate the mushrooms in order to discover the origins and nature of sickness and misfortune and to vanquish them if possible. These men and women took some of the suffering of the sick onto themselves, vomiting out the illness if a patient was too weak to do it. It took staying up all night with candles and incense and mushrooms, singing and clapping and whistling and dancing to effect a cure. It was hard work, and it was perceived as very pure and holy, as well as dangerous.

A dozen years after Serapio's death, María Sabina was again sought in marriage. She was doing well on her own, but her family was anxious to have a man join the household, and the suitor had some skill as a sorcerer. Acceding to her mother's wishes, she agreed to the marriage on condition that her second husband come to live with them. She was not willing to move in with him.

Unfortunately María Sabina's forebodings were realized. This new man, Marcial, was a drinker and a wife beater who was not even particularly good at farming. In thirteen years María Sabina bore six children by him, and four of them died at birth or soon after. She couldn't take the mushrooms to try to save them, because she could not keep her husband at bay for the eight to ten days of abstinence that had to surround the ritual. And alas, like her first husband, this one too was promiscuous. Finally Marcial was done in by an aggrieved husband.

Widowed again, María Sabina chose to follow her mother's own course and remove herself permanently from the marriage market. No one could fault her now that she was middle-aged, twice widowed, and mother of five surviving children. Throughout the years of her unhappy marriage she had been saving money, and now Catarino, her son by her first husband, was grown and contributing to the family income by working, like his father before him, as a traveling merchant. With accumulated capital María Sabina built a new house for the family and set up a small store there. Soon she was also serving meals, beer, and cane liquor at her house. And then she began to return to the mushroom rituals.

When María Sabina had eaten the mushrooms in order to save her sister, she had had a vision in which she was shown a great book and was called to read from it. She remembered carrying Serapio's note to the neighbor to read, ashamed of her own illiteracy. Now in her vision she was reading the holy book for herself, and when she had done so, all the wisdom of the book was hers. In later visions she would sometimes see the shining white book on its altarlike table and other times not, but it was of no consequence, since the wisdom of the book was now within her. As she put it, "I had attained perfection."[79]

When she was a child, the mushrooms had relieved María Sabina of the very concrete griefs of hunger and fatherlessness. As an adult she found a way through them to rise above more abstract hardships. In her visions she saw herself freed from the constraints of her world. Illiterate, she absorbed wisdom from books. Nearly monolingual in Mazatec, she completely transcended worldly Spanish and rose to proficiency in a divine language. A person who had done hard labor all her life, she acquired power not by physical or mental effort, but as a gift that came to her because she had been chosen. A woman in a society that was not supportive of women, she became a Wise One, far above all ordinary women and men. "In truth," she said, "I was born with my destiny."[80]

Assertions of such special status were not unfamiliar to the Mazatecs. In fact, it was common among Indians all over Mexico and Guatemala for individuals to claim to be conduits for messages from another, hidden world. That was how Doña Marina had been perceived by some, as a human mouthpiece for the mysterious "Malinche." It fit, too, with María Sabina's family history, so it was no surprise when she assumed for herself a place at the very top of the three-tiered company of sorcerers, curers, and Wise Ones. Some Mazatecs sought her out, compensated her for her services, rewarded her. Others were suspicious or envious, and in times to come that would bring her to grief.

She built up a practice treating sick children, people with toothaches, and people who were suffering from malicious sorcery. She also practiced midwifery, although she did not need the help of the mushrooms to deliver babies. There were other curers and Wise Ones in town, even in her own barrio, but she did not deign to consult with them, even for her own aches and pains. She looked out for her own well-being with the mushrooms, just as she did for other people's.

The first half of her life was behind her. It had been hard, but everything had worked out. She had her home, her family, and her profession. She had recently become a founding member and active participant in a lay Catholic service organization, and she was a respected senior member of her community. No one could have imagined what was to come.

In the 1950s, María Sabina was in friendly competition with a Mexican physician, Dr. Salvador Guerra, who was doing his rural medical service in Huautla. To his credit, he had learned how to greet his patients in Mazatec and to make small talk with them. Both knew they were sometimes treating the same patients.

Then circumstances brought them face to face. María Sabina's daughters had married and moved away, but Catarino still stayed at home with his mother when he was not on the road. He was home one day when a drunken man came around and provoked a fight. The drunk insisted that Catarino drink cane liquor with him, and Catarino wanted to drink beer. The drunk pulled a gun, María Sabina intervened, and he shot her three times. At his clinic in Huautla Dr. Guerra injected a local anesthetic and extracted the bullets. María Sabina's estimation of him soared. "Doctor," she told him, "you are as great as me."[81]

Two weeks later María Sabina, who had moved since childhood between the everyday world of the Mazatecs and the visionary world of the mushrooms, placed her foot on the slippery slope into yet another world, the world of blond people.

Twentieth-century Huautla was not so remote in the heart of its mountains that it was untouched by the outside world. The Carrancistas and Zapatistas had no trouble finding it during the revolution. The 1941 Oaxaca Indian State Fair had drawn people from the mountain villages down to the provincial capital, and they brought back a great deal of new information about each other and about the foreigners who had come to see them. In 1950, impatient for the road that would connect them to a main highway, the citizens of Huautla built an airstrip, and Mazatec men, women, and children had grown used to air travel before the road finally arrived.

The American collectors Donald and Dorothy Cordry had documented the men's and women's folk costumes of Huautla, and examples were on display at the museum in the state capital. In the Indian towns of Oaxaca women had always devoted a great deal of time to weaving and embroidery, although changes were underway. Once the road was open, the merchants of Huautla brought cloth from the city, and local women did less spinning and weaving. Yet an important part of the trading inventory of María Sabina's oldest son was still embroidery thread, just as it had been for his father. By the traditional embroidery pattern of her huipil blouse, it was easy for people in Oaxaca to tell what language an Indian woman spoke and what town she was from.

Before the turn of the century coffee cultivation had been successfully introduced, and after the Mexican Revolution Huautla acquired schools, a clinic, and electric lights. In anticipation of the arrival of the road, a local entrepreneur opened a hotel for travelers. Besides the courteous Dr. Guerra, the town also had a priest who tolerated the local folk Catholicism. Moreover, members of the Summer Institute of Linguistics, a Protestant organization dedicated to translating the Bible into all the languages of the world, had arrived in the mid-1930s to work on Mazatec. The priest, the physician, and the Protestant missionaries all knew about the Wise Ones and the mushrooms.

And so, in a limited way, did the world. Robert Weitlaner, an Austrian who had moved to Mexico, had acquired some mushrooms in Huautla in 1936 and sent them off to Harvard University. In spite of clear descriptions in colonial-period documents, controversy had arisen in the scholarly world about whether mushrooms had ever been used in Indian religious rites. Since it was hardly any secret in Huautla that mushrooms helped people see into the future and discover secrets, an analysis of some actual mushrooms seemed in order. In response to Weitlaner's shipment, Richard Schultes, a Harvard ethnobotanist, came to Huautla during the summer rainy season of 1938 to study them fresh in place and to identify them. From this field trip he soon published two articles, one in a journal with a large readership.

On a July night in 1938 four other non-Mazatecs—Weitlaner's daughter, her anthropologist husband, and two associates—attended a mushroom ceremony held especially for them. An article came of this experience too, published in Sweden in 1939. The mushrooms and the Mazatecs had made their international debut, but the world was preoccupied by war, and it was not until the beginning of the 1950s that a man obsessed by mushrooms came upon the Schultes paper, got in touch with Schultes and Weitlaner, and by the end of the decade had focused public attention on the slight figure of María Sabina, the Wise Woman of Huautla de Jiménez, Oaxaca.

R. Gordon Wasson was about the same age as María Sabina. Born in 1898 in Great Falls, Montana, he was the son of an Episcopalian minister and identified himself as culturally Anglo-Saxon to the bone. In 1920 he graduated from the Columbia School of Journalism and went off to London, where he met a young Russian emigré woman who was studying medicine and was to be one of the two great loves of his life. Theirs was a five-year courtship, during which she completed her medical training, and he worked his way up through a series of teaching, writing, and editing jobs in the United States. When they married in 1926, he was a financial reporter covering Wall Street.

Wasson took his bride on a honeymoon trip to the Catskills, and there she gave him the scare of his life. In a story that she told once in print and he told over and over in his publications, Wasson and Valentina Pavlovna were strolling arm in arm through the August woods when she saw something under the trees, left him, and went running. Following after, he found her kneeling, overcome with joy at seeing woodland mushrooms for the first time since the Russian Revolution had put an end to her childhood's happy country summers. They had quite a fuss, he insisting that they were dangerous and disgusting and that she would poison herself; she ignoring her husband, and eating them for dinner. According to them both, he was beside himself with apprehension. When she proved right and he mistaken, they were mesmerized by the cultural gulf that separated Anglo-Saxon Wasson from his Russian wife.[82]

The fascination occupied them for the rest of their lives. They generalized their personal cases of what they called "mycophilia" (a warm emotional attachment to wild mushrooms) and "mycophobia" (the suspicion that just about all mushrooms are deadly poisonous) to entire nations and ethnic groups. Just as surely as the people of sub-Saharan Africa have dark skin and Scandinavians are pale, so the Wassons saw Russians and Basques as mycophiliac, Anglo-Saxons and Germans as mycophobic. They were sure that the mycophobes needed to be rescued from their benighted state. Wasson already had been; when she abandoned him for the carpet of mushrooms in the Catskills, Valentina Pavlovna had introduced Wasson to the other great passion of his life.

At first they thought to write a book about Russian cuisine with its mushroom stuffings, mushroom sauces, and salted and pickled mushrooms. But one day when their son and daughter were nearly grown up, they looked at their twenty-five year collection of mushroom lore and decided to write a mighty book about the prehistory of European religion instead.

Soon after their marriage Wasson had moved from reporting about the banking world to earning his living there. He secured a position with J. P. Morgan and Co., eventually becoming a vice president in 1943. His promotion certainly could not have been hurt by the publication of his first book, *The Hall Carbine Affair,* in 1941. In it he took upon himself to debunk the belief that during the American Civil War J. P. Morgan had sold defective rifles to the government at premium prices, endangering Union soldiers while making a handsome profit. It was a tour de force of a banker defending the reputation of a banker, and all of Wasson's style of writing and argumentation are already to be seen in this book—his piling up of piece after piece of supporting evidence for his own position while bashing the people with whom he disagreed. Throughout his life Wasson was never a man with an open mind for alternatives. Nor, except for his obsessive recounting of that traumatic twenty-four hours in the Catskills, was he to admit in print to having been mistaken about much of anything in all his life.

Through the banking business and through Russian emigré connections, the Wassons cultivated a cosmopolitan circle of friends. One of them directed Wasson to Schultes, the Harvard ethnobotanist who had been to Huautla in the late 1930s. The immediate consequence of talking with Schultes was to divert the Wassons from ancient Europe and send them off to contemporary Mexico.

The idea that they were developing was that there had been an original Old World religion that venerated mushrooms, and that vestiges of this ancient religion survived among mushroom-loving people like the Russians, while it had been driven underground and made into the satanic opponent of "true" religion among mushroom-fearing people like the Germans and their English cousins. In the Wassons' opinion, positive and negative feelings about mushrooms ran too deep to have their roots in anything less than religion. But whereas in Europe their conjectured original mushroom religion was buried in millennia of cultural and religious developments, in Huautla they had the prospect of meeting a living mushroom religion face to face.

In response to a query, Wasson received a long, enlightening letter from Eunice Pike, a missionary linguist who had lived in Huautla off and on since 1936, in which she described the Mazatecs' practices and beliefs with respect to the mushrooms. She and her colleagues had not participated in the rituals, but the Mazatecs were not particularly secretive about them either, and in light of what Wasson was later to learn, she was well informed. She also reported that the Mazatecs were far from unanimous in their belief in the mushrooms' power, and while some were convinced that the mushrooms let them look into heaven, others compared experiencing mushroom visions to going to the movies.[83]

A few months later, in the summer of 1953, Wasson and his wife and their sixteen-year-old daughter Masha set out, leaving her brother Peter behind. In Mexico they met Robert Weitlaner, and continued on to Huautla. The road was not yet open, and it was a hard trek. Along the way they observed people communicating by the whistle language the Mazatecs share with their neighbors the Chinantecs. Local arrangements had been made by Florence Cowan, a linguist with the Summer Institute of Linguistics, and they were put up with the local school teacher. Wasson's excitement was palpable. "After all," he wrote, "it was a bold thing we were doing, strangers probing the innermost secrets of these remote people."[84]

On this, the first of ten trips to Mexico, the Wassons did not meet María Sabina, but at the last moment they got to witness a ritual where mushrooms were used. On the evening before they were to leave, Weitlaner persisted in questioning a Mazatec man named Aurelio Carrera until he agreed to help the Wassons check on the well-being of their son Peter, about whom they claimed to be worried. According to Wasson, that night vigil "confirmed in all essentials" the report of the four outsiders who had one done for them in 1938.[85] Valentina Pavlovna and Masha begged permission to withdraw after a while, but Wasson stayed on to the very end. The local compensation for a vigil at the time was twenty or twenty-five pesos. The Wassons paid Aurelio Carrera 120 pesos for their vigil and left town in the morning.

In the summer of 1955, Wasson had the second formative mushroom experience of his life. He and his wife and daughter again went to Mexico City, and Wasson and Allan Richardson, a friend of his whom he described as "a New York Society photographer,"[86] went ahead by plane to Huautla. This time they were put up by a Mazatec couple willing to help them participate in a mushroom vigil. Upon arrival they were taken to a ravine where a prime cluster of the mushrooms was growing. They filled a box with them and carried it to the home of María Sabina. Wasson wrote, "Neither she nor her daughter spoke a word of Spanish. We do not know whether they had been told to expect our visit."[87]

According to María Sabina, she was expecting them. Wasson's and Richardson's host on this occasion was the *síndico*, a town official second in command after the municipal president. He had visited María Sabina and told her that blond people had come to the municipal building looking for a Wise One. To his amazement, one of the men knew the Mazatec name for the mushrooms. The síndico told them he knew an excellent Wise Woman, and with María Sabina's permission he would bring them to her.

María Sabina claimed that the mushrooms had already warned her about this visit, but she did not understand the warning, although it made her uneasy. Now that the strangers had arrived, she felt she had to cooperate with her colleague, the town official.

When Wasson and Richardson arrived with the box of mushrooms, María Sabina, who was still recovering from her bullet wounds, had her daughter Apolonia waiting with her. Wasson observed that Apolonia was up and about but that María Sabina was lying down. It did not register with him that she was injured. "I told the foreigners that I was sick though not precisely that a drunk had wounded me with a pistol," she said later.[88] In urgently requesting a vigil that very night, Wasson again used as the reason concern for his son Peter, now serving in the army, and she agreed to do it.

That night, as María Sabina portioned out the mushrooms, she divided them into thirteen pairs each for herself and Apolonia, and four, five, or six pairs for the other adults present. To Wasson and to Richardson she presented six pairs each. Of himself Wasson wrote, "Our readers will imagine his joy at this dramatic culmination of years of pursuit."[89] Richardson had come along with the express understanding that he would not eat mushrooms, but now he found no way out. They both chewed and swallowed the mushrooms. The two men spent the rest of the night lying on the floor seeing visions, occasionally vomiting, and listening to María Sabina's chants, claps, clicks, and dances in the dark, backed up by Apolonia's singing.

Of that night's events María Sabina later said that the vigil was fine. She believed that she had gone to see the city from which the foreigners had come. She hadn't seen anything like it before.

Wasson never ceased to rhapsodize over his first direct experiences with the mushrooms. He told his story over and over again in print. "There is no record," he wrote, "that any white man had ever attended a session of the kind we are going to describe, nor that any white men had ever partaken of the sacred mushrooms under any circumstances."[90] He had seen spectacular colors and patterns and been swept with feelings of awe. Once he felt that the doors of heaven were about to open for him. He wrote, "The effect of the mushrooms is to bring about a fission of the spirit, a split in the person, a kind of schizophrenia, with the rational side continuing to reason and to observe the sensations that the other side is enjoying." "Clearly the visions come from within the beholder, either from his own unconscious or, as some will surely think, from an inherited fund of memories of the race."[91] Wasson's writing was seductive; any reader with an ounce of imagination would, however momentarily, want to try the mushrooms. And many, many of his readers wanted to join him in what he characterized as sheer ecstasy.

His host had promised that María Sabina was a first class Wise One, and she gratified Wasson's most cherished desire when she presented him with his own six pairs of mushrooms. She had given him just what he wanted, and he adored her for it. With all those present that first night, he felt brotherly love. Ever after, he referred to that shared experience as "agape," the Greek word for a love feast.

Their interpreter had vanished, and neither Wasson nor Richardson understood a word of the singing or intermittent conversations in Mazatec going on around them, but Wasson was sure he had now met in María Sabina "one of the finest exponents of the old tradition."[92] To him her voice was magnificent, her integrity unbreachable. When he wrote about this first vigil (or *velada,* as he preferred to call it, using the Spanish word), he went on and on about "archaic" languages and cultures, sure that the content of the chants would be of enormous interest and importance for specialists in the Mazatec language. Yet the Bible translators had quite a different research agenda, and in years to come he felt he never received sufficient recognition for his discovery.

Now Wasson wanted photographs. He requested that María Sabina do another vigil and that she permit Richardson to take pictures with flashbulbs. She had no objections to his photographing her and Apolonia by day in her home, but allowing a vigil to be punctuated by blinding flashes that revealed her and her associates while the mushrooms were working through them was an immense concession. Moreover, although courtesy kept her from mentioning it, her dancing at the first vigil hadn't done the healing bullet wounds any good. According to María Sabina, she felt that in agreeing to the second vigil, she was continuing to act in accordance with the wishes of the town síndico.

Valentina Pavlovna and Masha flew in between the two vigils, but they did not attend the second one. Nor did Richardson eat the mushrooms, on the excuse that he needed to keep his head clear to handle the photography. Just Wasson and a few Mazatecs joined María Sabina and her son Aurelio in eating them.

This time the night vigil was directed toward Aurelio, whom Wasson perceived to be "in some way ill or defective." He described the ritual as scaled down and different in content from the previous one. Under the influence of the mushrooms María Sabina sang to Aurelio and carressed her near-adult son in a way that gave Wasson pause: "We should have been embarrassed, had we not seen in this *curandera* possessed of the mushrooms a symbol of eternal motherhood."[93] In an interview some years later María Sabina said that it had been a painful experience for her, because during the vigil Aurelio had a premonition of impending death.

In the morning, having eaten Psilocybe mushrooms twice in three days without ill effects, Wasson concluded that the mushrooms were perfectly safe, and he wanted his family to share his experience. The Wassons' intention had been to depart immediately after the second vigil, but the summer rains kept them from leaving for several days. On Tuesday Wasson prevailed upon his wife and daughter to try the mushrooms. It was done without ceremony and without any Mazatecs present. While Wasson and Richardson stood by, Valentina Pavlovna and Masha made themselves comfortable in their sleeping bags, chewed, and swallowed. "This was the first occasion on which white people ate the mushrooms for purely experimental purposes, without the aura of a native ceremony," Wasson reported. "They too saw their visions, for hours on end, all pleasant, mostly of a nostalgic kind. They felt little or no nausea. Their pupils dilated and failed to respond to our flashlights. The pulse showed a tendency to slow down. There were no auditory hallucinations." [94]

Finally the rain let up. Wasson paid María Sabina 100 pesos for her two nights' work. The síndico and his wife refused to accept any payment. The party of blond people departed, on their way to visit other towns where they hoped to find more practitioners of mushroom rituals.

In New York in mid-August, during a hurricane, Wasson tried eating dried mushrooms he had brought back with him. He was gratified to discover that drying did not destroy their potency. One might think a hurricane sufficiently awe-inspiring on its own, but with the storm outside and the mushrooms inside, Wasson felt he was transported to El Greco's Toledo.

María Sabina and the síndico may have thought they had seen the last of the foreigners, but they were mistaken. The next summer the Wassons came back with Richardson; Roger Heim, a French mushroom expert; a French anthropologist; an American chemist; and equipment to record María Sabina for Folkways Records. Once again she had to do everything twice. They recorded the second vigil, which Wasson judged a failure. In the liner notes accompanying the record, he attributed the disappointing performance to poor-quality mushrooms, the presence of microphone cables, and Richardson's flash bulbs. He also noted that something un-pleasant had recently come between María Sabina and her neighbors, and as a result only one Mazatec attended the second vigil. In New York in the fall Wasson had Eunice Pike and a colleague listen to the tapes, which Pike partially transcribed and translated for the liner notes. Folkways put the material out on a single disc within the year, and Wasson saw to it that María Sabina received a record player and a copy of the record.

Right after Wasson and his recording team left Huautla, an Italian-born scholar named Gutierre Tibón arrived there at the recommendation of Florence Cowan's husband George to study the whistle language. From then on Tibón's and Wasson's paths were destined to cross and recross, as Wasson developed his theories about mushrooms and pre-Columbian Mexico and Tibón went on to create the *Enciclopedia de México*. Tibón's broader description of the town and its people, including María Sabina, afford some perspective on Wasson.

María Sabina was now entering into a maelstrom. At a vigil during "the days when Wasson came to Huautla" she had a disturbing vision of a stinking animal skin and a neighbor boasting of murder. It was a Thursday night, and Aurelio was out of town, but he came home for the weekend and spent Sunday afternoon drinking with the neighbor and some friends. Once again in María Sabina's house a drunken fight broke out. This time she was not quick enough to interpose her body. Aurelio, his throat slit, died in her arms.

For months María Sabina wept for her son, though this was not the end of her torment. One day she and her surviving children went to sell bread and candles at a fiesta in another town. When they returned, they found María Sabina's house burned to the ground. "Along with my house, my little store burned together with the corn, beer, aguardiente, the toasted seeds and cigarettes I sold, my huipils and shawls. . . . Christ! Everything," she exclaimed.[95]

They moved in with relatives. People gave them a few utensils, and they got by with wild foods from the woods to make up for the lost corn. María Sabina had to start from scratch accumulating enough money to build a new house, but she managed to replace the wood and thatch one with an adobe house roofed with tin.

Who had become her enemy, and why? "I don't know the reason why they did it," she said. "Some people thought it was because I had revealed the ancestral secret of our native medicine to foreigners."[96]

A principle suspect in her mind was Evaristo Vanegas, a competitor who, she believed, begrudged her Wasson's patronage. And worse yet, the rumor was going around that Wasson had insulted his professional integrity. It had gotten back to María Sabina that "Wasson had left marvelling, and that he went so far as to say that another person in Huautla who claimed to be a Wise One was nothing but a liar. In reality he meant the sorcerer Vanegas."[97]

How completely the secrets of the mushrooms had been revealed neither María Sabina nor her neighbors could have fathomed. During the course of all their married years the Wassons had been gathering material about mushrooms and religion in Eurasia, and they had more than enough for a book. To that accumulation they added the material from their visits to Mexico. They were now in a hurry to publish, because Valentina Pavlovna was diagnosed with cancer. They pulled everything together into a lavish two-volume work published in 1957. The title was *Mushrooms, Russia, and History,* but the real theme was hallucinogenic mushrooms as the root of universal human religion. They gave over much of volume 2 to the use of Psilocybe mushrooms in Mexico. It was illustrated with Richardson's photographs of María Sabina's vigil for Aurelio.

Before he had left Huautla that summer María Sabina had asked Wasson not to show the pictures around. This is what he writes in *Mushrooms, Russia, and History*:

On the morning after, a messenger came to us from her. We were welcome to the pictures, she said, but would we please refrain from showing those particular ones to all and sundry, *sería una traición,* it would be a betrayal. We are doing as the Señora asked us, showing these pictures only in those circles where we feel she would be pleased to have them shown. In order that she not be disturbed by the importunities of commercially minded strangers, we have withheld the name of the village where she lives, and we have changed the names of the characters in our narrative. On our next visit we shall ask for permission to publish our pictures for general circulation.[98]

But María Sabina really was María Sabina. He used the real names of the síndico and his wife and included a photograph of their house in Huautla. Wasson speaks of seeking permission for future publication of the pictures in the very book where he publishes them, a book with a 500-copy print run, marketed by a commercial publisher.

Perhaps Wasson and his wife felt that only the most sincere mushroom scholars would invest in their expensive book (as only a few people would buy the Folkways record). But the other thing that Wasson did with the pictures is—in a word often abused, but not in this case—incredible.

On May 13, 1957, *Life* magazine printed the "Third in a *Life* Series: 'Great Adventures'" on "Seeking the Magic Mushroom. A New York banker goes to Mexico's mountains to participate in the age-old rituals of Indians who chew strange growths that produce visions. By R. Gordon Wasson." The article was illustrated with color prints of Richardson's photographs, and there among them for all the world to see was María Sabina caressing a startled Aurelio, his eyes caught staring in the camera flash. An outdoor photograph of Wasson and his French colleague Heim against a sweep of hillside was identified as being near the village where the vigils were held. *Life* also printed a two-page spread of Heim's full-size, color paintings of seven hallucinogenic mushrooms that could be found in Mexico.[99]

The first piece of information in the article was that *Mushrooms, Russia, and History* was obtainable for $125 from Pantheon Press. Whatever else it may have been, the magazine article was an advertising bonanza for the publisher. Wasson continued the hype: "Richardson and I were the first white men in recorded history to eat the divine mushrooms, which for centuries have been a secret of certain Indians living far from the great world in southern Mexico. No anthropologists had ever described the scene that we witnessed."

Wasson informed the readers that he had changed names in the article to protect people's privacy, but he was only paying lip service to María

Sabina's anonymity. In this *Life* version he called her "Eva Mendez." The name of her language he gave as "Mixeteco," a made-up word that suggests the real Mexican Indian languages Mixe and Mixtec but is also close to the Spanish form of the real name, Mazateco. He placed her village at 5,500 feet above sea level in the fictitious "Mixeteco Mountains." (It is located in the Sierra Mazateca.) This is a very thin disguise. In Richardson's photographs María Sabina's traditional huipil identifies her as a Mazatec, and Wasson's approximation of the pronunciation of the local name for the mushrooms as "nti sheeto" would identify the language as Mazatec for anyone willing to do a little research. Seekers of what Wasson called "the divine mushroom" had only to take a copy of that issue of *Life* to Oaxaca, go to Huautla, look for the right hillside and houses, and show people the pictures to get to María Sabina's door as easily as Wasson had in 1955. For less adventurous souls uninclined to knock about the high country of Oaxaca without names and addresses, *Mushrooms, Russia, and History* with María Sabina's real name and clear directions for how to get to Huautla was available, albeit at a high price. Sure enough, a photographer from San Francisco, after spending a couple of fruitless weeks searching through Mixtec country, went to the Oaxaca state museum, identified María Sabina's huipil, and was at the door of Dr. Guerra's clinic less than three months after the *Life* article appeared. Guerra deflected him to a hundred-year-old woman named María Antonia, and he went on his way without meeting María Sabina. But her identity could not be shielded. Even before Wasson, Gutierre Tibón had published her name in the popular press.[100]

What even semiadventurous reader of the *Life* article would not want to go in search of the divine mushrooms? After recounting his honeymoon story, Wasson tells how his wife and teenage daughter ate the Mexican mushrooms and how he did so at home in New York. No harm had come of it; the mushrooms were not addictive, there were no after-effects, and there was much to be gained from the experience, as he assured the readers of *Life:*

> In man's evolutionary past, as he groped his way out from his lowly past, there must have come a moment in time when he discovered the secret of the hallucinatory mushrooms. Their effect on him, as I see it, could only have been profound, a detonator to new ideas. . . . One is emboldened to the point of asking whether they might not have planted in primitive man the very idea of a god. . . . At all times there have been rare souls—the mystics and certain poets—who have had access without the aid of drugs to the visionary world for which the mushrooms hold the key. . . . But I can testify that the mushrooms make those visions accessible to a much larger number.

A few weeks later *Life* published a selection of letters to the editor about Wasson's great adventure. Predictably there was a denunciation from a clergyman balanced by a letter from a broad-minded reader proclaiming the article utterly fascinating. Among the other letters printed were several paeans to the similar effects of peyote, complete with information about price, dosage, and how to get it from a mail-order business in Texas. The drug culture of 1960s America was aborning, and Wasson was serving as one of its midwives.

The following summer, although Valentina Pavlovna was in the last months of terminal illness, Wasson went back in Huautla to photograph and tape yet another vigil. By then María Sabina was deeply worried about her local enemies.

Concern for the absent Peter Wasson was wearing out as a justification for holding vigils. The boy was grown up, and why would his father travel all the way to Huautla to seek information about him when he had access to mail and telephones in New York? There had to be a new rationale. Aurelio Carrera, who had received 120 pesos from Wasson for his services in 1953, had recently taken on a young assistant, but the boy was useless. Before coming up to Huautla, he had been working in the tropical lowlands, where he had taken sick. The illness dragged on for months, and he had tried to escape it by seeking work in a cooler, healthier place, but to no avail. It was agreed with Aurelio that Wasson would pay for María Sabina to conduct a vigil for the boy, whose name was Perfecto. If the boy were helped, Aurelio would benefit. If he were not, Aurelio would lose nothing. In any case Wasson would have his photos and tapes.

Wasson put the tape recorders in a room adjoining the one where the vigil was to take place and set up a microphone to catch the voices of María Sabina and the people closest to her. Because of the recording session for Folkways, this was not entirely new, but Wasson did not credit the Mazatecs with much understanding of his enterprise. "In 1956 I had taken pains to explain to María Sabina and others in her circle what I was doing with my microphone and battery-run tape recorder, and they said they understood, but then and later it is more than doubtful whether they grasped the function of the microphone in recording all their conversation. They spoke without self-consciousness, with entire abandon, as though secure behind their language barrier against eavesdropping by outsiders."[101]

The photographer was in the room with María Sabina, Aurelio, Perfecto, and the other Mazatecs in attendance throughout the vigil, but Wasson was in the next room monitoring the recording. He saw nothing nor did he understand anything of the Mazatec he was hearing through his headphones. He was not to learn what went on at this vigil until years later, when George and Florence Cowan completed a transcription and translation for him.

María Sabina's enemies were much on her mind that night as Wasson and Richardson did their work. Off and on throughout the night, she returned to ruminations on her suspicions of Evaristo Vanegas. She and Aurelio Carrera also used the occasion to get in many jibes at her daughter Apolonia, who was assisting at the vigil. But the main work of the night was to find out what was ailing Perfecto. Conversation ranged over the possibilities of dropsy, yellow fever, homosexuality, bewitchment, the lingering effects of having taken fright. María Sabina had a vision of his soul being consumed by a lion. Perfecto asked for confirmation of this, and she assured him that it was so, but discussion continued of other possible reasons for his illness. Later, in publishing the transcription and translation of this vigil, Wasson made much of the tenderness that Perfecto's employer Aurelio Carrera demonstrated toward the sick boy.

With their night's work done, Wasson and Richardson moved on. After they left, Perfecto died. But according to María Sabina, it need not have turned out as it did: "Weeks went by and someone informed me that Perfecto had died. They didn't take care of him as they should have. If they had done several vigils he would surely have gotten well. They didn't do it." [102] The only investment Aurelio Carrera made in Perfecto after Wasson left town was the cost of a decent burial.

When Wasson finally had the Cowans' translation of the vigil in his hands, he perceived things quite differently. He focused on the moment when María Sabina reported that she saw a lion eating Perfecto's soul, making all else prelude and denouement: "We can watch the sick boy as he enters by stages into the full import of the pronouncement. He is visibly shaken by what he overhears and suddenly the others are alarmed by the effect on him. He loses color, collapses." Wasson goes on, "He died just as María Sabina had predicted. We cannot say whether her prediction led to his death or whether his illness, never diagnosed, was destined to end in death." [103]

Wasson made high drama of being present at the delivery of a death sentence, however unaware he was at the time. Since he gave credence to the possibility that Perfecto died because María Sabina told him he would, we might expect Wasson to have been conscience-stricken for having set up the vigil where it happened. But there is no evidence that he felt any personal accountability. In his introduction to the transcription and translation of the 1958 vigil, he only goes so far as to say, "Indirectly the harrassment by an enemy of María Sabina could be attributed to me, since my patronage was what he was coveting, and therefore the slow start of the performance as she worries about her 'enemies' can be partly laid to me."[104] It seems that his apologies are directed not to María Sabina or to the dead boy but to the reader, who must wade through tedious preliminaries before getting to the sensational pronouncement of Perfecto's doom.

The people Wasson brought along to Huautla with him were the leading edge of a tidal wave. During the summer of the vigil for Perfecto, Dr. Guerra sent word to María Sabina that a foreign woman who knew Gutierre Tibón wanted to meet her. María Sabina assumed that this latest visitor also wanted to consult the mushrooms, and she was right. Dr. Guerra arrived with a British artist. Indeed the blonde lady wanted to eat the mushrooms herself. María Sabina readied some for her colleague, the young doctor, as well. Now he found himself in the same position as the photographer Richardson had a few years before. He tried to refuse the mushrooms and was given no options. María Sabina demanded professional courtesy; she had allowed him to inject her with his anesthetic, and now he must partake of her medicine. Somehow Dr. Guerra managed to drive his jeep back to town afterwards amidst hallucinations of dancing trees.

Many more foreigners, blond ones and brown ones, were on their way to Huautla, for Wasson's article in *Life* had also been published in the magazine's international edition and in Spanish in *Life en Español*.

In New York City Valentina Pavlovna was slipping away, and on the evening of the last day of 1958 she died. Few married couples share such a compelling interest as the Wassons had in mushrooms and religion. Many another person, widowed after such a long marriage, would have been incapacitated, but Wasson was not. With the help of his many well-placed friends, he carried on alone. Heim immediately saw into press a joint work by himself and Wasson on the Mexican mushrooms and dedicated it to Valentina Pavlovna. Schultes, for his part, arranged a lifetime courtesy appointment for Wasson at the Harvard Botanical Museum, which provided a room for the Wassons' accumulated reseach material as the Tina and Gordon Wasson Ethnomycological Collection.

In 1962 María Sabina found herself face to face with Wasson and a friend of his yet again, and again Wasson wanted something new. Schultes's colleague Albert Hofmann, the Swiss discoverer of LSD, had also isolated the active agents in the Psilocybe mushrooms and synthesized them. Wasson got Hofmann to accompany him to Huautla, where they gave María Sabina some psilocybin pills and had her conduct a vigil using them instead of mushrooms. It was the last María Sabina was to see of

Wasson for a while; the next year he retired from banking and went off to study mushroom use in Asia. For more than a decade he devoted himself to mushrooms and religion in India, Siberia, and ancient Greece.

Wasson had left the municipality of Huautla with a problem on its hands. As María Sabina related:

> The day that I did a vigil for the first time in front of foreigners, I didn't think anything bad would happen, since the order to give a vigil for the blonde ones came directly from the municipal authorities at the rec-ommendation of the síndico, my friend Cayetano García. But what was the result? Well, that many people have come in search of God, people of all colors and all ages. The young people are the ones who have been the most disrespectful. They take the *children* [the mushrooms] at any time and in any place. They don't do it during the night or under the direction of the Wise Ones, and they don't use them to cure any sick-ness either.[105]

Of the people who came to Huautla to seek out María Sabina for medical problems, some sought alternative treatment for diabetes and others hoped for recovery after unsuccessful surgery. Some foreigners brought their children to her. She did her best for these people, but she was outraged by the people who bypassed her: "Later I found out that the young people with long hair didn't need me to eat the *little things*. Fellow Mazatecs weren't lacking who, to get a few centavos for food, sold the *saint children* [the mushrooms] to the young people. . . . These young people, blonde and dark-skinned, didn't respect our customs. Never, as far as I remember, were the *saint children* eaten with such a lack of respect. . . . Whoever does it simply to feel the effects can go crazy and stay that way temporarily."[106] These people were eating mushrooms by daylight out on the edges of cliffs. They were not observing sexual absti-nence. It was hardly any wonder that misfortunes befell them.

Past sixty, María Sabina, born at the turn of the century, might have begun feeling her age, but Valentina Pavlovna's death and Wasson's depar-ture for Asia marked the beginning rather than the end of events that kept her life moving along in high gear for the next twenty years. For María Sabina and her community, the 1950s had been the decade of Wasson. The 1960s were shaping up as the decade of chaos, to be followed by a decade of recovery and reconciliation. It was a time of losing old allies and finding new ones, having quarrels and patching them up, being arrested and released, enduring loneliness and celebrity. The 1960s were marked by a great deal of trouble for María Sabina, while the 1970s brought a measure of help, accomplishment, and satisfaction.

In 1960 Dr. Guerra concluded his service in Huautla and left to practice cardiology in Mexico City. María Sabina took pride in his farewell Mass in which she and the physician knelt side by side and acknowledged each other as equals. The Mass had been arranged by the priest who had served Huautla for most of two decades. He had his own copy of the Folkways record, and he assured María Sabina that it was of great worth. Now, soon after Dr. Guerra's departure, the priest also left. María Sabina had lost two friends and supporters.

But the 1960s also brought new people who would touch her life in positive ways. Among the Americans who sought her out for vigils was a young man who twenty years later would serve as the book designer for her autobiography. A man named Fernando Benítez conducted three interviews with her through an interpreter and included what María Sabina told him about her life in a four-volume work on the Indians of Mexico published in 1970. An Australian came to town to settle in. Like Wasson, Henry Munn had no anthropological training but a strong interest in hallucinogenic plants and religious ritual. Unlike Wasson, he became part of the community, married into the local Estrada family, and began to study the practice of Wise Ones up close on a day-to-day basis.

But for the most part, daily life in the 1960s meant contending with the endless stream of young Mexicans, young Europeans, and young Americans looking for God, as María Sabina wonderingly put it. "Before Wasson," she said, "nobody took the mushrooms only to find God."[107] The market price for a kilo of the mushrooms, a commodity that had never been on the market before Wasson's article, rose to 100 pesos. A storekeeper on the main street of Huautla approached likely looking foreigners to offer both mushrooms and vigils, much to Wasson's disgust. Wasson characterized the people who patronized the local purveyors of the mushrooms as "hippies," "oddballs," and "the riffraff of our population,"[108] but he himself more and more openly advocated the mushroom experience as imperative for anyone wishing to really understand pre-Columbian America. According to Benítez, Wasson on his own initiative extracted him and his friends from an agreement with the Huautla storekeeper and arranged a vigil for them with María Sabina instead. On a second visit to María Sabina, Benítez offered her four hundred pesos for a vigil. There had been tremendous inflation since the days before Wasson when a Wise One typically received twenty to twenty-five pesos for a night's work.

With time the volume of God-seeking, mushroom-eating outsiders exceeded anything the local authorities could hope to control. The area was placed under the jurisdiction of federal law enforcement officers. One day María Sabina found her house full of strangers, who had come with a

Mazatec interpreter. They ransacked her belongings, examining her record player and the Folkways record, looking through her collection of photographs and newspaper clippings, and asking through the interpreter about the mushrooms and tobacco powder she kept openly in her house. Then they arrested her on suspicion of selling dangerous substances and drove her off to the municipal building. There, workers with the National Indigenist Institute got her released and sent her home, but her record player, record, and clippings were confiscated.

This arrest was the most traumatic of María Sabina's several encounters with the law, but a literary figure far away in Spain conceived a much worse fate for her. In 1965 the Spanish poet Camilo José Cela was inspired by Wasson's writings to compose an oratorio about her in which she is condemned to be hanged, a fate from which "she cannot be saved by the wailing of Valentina Pavlovna Wasson." It is a piece replete with images of sexual violence and degradation in which two choirs, one of thirty-three virgins and the other of thirty-three whores, sing of her community's desire to swing on the feet of the hanged woman and to sniff her last sweat. Flanked by the choirs, the character of María Sabina sings such lines as: "I am a woman who daydreams while a man rapes her, I am a woman who always gets raped again. . . . I am a woman who was buried alive, I am a woman who enjoyed being buried alive, I am a woman who drinks her father's semen in the flower of the mandrake."[109] Cela's misogynist text brought him international acclaim. He and the Spanish composer Leonardo Balada collaborated on turning it into *María Sabina: A Symphonic Tragedy,* which had its world premiere at Carnegie Hall in the spring of 1970 under the auspices of the Hispanic Society of America and then moved on to its European premiere in Madrid. The music reviewer for the *New York Times,* noting that María Sabina was still alive in Oaxaca, extolled the musical setting of her execution. María Sabina, whose chants were devoid of sexual reference and for whom abstinence was the watchword in any dealings with the mushrooms, would have been shocked and appalled, but she would have agreed with Cela that some people in Huautla would not have minded seeing her come to a bad end.[110]

According to María Sabina the municipal president revealed to her that she had been denounced to the outside authorities by a fellow Mazatec. She was cut to the quick and vociferously defended herself and her dealings with foreigners, threatening blood revenge against her accuser. The president urged her to drop her grudge against him, since the matter had been settled, and he warned her of the ill effect outsiders were having on local traditions.

María Sabina was not an easy person to get along with. She quarreled with the schoolteacher over money and criticized her for feeling superior. She put the síndico's brother on her enemies list. Her criticisms of her daughter during the 1958 vigil were humiliating. It is hardly surprising that after her aged mother died in the 1960s, María Sabina found herself alone: "My children have gone their separate ways: each one of them is dedicated to his or her family. I've remained alone. My children hardly visit me."[111]

To the degree that María Sabina felt alienated from Mazatec society in Huautla, she had become dependent on the attention of people who came from far away to see her. That they undertook the difficult journey was a vindication of her worth, neglected as she was by her children and plagued by her enemies. Someone had even stolen the pet bird she had bought to keep her company. In its place, journalists, flower children, and rock stars provided her with companionship. (According to the press, John Lennon, Mick Jagger, and Bob Dylan all made the trip to Huautla.)[112] She grew weary of answering the same questions again and again, but it helped pass the time.

Besides local resentment of the foreigners she attracted, another thing that distanced María Sabina from other Mazatecs was the way mushroom language had invaded the fabric of her everyday discourse. In the vigils, the mushrooms were supposed to speak through her, and when she listed her credentials as a clean, well-prepared woman with the heart of Christ, a woman wise in medicine, a lawyer woman, a woman of affairs, a personal associate of Oaxaca's hero Benito Juárez, it was not to be taken as personal boasting. But relating the story of her life, without eating the mushrooms, she nonetheless injected her narrative with claims of her wisdom and special status: "I am the daughter of God and elected to be wise." "Apolonia and Viviana, my two daughters, will never be Wise Women. They will not receive the Book from the hands of the Principal Ones. I, on the other hand, am known in Heaven, and even the holy Pope knows I exist." "You had to go to school many days to know what you know; but you should know that I didn't have to go to any school to be wise."[113] Such talk is not calculated to keep friends. The foreigners partook of a little of it through interpreters and went on their way feeling enlightened. María Sabina's neighbors were less impressed. Luckily for María Sabina, there was a Mazatec who was sympathetic. He was Alvaro Estrada, a Huautla-born engineer who was Henry Munn's brother-in-law. During the 1970s Alvaro, his sisters Natividad and Eloina, and Munn devoted themselves to the study of the Wise Ones in their own family and also of María Sabina.

Alvaro Estrada lived and worked in Mexico City and only came back on visits, but his sister Eloina lived in Huautla and assisted her brother-in-law. Munn owned a copy of the Folkways record and was not satisfied with Eunice Pike's incomplete English translation. Eloina translated the whole text from Mazatec to Spanish for him in 1970. She also translated a new recording of a vigil made in July of 1970. On this occasion María Sabina was assisted by her niece María Aurora. Munn and some Mazatecs made the recording for themselves, and no outsiders were present. The study of Mazatec culture was beginning to pass into the hands of local people.

George and Florence Cowan were also consulting with María Sabina. Wasson had engaged them to transcribe and translate the tapes from the 1958 vigil for Perfecto, and they in turn asked for her help. The result was a much more polished product than the liner notes for the Folkways record, because María Sabina not only listened to the tapes with the Cowans and explained to them things they did not understand, but she also revealed what was going on during the vigil.

Wasson himself, in the company of Weitlaner's daughter, dropped in for a brief visit, but he made no new demands. He assured María Sabina that he and she both had many years of life ahead of them, and as it turned out, he was right. *María Sabina and Her Mazatec Mushroom Velada* was published in 1974 in the no-expense-spared style of all Wasson's productions. The book, in a binding printed with traditional Mazatec embroidery patterns, contains a prologue by Wasson; the Cowans' transcription of the Mazatec with both Spanish and English translations and commentary; Richardson's photographs; an essay on the Mazatec language by George Cowan; and notes on the music by Willard Rhodes, a musicologist. Moreover, the book was packaged with a set of records of the vigil as it had been recorded in 1958 and a complete musical score by Rhodes.[114] When Wasson wrote in the prologue, "Never before has a shamanic performance in the New World been presented with anything like the completeness of this one," he was undoubtedly right. A dozen years later, just before he died, Wasson remarked with some bitterness, "So far as I am aware, no one has paid the slightest attention to *María Sabina and Her Mazatec Mushroom Velada,* but I am prouder of it than of anything else I have done."[115] And in this he was justified. In the long run the book will probably turn out to be the most enduring contribution to linguistics and anthropology that Wasson ever put together, simply because it allows María Sabina to speak at length in her own voice. For once, most of the book is María Sabina's chants and conversation, not Wasson writing about his ideas of María Sabina. It stands as a sober memorial to her and to poor Perfecto. The deluxe special-edition copies bound in leather were printed in Italy. As soon as they were done, Wasson sent a copy to Henry Munn to present to María Sabina. She was very pleased.

During 1975 and 1976, Alvaro Estrada began interviewing María Sabina about her life and experiences. She gladly told him about the conventional hardships of the first fifty years of her life and the unconventional ones of the last twenty, since she met Wasson. She repeated some of the stories she had told Fernando Benítez several years before, but now it came easier without an interpreter. Alvaro not only came to talk to her in Mazatec and to record their conversations, but he also helped her in practical ways. Because she had continued to receive summonses to appear in court after her arrest, he took her to Mexico City and arranged interviews to win public sympathy and support for her.

He also took her to the new National Museum of Anthropology, where the second floor of the museum is given over to exhibits of the country's Indians. At the Mazatec exhibit there is a dramatic photograph of María Sabina herself, and the Folkways recording plays ceaselessly. María Sabina was very well pleased with the exhibit and with being recognized by visitors to the museum.

The nuns of Huautla took her on a visit to the shrine of the Virgin of Guadalupe, and in 1979 she was brought back to the capital again for the premiere of a documentary movie about her.[116] The attention she was receiving had taken a decided turn for the better in the 1970s. Back in her home state she visited with the governor, and he presented her with two mattresses to afford her aging body a bit of comfort. Never until then having slept on anything but a mat rolled out on the floor, she confessed to having fallen off her mattresses more than once.[117]

When Alvaro Estrada had prepared María Sabina's dictated autobiography for publication, he sent a copy to Wasson and asked him to write an essay to serve as a prologue. This was the first time the language barrier between Wasson and María Sabina was lifted, revealing her as a genuine person, and Wasson admitted that it made him wince to learn of the damage he had done. But Wasson was unrepentant. Even with the evidence before him of what she had suffered, he thought in terms of himself: "At the time of my first velada with María Sabina, in 1955, I had to make a choice: suppress my experience or resolve to present it worthily to the world. There was never a doubt in my mind. The sacred mushrooms and the religious feeling concentrated in them through the Sierras of Southern Mexico had to be made known to the world, and worthily so, *at whatever cost to me personally.*"[118]

Wasson was convinced that the mushroom ritual was, in any case, doomed to extinction in a matter of years by the advance of modern education. María Sabina was one of the last practitioners of an ancient form of religion that would be lost completely if Wasson did not document it for posterity, thereby supporting his most cherished ideas about mankind and religion. And whoever would have imagined that there would be so much unworthy riffraff in the world?

Wasson gave much credit to Estrada for transcribing María Sabina's autobiography, and Estrada in turn gave credit to Wasson for his pioneering work in "ethnomycology" (the role of mushrooms in traditional cultures). María Sabina's life story is flanked on one side by Wasson's essay and Estrada's introduction and on the other by translations of ritual chants.

The Mexican edition of the autobiography was a success, and an English edition soon followed. Henry Munn did the English translation; the poet Jerome Rothenberg added a preface; and Frederick Usher, who had visited María Sabina during the 1960s, was responsible for the attractive book design. Unlike Wasson's expensive volumes, it is a book for the ordinary bookstore patron, a nostalgic book for those many people now in middle age who had made their way to Huautla when they were very young and searching for God.

And how does María Sabina's life story end? In her autobiography she complained that she had lost teeth and was ashamed of her appearance. Worse still, she had trouble eating and talking. She had been on good terms with her mother, María Concepción, when she died, and now María Sabina was looking ahead to her own death, when she would go to join Benito Juárez. The details of her funeral were pleasing to anticipate. Although his idea of her dominated Wasson's life, he does not loom very large in her memoirs. In his essay Wasson writes, "Not once does María Sabina reproach me,"[119] but this is what she has to say about the ultimate price she paid for their collaboration: "From the moment the foreigners arrived to search for God the *saint children* lost their purity. They lost their force; the foreigners spoiled them. From now on they won't be any good. There's no remedy for it. . . . Before Wasson, I felt the *saint children* elevated me. I don't feel like that anymore."[120]

The mushrooms that had brought hope to her and to her sister when they were hunger-stricken children lost the power to comfort her as a toothless old woman.

Late in 1985 María Sabina died in a hospital in Oaxaca of old age exacerbated by bronchitis, malnutrition, and pneumonia. In the months before she died, according to one of her obituaries, she had been making efforts to obtain some legal restitution from "people who allegedly earned large sums of money by publicizing her knowledge about the mushrooms."[121]

Wasson saw one more book into print in 1986 and died at the end of the year. One of the last published photographs of María Sabina, taken in 1980, faces the title page of the English edition of her autobiography. A photograph of Wasson is on the back cover of the paperback edition of his 1980 book, *The Wondrous Mushroom: Mycolatry in Mesoamerica*. There they are, two very tough old people who both desperately needed the mushrooms to take them to another world, because the worlds they were born into were too small to contain their immense egos.

THESE THREE WORDSMITHS

The room was pervaded by a marvelous atmosphere. The suggestive rhythm of the primitive melody transported me back centuries in time. I was somewhere in Finland's primeval times, in the realm of Kalevala, where stories and tales have life and substance. . . . Every step I have taken in wending my way through forest and swamp . . . in the far-off borderlands has brought me decades, indeed centuries, back in time.
—*IMPRESSIONS OF A VISIT TO A KARELIAN HOME*[122]

Paraske, Doña Luz, and María Sabina were exceptional people, artists who stood head and shoulders above other members of their communities. Others sang, but Paraske possessed more songs than seems humanly possible, and her forceful personality so invested her performances with emotion that no audience could remain unmoved. Many a resident of Milpa Alta could relate traditional folktales, but only Doña Luz, whose physical presence had set loose the creative energies of a generation of artists in Mexico, spun the new stories of the Centennial and Zapata and President Cárdenas wading through the muddy debris of San Pedro Atocpan. As for María Sabina, such was the power of her chants that Wasson, understanding not a word, thought they might convey him to heaven. Without recourse to the mushrooms, perfectly sober visitors to the National Museum of Anthropology are stopped in their tracks by her recorded voice.

Unlike the interpreters, who had to react on the spot to every atom of incoming information, these artists could lose themselves in their performances, as though flying on automatic pilot; such was Paraske's weeping, Luz's spinning of the zazanilli, and María Sabina's mushroom talk. They seem to have differed in the extent to which they separated their art from their lives. The speech of María Sabina, studded with Wise One pronouncements even outside the mushroom rituals, brings to mind others for whom religious consciousness pervades every aspect of daily life—fundamentalist Muslims, evangelical Protestants, charismatic Catholics. People who knew Paraske remarked on her humor and compassion. Directly from Paraske herself we have so little other than the great collection of her songs that we can hardly know whether the stylized language of her verses and their emotional volatility shaped her everyday discourse. As compelling as her presence was for people mesmerized by the distant past, there was something about her that greatly discomforted her son Vasle and his wife. Doña Luz could switch modes, from performance to fine-tuned acuity, and her letters to Charlot are solidly in the latter mold, as she writes about whom she has seen, what they said, and—during the early 1940s—her concern for Charlot's relatives still in France. For her, the Indian woman persona seems to have been like a shawl she could wear or put off at will. Paraske and Luz never imagined that they were conduits for things passing through them from another world. On the contrary, they were very clear about which things they had learned and from whom and which things they had composed themselves. They found solace in religion, but their art was not religious, and that is a fundamental difference between them and María Sabina.

Like their interpreter sisters, these women were engaged in barebones survival. Barge-hauling, ditch-digging, and domestic labor were by no means their unique misfortunes. According to a survey published at Finnish government expense in 1894, in that small country alone 550 women were working as bricklayers and 600 as builders and carpenters; 765 were unloading ships, and 1,136 were laundresses.[123] Working with investigators was one more way of getting by from day to day. When the exhausted body demanded a respite, the mind could go on a while longer.

In the face of relentless need, the income to be earned from offering interested parties a glimpse of vanishing folkways could be the last bulwark against illness or starvation, and it might still prove inadequate. As she coughed her life away in Sakkola, Paraske could not afford medicine that might have brought her some rest. Despite social welfare programs in Mexico, Doña Luz suffered for months with an untreated eye infection, and in badly deteriorating handwriting she had complained to Charlot of impaired vision quite some time before she finally lost her life to the car she did not see coming.[124] In the mid-1980s, a half-century since dentures had become a commonplace, malnutrition hastened toothless María Sabina's life to its end. Although people in their home communities thought these women enjoyed special advantages, not one of them escaped poverty by working for outsiders.

The experiences of these verbal artists were notably different from those of the three women interpreters. Like them, they led unspeakably hard lives in a world haunted by violence, but the men they fell in with—artists and academic investigators of folklore, linguistics, and religion—were well-meaning people. More to the point, perhaps, the men did not treat them as means to an end but as an end in themselves. In these flesh-and-blood women they felt there was embodied something abstract and elusive, something they wanted terribly to grasp.

There was more to the investigator-informant enterprise than cash for data. Heirs to centuries of ill-treatment as ignorant peasants, the women found themselves the objects of the respect and admiration of attractive men with grand ideas. National romanticism, whether Finnish or Mexican, painted—in the words of a Kalevala scholar—"a new vision of a nation whose common people were not, after all, passive, subjugated, clumsy and ungifted, but the inheritors of magnificent powers of the mind and spirit that had gone unnoticed until now."[125] This was the spirit in which Neovius set out for Sakkola, the attitude Barlow and Horcasitas brought to their work with Doña Luz, and Wasson's approach to María Sabina as a practitioner of ancient religion.

In these working relationships, both investigator and informant were operating outside their respective cultures. The men put aside the prejudices of their society to find value, things of interest, and worth in their informants'. The women, in turn, conceived the possibility of other ways of doing things. Consider, for instance, the flying cultural leap young Luz made when she took off her clothes and presented herself naked to the artists, and the one she made later with Whorf when she learned how to break up and repeat her speech phrase by phrase so he could transcribe it—the same skill Paraske had learned for Neovius. Consider the equanimity with which María Sabina accommodated Wasson's cables and Richardson's flash bulbs and Hofmann's psilocybin pills. Few members of their communities would or could do such things.

The men they worked with nourished these intellectually flexible women not least by introducing them to revolutionary ideas. The influence of the 1860s liberal movement in Russia, which sought to break down traditional structures of power at every level, from within the family to the highest levels of government, carried forward through the rest of the century and across borders. It gave impetus to women's organizations in Finland in the 1880s, among whose products were the published statistics on women at work and the biographical dictionary of women where Neovius placed Paraske's life story. The Bolshevik Revolution inherited much from Russia's "men of the sixties," and Diego Rivera, who went to Moscow to see the revolution firsthand, brought their ideas home to postrevolutionary Mexico, to his fellow artists, and to Luz.

Unlike the explorers, military commanders, evangelists, and bureaucrats who employed the interpreters and civil servants we have met, the men who worked with Paraske, Doña Luz, and María Sabina were skep-

tical of the superiority of their own societies. Where others saw superstition, paganism, lack of economic success, and lack of power, these
investigators found valid beliefs, sincere and sustaining religious foundations, and clarity of vision. From the outset they shared fewer of their
societies' assumptions. Wasson, in particular, delighted in portraying himself as an intellectual maverick, repeating with relish the establishment put
downs he had endured. In *The Road to Eleusis* he writes of a warning he
received after giving a paper in 1956 "to beware of seeing mushrooms
everywhere."[126] They differed among themselves too: the artists and
folklorists appreciating performances and survivals from the past, while
the linguists and anthropologists were more interested in spontaneity and
how present systems work.

Unlike some of their colleagues who were given to identifying their
informants just by first name or hometown or even as "a peasant woman,"
"a young man," "a girl," or the like, Neovius and Wasson promoted
Paraske and María Sabina as their personal discoveries, important individuals deserving of the world's attention. As for Doña Luz, long before her
verbal gifts were recognized, the artists of Mexico had covered canvasses
and walls with her face and form and invited the public to see. There was
nothing anonymous about these three women. Paintings and photographs
of them were in museums and galleries, and strangers recognized them on
the street. What Sarah Winnemucca had tried to do for herself with her
costumes and publicity photographs and press conferences had been done
for them; the men who admired them had made them celebrities.

Public reaction to celebrities is hardly objective. The English travelers
Mrs. Tweedie and Mrs. Clive-Bayley clung to the persistent stereotype of
Finns as small-eyed, high cheek-boned, tip-nosed, Asian-looking people
of Mongol affinity, and yet they managed to see beak-nosed, lantern-
jawed, deep-eyed Paraske as quintessentially Finnish.[127] In the borrowed
antique costume and holding a borrowed kantele, she symbolized for
Finns both the passing of an age and the roots of a new nation for whom
day was just dawning; she validated them all as not-Swedish, not-Russian.
They went to exhibitions to see the paintings of her and were pleased to
catch a glimpse of her on the streets, but they did not flock to buy the
first volume of her collected verses.

For Charlot, Leal, and Rivera and for that segment of the public that
appreciated their work, Luz as the primordial Indian woman symbolized
the wellspring of the un-Spanishness of Mexico. In the 1920s, as indeed
today, there were Indian women to be seen everywhere in Mexico City
and the surrounding countryside, but it was Luz who embodied the
enduring, monumental qualities that tapped a depth of feeling in them,
inspired some sense of joyous recognition.

Wasson considered himself both scholarly and deeply religious, and in his prolific writing he addressed himself to like-minded people. He was surprised and dismayed to see a very different sort of people enthusiastically take up his lead. Yet they represented themselves to the people of Huautla as seekers of God, and who is to say that young and uninformed though they might have been, they were not sincere? Still, what they came for was the intense personal experience Wasson promised they could find through the mushrooms, and few took the trouble to learn about the Mazatecs or to know María Sabina's real-life situation within her community.

Practical and down-to-earth though these women were, in other people's imaginations they went about enveloped in an aura of nostalgia. They represented the past, something almost gone and yet still—miraculously—available in their persons. Caught up in the dizzying rush of modernization, the women themselves believed that they would carry with them to the grave ancient ways of life that their children were rejecting. María Sabina had announced that her daughters would not be Wise Ones, that the great book of wisdom would never be opened to them, and by the end of her life she said with resignation that the mushrooms had even ceased to talk to her. Doña Luz told Horcasitas and his assistants stories of the life in the old Milpa Alta that was destroyed in the Revolution.

Yet the pervasive idea of cultures dying out was to some degree exaggerated by investigators and informants alike. Back in 1834 one of Lönnrot's informants had said to him, "Not one of my sons will be a singer after I'm gone, as I was after my father. People don't like the old songs any more, as they did in my childhood."[128] He was mistaken; his son became a singer, and he was followed by many more. As late as the 1930s, heirs to Paraske's tradition continued to arrive in Helsinki hoping to earn money from appearances at schools and festivals. One of them sang for the king of Norway and then went on to an appearance in Budapest dressed in a reconstructed costume based on a thousand-year-old grave find. Described as a museum piece with the self-same thousand-year culture in her very soul, she shared with María Sabina the experience of serving as a living exhibit.[129]

The irony of seeking the past in living people is that it leads to not dealing with their perfectly contemporary problems. In these investigator-informant relationships we sometimes see an odd mix of intimacy and total strangeness, most markedly in the case of Wasson, less in the long-term commitments of Neovius and Charlot. But even these two well-meaning men failed to protect the women they valued so highly from destitution and humiliation. They stretched their personal resources to the limit to send money for one emergency after another, but the women had to keep asking for it, apologizing for their needs again and again.

It is little wonder that the women could not get by on payments doled out piecemeal from supporters' pockets. What they needed was regular income, and although all of them—Paraske, Doña Luz, and María Sabina—had been recognized as national treasures during their lifetimes, dependable pensions were not forthcoming. That no one was willing to take the long view, to find out their true circumstances and see what was needed to change things for the better, bespeaks a tragic failure of imagination. From the perspective of a century, it seems obvious that Paraske needed the government to provide her a life-right to Larila and a modest pension for no more than a decade, a small return on her contribution to the nation's cultural treasury. It was not something Neovius could give her, but it would have cost the government little had Paraske's Helsinki friends and supporters lobbied for it effectively.

María Sabina told Benítez in 1970 that she was the main support of her grandchildren and what she wanted was another little store like the one that burned down.[130] Operating a store would have afforded her an alternative to earning income from veladas for foreigners. What she needed was capital, which Wasson could have provided, had he understood her situation and been willing to help. Unlike Neovius and Charlot, he was a wealthy man. But he offered his informant no ongoing support; he paid María Sabina generously for her time and moved on.

Doña Luz was pleased when, some twenty years into their relationship, Anita Brenner proposed to pay her a monthly wage of twenty-five dollars. She had recently been bitterly disappointed in her expectations for a return on a children's book based on her stories and published in New York in 1942. Anita Brenner had written the English text, adapting Luz's stories to Anglo-American sensibilities, and Charlot had illustrated them. Doña Luz had assumed that she would earn both recognition and a share in profits from the enterprise, but to her chagrin, she only extracted money from Brenner by badgering her, and months after its publication, she was told she would have to pay to obtain copies of the book for herself. A regular salary would mitigate the hard feelings she bore toward her *comadre,* but half a year later she gave up waiting for back wages and hoping for any future ones.[131] In years to come she could count on thirty pesos for each work session with Horcasitas and his assistants, but they were still paying out of pocket, recording at the end of each transcription which of them had paid and who would pay next time.

When the investigators began work with these women, they had no expectation or (except for Wasson) the means of making anything but hourly payments or payments per session. Only in the compact of compadrazgo that Charlot and Brenner entered into with Doña Luz was there an acknowledged long-term commitment. The informants, their family members, and their communities may have hoped and imagined that they were forming sustaining lifelong relationships. What they were actually engaged in was contract labor.

All these women lived in or on the edge of poverty, and working as informants did not make them rich. But they did receive positive recognition. Shabbily treated at home in Sakkola, Paraske could recall the wonders she had seen, the respect and comforts she had enjoyed in Helsinki and Porvoo. Even as her house was being sold away, she was entertaining visiting ladies in it. María Sabina could remind her enemies that she was known worldwide, and she had the newspaper clippings to prove it. In the last years of her life Doña Luz was interviewed about working with the Mexican muralists, and she appeared on television.[132] In the course of their work they had gained perspectives on their communities and an independent vision of themselves and their art. Explaining why she performed veladas for Wasson, María Sabina said in her own defense that she had been cooperating with the town síndico, and then went on: "Yet I think now that if the foreigners had arrived without any recommendation whatsoever, I would still have shown them my wisdom, because there is nothing bad in that."[133]

C h a p t e r   F o u r

More Lives, Familiar Stories

W hen Cortés reported in his letters the discovery of the great empire of Montezuma, he and his audience might have thought it unique. Then in 1532 came word from Peru of Atahuallpa's realm, setting off decades of exploration north into the deserts, south toward the cold tip of South America, east into the basin of the Amazon. If there were two, there must be more, went the reasoning. But the Spaniards never found another to conquer. In light of this example one might ask, what can we learn from these nine exceptional individuals, however heroic? Perhaps there is not a tenth like them, no generalization to be drawn about life between worlds. In this chapter we will meet others from around the globe whose experience as interpreters resonates with the lives of the women and men we have already met. Here again we encounter the themes of prior marginalization, engagement with outsiders, and yet more alienation from the home community.

AFRICANS AND DUTCH AT THE CAPE OF GOOD HOPE:
Eva (ca. 1642–1674)

European settlement of the southern tip of Africa began at the Cape of Good Hope in the 1600s. At the time, it was inhabited by the Khoikhoi, a brown-skinned people who traveled with herds of cattle and sheep if they were fortunate or lived by hunting and beachcombing if they were not. The Dutch who established a colony on the Cape in the mid-1600s called the poorest of these the "beach wanderers," and it was from among the beach wanderers that Europeans obtained interpreters for their dealings with the Khoikhoi herdsmen.[1]

Just as the Spanish had done off the coasts of Yucatan and Peru, so the English and Dutch snatched people from the shore of the Cape to make interpreters of them. In 1613 an English ship carried off a pair of Khoikhoi men. Aboard ship one died, but the other made it to England, where he suffered desperately from homesickness through a long winter before being returned to his shore. Thereafter, the fleet expected to restock their provisions with meat bought from the Khoikhoi with his help whenever they put in at the Cape, and for a dozen years the arrangement worked fairly well. Then their man disappeared, and the English took another man off with them, this time on a cruise east to Dutch-held Java.

Their intention was that this new agent, whom they called Harry, would serve as their postmaster, receiving letters from passing ships and holding them for later arrivals. To this end they stationed him and some other cattleless beach wanderers on an island at the mouth of the harbor. There they could subsist on the meat of seals and penguins and be safe from the mainland Khoikhoi, who lacked the means to get to off-shore islands. Very soon after the English placed Harry and his companions there, another group of beach wanderers asked the Dutch to take them out too. The postal service worked for a number of years, with Harry looking after mail and local information for both the English and the Dutch, but by the end of the 1630s the beach wanderers had eaten the island nearly clean of seals and penguins and returned to the mainland.

In the meantime, the Dutch continued the practice of taking Khoikhoi men off to Java to acquire interpreting skills. The English and the Dutch alike perceived African "click-languages" with their percussive consonants as virtually unlearnable, and they depended on Africans to learn European languages, however imperfectly, in order to do the necessary interpreting.

Khoikhoi women learned European languages in different circumstances. By mid-century, the Dutch East India Company had established a permanent mainland post at the Cape with Jan van Riebeeck as resident commander. Most of the employees who manned the new post were men who did not bring along their families, but Commander van Riebeeck did. In his household and a few others Khoikhoi girls received training as domestic servants. Their experiences were probably much like those of Sarah Winnemucca and the other Paiute women taken into settlers' homes to clean and cook and do the laundry, the sort of experiences young Luz Jiménez sought to avoid after the people of Milpa Alta were driven from their homes.

Among the Khoikhoi servants were two children, Sara and Eva. The story of Sara's life is quickly told. She was brought up from childhood to dress as a servant in a Dutch home and to attend church services. She learned to speak both Dutch and Portuguese, and she was paid wages for her work, which came to include sexual as well as domestic service. At age twenty-four, she committed suicide. The Dutch, having concluded that the Khoikhoi did indeed have souls and therefore were responsible for their sins, accorded her the same treatment they extended to their own suicides. They dragged her corpse through the streets and out of town, where they impaled it on a pole to rot away and be eaten by birds.[2]

Eva's story is a little longer in the telling. Richard Elphick, historian of the Khoikhoi, has described the beach wanderers as the most poverty-stricken members of Khoikhoi society, and also "refugees, outcasts, orphans, and other persons without family."[3] Yet Eva had family ties. Perhaps the Khoikhoi did not mean precisely what the Dutch did by kin-terms, but Eva was understood to be the niece of Harry, and among the better-off inland Khoikhoi she had a mother, a sister or female cousin, an aunt, and an uncle. For them her name was not Eva, but Krotoa.

That was one of her worlds. Her other world was the family circle of the van Riebeecks, where the Commander's wife raised her and educated her and instructed her in the Christian faith. The circumstances under which she had been handed over to the van Riebeecks are unknown, but like Sara, she grew up bilingual in Dutch and Khoikhoi and competent in Portuguese. And while she was still a child, Commander van Riebeeck began to use her services as an interpreter and advisor.

Five years or so after van Riebeeck took command, relations between the Dutch and the Khoikhoi were deteriorating. The East India Company sought to relieve the Cape post of its reliance on rice imported from Java by setting up farms around the fort. When the Khoikhoi saw their grazing land plowed up for planting and their herds' access to water restricted, they became alarmed. Moreover, the Khoikhoi on the peninsula immediately surrounding the Dutch settlement had profited from serving as middlemen between Europeans and the Khoikhoi of the interior. Now, through van Riebeeck's and Eva's diplomatic efforts, the Dutch were trading directly with inlanders to whom Eva had family ties.

As the local situation grew ever more hostile in the early summer of 1658, van Riebeeck, at Eva's advice, seized several prominent hostages in order to keep the threatening Khoikhoi in line. One of them was her uncle Harry. Eva testified against him, claiming that he had engaged in thievery and fraud against the Company. The herds that he had accumulated during his long career as agent for the Europeans were confiscated, and he was banished to the island at the mouth of the harbor.

Joining Eva in the testimony against Harry was another interpreter named Doman, just returned from a Dutch training trip to Java. What he had seen there, and what he now saw in van Riebeeck's use of hostage taking to manipulate the Khoikhoi, turned Doman against the Dutch and against Eva, whom he henceforth took every occasion to brand as a traitor.[4]

Shortly after the hostage crisis in which, despite being a very young girl, she had played a central role, Eva left the Dutch fort and went inland. Because she was then in her mid-teens, Elphick speculates that it was the occasion of her first menstruation, and she went to undergo initiation rites among her relatives.[5] She received a hostile reception; shunned by her mother, she was attacked, robbed, and driven off. Fortunately, she found refuge with her sister,[6] the wife of an influential Khoikhoi leader. During her stay with them, both Eva and her sister fell ill, and Eva took the occasion to demonstrate the power and consolation of Christian prayer. Upon the recovery of both women, Eva enjoyed marked respect in both the worlds she inhabited, much as Doña Marina is said to have in Mexico between the fall of Tenochtitlan and the fateful march to Honduras.

In the spring and summer of 1659 a one-year war began in which the Khoikhoi attempted to drive the Dutch from the peninsula, much as the Maya had tried to oust the Spanish from Yucatan. The Dutch were so concerned they brought Harry back from his exile to help, but it was Eva and a Dutch farmer who had maintained good relations with the Khoikhoi who conducted the negotiations that brought hostilities to a close.

Like Doña Marina's, Eva's life was destined to be short, and her descent was precipitate. Among the Khoikhoi, Doman worked against her, seeking to undo whatever she and van Riebeeck accomplished and making poisonous attacks upon her character and her religious beliefs. Ultimately he undermined his own position, but—judging from sub-sequent events—he must also have sowed seeds of doubt and despair in Eva.

The seeds germinated in the years after the conclusion of the war. Recurrent epidemics, unchecked by Christian prayer, struck the Cape three years in a row, beginning in 1661, greatly afflicting the Khoikhoi. In the midst of the misery van Riebeeck and his family moved on to a new post in Java, and Eva was left behind without a protector. Her brother-in-law, seeing no further use for her once van Riebeeck departed, grew unfriendly. Eva, who had so recently enjoyed positions of honor in two homes, found herself with none and joined other Africans who sold themselves on ships in the harbor.[7] Out of wedlock she bore one child and then another. Barely past twenty, she was by the moral standards of both the Dutch and the Khoikhoi utterly disgraced.

Yet a European reached out to save her, a respectable young Danish surgeon with a strong interest in the Khoikhoi. The two were married in a Dutch ceremony, and Eva received cash compensation for her past service to the Company. Together they moved out to the island where Harry had once been confined, and Eva resumed childbearing—three children in four years. But her world came crashing down again when her young husband was killed on an expedition to Madagascar, leaving her a widow with fatherless children to support.

Life was now hard indeed. The Dutch provided the family minimal housing at the fort and a modicum of social recognition, but Eva returned to prostitution and drink. Like Sarah Winnemucca, she grew bitterly critical of the people who had once fostered her, and with her drunken railing she made herself offensive to the Dutch. In her behavior they perceived sure evidence that Khoikhoi could not be civilized, no matter what advantages they were given. Threatened with banishment for her public criticism of the Dutch authorities, she deserted her children and attempted to flee to the Khoikhoi, but she was apprehended and shipped out to the island, where she lingered on for five years before dying in her early thirties. Since she had not taken her own life, the Dutch brought her body back to the mainland for proper Christian burial.[8]

Two Survivalists: *Dersu Uzala (ca. 1850–1908) and Ishi (ca. 1860–1916)*

The 1800s saw not just the exploration of the American West, but of the Asian Northeast as well. During the century European explorers of many nations fanned out through central and northern Asia, wherever the local populations did not prevent their passage, collecting and surveying as they went and publishing thrilling travel journals for audiences back home. As in North America, the travelers represented themselves as first visitors to new lands, not taking into account their guides and provisioners and the local peoples to whom Asia's vast expanses were as well known as the Great Basin was to the Paiutes and the Great Plains to the Sioux.

A Russian military surveyor named Arsenjev was the exception. While mapping the Pacific maritime province north of Korea and east of Manchuria he met a man named Dersu Uzala who became his guide and friend. Arsenjev was devoted to Dersu from the first and shared his

Russian home with him even as Dersu shared his forest life in the *taiga* with Arsenjev. When Dersu was murdered, an inconsolable Arsenjev published his account of their life together as a memorial.[9]

Russian explorers had entered the maritime province in the 1850s and met there aboriginal people known as the Goldi.[10] It was at about this time that Dersu was born. By the time Dersu and Arsenjev met a half-century later, northeast Asia was full of outsiders conducting scientific expeditions, making maps and laying out railroads, building towns and setting up businesses. Whole communities of Russian "Old Believers" had fled to these remote parts to avoid contact with the established Orthodox church, on which they perceived the mark of the anti-Christ. When he and Arsenjev met, Dersu spoke fluent, although nonstandard, Russian.

Dersu and his fellow Goldi had seen terrible changes during that half century. To newcomers, the taiga seemed a wilderness nearly empty of inhabitants and the Goldi a wild people living miserable lives. Just as the Dutch found the appearance and habits of the Khoikhoi offensive and Lewis and Clark were repelled by the looks of Northwest Coast Indian women and the circumstances of their lives, so were Russians—including Arsenjev—appalled by the tiny Goldi communities where the men always outnumbered the women, the women were addicted to opium, and parasite-ridden toddlers learned to beg tobacco before they stopped nursing at the breast.[11] Probably for Arsenjev one of the most attractive, ennobling aspects of Dersu was that he lived a solitary life outside these communities.

Yet the Goldi had not always been what Russian visitors found them to be in 1900, nor was the taiga of 1900 the same as the taiga of 1850. Through conversations with Dersu and with other forest people, Arsenjev pieced together the story of an all too familiar catastrophe.

The first round of Russian exploration of the Goldis' territory had been halted by Chinese who were there hunting ginseng root. Only after most of a decade were the Russians able to force their way back in and establish the ports of Vladivostok and Khabarovsk. In those early days, the Goldi and their neighbors had been much more numerous, but the ginseng hunters had found it easy to take their young women away from them, just as the Spanish had taken Andean Indian women for themselves. In the Chinese settlements, the women forgot their language, learned new ways, and raised children fathered by the Chinese. Disputes led to warfare among these communities, and then smallpox arrived and decimated the Goldi. To the demoralized remnant the Chinese introduced tobacco and opium, and the Russians brought alcohol. The people Arsenjev met on his expeditions were the dazed survivors.

The once well-inhabited forest had reverted to wilderness overrun by crashing packs of wild pigs that neither the Goldi nor the Chinese nor even the Siberian tiger could keep in check. But while the pigs increased exponentially, the wild game of the taiga was fast disappearing. Dersu predicted that the sables, elk, and squirrels would be driven to extinction in a decade, and Arsenjev agreed, noting that outsiders—Korean and Chinese—acted without feeling for conservation of resources. "On every side," he wrote, "one sees nothing but robbery and exploitation. In the not-distant future this land of Ussuria, so rich in animal life and forest, will be turned into a desert."[12] By the end of his account, he had tacitly added the Russians to his list of despoilers.

Within this vast forest once stable and sustaining, now unpredictable and dangerous, Dersu lived by himself without companions or permanent shelter. He was by no means antisocial; Arsenjev noted that he knew a great many people who were glad to see him and welcomed him into their homes. His personality was warm and outgoing, but he was also exceptional. Circumstance had marked his life with tragedy, and like his American contemporary Charles Eastman, Dersu sought solace beyond the reach of human society. Sleeping outdoors in storms and cold weather, owning practically nothing, meeting his own needs from whatever was at hand, reading signs and being exquisitely sensitive to all that transpired about him—for him as for Eastman, these were a source of spiritual power. And yet he was a man of words, and in Arsenjev he found an avid listener.

By Arsenjev's account, Dersu simply walked into camp one night in 1903, addressed Arsenjev as "Captain," and accompanied the expedition to its end, greatly facilitating work for Arsenjev and his company of cossacks. From the first evening, the two men sat up until all hours of the night and early morning talking while the men under Arsenjev's command slept. By the campfire, smoking his pipe and brewing tea, Dersu told the story of his life and the life of the taiga.

Once he had parents and a sister. Thirty years ago he had been a young family man himself with a wife and son and daughter. Smallpox had taken everyone away. No one must go near where they were buried. From his father he had an old rifle, and he traded with the Chinese for ammunition and his few other necessities. He conserved shells by trapping and snaring whenever possible and never wasting a shot. But when he did shoot, he was a crack marksman. His contempt for people who were wasteful, especially of the lives of animals, was boundless. Expecting to find a use for anything that came his way, he collected into his backpack whatever others discarded in the forest, and he collected languages too, in order to get along with outsiders.[13] From talking with an old Chinese hunter he had learned how to locate ginseng roots, and over many years he had transplanted the ones he found to a remote place where they were growing undisturbed as a sort of insurance policy for his old age.

Dersu astounded the Cossacks with his ability to read from the smallest signs of disturbance what had happened in the forest. From a partial footprint, he would weave a scenario of the traveler's ethnicity, where he had come from, where he was going, what he was carrying, and on and on. Pressed for an explanation of how he knew all this, he would analyze the evidence in the manner of Sherlock Holmes, convincing everyone and asking in some exasperation why they could not see for themselves. As Arsenjev put it, Dersu had learned "from lifelong habit, never to overlook details, and to be attentive to everything, and always observant. If he had not learnt from childhood to understand the art of tracking, he would have died of hunger."[14] In matters of woodcraft, Dersu and Charles Eastman would have been soulmates, although there was nothing whatsoever of the warrior in Dersu.

Arsenjev, for his part, was a naturalist who kept careful records of birds and plants he encountered, identifying them by their common and Latin names. From Dersu he learned meticulous observation of animal behavior. For plants he learned the uses to which the Goldi put them. Dersu also taught Arsenjev and his men how to anticipate weather changes, when to press forward in spite of rain, and when to stop and wait for storms to come up and blow over. The mighty winds that sent huge trees crashing down around them impressed the company even more than the winter cold, and most of all Arsenjev was impressed by the immense blackened swaths where forest fires set off by lightning strikes had burned themselves out unimpeded. Slowed to a crawl by an infected foot, Arsenjev was overtaken by one of these fires and only escaped through Dersu's level-headed assistance.[15] Day by day Dersu added to Arsenjev's abstract knowledge a virtuoso stock of survival skills. Arsenjev was pleased to learn, and Dersu—who had lost the opportunity to impart his knowledge to his own son—was anxious to teach.

Arsenjev regarded the Goldi as primitive people, and Dersu's behavior confirmed him in his belief. Dersu talked to animals and fire and the earth itself in the same conversational style he used with people, and he described as animate, and even human, things that to Arsenjev were obviously neither. To Arsenjev this was "animism," a clearly primitive religion. At one point in their travels, Arsenjev encountered a genuine shaman at work, but he looked upon the aboriginal religion of northern Eurasia as childish superstition.[16]

Despite Dersu's renown among the taiga dwellers and his tremendous powers of concentration, there is nothing in Arsenjev's account to suggest that he was a practitioner of María Sabina's flamboyant art. The governing principles of his life as Arsenjev observed them were of a piece with Charles Eastman's: perpetual alertness, rational understanding of what one observes, and solitary seeking of unity with the natural world. Arsenjev wrote, "Dersu worried his head not only about men, not only about animals, but even about such tiny creatures as ants. He loved the taigá itself with all its inhabitants, and took every kind of care of it." [17]

Locked as he was into his own cultural assumptions, Arsenjev nonetheless remarked time and again on how Dersu morally outshown his supposed superiors. When the Cossacks upon breaking camp of a morning tossed unused firewood onto the fire, Dersu chided them for wastefulness. When they had stayed at an empty house overnight, Dersu made sure that they left firewood, salt, and matches for the next person who might need to take shelter there. When they came upon abandoned pitfalls in the forest, Dersu saw to it that they filled them in. Arsenjev wrote, "Here was this savage far more thoughtful of others than I. Why is it that among town-dwellers this forethought for the interests of others has completely disappeared, though no doubt it was once there?" [18] Dersu, for his part, was astounded to learn that in Russia with its advanced civilization, just as in China, there were brigands, whereas the Goldi, totally lacking in bureaucracy, were also free of organized crime.

Such were the mutually exploratory conversations Dersu and Arsenjev carried on over five years. At the end of the first expedition in 1903, Arsenjev was distressed when Dersu bid the company farewell and went off about his own business. Arsenjev was kept from his surveying work while Russia fought and lost the brief Russo-Japanese War, but when he returned to the forest in 1906, Dersu soon located him. As Arsenjev had occasion to notice more than once, information traveled fast through the supposedly empty wilderness. When work ended for the year, Arsenjev and the Cossacks went to the Russian settlement of Khabarovsk, now accessible by railroad, and Dersu once again withdrew to the forest. After the third expedition in 1907, however, Dersu accompanied Arsenjev to Khabarovsk.

The circumstances that overcame Dersu's repugnance for urban life were the sum of traumatic experiences that had bound him and Arsenjev ever closer. In 1903 the two had been caught alone out on a frozen lake in a blizzard, and Dersu had saved them both by making a den for them. Under the snow, insulated by bundles of reeds Dersu had tied together after Arsenjev collapsed, the men kept each other warm as they slept out the storm.

Not long after, while hunting, Arsenjev caught a glimpse of Dersu, mistook him for a wild pig, and opened fire. Dersu was only bruised by his shot, but Arsenjev was distraught: "I could not forgive myself. The thought that I had shot the man to whom I owed my life was a torment. . . . That lifelong night I could not sleep. I could see nothing, hear nothing, and think nothing but the trees, the boars, my shot, the bush where Dersu crouched, and his cry of pain. . . . I tried to console myself by the thought that Dersu was, after all, alive and still with me, but it was of no avail."[19]

They had many more adventures and death-defying scrapes along the way, but the crisis that came down upon them during the 1907 expedition was at last one that Dersu could find no way out of. He was approaching the age of sixty, and over a six-month period his vision began to fail. When he realized that he could no longer hit a target, his composure deserted him. Shaken, he confided to Arsenjev that he had no idea how to live as anything other than a hunter. He had no heirs and only one significant possession, his ginseng plantation, which he now bequeathed to Arsenjev. Arsenjev, for his part, assured Dersu that they would live together in Khabarovsk and all would be well.

But what was possible in the taiga was not easily accomplished in a Russian town. They moved in together, but Arsenjev's Russian friends found Dersu a curiosity, and Dersu felt, as Arsenjev put it, "out of his element." Still, the two men continued to learn from each other. It came as a surprise to Dersu that Arsenjev put in long days of work in town just as he did in the field. Arsenjev, who had tried to collect wordlists from people he met in the forest, took the opportunity to make recordings of Dersu's speech: "He quickly understood what was wanted of him and made a long speech into the receiver which filled up almost the whole cylinder. Then I changed the film for a pronouncing one, and turned the machine on again. Dersu, on hearing his own voice coming back again out of the machine, was not the least surprised, and not a muscle of his face stirred. He listened attentively to the end and then said: 'Him,' pointing to the apparatus, 'talk true, not leave out one word.'"[20]

Arsenjev, despite his recording machine, was not a professional linguist and read a whole worldview into Dersu's choice of pronoun, concluding, "Dersu was incorrigible. He humanized even the phonograph."

Although he regarded the phonograph with equanimity, town ways distressed Dersu. He was uncomfortable indoors and got in trouble with the authorities when he went out. Having arrived in Khabarovsk in early January, he decided in early March to go back to the taiga and slipped away one night without saying good-bye. Outside town some riflemen saw him striding along looking happy. A few days later he was found murdered. Robbers had killed him as he slept, searched his body for money, and taken his old rifle.

Arsenjev was called to the place, not far from a railroad line. Technology was penetrating Dersu's taiga in disorienting ways with trains and steamboats and telegraph stations and even movies. As he waited for Dersu's grave to be dug, Arsenjev said, "I sat down by the road and buried myself in memories of the friend whom I had lost. As in the cinema, all the pictures of our past life together were unrolled before the eyes of my memory."[21]

In the spring of 1908 Dersu was buried where he had died in the midst of beautiful forest, his grave marked by two tall pines. Two years later Arsenjev returned to visit his grave only to find that the town had spread over the place. The trees were gone, and there were no landmarks. All around were dumps and quarries and embankments. Dersu's resting place was lost in general uglification.

Less than ten years after Arsenjev sat remembering his forest life with Dersu as though he were watching a movie, a man known as "the Last Wild Indian in North America" really was filmed demonstrating the sort of skills the Goldi had practiced a half-century earlier, the same skills Charles Eastman was just then trying to perpetuate by teaching them to the Boy Scouts and the Campfire Girls. For the camera the thoughtful-looking man who appeared anything but wild made fire with a drill, flaked arrow heads, shot with a bow, and showed how to construct a brush shelter.

He was known as Ishi, and he was a permanent resident in the museum on Parnassus Heights in San Francisco, where he demonstrated crafts to visitors and worked with University of California anthropologists who were investigating the structure of his language. He was the last person to speak it, the last Yahi Indian left alive. Until recently he had lived even more out of touch with white society than Charles Eastman had during his boyhood in the Canadian woods, far more apart than Dersu had ever lived from Chinese and Russian society.

At age fifty Ishi had been completely monolingual in Yahi, completely without skills for living in a city. Yet in a short time he had become a successful urbanite, traveling alone on trolleys and ferries, going to theaters and Wild West shows, shopping for his own groceries, earning wages and saving a portion of them. Life in San Francisco was far more tolerable for Ishi than life in Khabarovsk had been for Dersu just a few years before.

His protectors and companions were men of goodwill like Arsenjev, men who loved and admired him as Arsenjev had Dersu, and these Americans had more than their homes and friendship to offer Ishi; they had an institution with buildings and a budget and a public mission. Also contributing to Ishi's adjustment to life in the museum was the certainty that he could not go back home as Dersu had sought to. No matter where he went in all the world, there were no other Yahis. Completely alone, he could no longer survive on his ancestral lands. Ishi had the choice of living among strangers on a California Indian reservation, victimized like the Paiutes at Yakima, or staying with the anthropologists who held him in high esteem. Ishi listened to the alternatives proposed by a representative from the Bureau of Indian Affairs and stated that he would live in the museum to his dying day, and so he did.

When Ishi came to the museum in September of 1911, he was a half-century old and had lived in hiding since childhood. Throughout all those years he had observed white men and women go about their lives. He knew about their houses, because he sometimes broke into them in search of food. He was familiar with their domestic animals, because he and older Yahi men—when there still were others—stole them for meat and skins. He scavenged their abandoned camps and their dumps for glass bottles from which he made points for his arrows. And he knew about their railroads, because the sound of train whistles and the sight of steam and smoke plumes punctuated his days. But contact with white people had always been fatal to the Yahis.

The Yahis were part of the Yana Indians of northern California. In the twenty years after the 1849 gold rush, the other Yanas had been killed off. Like the Paiutes, they died of starvation as their traditional sources of food were destroyed by new settlers. They died of infections they had never before known, both childhood diseases and venereal diseases. Those who were removed to reservations for their own protection died there, and the ones who fled from the reservations or managed not to go to them in the first place were hunted down by armed vigilantes. Only the Yahis remained.[22]

The Yahis had a fearsome reputation among the settlers along Mill Creek and Deer Creek, the watercourses that defined their small territory. Although the warrior-worship and prideful coup-counting of the Plains Indians had no place in their culture, there is no doubt that they killed some settlers and stole much livestock and robbed many houses and camps. But the day came in 1870 when so many of them had been run to earth and killed that the few survivors tried to approach the white settlers and lay down their arms. Then at the last moment they lost confidence in their own peace initiative and fled.

At that point there were only twelve Yahis left on the face of the earth. Ishi was one of them, and he was about ten years old. For the next forty years he and the others kept the secret of their existence with such care that it would have been a challenge for even Dersu to track them. One by one their numbers diminished until they were only five: an old woman, a young woman, two older men, and Ishi. As with the Khoikhoi, sisters and female cousins were grouped together by the Yahis. Ishi and the young woman, whether she was sister to him or cousin, were prohibited from becoming man and wife. They all knew that they had outlived the time of Yahis on earth. After a while they were only four, an old man and woman and a no-longer-young man and woman.

In 1908 a company of surveyors planning a dam happened to walk straight into the Yahis' hidden home. Ishi's sister fled, dragging the old man with her. Ishi hid. His mother, too old and sick to flee, remained hidden under a pile of covers. The white men found her and left her unharmed, but the locals—in retribution for all the times the Yahis had raided their supplies—stripped the camp of everything that could be carried off. (This was an easy task, for the Yahis had almost no material possessions besides the men's fine arrows and the women's exquisitely woven baskets.) When they had left, Ishi carried his mother away to safety. He never saw his sister and the old man again, and his mother did not live much longer. Then Ishi was totally alone. In mourning he hacked off his hair, burned away what was left down to the scalp, and coated his head with pine pitch. For two years he lived on, already half-ghost, waiting to join the company of Yahis in the land of the dead. Finally weary of waiting, he walked out into the white world and gave himself up to whatever death they might deal him.

Instead he was taken into protective custody, given clothes, and offered food. He refused to eat, understood nothing of what was said to him, and waited for what might come next. What came was a graduate student from the University of California at Berkeley with a Yana wordlist. The Yana dialect was different from Ishi's Yahi, but the graduate student was gentle and patient, just as it turned out that Ishi was gentle and patient, and together they found words on the list that were enough like Ishi's for both to recognize them. Ishi gave his pronunciation; the graduate student, whose name was Thomas Waterman, adjusted his pronunciation to Ishi's example; they both understood, and a friendship was born. With Waterman, Ishi boarded a train (a monster he found as intimidating as young Charles Eastman had) and went to San Francisco to live at the museum.

In a short time, Ishi had not just one friend, but many. Besides

Waterman, the two closest were Professor Alfred Kroeber, head of the university's museum and anthropology department, and Dr. Saxton Pope, a teacher at the medical school next door to the museum. Ishi also had an admiring public, people who came to the museum to see him and returned again and again. Kroeber kept hoards of potential exploiters at bay, but Ishi appeared at museum receptions and went out in public to the theater and on sightseeing tours where he came into contact with large numbers of people.

Within a month of his arrival in San Francisco, Ishi was suffering from the first cold of his life. That winter he experienced pneumonia for the first time. Dr. Pope, who examined him and wrote a monograph on Ishi's medical history, found no evidence that he had ever been infected with any of the childhood diseases. Ishi recalled none and had no scars from chicken pox, much less smallpox. In fact, he had no scars at all. Nor were any of his teeth decayed.[23] Ishi was perfect, and that meant he was perfectly vulnerable.

Yet for a while he was spared. Choosing and preparing food to his own tastes, he gained weight. With medical students half his age, Ishi showed that he could climb a rope faster than anyone. Three years after he had given himself up for dead, he accompanied his university friends and Dr. Pope's eleven-year-old son back to the land between Deer Creek and Mill Creek and let them play Indian with him on a camping trip the likes of which they would never know again. The photographs taken that summer show Ishi living nearly naked, his hair grown out long and soft and shiny, a picture of health.

There in his home canyons he showed the anthropologists firsthand where and how the Yahi had lived and regaled them with stories and jokes. For Ishi was also a storyteller, and for years he had had no one to appreciate his art. With an audience at last, he told his friends at least forty different stories. Just as Dersu and Arsenjev had entertained themselves telling each other yarns all through the night, Ishi traded his stories for silly songs and dramatic poetry recitations around the campfire. A man who had had so little chance to share it, Ishi loved talk—his own and his friends'. As they hunted and fished and swam together in the summer of 1914, the party of men from the University of California were living out Charles Eastman's dream a year before Eastman opened his own summer camp in New Hampshire.

While his friends were engaged in all the ebullient horseplay, Ishi seemed entirely at one with them. Yet he had resisted the idea of returning to the creeks and canyons, and as the last days of the trip drew near, he grew anxious to get back to his museum home. Unlike them, Ishi lived in a world bounded by prohibitions. The anthropologists knew about them, but they did not observe them in their own lives, and their lack of observance spilled over onto Ishi at times. Yahi culture, for instance, was very protective of names. Ishi never told his friends what his name was. Under pressure to give the public something to call him, Kroeber said he should be referred to as *ishi* 'man', and thereafter, Ishi ceased using that word in his own vocabulary, a consequence Kroeber certainly did not have in mind.

Ishi would also have avoided menstruating women if he possibly could, but white women did not withdraw into seclusion as Yahi women had. No matter how much he kept to the company of men, Ishi was constantly exposed to their wives, to the nurses at the teaching hospital, to women on the streets and in stores. That the medical students performed autopsies and the anthropologists handled bones and mummified bodies in the museum collections also filled Ishi with anxiety, and his friends' enthusiasm for having him return to where all his people had died troubled him even more. Yet he placed his confidence in their superior powers and cooperated with them.

During the winter after the camping trip, Ishi began to exhibit the first symptoms of tuberculosis. By spring of 1915 the diagnosis was confirmed. At the time there was no other treatment for the disease but rest and nourishing food, and Ishi went to spend the summer with Waterman's family. The eminent linguist Edward Sapir came to Berkeley for the purpose of recording as much of the Yahi language as possible from its last speaker. By September Ishi was hospitalized under Dr. Pope's supervision, but nothing could be done to save him. His friends took him home to the museum next door to live out what remained of his life. Early in the spring Ishi drew his last breath, and left his public bereft. Letters came from all across the country. Waterman wrote, "He was the best friend I had in the world," and blamed Sapir for working Ishi too hard during his last summer, although it seems that it was Ishi rather than Sapir who was driven to get down as much of the Yahi language as possible while he still could.

Before his death Ishi's speech was captured both in writing and in recordings. In time the film of him demonstrating Yahi crafts self-destructed, but the sound recordings were successfully transferred to archive tapes, and so his voice remains in the world today. Theodora Kroeber, Kroeber's wife, became Ishi's biographer, producing a beautifully written, thoughtful book about American Indians, California history, and the deeply emotional and often joyful association of Ishi and his friends in the last years of his life. The title of her book is *Ishi in Two Worlds*, and in it she returns more than once to the theme of Ishi moving from a Stone Age world to ours.

One of Ishi's worlds ceased to exist when he lost the other three Yahis in 1908. The 1914 camping trip had been a recreation during which Yahi prohibitions had been flaunted. Not only did the party visit the sites of Yahi deaths and talk about them, but Kroeber and Pope had killed, cooked, and eaten a rattlesnake. Ishi expected them to die, but they had not. Even though he had refused to participate and convinced others in the party that they should not, did Ishi feel himself contaminated?

As he lay dying in his room in the museum, did he suspect that after all he had been right, and his friends' carelessness had killed him? Lacking the knowledge we have today about vulnerable immune systems and the transmission of infection, they had unintentionally doomed him when they taught him to stand in reception lines to greet people and shake hands with them, touching their skin, breathing their breath. Their world, however delightful, was a very dangerous one for Ishi, and he could not long survive in it.

Two Australians: *Chloe Grant (ca. 1903–1974) and George Watson (ca. 1899–1991)*

Australian Aborigines peopled their continent so many thousands of years ago that they have every right to say, "We have always been here." But like Sacajawea's and Sarah Winnemucca's peoples, Australia's original people lived so broadly on their home territories that Europeans did not recognize them as being connected with the land at all.

Therein lay nearly two centuries of troubles. European law required an owner to establish physical boundaries, clear land, erect buildings, and stay put. Places that were only visited at certain seasons, resources that were tapped without transformation of the landscape—such land was empty, ownerless, and available to be claimed. No matter that every inch of it was known and named and traveled. First with bullocks, then with dynamite and bulldozers, white newcomers have subjected Australia to development—clearing, fencing, obliterating the Aboriginal world.

Australia until the end of the 1700s was like the mainland Cortés reached in the second decade of the 1500s in this respect: although the people already there spoke more than two hundred languages that differed greatly among themselves, they had many cultural features in common. In the lands through which Doña Marina and Cortés passed, such features were readily visible: pyramid temples, sculptures of feathered serpents, painted books that folded between their covers like fans. In Australia the common cultural heritage was largely hidden from outsiders who did not know any of the languages. It lay in social and ritual organization so complex we could hardly keep track of it without a computer. And it was expressed in stories of the remote "dreamtime" when the vastness of the continent was charted and punctuated with landmarks, the time when places received their names. Even sparer in material culture than Ishi's people, the Australian Aborigines possessed an intellectual heritage that white society did not perceive until encountering it in their paintings. By the time dreamtime paintings began to appear in art galleries around the world, however, and Aboriginal artists had become celebrities, there were not many Aborigines left. The survivors no longer lived as they once had, and the languages were flickering out one by one.

R.M.W. Dixon, a linguist from Britain, recorded not one but many of northeast Australia's languages on the brink of oblivion, and among his Aboriginal partners in this enterprise were two remarkable people. In their working relationship and in their friendship with him, we catch resonances of Paraske and Neovius, Dersu and Arsenjev, Ishi and his friends at the museum.

Chloe Grant was born shortly after the turn of the century, probably in 1903, of an Irish father and an Aborigine mother. Her mother died in childbirth, and an older Aborigine woman took the infant girl to raise as her own. Chloe's childhood was passed in a less disturbed Aboriginal setting than those of many of her contemporaries because the mountain-ous rain forest of coastal Queensland did not attract large numbers of settlers. So it was that she learned a great deal of Aboriginal lore along with different dialects of Dyirbal, the language of the area. But it was not just freedom from white society that made Chloe so quick to learn about everything in Aboriginal society: styles of talking, ways of reading nature, Aboriginal law, stories from the beginning of time. She had a mind both receptive and critical, which manifested itself from childhood. Challenged by fearsome stories adults told to keep children in line, she would boldly test them and show them to be humbug. Her disruptive behavior was punished by ostracism and taunts about her ancestry, but she was not abandoned, as children of white fathers sometimes were.

Chloe was twelve before she was informed that her birth mother had died and that she had been adopted. She found the news unbelievable, but presented with the evidence of her mother's grave and her own lack of family resemblance to the people with whom she had grown up, she gradually accepted her new identity. What was important was how she had passed her childhood in the Murray Upper valley. Chloe could, in fact, speak more than one variety of Dyirbal: her mother's Girramay, her foster mother's Jirrbal, and Gulngay as well. When she discovered that Dixon imagined Dyirbal to be the same everywhere, she set about straightening him out, and so their work began. But that was in 1963, when only about sixty Aborigines were left living in the valley. Chloe was a widow by then.

Disruption of traditional ways of life had come to the area in 1913, four years after the Aborigines Protection Act was put into law to limit where Aborigines might live and travel. It also gave the Aborigines Protection Board the power to remove children from their families without showing cause, and soon all over the continent children were being taken away from their parents and sent to boarding schools to be trained as laborers and domestic servants. This was just the system Sarah Winnemucca had unsuccessfully opposed decades earlier in Washington. Now it had the full force of law in Australia.

Chloe was placed in a household to be a white child's companion, much as Sarah Winnemucca herself had been. There she learned to lay a table and wait on dinner guests, and of course she also became fluent in English, which she spoke not with the cultivated perfection of Eva's Dutch, but with color and imagination and wit. When a storm destroyed the mission to which she had been sent, teen-aged Chloe took advantage of the confusion to run away and save herself from a lifetime of doing other people's housework and looking after other people's children.

Within a couple of years of escaping back to Aboriginal life, Chloe was married. The marriage was long-lasting, and through it all the couple worked hard, taking jobs where they could find them. At least at the end of the working day, Chloe had a home and husband to return to. And the years brought many children: eleven, of whom eight survived infancy. When Dixon met Chloe, the youngest were still living with her, and she was looking after grandchildren as well.

Dixon's impressions are telling. He wrote, "The Europeans looked askance at Chloe, certainly the most knowledgeable and intelligent person we met in Murray Upper; she was too sassy by far." Her sassiness expressed itself in her refusal to be pushed around; when Dixon first came to visit, Chloe—like Paraske—was resisting eviction. It also was there in her exasperation with what other Aborigines had been providing to Dixon. "They should have more sense," she snapped. "You didn't come all the way from London for: 'Where are you going? Oh, going up.' You wait till I tell them what I think of what they say into machine." She herself provided long stories, switching easily from dialect to dialect, voice to voice for different characters. Among them was a grand story about the coming of Captain Cook to the coast of Queensland, of the distaste of the people he met there for his tea and johnnycake, and their desolation when he sailed away.[24]

Dixon was fortunate in having met Chloe at the very beginning of his acquaintance with Australia's Aborigines and their languages. For over eleven years they worked together, Chloe providing, criticizing, and correcting. At one point, recording her life story, she added to the end a message to the government expressing thanks for sending "Robert Dixon, out from England to learn our language."[25]

They both loved what they were doing. Dixon said, "Chloe was a natural linguist. Given the proper educational opportunities she could well have been doing my job."[26] Describing their work, Dixon wrote of himself, "Chloe Grant became his main teacher (and his best friend), working hard each and every day at recording texts, helping to transcribe those others had given, and going through a large vocabulary with a sample sentence for each word. Chloe combined intelligence, ebullience and a great gift for explanation with a wicked curiosity."[27] That curiosity reached a deeply personal level: "Chloe and I knew about as much about each other's lives and families and beliefs and ideas as any two people could."[28]

The strength of her personality and the warmth of her friendship with Dixon—forty years younger than she, just married and starting a family as well as a career when they first began their collaboration—suffuses Dixon's memoirs, which he published a decade after her death. After its publication he wrote that he considered *Searching for Aboriginal Languages: Memoirs of a Field Worker* to be "effectively a biography of Chloe Grant."[29]

Although none were quite as close to his heart as Chloe, Dixon had many Aborigine friends—people he respected and whose company he enjoyed. Perhaps first among his men friends was George Watson. Like Chloe, George had a white father. By George's own account, his mother intended to kill him at birth, but her sister, who had also borne a child fathered by a white man, intervened and said she would raise the two children together. In the end, it was his grandfather, whose wife had been murdered by yet another white man, who looked after the little boy and taught him how to live the traditional Aboriginal life.

As he grew up, however, George had to find a way to make a living for himself, and so he went to work for white settlers. Then it happened that a character trait that should have been an asset became a millstone around his neck. He was such a strong and steady laborer that whoever employed him did everything possible to keep him from leaving, and the law restricting the movements of Aborigines was on their side. To begin with, it was a matter of persuasion. He was told that he was such a good worker that he should never even think of going back to Aboriginal life. This had its intended effect, and when his relatives came to see him, he refused to go off with them.

Not so long after, persuasion turned to compulsion. Now a full-grown man, he took up with an Aboriginal woman who was in service to the mistress of the local train station. Concerned about the consequences of their relationship, George worked even more for extra cash. When he was paid, he bought supplies and moved on, but his companion was not so easily abandoned. She, too, ran away and joined him in the bush, where they camped together and avoided the search parties looking for her.

News that his mother was dying brought George back to the edge of town, where he disarmed a policeman who tried to apprehend him. In the end a whole party of police caught and arrested George and his woman friend. She was sent back to her employer, and he was sentenced to a term on Palm Island, a semi-penal colony off the Queensland coast. "When I went there," he recalled, "I was really a slave, working all the time." He was set to clearing forest with bullocks, and later became a bulldozer operator. Now as before, his diligence was his undoing. He heard secondhand that the managers said among themselves, "He's a good man. We'll keep him here. We won't let him go home." With quiet irony he remarked, "I got a bit tired after being there forty years."[30]

When they were still children, Chloe Grant had been promised in marriage to George Watson, but he had been sent away, and she had chosen her own husband. This was just as well, since George found the Murray Upper valley a gloomy place and preferred to live in more open country. Moreover, his type of Dyirbal, Mamu, was different yet again from the upcountry dialects Chloe commanded, and it was for this reason she highly recommended George to Dixon.

When Dixon went to Palm Island to meet George, he found him married and living with his wife in a settlement of about a thousand Aborigines from all over Queensland. The residents of Palm Island were not just men convicted of such crimes as resisting arrest, but also women and children. On the island, children were moved into dormitories at age eight and permitted only brief weekend visits with their families. Compliance with the rules of the settlement were enforced by carrot-and-stick: small payments for each task performed, jailing for infractions—methods not so different from the ones used in Milpa Alta to get parents to give up their traditional way of dressing and to send their children to school. Aboriginal languages could not be used as a means of communication on Palm Island, and the children learned little of their parents' traditions.

The island was a linguistic and cultural death camp, yet it was also beautiful and relatively safe from violent crime. From time to time, when George approached the authorities about leaving, he was told that life on the outside was perilous and he did not know how to manage it. Instead, he was recruited to the force of native policemen who kept peace on the island and was eventually promoted to the rank of sergeant.

In spite of the restrictions placed on his life, George Watson had served as a linguistic informant for a Catholic priest-linguist in the 1940s. He had given the priest one of his several Aboriginal names, and he gave Dixon another, so it came as a surprise when George recognized a published text in Dixon's possession as a story he himself had told twenty years before. At the time he had left pieces out of the story out of respect for the priest's sensibilities, and he relished the opportunity to go over the priest's transcription and translation—correcting, explaining, and amplifying for Dixon. Given the chance, he plunged into linguistic work with the same inexhaustibility he brought to clearing brush, hauling logs, and building dams.

Dixon's company strengthened George Watson's resolve to leave Palm Island once and for all, and he acted to loosen the hold of the supervisors. In defiance of the strict racial separation maintained on the island, George insisted that Dixon come to do his recording at his home and to share a meal with him and his wife there. When the staff perceived him as developing into a potential troublemaker, they were willing to let him and his wife leave. Settled on the mainland, they had the opportunity to renew contacts with Aborigines in their home territories and to visit with Chloe Grant after a lifetime of separation.

Dixon wrote of his two Aboriginal colleagues, "Chloe and George both had extraordinarily intelligent minds, but used them very differently. I could get through things more quickly with Chloe—her responses were immediate, almost instinctive. George, on the other hand, would always think a question through and give a measured, deliberate answer. Chloe would sometimes go back and correct what she had just said, or think a question through in the evening and tell it to me from a different angle the next day. George rarely did." [31]

George's wife died in 1970, but he continued an active life on the mainland for another fifteen years. From 1977 to 1984 he accompanied Dixon on yearly field trips to compile a comprehensive dictionary of all ten dialects of Dyirbal, assisting him in locating speakers of varieties other than those he and Chloe spoke and getting them to cooperate with Dixon. When old age finally caught up with him, he returned to Palm Island, where the management had by then passed into the hands of the Aborigines who lived there. For a while he lived with his daughter, and then he took his place at the Old Men's Home. There his life concluded in just short of a century.

FROM THE AZORES ISLANDS TO PEMBROKE COLLEGE:
Laurinda Andrade (1899–1980)

On the other side of the globe from the island continent of Australia lies the Azorean island of Terceira. In a small village on that small island another intellectually gifted child was born at the turn of the century. Her family was disappointed that the baby was a girl, and in years to come they were more bothered by her brilliance than pleased about it. Like her age-mate Luz Jiménez, Laurinda Andrade had a craving for schooling from the time she could walk, a passion for knowledge, and a career dream. Like Doña Luz, Laurinda's ambition was to be a teacher, and despite world war and world economic depression, in the face of obstructionism, prejudice, and virulent jealousy she succeeded in becoming a teacher of Portuguese language and culture in New Bedford, Massachusetts.

Late in life she, too, wrote a book about her journey away from the community into which she had been born, a world rich but inflexible in its traditions, to a different world of ideas and individualism. For her the break was profound and irreversible. In the first part of *The Open Door*, she writes about herself and her Azorean childhood in the third person. In the second and third parts, after she has stepped through the door by emigrating from her island to the U.S., she continues her story in the first person. Now, at last, Laurinda becomes "I."

Yet in the U.S. she capitalized on being Portuguese. She found housing and community among Portuguese factory workers, made her way through high school and college as an immigrant prodigy, took her degree in Romance languages, got her start in employment after college working on Portuguese newspapers, moved on to a Washington job assisting the Portuguese envoy, and finally was able to establish Portuguese classes in the New Bedford school system. All along the way she broke the ice with strangers by telling fortunes, as she had learned to do as a child in the Azores. Being Portuguese was her meal ticket as being Indian had been for Doña Luz.

The fortune-telling part she resented even as she made use of it; the rest was central to her worldview. It seemed obvious to her that the United States with its large Portuguese immigrant communities should take a strong interest in Portugal and Brazil and that she should be professionally employed in a way that made use of her cultivated Portuguese/English bilingualism. She had something of the air of Guaman Poma as she insistently presented her arguments and her credentials, trying to get the attention of potential employers who appeared oblivious to the facts that their schools were full of Portuguese-American students, that their courts needed interpreters, and that their banks needed people to manage their Brazilian accounts.

One of her few moments of uncompromised triumph was commencement day in June 1931, when Laurinda Andrade, at age 31, received her baccalaureate degree from Pembroke College in Rhode Island. Looking back on her life from that point her accomplishment was remarkable.

She had been born into a society that advanced its boys and kept its girls at home. Her father vacillated between treating her like a son and treating her like a daughter. Whenever she managed to get into school, she did not know how long she might stay before he pulled her out. As a very small child she conceived a resentment of boys and picked fights with them. More than once she was expelled from school for being disruptive. Yet her well-to-do godparents saw her potential and sought to give her refuge and the opportunity to be educated. Unfortunately, their special attention drew envy and criticism down on Laurinda. She knew that she was bright, but as she recalled, her relatives and neighbors worked incessantly at convincing her that she was odd, unlikable, and destined for failure.

Two childhood revelations, one provided by a cow and the other by a curate, comforted and sustained her in the face of harassment. One day at the village fountain, local women teased her about "the fancy idea of becoming a teacher." Just then a farmer came to water his cows. While the others drank from the trough, one cow lifted her head and drank straight from the fresh stream of incoming water. The farmer and the women at the fountain laughed at the cow and called her *esquisita* 'strange', the same adjective they often used to torment Laurinda. In an instant Laurinda realized that being out of the ordinary might mean taking a higher road.

Her other liberating experience came in the course of instruction for first communion. She wrote: "Significant here is the fact that under the zeal and guidance of that inspiring curate, Laurinda got the answer to her most perplexing question. God had made her! Boys and girls were both made by Him. He and He alone determined Who and What, without inferiority or superiority. . . . Let people talk and look down on females, it would not matter any more." Later on she refers to "my life-long belief in the general intellectual equality of both sexes."[32] Throughout her autobiography she emphasizes the sustaining role that Catholic devotion of a very personal sort—unmediated, it seems, by any male authority fig-ure—played in her life.

She never had any ambition to marry. On the contrary, the flame of her ambition to become a teacher was fanned by her desire to avoid marriage. Not only did her father thwart her consuming desire for learn-ing, but her parents' marriage was far from happy. Her father's betrayals and autocratic ways hardened her resolve never to be dependent on a man. Her later experiences with other Portuguese men in the U.S., even very well meaning ones, convinced her that traditional Portuguese family structure was pernicious, and she wrote a newspaper column to that effect. As for non-Portuguese men in the U.S., she apparently never took them seriously, nor on the other hand does her autobiography record any inclination toward becoming a nun. Her single stated goal was, as she wrote it with capital letters and exclamation point, "EMANCIPATION!"[33]

In the spring of 1917, in a world engulfed by war, she emancipated herself by walking onto a steamboat headed for Rhode Island. Sons of Azorean families had been taking this step for decades, launching forth for Brazil, New England, California, Hawaii. For several years Laurinda had been providing a reading and writing service for these emigrant Azoreans and their illiterate relatives left behind on Terceira. Through the letters she read aloud, she had learned a great deal about the world at large, and she was ready to go forth to it herself.

Other Azorean women and girls who set out across the Atlantic were on their way to join male relatives who had gone on ahead. Laurinda was on her own and had to attach herself to people who were not kin and often felt little responsibility for her. For the next several years she often would find herself left behind, slandered, shut out by people she had looked upon as protectors, but eventually she found a place for herself with a Portuguese landlady and her dressmaker daughter, women who became her loyal adopted family without whose support her subsequent educational achievements would have been impossible.

Beginning was difficult. Laurinda took her place among the other Portuguese laborers in New England textile mills, and within a year she was felled by tuberculosis. Undernourished and inadequately dressed, sleeping in crowded boarding houses and spending the days in great halls of workers, she succumbed to the omnipresent infection sooner than Ishi had, but she had youth on her side and within months recovered enough to return to work. In the meantime she had been housed, fed, and cared for *gratis* in a Portuguese workers' boarding house, and she had used the empty hours of her convalescence to study English on her own through books and conversation with American-born Portuguese.

While she was still bedridden, her father demanded that she return home to take the place of one sister who had recently married and another who had died. "He had never grasped the extent to which his daughter's mind had been stretched to the idea of finding freedom through knowledge," she wrote. With no resources of her own and dependent on charity, her answer to him from the boarding house was that she had left "for better or for worse and for good." When fellow workers took up a collection to pay for her passage back to Terceira, she used the money to buy a coat instead.[34]

Soon after that Laurinda rented a room from an ambitious family that had taken over an abandoned house. At the time Francisco Garcia and his wife were living there with their factory-worker son Frank, their seamstress daughter Albertina, and their American-born daughter Alice. By joining in the hard work of renovation, Laurinda made herself welcome, and the Garcia family became her own for the rest of their lives together. Although her brother arrived from Terceira, following in his sister's footsteps three years after she had emigrated, the siblings saw little of each other and went their separate ways.

Laurinda's position in the Garcia family was strengthened by the deaths of both Francisco Garcia and his son followed in a matter of months by Alice's, apparently all victims of tuberculosis. Senhora Garcia and her surviving daughter, who chose to go by the name of Albertina Grace, managed to keep their house by taking in more boarders and building up Albertina's dressmaking business. In the midst of this, Laurinda announced that if she could just manage to go to school, she was sure she could complete teacher's training in English and work as a professional. Unlike other Portuguese women who ridiculed Laurinda's ambition, Albertina Grace and her mother helped her find the tutoring she needed to attend high school.

From that point on, Laurinda's progress was mercurial. Teachers in New Bedford High School found nothing odd about her desire for education. They encouraged her, praised her, and moved her on. As she approached graduation, her history teacher dismissed her plans to enter a two-year teacher's training program and told her that the place for her was in a four-year liberal arts college. He assured her that there were scholarships available and that he and his wife would provide her with a supplement if one were needed. Laurinda's high school graduation was marked by publicity in both English- and Portuguese-language newspapers, and a scholarship did indeed materialize. In the fall Laurinda moved into a Catholic women's residence in Providence and matriculated at Pembroke College.

College years were marked by exhaustion, a tubercular relapse, and other health problems along with anxieties about courses and about the collapsing world economy. Yet Laurinda survived her required composition, mathematics, and geology courses and insisted on majoring in Romance languages, adding French, Italian, and Spanish to her native Portuguese. During her undergraduate years she satisfied her yearning for teaching by taking on Americanization classes for newly arrived adult immigrants, and she herself learned a great deal more about the U.S. beyond the Portuguese community from her younger Pembroke classmates and their families. One of the things she and her classmates came to see and dread was that they were about to graduate into the Great Depression. There might have been a job for a woman who had taken a two-year teacher's training course and received a teaching certificate. For the young women graduating from Pembroke in 1931, prospects were bleak.

It would be another eleven years before Laurinda would be able to begin teaching. In the meantime, she tried everything, offering her language skills to courts, banks, and businesses. Time and again she was told to acquire secretarial skills, which she did, but no matter what skills she brought with her, she was told that others were needed. When she had received U.S. citizenship, the presiding judge had said, "You are completing your college education, and you intend to remain here as an American citizen. Well, we are glad to have you as one of us, Miss Andrade." Once out seeking employment, she encountered an altogether different American attitude. "We gave you an education," said one interviewer; "Why don't you go back to your country and use it there?"[35] She was told that her "appearance and bearing" worked against her, and she was advised to practice shorthand. Although she buries the matter in euphemism, her autobiography suggests she was propositioned by prospective employers. Only fortune telling seemed to interest people, and that she steadfastly refused to do for income.

A job with a Portuguese-language newspaper saved the day, and from there Laurinda moved on to a secretarial position at the Portuguese legation. In Washington she resumed her life of frequent changes in living quarters while maintaining her base with Albertina and her mother in New Bedford. In 1937, as the Spanish Civil War cast apprehension over Portuguese communities everywhere, the three women made a trip together to Terceira, where Laurinda found herself estranged from the family she had left twenty years before. Emigrant children were expected to send money back to their families, and she had not, nor did she intend to begin. She was hurt by her relatives' expectations and turned away from them, going off to visit the other islands of the Azores and on to Lisbon, a tourist in the country that so totally defined her identity.

Returning to the U.S. as the world plunged once again toward global war, she urgently sought employment teaching Portuguese in the New Bedford schools, and days after the Japanese attack on Pearl Harbor, she at last received a contract. Leaving wartime Washington behind, she finally began her teaching career in January 1942.

RAIN FOREST WOMAN: *Dayuma (ca. 1932–)*

In the twentieth-century life of Dayuma, a woman of the Ecuadorian rain forest people known as the Huaorani,[36] the experiences of all the other individuals we have met heretofore come together. She was a guide into unmapped territory, an interpreter and teacher of her language, a missionary assistant, a native informant for linguists, a person violently separated from her people and made a participant in a world of undreamed-of technology. A New York publisher brought out her biography in 1960, with an update in 1973, and her stories—both traditional ones and retellings of biblical stories—have been preserved on records and in print. Like Ishi she was said to have emerged from a Stone Age culture, and for a while she was a celebrity.[37]

Dayuma's world lies over the Andes from Guaman Poma's in the Amazon Basin, a jungle-and-river vastness rich in animals and fish, richer yet in insects and flowers, bushes, vines, and trees. Until very recently it was regarded as a green monster to be tamed. Only now, almost too late, has the outside world begun to perceive it as a storehouse of riches to be protected.

The Huaorani, on the other hand, have been fighting to protect their piece of the rain forest for centuries on end. Until the latter half of this century, they had been more successful than the Aztecs, the Sioux, the Goldi, the Khoikhoi, the Dyirbal, or any of the other peoples we have met in these pages, and they paid the price for their implacability in blood and in public opinion.

In the Ecuadorian lowlands there are two words for Indians; those Christianized and acculturated are known as "Quichuas," and the rest, the wild Indians, have been called "Aucas." "Quichua" is the local form of the word "Quechua," and reflects the perception that all civilizing influences have descended into the Amazonian forests from the Peruvian highlands. Quechua was the language of the Inca state, and then it was the language of the Catholic evangelists. To become a Quichua was to accept a language and a religion and a manner of dress and a place within a money economy, all imposed by outsiders.

"Auca" is a Quechua word that means 'enemy'. To be an Auca was to speak one's own language, maintain one's own beliefs, decorate one's body according to the customs of one's kin, and enjoy self-sufficiency from one's own garden and the abundance of the rain forest. People who lived on the margins of the forest and sought to exploit it perceived the Aucas—the Huaorani and many of their neighbors—as murderous primitive people. This perception was shared by those who saw in the Huaorani souls to be saved. Because they turned violence in upon themselves as well as outward against the invaders, the "Aucas" appeared to be first and foremost their own worst enemies.

The events of the last decades have shown that however much the rain forest people wrought havoc upon each other with blood feuds, their intuition that foreigners would ultimately spell their doom was on the mark. Today the Amazonian rain forest has been despoiled by oil exploration, gold mining, and monoculture plantations, each with its own kind of toxic waste. A vast national forest and a reserve for the surviving Huaorani were established by the Ecuadorian government, yet the burgeoning population and the pressing economic need of the rest of the country continue to bear down on what is left of the realm its defenders guarded so fiercely and so long.

When Dayuma was born in the 1930s, outsiders seeking new sources of rubber, gold, and petroleum had been persistently intruding into Huaorani territory for more than half a century, and the Huaorani were resisting these incursions with the only help they had: their fearsome reputation, their spears, and the impenetrability of their forest. But explorers kept forging down the trails, and overhead there was ever-increasing air traffic. Like any endangered species in a shrinking habitat, the Huaorani came more and more often into contact with outsiders who plundered their homes and food supplies, with armed work crews who shot at them with their guns, and with settlers who were terrified of them. These moments of contact were fraught with heart-stopping fear, desperation, and frequent violence. The Huaorani experience was much like that of the Yahi in northern California.

The stress was taking its toll on Huaorani society. For a period in the past, they said, they had lived peaceably with each other, but about the time Dayuma's baby teeth were being replaced by permanent ones, the Huaorani men began a new round of savaging each other. If a man took multiple wives, sooner or later jealous bachelors would do him in. Likewise a man put his life in danger by spurning an invitation to go raiding against the invading "foreigners." (The Huaorani made no distinction between Quichuas and non-Indians, but the Quichuas were easier targets.) Uninvolved relatives were not spared, and neither were women and children. The spears struck at all: foreigners and Huaorani, men and women, adults and children.

Even in more normal times, the lives of rain forest children were precarious. They shared the forest with boas and jaguars, and when storms struck, huge trees crashed down around them just as they came down upon the Goldi in Dersu's far-away taiga. Family groups were vitally dependent on their men; starvation or violent death loomed for a widowed woman with little children unless she could persuade another man to take them all under his protection right away. Rather than risk the chance, a dying father might order that some or all of his children be buried with him in his grave, or mothers would take the initiative of strangling the youngest or weakest of them. If a child would slow flight from danger or expose its mother's hiding place by crying, the only solution at hand was to abandon it. And, despite the shortage of marriageable women, female infants might be dispatched at birth for no more reason than their gender.

Adult life was also bedeviled. Night brought the fear of malevolent blood-sucking spirits to the Huaorani, and they believed that some individuals had the power to kill by curse alone, without resort to spears. Even people with no ill intent might be possessed by animal spirits that wore them out with wrangling and left them suffering from headaches and exhaustion. Such was the fate of Dayuma's storyteller grandfather, who had to contend with a pair of internal jaguars constantly snarling and spitting and predicting doom to the Huaorani.

But as a little girl, Dayuma lived in mortal terror not of her grandfather's jaguars but of being done to death by her own mother. All her life, she said, was shadowed by the memory of the time her father had been missing for several days and her mother informed her that after one more day of his absence she would strangle and bury her. Her father returned, and the child was spared, but her trust was never restored. From that time she was inclined to take her chances with the foreigners, despite rumors that they ate human flesh. Against that day she began to learn Quichua words from a captive kept by her family, and when her father did fall to Huaorani spears, Dayuma and one of her cousins fled with the Quichua girl to the outside world.

Her father and little sister and their relatives were dead—speared or hacked to pieces. Her mother had survived but refused to leave the forest. In 1947, at about the same age as Doña Marina and Sacajawea had been when their lives were violently redirected, Dayuma ceased to live with her family and passed into involuntary servitude.

Her fate could have been worse. She and her two companions walked into a rubber camp established by Don Carlos Sevilla, a colorful landholder who was known as "the Daniel Boone of Ecuador." Sevilla had carved out haciendas and personally led rubber exploration parties in the Huaorani forest, over the years accumulating battle scars and adventure tales to go with them. He had also accumulated a work force of Quichuas for his enterprises and was inclined to accumulate "Aucas" as well. He went out to meet the employees who had received Dayuma, her cousin, and the Quichua escapee when they came out of the forest and took the girls back to his Hacienda Ila, where he put them to work as field hands toting bananas.

Three times Dayuma tried to leave, and three times she was brought back. Later, telling her relatives about her long sojourn in the outside world, she explained, "I was not able to return. I lived in another foreigner's house. I told him I would return to my family. He was angry." [38]

Giving up on escape, teenaged Dayuma became the wife of one of Sevilla's Quichua laborers, a man named Miguel. She bore two sons before a measles epidemic carried off her husband and their infant and nearly killed Dayuma herself. Oblivious to her surviving son, she sought escape through suicide but found herself too weak to get to water to drown herself and unable to maintain her death fast to the end. When, in spite of herself, she began to recover, she went back to the hard labor of the hacienda.

In 1955 Dayuma had been away from the forest for eight years. She was an adult woman with a six-year-old son, and she was finding her widow's life hard. She was completely dependent on Sevilla to provide subsistence for her and the boy Ignacio. Since she had to leave him to fend for himself while she worked long hours in Sevilla's plantation fields, Ignacio had learned only Quichua and none of his mother's native language. Even for her it had grown rusty with disuse. Drunkenness and sexual predation were part of the fabric of everyday life. When death came yet again and claimed Miguel's aunt Olimpia, with whom she and Ignacio had taken refuge, Dayuma belligerently demanded a gun from Sevilla so that she could return to the forest to take vengeance on her father's murderer. She was on the way to joining her fate with all those Maya and Sioux and Khoikhoi and Aboriginal Australians who had given up on life, drunk until their livers burned out, and died of "sullenness." The year 1955 marked a nadir and a turning point for Dayuma.

Her desperation on the day she confronted Sevilla distracted her from a new job assignment. Sevilla was on cordial terms with members of the Summer Institute of Linguistics (SIL), the same Bible-translation organization that was at work among the Mazatecs in María Sabina's hometown in Oaxaca. In Ecuador Protestant missionaries had for quite a while enjoyed a working relationship with the oil companies, making use of their bases to spread the gospel to the local Indians. A man with an eye for opportunities, Sevilla had bought up machinery from Shell Oil when the company, under relentless attack by the Huaorani, gave up on exploration in the area. In 1955 the machinery was still stored at the Hacienda Ila for future use, and trucks were rusting away out on an overgrown road. Sevilla saw clearly that aircraft were the way of the future. The Protestant ministry was supported with planes and radio equipment, and Sevilla lay plans for building airstrips and attracting them to his holdings. The "Aucas" at Hacienda Ila were a magnet for the Bible translators, and Sevilla permitted two of their linguists to come there to work on the language. As their native informant he chose Dayuma from among the Huaorani living on his haciendas.

The beginning phase was not easy. The first work session was interrupted by the news of Olimpia's sudden death and Dayuma's demand for a gun and her freedom. As she began to regain her composure, and the linguists Rachel Saint and Catherine Peeke got to know her, they learned that Dayuma was to have no released time from her unremitting field labor to work with them. Rachel Saint expressed day-to-day frustration as she watched Dayuma weed fields and haul heavy loads from sunup until she sank down in exhaustion at night. Yet nonetheless, armed with what little was already known about the language of the Huaorani, and through Catherine Peeke's and Dayuma's shared knowledge of the language of the Quichuas, the language-learning enterprise was begun.

Dayuma's physical exhaustion was not the only barrier to their efforts. She had been immersed in the Quichua world for eight years. Her husband, son, and in-laws all spoke their language, and so did the people at the hacienda, from fieldhands right up to the *patrón* Sevilla himself. It seemed at first that her own native language was moribund. But believing it to be impossible to lose one's first language, Rachel Saint set about helping Dayuma remember the language of her parents and family. As they went along, Dayuma recalled ever more vocabulary and began speaking in whole sentences, telling about her childhood in the rain forest. There was just one part of the language of the Huaorani that she seemed unable to recover. Rachel Saint wrote, "There is a rhythm and melody to this language that Dayuma has lost through the years outside the tribe." Later Saint evoked gales of laughter from Dayuma's forest-living relatives as she tried to learn that elusive melody.[39]

According to Ethel Emily Wallis, who was assigned to write about Dayuma's life and work with Rachel Saint, informant work from the beginning was congenial to Dayuma: "She began eagerly to anticipate the few hours when she was free to teach her language. . . . It became a game and Dayuma joined the fun with zest." And more, it provided a welcome diversion from preoccupation with loss, grief, and anger. In teaching them her language, Wallis says, Dayuma "found an unexpected motive for living."[40] The various linguists who had contact with Dayuma over the years found her to be ever-cheerful, outgoing, obliging and helpful—the sort of virtues we have seen attributed to Doña Marina and Sacajawea and that were most certainly characteristic of Doña Luz, Paraske, María Sabina, Dersu, and Chloe Grant. Like them, Dayuma combined an extraordinary memory with infinite patience for repetition and explanation. These are traits that make for harmonious, often joyful working relationships. In Doña Luz they undeniably gave her an air of girlishness even when she was a grandmother. In the case of Dayuma, the SIL workers always thought of her as a "girl" and a "little sister" although she was manifestly a mature woman and mother as well as an individual of incisive intelligence whose life had been replete with violence.

One thing that Dayuma was not was a free agent. Over time Sevilla conceded more of her time to the missionaries, until in 1958 he released her and Ignacio to Rachel Saint for full-time evangelical work, causing Dayuma some anxiety about who would feed and clothe the two of them in the future. The SIL workers, too, had a claim on Dayuma's life, albeit in more subtle ways than Sevilla had. In the beginning she worked with them because she was told to. Then, as their relationship matured, she was bound to them by other ties. Their shared interest in locating Dayuma's family group offered her a chance of leaving hacienda life behind permanently. Then came bloodshed.

In January 1956, less than a year after Rachel Saint began language study with Dayuma, her brother and four fellow missionaries who been flying over Huaorani territory landed their plane and made contact with some of Dayuma's relatives in the forest. Huaorani men speared all five missionaries and destroyed their plane. News of the young men's deaths drew worldwide attention to the Huaorani and brought journalists to Sevilla's haciendas seeking Dayuma's services as a guide. Rachel Saint, who had been away at the time, returned to continue work with Dayuma, whom Sevilla transferred to a different hacienda and promoted to house girl. Now the two women were bound by the fact that Rachel Saint's brother was dead, and Dayuma's people had killed him. Within Huaorani culture this would have meant inevitable blood revenge. For the missionaries it was an opportunity to teach the lessons of Christian forgiveness.

It was suggested that Dayuma herself fly over the forest in a plane broadcasting messages through a loudspeaker, but Rachel Saint argued against it on several grounds: first, that Dayuma was only beginning to learn about the Christian message; second, that the SIL workers did not yet have sufficient grasp of her language to understand what she might say to people on the ground; and third, that they could not afford to put at risk their only native informant.

Rachel Saint's arguments prevailed until the following spring, when a new scheme was presented. She and Dayuma were to fly to Hollywood to appear with Sevilla on the *Daniel Boone* television show where, like María Sabina and Ishi, Dayuma would serve as a living exhibit and Rachel Saint would be her interpreter.

By the 1950s it was well known that individuals from isolated populations such as the Yahi and the Huaorani are profoundly vulnerable to infections that are at most a nuisance to people who live in dense populations, and Dayuma had already nearly lost her life to measles. Rachel Saint was apprehensive for Dayuma's health and also for the effects of culture shock. A television appearance seemed, however, a heaven-sent opportunity to gain support for the efforts of the Bible translators. Rachel Saint sought and found through prayer assurance that Dayuma would survive. Ignacio was left in the care of others on the hacienda, and the two women set out by plane from the Amazonian lowlands of Ecuador to the Los Angeles Basin.

As it turned out, the call to appear with Sevilla on the *Daniel Boone* show was a ruse to bring Rachel Saint to Hollywood to be featured on Ralph Edwards's *This Is Your Life*. A year and a half after the deaths of her brother and his four companions, her life and career were relived with her parents, surviving brother, and SIL colleagues before an audience of thirty million television viewers.

Before the cameras Dayuma was joined by Tariri, a Shapra Indian flown in from the forests of Amazonian Peru, a man with whom Rachel Saint had worked before dedicating herself to the Huaorani. After the broadcast, Tariri and Dayuma were taken along with everyone else to a public reception where they were surrounded by crowds of curious people before they were finally able to escape to hotel rooms. Not surprisingly, by the next day Dayuma was burning with fever.

Rachel Saint did not look for help from the hotel's house physician nor at a hospital emergency room, but from a Christian cardiologist who solicited from Dayuma a testimony about her faith and, having received it, sought healing through prayer. Half a year later, when Dayuma fell ill in the 1957 influenza pandemic, Rachel Saint took a similar course, calling across country to a Christian physician with experience in Peru rather than committing Dayuma to local medical practice.

When Dayuma had left Ignacio behind in Ecuador, she and Rachel Saint expected to return soon. But now that Dayuma was in the U.S., they undertook air travel back and forth across the country, visiting members and supporters of the Bible translators, Rachel Saint's relatives, and SIL facilities where Dayuma worked long hours teaching her language. In New York City Dayuma was brought before Billy Graham's crusade in Madison Square Garden to give her public testimony.

From time to time Dayuma was besieged by homesickness and anxiety, but she was kept busy with work, air travel, sightseeing, and Christian instruction. Far from Ecuador and her son, a receptive Dayuma was being persuaded that the Huaorani lived in darkness and that she could lead them into the light of salvation. Return was delayed and delayed yet again, and then Dayuma collapsed, stricken by influenza.

During her long convalescence Dayuma asked with ever-increasing importunity for Ignacio to be brought to her. Finally she made a direct appeal to one of the evangelist pilots, who fetched her boy to her nearly nine months after she had left him behind.

As Dayuma experienced autumn and winter weather for the first time in her life in Arkansas, more Huaorani women left the forest back in Ecuador. Missionaries joined them, including Elizabeth Elliot, widow of one of the men who had been killed with Rachel Saint's brother. Too weak to travel home, Dayuma exchanged tape recorded messages with the women and learned what had happened after she left the forest a decade before. Many of the people she asked about, relatives and enemies alike, were dead, but others had survived, and the speakers on the tapes arriving from Ecuador were relatives of Dayuma's mother.

In the spring of 1958 Dayuma requested baptism and was flown to Illinois for a multilingual ceremony in which she also dedicated Ignacio to her new faith. She was now to return to the Huaorani as a missionary. At last, nearly a year after she had left Ecuador, she was returned to the SIL base at the edge of the rain forest. Soon after her arrival, a plane brought Elizabeth Elliot and the two Huaorani women to meet her.

From them Dayuma learned that her mother was alive and had made persistent efforts to learn about her daughter's fate. The women also told their version of the missionaries' overflights, Huaorani ambivalence about the gifts they had dropped down to them, and the lucid argument that led to their deaths: "There are only five of them now, but more may come. They might kill us all."[41] And so it was that Rachel Saint's brother, Elizabeth Elliot's husband, and their three companions were speared to death on the river beach next to their plane.

In three years of working with Rachel Saint, Dayuma—the granddaughter of a noted storyteller—had become adept at hearing biblical stories and retelling them as Huaorani stories are told. She had done this to great effect in Madison Square Garden. Bernal Díaz tells us that Doña Marina skillfully recast messages from Cortés to Nahuatl speakers, but we have no sure examples of her public addresses. Dayuma's narrative art, like that of Doña Luz Jiménez, has been recorded and published.

At the SIL base Dayuma practiced her missionary skills on her aunts, but she hesitated to return to the forest, apprehensive that after her twelve-year absence she would be treated as an outsider. Finally, committing Ignacio to the care of Rachel Saint, she set out to rejoin her Huaorani family.

A month later she returned safely and prepared to take Rachel Saint, Elizabeth Elliot, and the Elliots' four-year-old daughter into the forest to meet the Huaorani. She had left instructions for one of her kinsmen to build a shelter for the women she had gone to fetch. Little did she know that he had been warned that the hut he was building would be his own grave.[42]

Resentment toward Dayuma had been kindled not because she had been forgotten or had grown too strange during her absence, but because she and her aunts had brought respiratory infections back with them. Everyone came down with running noses and fevers, and people began to die. The Huaorani discussed spearing Dayuma and anyone she brought with her on a subsequent trip. But instead they welcomed the missionary women with the blonde child, although they found them peculiar with their blue eyes "like rain" and "dry" tongues that spoke their language strangely.[43]

In the course of several visits, Dayuma instructed her relatives in her acquired faith and taught them prayers and hymns, while the visiting women continued to learn the language. Beyond the forest, Ignacio was in school, but eventually he was brought into the forest and began to learn to speak the language of his forest kin. He took on teaching the Huaorani how to operate a wind-up record player and play records of Dayuma telling biblical stories in their language and provided company and reassurance to two of the group who were flown to the town of Limoncocha for a month to see how the foreigners really lived.[44]

On Dayuma's initiative her family group cleared an airstrip close by their houses and gardens. This place called Tiwaeno was to be an outpost from which light might spread to other Huaorani downriver deep in their spear-wielding heart of darkness. The missionaries saw it as not only a place where Christian instruction could go on, but also as a safe haven for the Huaorani from the oil explorers entering their territory. On their map of Huaorani territory, they labeled the corner around Tiwaeno "Dayuma's

Auca Protectorate," and late in the 1960s, they managed to get the government of Ecuador to so designate it.[45] From their point of view, it was not so much a matter of protecting the Huaorani from injury and death at the hands of the outsiders, but of saving the Huaorani from the sin of taking lives. Tiwaeno represented a dual effort: to wean the Huaorani from killing each other and to dissuade them from killing intruders.

What had been created bore resemblance to the earlier Catholic *congregaciones* and the North American Indian agencies where Indians were concentrated for instruction and assimilation out of the way of non-Indians. Like Sarah Winnemucca a century earlier, Dayuma and other members of her group went forth repeatedly to bring in their free-roaming relatives from their now perilous traditional area.

The forest-dwelling Huaorani were now being approached on three fronts. As the oil explorers went on cutting trails, and the Tiwaeno Christian Huaorani came down streams and footpaths seeking them, overhead the missionaries' planes flew low over the forest on the lookout for garden clearings and thatched roofs. When they found Huaorani, they called to them with loudspeakers and dropped radio transmitters into their midst. Subjected to constant overflights of small planes and helicopters, the Huaorani began to respond to the message to come to Tiwaeno, and there they came to realize their long battle was lost. At Tiwaeno the missionaries maintained a map of Huaroani territory on which they recorded the advance of the oil trails. When a man recently arrived from downriver understood it, he fell to the ground and upon recovery declared, "Fearing for my children, I got fainthearted."[46]

Although the missionaries had not planned for it, there was as much to fear at Tiwaeno. The arriving groups of downriver people needed more food than the existing gardens and immediate forest area could provide, and the community became dependent on relief supplies flown in from outside. Overcrowding and the differing practices of Christian and traditional Huaorani strained everyone's patience. Increased contact between Huaorani and outsiders brought waves of respiratory infections, and then in 1969 polio came to Tiwaeno. Even Rachel Saint fell victim to it. A group that had come from downriver departed again, declaring that Tiwaeno was "a place of death."[47]

Dayuma had made an irrevocable commitment to Tiwaeno. In 1962 she married a Huaorani man there and resumed childbearing. As others became active in advancing the Christian message, she led a more circumscribed life, staying at home while her husband and another Tiwaeno man accompanied Rachel Saint to Europe in 1966. She also remained behind when her son made a return visit to the U.S. in 1971 to speak at rallies and appear on television. While looking after her children, one of them born blind, she was assisting in the translation of the New Testament. More resilient than Ishi, Dayuma had survived measles, influenza, and difficult childbirth to live and raise her second family amidst the transformation of traditional Huaorani life. Her family withstood the 1969 polio epidemic that decimated other families, but in 1972 her blind daughter drowned.

In retrospect Elizabeth Elliot expressed some skepticism about the enterprise in which they had engaged Dayuma. She wrote, "I think of the Indians themselves—what bewilderment, what inconvenience, what disorientation, what uprooting, what actual diseases (polio, for example) they suffered because we got to them at last!"[48]

Rachel Saint lived with the Huaorani for twenty years. Toward the end of that time a Catholic missionary, Alejandro Labaca Ugarte, took up the challenge to reach the same people. For a decade he shared their forest life as Rachel Saint had done. He also brought in others—in this case nuns—and arranged for young Huaorani to visit Catholic schools to learn about the outside world. Building on the policy of the Protestant missionaries in previous decades, Labaca successfully worked for the establishment in 1979 of the Yasuní National Forest and reserve to protect the Huaorani. Then one day in 1987, hoping to reach an as-yet-uncontacted group, he had himself and a companion flown in to where an unfamiliar thatched roof had been spotted from the air. Within hours the two were speared to death just as the five Protestant men had been more than thirty years previously, before the mission to the Huaorani began.[49]

Fewer than 1,500 Huaorani have survived into the 1990s. They recently joined with other Ecuadorian Indian groups in a confederation to reclaim traditional lands, and then, unsure of who might have their best interests at heart, withdrew again. In 1990 the Ecuadorian government granted them legal title to an area ten times larger than the overcrowded protectorate to which they have been confined for so long. Joy in this apparent victory turned to disillusionment, however, when the Huaorani discovered that they had only received title to the surface of the land and were prohibited by law from interfering with extraction of oil from beneath it. Oil rights within the Yasuní National Forest were granted to Conoco, and almost all the Huaorani traditional lands fell within the concession. Under intense public scrutiny and protest, Conoco withdrew, and now another oil company has come forward with promises of environmentally and socially responsible exploration and extraction. Only time will tell if this is feasible. Although the Yasuní National Forest has been designated a world center for plant diversity, the forest's people have not been similarly well served by the civilization to which they were brought so unwillingly. Some Huaorani are now living in towns, buying rice instead of cultivating their gardens, while their men work for the money they need by clearing trails and detonating explosives. Such is the legacy left to Dayuma's children and grandchildren.[50]

There is, however, a second legacy. In the last five hundred years many of the languages of the world have died, leaving behind barely a trace of themselves. Like extinct species of plants and animals, these languages cannot be recovered. For that we are all the poorer, since with each extinction we lose information about the potential diversity of life and language. Through Dayuma's work with the missionary linguists, the language of the Huaorani will be preserved whether or not the Huaorani continue as a distinct people.

What Was Won
and What It Cost

It is said we have an indentation between upper lip and nose because as we come into the world all-knowing, an angel places a finger to our mouths and whispers, "Shhh." The individuals we have met here were born under other auspices. Attendant at their births was a spirit that touched their tongues and ushered them into interesting times. So it was that they were fated to speak of worlds in collision and of encounters that brought both rewards and ruin.

Broadening though it was, it was not their work as interpreters that made unconventional people of them. For one reason or another, they had already been set apart before they began to speak to outsiders, and it was their very isolation that rendered them available and capable of doing the job. For some of these people the marginalization process had been brutal: Doña Marina given as a child into the hands of strangers and traded as a piece of merchandise, Sacajawea treated in much the same way, Dayuma fleeing from forest violence to plantation bondage. For others the dominant note is tragedy: the solitude of Dersu and Ishi left behind after everyone else had died. Gender has its particular role; among these interpreters are single women and widows, women with no children or few children or children already grown, individuals less bound to home and community by the conditions that circumscribe other women's lives.

Some of the circumstances that set these people apart were strongly positive ones: a special aptitude for language-learning, an unusually reflective turn of mind, striking intellectual acuity. In societies where such traits are cultivated only in men, a woman so gifted is congenitally marginal. Worse yet, conspicuous brilliance, especially when accorded public recognition, seems to attract malicious treatment with depressing inevitability. Laurinda Andrade, so beset as a girl growing up in the Azores, stands as a particularly unambiguous case, but all the people we have met here impressed others with their out-of-the-ordinary intelligence, and most of them suffered for it.

Nancy Farriss, writing about the life of the Maya in colonial Yucatan, speaks of the perceived threat represented by men like Gaspar Antonio Chi:

> Such marginal people can be dangerous not merely in the symbolic sense of taboo . . . but also in a very practical sense that may underlie the taboo. These people make others uneasy by challenging an orderly system of classification. . . . If the Spanish were not prepared to grant full equality to talented Maya nobles, . . . they were wise to see the risk in granting them the semblance of it. For if such men ceased to think of themselves fully as Indians, yet were not accepted as Spaniards, their equivocal social identity and sense of frustration would simply make them more likely to challenge the system, and their understanding of Spanish ways would make the challenge that much more dangerous.[1]

This applies as well to other Indian men—Guaman Poma de Ayala among them. Far north of the Rio Grande in Anglo-America similar apprehension underlay the repellent bureaucratic mistreatment of Charles Eastman.

And the women's rewards, if such they may be called? Sarah Winnemucca was branded a whore in her lifetime, Doña Marina mythologized into a traitorous whore after her death, Eva abandoned to prostitution, Paraske ostracized in Sakkola, María Sabina burned out of home and livelihood in Huautla, Chloe Grant resented by her Aboriginal cousins and by white society alike for being too uppity. Like Dayuma, they all must have intuited—sooner or later, and for the most part sooner—that people were out to get them and that without powerful allies, they had no future.

Anxiety must have been no stranger to all these interpreters, men and women alike, as they balanced precariously on the margins of their several worlds. Unprotected by their own communities and at the mercy of powerful external forces, they formed connections with outsiders for better or for worse. I would compare the experiences of Doña Marina and Gaspar Antonio Chi to that of Patty Hearst. While very young—and initially involuntarily—they were incorporated into ideologically rigid groups dominated by men who used violence as a tool to achieve their goals. Others—like Ishi and Dersu, Paraske and Doña Luz—became attached to people of transcendent, albeit sometimes ineffective, decency. In the face of shifting loyalties all around them, some—like Doña Marina—remained steadfastly loyal to the end. Others—Gaspar Antonio and Guaman Poma, for instance—detached themselves from their early associations. And a number—Guaman Poma, Eva, Sarah Winnemucca, Charles Eastman, and María Sabina—gave bitter voice to their disenchantment.

Where had they come from? What had they hoped to gain? And in the end, for each of them, what had the enterprise cost?

The worlds into which they were born had been none too comfortable before the advent of the collisions. Although the successors of Columbus have brought disasters of hideous proportions upon indigenous peoples, right up to the present-day devastation of the forest peoples of the Amazon Basin, they have had no exclusive monopoly on intolerance, exploitation, violence, and disease. Khoikhoi and Goldi and Australian Aborigines; Andeans and Aztecs and Maya; Sioux, Shoshones, and Paiutes; even, perhaps, those remote Karelians who lived at the edges of the White Sea—all had generally better health so long as they remained unexposed to epidemics spread from the dense population centers of Eurasia. But while indigenous peoples enjoyed the benefits of relative isolation, they also endured as a matter of course periodic famine, commonplace encounters with dangerous animals, and the natural disasters of floods and wildfires, violent storms and volcanic eruptions. Death was a familiar companion, whether swift, lingering, or helped along in the name of expediency or compassion. In sum, not all suffering has been visited upon the world's peoples by urbanization and the age of discovery.

Besides such external sources of distress, the various traditional societies from which these interpreters came were all replete with mechanisms of social control that to a greater or lesser degree impinged on the lives of individuals. Some kept warfare out on the borders, as did the Inca Empire before it was afflicted with civil war, but in others—the nineteenth-century Sioux and the twentieth-century Huaorani, for instance—bloody deeds could be expected to visit home and hearth without warning at almost any time.

Within families, emotional attachments were contravened: parents' for children destined for the ruler or the gods; childrens' for parents who might leave them behind or let them be taken away; wives' for warrior husbands; relatives' for individuals accused of social transgressions; young Ohiyesa's for his beloved dog.

Nor was rigid class structure solely a European invention. It was a core feature, as we have seen, in the Inca state and among the Maya and

Aztecs. Class consciousness went hand-in-glove with contempt and lack of compassion for those perceived to be situated lower down the social scale. Chimalpahin, one of the great Nahua historians, wrote in considerable disgust that there was no way to know whether a particular Spaniard was of noble or common descent back in Spain, and that these men indiscriminately impregnated Indian noblewomen and poor commoners alike, producing mestizos who generally had a better opinion of themselves than they deserved.[2] As witnessed in the writing of Isabel Ramírez Castañeda from Milpa Alta, distinction of elite and commoner survived within Mexican Indian communities into the twentieth century. Among the Khoikhoi, the well-born and well-connected despised the beach wanderers, and lineage was a central preoccupation of Australian Aborigines and Sioux alike. Charles Eastman, who demonstrated so much sensitivity to Sioux kinship in devising European-style family names, was no democrat. In the same vein as Chimalpahin, he wrote that white intermarriage with low-class Indians inevitably produced contemptible half-breeds, whereas only a match between a superior Indian and a white of good breeding could come to any good.[3]

We should not romanticize self-contained, ethnocentric societies (including, most especially, our own) or turn a blind eye to their negative aspects. Broad perspective, tolerance, and willingness to find value in others' societies have been and remain more the exception than the rule among us humans. Consider Guaman Poma's hatred of so many groups: mestizos, women, priests, Jews, Englishmen. His anti-Semitism is to be found throughout the Americas, from which Jews were initially excluded in principle if not in fact. Its European counterpart made its way to the most remote Karelian and Ingrian villages, where folk poets wove lines into their songs about how "evil Jews, demons, and pagans" killed and devoured people. As late as the summer of 1936 an elderly grandmother traveled to Lubeck to sing such a song to an approving audience.[4]

Reflexive intolerance is to be found in many a culture, and where Christian evangelists have gone, they have capitalized on it. In battling indigenous religions in Europe and the Americas, they set up Jews and Muslims as the common enemy against whom church and new converts might unite. If there were few or no Jews or Moors or Mongols or Tartars around, all the better, for popular imagination can create them in fantastic form. Hence the enduring popularity of the flamboyant dances of Indian Latin America enacting battles between angels and Moors, shepherds and devils.

Stigmatizing of one's neighbors hardly needs religious missionizing to set it off, however. Ethnicity and language serve as well. Before Cortés planted foot and cross on the mainland, the peoples of Mesoamerica, from Yucatan to the Pacific and from the northern deserts to the isthmus, were organized into mutually hostile city-states. The last chapter in Book 10 of the *Florentine Codex* summarizes Aztec stereotypes of their neighbors: Huastec and Tarascan men went about with their genitals exposed, and neither Tarascan men nor women knew how to cook. The Tlalhuica were cowardly, the vain and gaudy Otomí were also stupid blockheads, and the Tlappaneca "were just like the Otomí; yet they were really worse."[5] People whose language was intelligible to the Aztecs had "clear speech" (*nahuatl*); everyone else spoke "gibberish" (*popoloca*).

On the other side of the globe, as the nineteenth-century scientific explorers traveled north and east from Moscow, they discovered languages related to Finnish spoken from the Kazan bend of the Volga River across the Ural Mountains to remote parts of Siberia. The easternmost members of this language family were spoken by people more like the Goldi and their neighbors than like Europeans, and the Scandinavian neighbors of the Finns seized upon this to brand the Finns "Mongols" and "Turanians." English travelers abroad in Finland in Paraske's time enjoyed imagining themselves in the company of fair-haired Chinese. Anxious Finns scrutinized themselves in mirrors for prominent cheekbones, pug noses, and epicanthic folds and then cast the slur onto their nearest neighbors, baiting Ingrians with the twin taunts of "Russkie" and "Mongol."

The Americas and Europe alike have been pervaded by fear of malevolent sorcery, the victims of suspicion likely to be old people, women without men in their households, and others who stand apart in some marked way. Doña Marina became associated early with La Llorona, the Mexican version of Lilith, a shrieking wraith of a woman who haunts deserted places and threatens men and children. The friars were convinced that their Indian students were concealing demonic practices behind an outward semblance of Christian devotion. The Protestant missionaries labored hard against Huaorani belief in the power of sorcerers, while they themselves had no doubt of the reality of satanic possession. Elaine Goodale did not believe that Sioux grandmothers had supernatural powers, but she respected and denounced their ability to frighten family and community with predictions of death and disaster. In Sakkola people edged away from acerbic old Paraske, and people in Huautla gave María Sabina good reason to fear. When her family urged on her a second marriage, it must have been in part because having a man in the house, even if he were himself a sorcerer, was safer than living with a widow who profited from the Wise Ones' art. And then there was the odd predicament of Laurinda Andrade; her academic credentials held little interest for potential employers who instead pressed money on her to tell their fortunes.

Not that everyone was an entirely innocent victim of baseless suspicion; María Sabina would have been the first to claim all the power of the Wise Ones. But it was in no one's interest to be shunned or persecuted. That treatment easily comes unbidden to people on the edges, even as it did to the poor wretches condemned in the seventeenth-century Salem witch trials.

Marginalization and its attendant dangers threaten both men and women, but the special vulnerability of women has been easy to overlook. A society's view of itself, the one transmitted by its offical historians, is not necessarily the way its women individually experience it. For instance, when a Maya writers' cooperative was established in Mexico some years ago, all its charter members were men. The productions of these men, laudably enough, focused on preserving Maya folklore and transmitting it as a living tradition to succeeding generations. Recently two women joined the cooperative, and they have since written searing social commentary dealing with alcoholism, domestic violence, and inequities of power within families. The men's goal, with its appeal to the wisdom of the elders and its nostalgia for the Maya past, has been conservative and didactic, while the women cry out for dynamic social change.[6]

Consider the widespread intolerance of children born out of wedlock and the condemnation of their mothers. The Aztecs and their neighbors condemned unsanctioned sexual activity, and punished it with death.[7] According to the *Florentine Codex,* a parent instructed a young daughter as follows: "My youngest one, dove, if thou art to live on earth, do not know two men. . . . If it become discovered of thee, thou wilt be cast on the road, thou wilt be dragged on the road, thy head will be crushed with a stone, thy head will be fractured."[8]

When Tenochtitlan had finally and irrevocably fallen to the Spaniards, Bernal Díaz writes that the Aztec ruler Cuauhtemoc requested of Cortés that the noblewomen carried off by the Spaniards be returned to their husbands and fathers, and Cortés agreed that any who wished to return home could do so. A house-to-house search was made, and many noblewomen were found, but according to Bernal Díaz, they—like Doña Marina—declared their hatred for idolatry. Besides many of them already knew themselves to be pregnant, so of them all only three took advantage of the opportunity to return to their families.[9]

Bernal Díaz may have fabricated or misconstrued the Aztec noblewomen's enthusiasm for deliverance from the indigenous religion, but what fate could they have faced had they returned pregnant to the homes of their husbands and fathers?

Charles Eastman and Mary Eastman before him relate the shaming of young Sioux women accused of inchastity. Elaine Goodale wrote of the

Sioux, "No virtuous girl or young married woman might venture abroad unaccompanied. To meet men openly, look frankly in the eye, walk, and talk with them and retain her reputation was, according to the old code, impossible."[10] The two children born to Eva before her marriage branded her a fallen woman in the eyes of Khoikhoi and Dutch alike. At one point Paraske tried to add an extra pair of helping hands to her household by taking in an unmarried mother and her child and was roundly censured by the people of Sakkola for doing so. Doña Luz never moved back to Milpa Alta after Concha was born.

And then there were the haunting memories of narrowly averted infanticide. Disposal of inconvenient children was by no means peculiar to the St. Petersburg foundling hospital and the rain-forest Huaorani. Sarah Winnemucca wrote that Paiute women so despaired of protecting their daughters from rape that they didn't even want to give birth to them. According to Bernal Díaz, Doña Marina's mother and brother were terrified when they learned she was still alive. George Watson, born at the very end of the nineteenth century, said that his mother intended to kill him at birth, and he was only saved when his aunt offered to take him. In similar fashion one of Charles Eastman's grandmothers rescued him from infanticide at the hands of his other grandmother.

It is hardly difficult to see why these bright, not very secure individuals would be ambivalent about their own societies and open to engagement with outsiders. Among outsiders they found protectors, allies, intellectual companions, and replacement for lost kin, to say nothing of employers. There is no evidence that Doña Marina was romantically in love with Cortés, but what he did for her was to raise her from slavery, protect her from other Spanish men by making her his own, unite her in legitimate marriage with one of his lieutenants, and endow their wedding with a substantial income. Lewis and Clark stood up for Sacajawea against Charbonneau on their trip to the Pacific Northwest, provided means for getting her a horse to ride, and nursed her when she was ill. They respected her wish to see the coast with her own eyes, and after their return Clark—for better or worse—supported and educated at least one of her children.

As a child Sarah Winnemucca found an affectionate second family in the Ormsbys, in whose home she learned English, reading and writing, and a model of behavior entirely different from that of the Paiutes, things she would put to use in her subsequent public life. Later the Parrishes and finally the Peabody sisters inspired her, supported her, and gave her at least a chance to realize some of her ambitions. Meanwhile a number of military men took on the role of her protector, employing her and writing letters in her defense when she came under attack, and some of them—the least competent—marrying her.

Gaspar Antonio Chi had the Franciscans to thank for his education, from which foundation he launched his civic career. When he broke with Diego de Landa, it was to pass into the protective sphere of another Franciscan, Bishop Toral, and when he had outlived them both, he advertised himself as the protégé of two bishops. His satisfaction in assisting the encomenderos of Yucatan in responding to the king's questionnaire must have been much like that of Chloe Grant and George Watson in their work with Dixon and much like Ishi's satisfaction as he patiently labored with Sapir during the last summer of his life.

Guaman Poma obviously did not have such friends as he composed his report for a distant king. But at some time in the past he had surely received education in a religious house, working as an assistant to evangelists and reading the books in their library before breaking off and perhaps assuming a new or altered persona in the process. His voice is of the sort of person Farriss describes, an Indian who has come to know and understand the colonizers and their ways on the closest possible terms; a disgruntled protégé turned bitter critic.

Sarah Winnemucca's experience was not so different, though perhaps less extreme. She too used the education she had received from the outsiders to verbally attack them, and she too created a persona for herself. Whereas Guaman Poma had to draw pictures of himself as he wanted to be perceived, Sarah had at her disposal the photo studios that followed along in the wake of white settlement. Like Guaman Poma and Gaspar Antonio both, she improved upon her family background, making claims for her immediate ancestors that were a bit more royal than real. And whereas Guaman Poma and Gaspar Antonio had at their disposal European paper and ink to make their statements in single vulnerable manuscripts, she had the advantage of book publishers, the newspaper industry, and the lecture circuit to take her case to very large audiences.

Charles Eastman also took his message to a mass audience, and to Sarah's one book, he had many. He had mentors, warm encouragement and support, and much positive publicity before he ran into the wall of racism and bureaucratic corruption. He and Elaine Goodale knew well how to use the public forum to make their views known, and they worked that forum to the ends of their lives, long after their political views had irreconcilably diverged.

Sharp as his criticism of white society was, Eastman never ceased to delight in taking part in its public ceremonies: leading Dartmouth processions, attending Mark Twain's seventieth birthday party, speaking at Oxford University, and at the age of seventy riding to the hounds in full English riding dress. As an earnest young man, he may have found public scrutiny irksome, and the mudslinging during the years when he tried to serve the Sioux had been an agony, but in the end he was as much sustained by his celebrity status as by his rather antisocial philosophy. On tour he made himself at home in great cities of the world—London, Boston, New York—and betweentimes he might live alone on his Canadian island; the one place he could not live (and this had probably been true since his midteens) was as a Sioux among the Sioux. Reunited in Canada with Mysterious Medicine twenty years after his father had taken him away, he wrote: "My uncle was so happy that tears welled up in his eyes. . . . The early days were recalled as we feasted together, and all agreed the chances were I should have been killed before reaching the age of twenty, if I had remained among them."[11] Perhaps what he had gained from the Presbyterian missionaries at Flandreau was a life.

The work of translation, informing, putting things on record—getting things down right, as Chloe Grant viewed it—was compelling for the interpreters. Most of them relished their work, even though it might be dangerous and exhausting. Bernal Díaz describes Doña Marina as ever ready to work and very good at it; the missionary linguists at the Hacienda Ila credited Dayuma's work as a linguistic informant with delivering her from deep depression. In between we find Gaspar Antonio's pride in his craft; Eva's brief period of triumph as she advised van Riebeeck and taught Christian prayer to the Khoikhoi; Larin Paraske's smiling self-satisfaction caught for all time in Järnefelt's drawing. There are Doña Luz's anxious attempts to obtain copies of the 1942 American publication of her stories as evidence that she was a person of substance,[12] and María Sabina's delight in receiving books and records of her chants that she had so willingly elucidated to the Cowans. We see Ishi pushing on past exhaustion to be sure that the Yahi language would survive him; Dersu, Doña Luz, Chloe Grant, and George Watson all patiently adapting themselves to recording their languages for posterity, all taking supreme satisfaction in doing it.

Even for the most distressed interpreters, their work was all-absorbing. Sarah Winnemucca made more public appearances on the East Coast lecture circuit than seems humanly possible. Guaman Poma went on and on writing of the abuse of the Andeans and drawing his appalling illustrations of the violence. Charles Eastman turned out book after book and traveled thousands of miles to speak to audiences across two continents. While seeking employment after graduation and again in her retirement Laurinda Andrade devoted herself to writing about growing up poor and female in the Azores and achieving emancipation against all odds.

No one doubted for a moment that they had something important to say, something that king and czar, president and pope, scientists and humanists and humankind in general would profit from hearing. Is it any wonder that many of the interpreters cherished partnerships with outsiders who gave their voices scope in the greater world beyond the ones into which they had been born?

Rescue, protection, sustenance, recognition, companionship—these, I think, are what the interpreters won. And beyond these personal benefits, many of them believed deeply that they were working in the best interests of their own people. Guaman Poma, Sarah Winnemucca, Charles Eastman, and Laurinda Andrade convinced themselves of this. Doña Marina, Gaspar Antonio, and Dayuma assisted evangelists who were utterly convinced that only through Christian conversion could people be delivered from eternal suffering. And Lewis and Clark, as they made use of Sacajawea, had as pure a faith in the democratic principles of the United States of America.

And what did the interpreters pay for their heady experiences? For one thing, they relinquished even more of such support as they might have claimed at home. Delicately self-sustaining communities, especially ones under stress from outsiders, must shepherd their resources very carefully. If someone in the community, especially someone exceptional— someone perceived as troublesome—receives support from outside, then the community is likely to withdraw its own more or less permanently. When Paraske returned to Sakkola to regale people there with her tales of coffee served in gold-rimmed cups, people did not hasten to welcome her home and make her comfortable. Dayuma, hesitating to return to the forest and worrying about whether in her absence she had become too foreign, might have been worrying less about whether the Huaorani would attack her than whether anyone would share meat with her. When van Riebeeck departed for Java, Eva was not reabsorbed by the epidemic-ravaged Khoikhoi; and the young Sacajawea, reunited for the first time with the Shoshones, found she had lost the place among them that her father had negotiated for her before the Minnetarees carried her off.

As a last case study let us look again at Laurinda Andrade. Although she thought of herself, and rightly so, as an authority on Portuguese culture, she was not an embodiment of it, and the more recognition she enjoyed outside the Portuguese community, the more resentment she encountered. Etched into her memory along with "esquisita" were such statements as, "If you want to be good, die or go away," and "Some of your people will never forgive you."[13]

When she left Terceira, she thought she might return as a teacher, but whether in America or Terceira, she intended to remove herself from the Azorean way of doing things once and for all. Returning twenty years later, she found no common ground with her family. Uninterested in marriage since childhood, she was not committed to supporting her parents and siblings either. By dint of extraordinary perseverance she had done modestly well for herself, but she did not feel that she was in a position to do things for anyone else. Between the time she set the date for her return home and her actual arrival, her father, who had not written to her in years, had died. She found her family living in an unfamiliar house, her mother blind and in the care of a daughter who had been born after teen-aged Laurinda's departure.

The family reunion was traumatic. In retrospect she wrote, "Before the day was over, I found myself a stranger in my own family. . . . Eventually it occurred to me that with the exception of my mother, I was simply a projection of America, land of dollars and material wealth. How much did I have, and how much could I give or send later was obviously transparent as their only interest." With that realization, she suffered a collapse and withdrew to another island to recuperate.[14]

In isolation this incident would not be particularly telling of the psychic cost of Andrade's emancipation, but it fits a pattern carried through her autobiography. She was without question a person of rugged constitution, yet her life was punctuated by collapses. On the steamboat departing from Terceira in 1917 she had a fainting fit that aroused suspicions that she was pregnant. Aboard ship it got her attention and extra food, but upon arrival in Rhode Island, she found herself deserted by the couple who had agreed to act as her guardians, and within a matter of days, the rumor also lost her the first lodgings she had found for herself. The next great crisis was tuberculosis, one year into her life in America. "The first two doctors consulted, probably misled by my healthy-looking pink cheeks and the husky appearance I gave, dismissed the case lightly," she wrote. She continued consultations; a third doctor threatened to send her to a sanatorium, and she moved on to a fourth who proposed a regimen of brief hospitalization followed by home care.[15] Once again, as on the ocean crossing, she called on the sympathy of people with whom she had no family ties to put her to bed, feed her, and tend her. When they took up a collection to buy her a ticket home, she didn't go. Some years later, having begun her studies at Pembroke College, she had a relapse, and this time Albertina Grace and her mother nursed her. At the beginning of her senior year, she was incapacitated by back pain, and lived the year taped, bandaged, and braced under the care of the nuns who operated the residence hall where she lived. The year after graduation she went to live with some of Albertina's relatives in order to take a social welfare job in Brooklyn, but no sooner had she begun than she obtained a certificate that she could not climb tenement stairs.

A year after her nervous collapse while visiting Terceira, Andrade was in an automobile accident. She seemed to escape unscathed but in the end spent two weeks in a hospital followed by lengthy nursing, yet again provided by Albertina Grace and her mother. Established as a teacher in New Bedford, a beneficiary at last of health insurance and paid sick leave, she spent weeks more in a hospital "with what was diagnosed as a heart attack."[16] Yet she worked another eight years and then enjoyed fourteen more of retirement before dying at age eighty-one.

None of these sometimes ambiguous incapacitations stopped her. She always returned to work, took all her examinations, graduated from college on schedule, stayed at her teaching job until retirement. In her autobiography she presents them as challenges she overcame, opportunities she seized to practice English, to find time to reflect and meditate. But she also dwells on the care and attention that followed each incident, the coddling, the gifts of food, the cards, the visits. As a young girl, she had triumphed repeatedly over her father's obstructionism. Once she was on her own, it was as though some internalized demon continued to throw up roadblocks, placing her time and again in need of being cared for.

As her autobiography documents her reliance on patrons and bene-factors, it also catalogues her accumulation of former friends, people who one day were, by her estimation, welcoming and generous and the next cold and rejecting. Returning from her first mill job, she discovered that the people who had taken her into their home two days before had changed: "The atmosphere was icy. No smiles and no conversation. . . . By the disturbed glances of Mrs. Mendes, pointedly searching my eyes, I knew something was ominously wrong. But what?"[17] Twelve more ad-dress changes followed before she reached the family of Albertina Grace, and even there she did not get off to a good start. But from inauspicious beginnings Andrade's one great lasting relationship developed as Albertina and her mother, devastated by a series of deaths in their family, made a place for her and devoted themselves to her education.

Out of college, Andrade launched forth again on her pattern of frequent moves. Having abandoned her social work job in Brooklyn, she took a tutoring job in exchange for board and room. When, at the end of three months, she found a paying job at a bank, she passed it up to return to New Bedford for an extended visit. "My friends in Brooklyn did not take kindly to this decision," she wrote," and reacted by shipping my belongings with a sharp and terse note, which ended with, 'Good luck to you in New Bedford.' Their door had been permanently closed."[18] Returning to New York after a while, she had a hostile encounter with the family of the physician who had helped her extricate herself from her previous job, "and quickly left their home for the last time."[19] Yet another

Portuguese couple helped her with lodgings in Brooklyn, where she lived until she landed a newspaper job in New Jersey. That parting, too, nearly ended in fireworks. Nor was her boss at the newspaper pleased when eight months later she left for Washington. Once there she continued moving frequently from one housing arrangement to another.

I would hazard a guess that people who initially offered Andrade hospitality almost immediately began to worry that in the absence of any family of her own, she would begin to draw on their limited resources, resources they no more wanted to share with her than she wanted to share with her own family back in the Azores. When, on arrival in the United States, she was first taken into a Portuguese-American household, she had been warned, "With neither money nor relatives to support you, you must go to work immediately. We are poor working people."[20] As soon as they got wind of her fainting and taking to bed aboard ship, they were anxious to have her move on. Albertina Grace and her mother had great gaping holes in their family that Laurinda Andrade could help to fill, but intact families perceived her as a threat. In her need for people to welcome her and tend her, to be to her what her mother and father had not been, she never seemed to anticipate the abrupt shutting of the door and turning out of the lights.

Returning to the broad picture, we see, paralleling denial of material support, withdrawal of trust and approval. Informants were open to intense criticism, slander, and shunning. Within her lifetime Doña Marina was imagined burning with Cortés in hellfire; over the centuries her reputation has, if possible, deteriorated further. The Maya rejoiced in their mistaken belief that Bishop Toral would punish Gaspar Antonio for his role in Landa's inquisition. Doman bedeviled Eva, publicly calling her a traitor. Bazil's mother on the Wind River reservation kept a low profile because Indian men resented a woman who would presume to take her place among them in council. Laurinda Andrade did not keep a low profile and saved up for her autobiography many a spiteful thing that had been said to her face or behind her back. In Huautla María Sabina suffered arson, and a fellow Mazatec denounced her to the federal police for drug dealing. Doña Luz's Milpa Alta relatives boycotted Concha's wedding.

Both Sarah Winnemucca and Charles Eastman met little thanks for their efforts on behalf of their respective peoples. They were characterized as self-serving, accused of enriching themselves at others' expense, suspected of diverting cash intended for direct payment to Paiutes and Santee. They were fiercely attacked, publicly jeered. Sarah went away from the Paiutes to die; Eastman went away from everybody.

Already marginal to some degree in the world into which they had been born, made more marginal yet by associations with outsiders, plagued by others' jealousy and suspicion, in one way or another many of these people suffered the additional blow of abandonment after they had rendered their services. The most poignant symbol of this is van Riebeeck's ship disappearing over the horizon, leaving Eva behind on the docks. But what of the others? Who is to know how Doña Marina viewed her separation from Cortés? He provided her with a dowry, but had she any inkling of the minimal credit he gave to her in his own account of the conquest of Mexico? As he told it in his letters to Spain, the conquest was his great deed, and she was an Indian girl who had been there. It was left to others—to Bernal Díaz and other conquistadors, to the Tlaxcalans, to the compilers of the *Florentine Codex,* and to the enduring Indian tradition—to tell her part in it.

Clark was conscience-stricken that he and Lewis had not paid Sacajawea directly for crossing the continent with them, but he was not embarrassed about seeking to take her son from her. In principle, at least, she was the indirect beneficiary of both the cash payment and the land grant that Charbonneau received, and then—if Sacajawea did die soon after—there was nothing more to be done for her. On the other hand, if the Shoshone tradition is true, Sacajawea made her way through a long life, living by her own wits, independent of the men for whom she had once worked.

Late payment, nonpayment for work done, and false promises of employment made to Sarah Winnemucca are too depressing to review, as likewise is the aborted medical career of Charles Eastman, who was misassigned, reassigned, and reassigned yet again before he even saw his first post, then forced out of one assignment after another.

We have seen the losing battle against destitution waged by Paraske, Doña Luz, and María Sabina in the last years of their lives. Of the three, the one with the ablest potential benefactor was María Sabina, and, walled off by a barrier of both language and culture, she did not grasp the extent of Wasson's wealth or expect him to share more of it with her. Only at the very end did she, according to reports, begin to suspect that others had turned her art to much greater profit than she had herself.

Many an informant shares this suspicion. It is not at all uncommon to hear the complaint that some anthropologist has built a reputation and a secure livelihood on the confidences of an individual or a community, and what, after all, has the work accomplished for the people who cooperated? By contrast, Chloe Grant and George Watson were satisfied in their working relationships with Dixon, while Dersu and Ishi received, so to speak, full retirement benefits. Dersu's inability to live in town and Ishi's lack of resistance to infection, tragic though they were, cannot be laid to irresponsibility on the part of Arsenjev and Ishi's museum friends.

Their experiences left the interpreters marked, both physically and psychically. There were the shortened lives and the hard old ages, but survival had its psychological cost as well. Moving between worlds with conflicting values, needing to get people to listen to strange, often unwelcome messages, the interpreters engaged in inventing and reinventing themselves, making themselves into what other people wanted them to be, what they themselves needed to be in order to succeed. The least insidious aspect of this, perhaps, was preoccupation with physical appearance. Hyper-aware of their roles as public people, at least some of the interpreters dressed very self-consciously. So long as this worked to their benefit, it was another shrewd means of communication, but sometimes the function of the costumes seems to have turned in on them: assertion, denial, invention, protection not for the audience at large but for the player.

One of Doña Marina's Indian servants testified that his mistress always wore the traditional garb of a proper Nahua matron, and early drawings of her bear him out.[21] This is the polar opposite of the twentieth-century definition of "malinchismo," namely forsaking one's own in order to embrace the new and foreign. By keeping to the fine huipil and the distinctively bound hair of the mature Nahua woman, Doña Marina seems to have been asserting her claim to good birth and respectability, not deriving her authority solely from her association with Cortés and the Spaniards.

On the other hand, Henry Brackenridge described the woman he met in the company of Charbonneau four years after the end of the Lewis and Clark expedition as "greatly attached to the whites, whose manners and dress she tries to imitate."[22] Such would not be inconsistent with the old woman of the Shoshone tradition who was a friend to white people, welcome in their houses, and in council a consistent champion for cooperation with the United States government. Had Sacajawea bought into Lewis and Clark's unquestioning belief that they were bringing improvement to the savages? Had she, in order not to be separated altogether from her son, done her best to put herself through the same civilizing program Clark had laid out for little Jean Baptiste?

Coming forward in time, we can clearly see in the photographs illustrating Wallis's two books how Dayuma's succession of attachments were expressed in her dress. Traditionally, Huaorani have ornamented their bodies rather than covering them, and their most distinctive ornaments are large balsa plugs they fit into their earlobes. Women and men alike cut their hair short from forehead back to behind the ears to show off their earplugs to best advantage. As a plantation worker and then wife and mother, Dayuma perforce adopted the characteristic skirt and cover-up smock of the acculturated Quichua women. She could do nothing about her earlobes, which had been stretched to large open rings while she was still a child, but she grew her hair long all around to hide her ears away. In her widowhood, promoted from field hand to indoor servant, she exchanged her Quichua clothes for a housedress. Then, in the fellowship of Protestant evangelists, she sewed her own dresses to wear in the forest as she called her fellow Huaorani to clothe themselves in pants and shirts and dresses along with Christian righteousness.

Like Doña Marina, Larin Paraske also dressed as a matron of her place, but not really of her time. To be received in Helsinki and Porvoo as a personification of folk culture, she attired herself in an old-fashioned way analogous to the way museum workers dress at Plimouthe Plantation and Colonial Williamsburg. Going yet further, Sarah Winnemucca created for her stage appearances a theatrical costume such as never a Paiute woman had worn, while off-stage she dressed according to Victorian fashion. An expert maker of ladies' gloves, she also knew her way with hair ribbons and ruffles, bodices and riding skirts.

Laurinda Andrade left the fashion sense to her dressmaker friend and companion Albertina, but she took considerable pride in the effect, in particular, of a red crepe evening gown she first wore to a Depression-era public function soon after her graduation from Pembroke. Justifying it, she wrote, "Dean Morriss, who was well acquainted with the source of my always fashionable and unusual wardrobe, enlightened some of the ladies by explaining what could be interpreted as an anachronism between the poor and still jobless college graduate and her luxurious appearance." When the wife of a Portuguese diplomat took an instant dislike to Andrade at another function, she wondered, "Did she react to my stylish brick-red-color evening gown or to me?"[23]

Men as well as women were exquisitely sensitive to the expressive function of clothes. Ishi took readily to trousers, shirts, and fitted jackets, even neckties, although he resisted shoes until his first mid-winter in San Francisco. (It isn't clear why moccasins were not an alternative.) Once he had adopted city clothes, Theodora Kroeber writes, "Ishi, to whom nakedness had been the normal and unmarked state, refused to have his picture taken except when he was fully dressed. Pictures of him in native undress had to await his return visit to the Lassen foothills."[24]

Charles Eastman's sense of costume was not limited to ceremonial eagle feathers, beaded shirt, and leggings. In his later years he cut a fine figure in beautifully tailored suits and full evening wear, to say nothing of the red jacket and breeches of the hunt, but his fascination with what he could make of himself by the clothes he put on was of long standing. He recalled how, as a Dartmouth undergraduate, he had perfumed himself with rosewater, donned a fez, and successfully passed himself off as a Middle Easterner. Newly arrived at spartan Pine Ridge, he was cheered to receive as a gift from friends in Boston a fashionable riding suit and boots, and to complete his dashing image he bought himself a part-Arabian white horse.[25]

For Gaspar Antonio and Guaman Poma it was their family trees rather than their persons that they adjusted for effect, Gaspar Antonio moving himself closer to the direct line of Xiu rulers, Guaman Poma systematically altering a document to make himself a prince.

Thoughtful people meeting one of these interpreters might well ask, who is the person behind the constructed image? The cheerful agreeableness of Doña Marina and Sacajawea, Doña Luz and Dayuma, even Paraske—was it a survival strategy? The extravagant expressions of gratitude and admiration in the writings of Sarah Winnemucca and Laurinda Andrade—can they be sincere? Here is what I imagine Doña Luz might have said in her heart to the many people she engaged with:

> To all and sundry: Yes, I will take you to Milpa Alta and to Chalma. I will show you Indian homes and Indian dances, and I will cook Indian food for you. I will be your tour guide. To the painters and photographers: Yes, you may look at me as much as you like. I will put on whatever skirts and smocks and shawls you like or take everything off and let you look at me naked. You may make of me what you will, portray me mountainous, dim, eternal, maternal, whatever qualities you associate with Indian women. I am someone else. I am somewhere else. To the folklorists, anthropologists, and linguists: Yes, I will tell you animal fables and ghost stories by the hour, every charming folktale I ever heard. And I will retell them as often as you need me to, almost verbatim. I will tell them with emotion and conviction and charm. I will also tell you of catastrophe and death and famous men, of Díaz, Sierra, Zapata, and Cárdenas. But for all your ideas about me, you don't know me.

I find it a relief that in her letters to Jean Charlot she did not keep up the facade of relentless agreeableness, that at least to him she could and did complain.

For others there is ready evidence of real damage to the person within. Having mastered the language, religion, and manners of outsiders, they were consumed by disillusion in proportion to their initial investment. Eva turned to drink and to rowdy criticism of the Dutch, and they responded by exiling her from their midst for the rest of her short life.

From the beginning of Sarah Winnemucca's public career, she wept in public as freely as Paraske, but unlike Paraske's tears, Sarah's were mixed with moral indignation and scathing personal attacks. Her intense emotional style had appeal in lecture halls but not at the Department of the Interior, where she was at a loss to find any other voice in which to speak. Finding his own articulate righteous indignation likewise ineffective in Washington, Charles Eastman largely ceased to look to white society for justice and took to writing angrily about its broken promises while elaborating in his mind an Indian Utopia.

Neither he nor Sarah was paranoid; they were not mistaken in perceiving corruption and hypocrisy on every side, enemies lying in wait everywhere. The tragedy of it was that the sympathetic audience for their discomforting messages was limited. The social ills to which they witnessed were of such immense magnitude as to exhaust most people's reserves of patience, influence, and disposable funds. On the most personal level, their rather unsuccessful family lives provided little refuge.

The same would seem to be true of Guaman Poma on an even starker scale. According to his account, he sacrificed his family to devote himself to what was, at least in the short term, a grandiosely unsuccessful project—addressing, like the others, an unwelcome message to an unresponsive audience. If what he says is true, he lost everything to his commitment to enlightening the Spanish king and in the end was denied his very identity. Suppose, on the other hand, in addition to fixing up a document to make a prince of himself, he invented his whole family history within the Yarovilca lineage. An impersonation of such magnitude appears to have no strategic value. What purpose, other than an intensely personal and internal one, could it have served?

Few of these people we have met were easy to live with, either publicly or privately. The last five centuries have seen unspeakable tragedies, and they were among the ones who mediated the tragedies, witnessed and reported on them. Gifted and attractive, they were also battered and scarred.

One of the things that set apart these individuals who, willingly or not, learned to live in two worlds, was the perspective that was forced upon them. It is a perspective now being forced on the many rather than being borne on the shoulders of a few. Thoughtful people today feel a profound regret that around the world aboriginal cultures with all their richnesses have been swept aside by the mobile, invasive, extra-national one unleashed by the voyages of discovery. We look upon the horrors that epidemic disease, modern warfare, and environmental degradation have visited on the peoples of the earth, the biological and cultural homogenization spreading via mass transportation and mass communication, and like the Huao man who fainted when he comprehended the oil-exploration map, we tremble for the future. Advances in human technology and burgeoning human population now impose a global perspective on us all.

What has been lost, is being lost, is a mixed bag. It includes narrative art and music and craftsmanship the like of which mankind may never reinvent—the high rhetoric of the Aztecs and the ingenious verses of the Ingrians; the transcendental unity of the Sioux and of the Goldi with their forests and prairie now wiped from the face of the earth; the wondrous textiles of the Incas and the equally wondrous basketry of the Yahi. But like those that have come rolling over them, these societies were not innocent of uninformed hatreds; ethnic separatism; enforced color, class, and gender lines; shaming and ridicule to keep individuals in line; enslavement or death for the unconventional; or remorseless culling of surplus population. Ethnocentrism has caused terrible local tragedies, but it now can cause and has caused irreversible damage reaching out to every nook and cranny of this planet. There is no safe haven to which we and our children can withdraw. Informed people everywhere know this, and the United Nations, together with supranational relief agencies, human rights organizations, environmental protection groups, and women's groups, is our twentieth-century response. Our many worlds we must now at last seek to transcend, for our planet's sake, for the sake of the world's children, and in commemoration of the lives of the people who worked so hard and paid so much to mark the way.

We can hardly look at the lives of these interpreters without a sense of harm done, wittingly or unwittingly, and great human potential squandered. What is there to do now but to apply ourselves to the double task of preserving what is left and building upon it, that we as human beings might at last find common cause in protecting who and what remains? Our planet and its inhabitants desperately require human commitment to global responsibility. Better than statue, monument, or mural, that would be the most fitting memorial for all those who have lived out their lives between worlds.

Epilogue

Their Children

If it is hard to be thrust into a world other than one's own and to learn to interpret between the two, it is as hard or harder to be born to a parent who already lives between worlds. The children of the individuals we have met here were vulnerable to alienation from their parents, either by outside forces or by their own discomfort with their parents' circumstances. Here is how some of the children made places for themselves in one or the other of their parents' worlds.

DON MARTÍN CORTÉS AND DOÑA MARÍA JARAMILLO

Of his several children born out of wedlock, it was to Doña Marina's son that Hernán Cortés gave his own father's name, Martín. By the time the boy could talk and toddle, his father and mother had departed for Honduras, while he remained in the care of one of his father's Spanish kinsmen. On the expedition his mother became the wife of another man and mother of his child. Soon after that she died, and her son was left entirely to the Spanish world, a world obsessed with genealogy and race.

Cortés took the six-year-old boy along with him to Spain when he went to court to answer charges of irregularities in the governance of the realms he had conquered for Spain with Doña Marina at his side. Both crown and colony were apprehensive that Cortés would attempt to seize power in Mexico and rule it as his own kingdom. For two years he defended himself, and in the end, he had to give up any hope of being named viceroy, accepting in grand compensation the title of Marquis of the Valley of Oaxaca, which came with an immense grant of Indian labor.

Blow though this was to his ambition, such was his fame and such the richness of his reward for the conquest of Mexico that it was not difficult for him to make an advantageous match with a young Spanish lady. Before their marriage, he petitioned the pope to legitimate his mestizo son Martín as well as Martín's half-brother Luis (who had a Spanish mother), and a half-sister of theirs as well. To young Martín, despite his mixed ancestry, came not only legitimacy but honor. As son of the conqueror of countless heathen, the boy was invested as a knight of Saint James, the Spaniards' bellicose Santiago the Moor killer. War was to be Martín's profession, and according to tradition, the Moors were to be the instrument of his demise.

Cortés and his new wife returned to Mexico and stayed there for a decade, raising a family. When a son was born to them, Cortés honored his father once again. Now there were two Don Martíns, half-brothers, the elder a legitimate son but a mestizo; the younger the son of a well-born Spanish mother. At that time and place there could be no question of which would enjoy first rights of inheritance. Martín the younger would succeed his father as marquis and principal heir to his estate; Martín the elder and his half-brother Luis would receive annual allowances dispensed by Martín the younger. Cortés also provided for his other children, legitimate and otherwise, but on further consideration, he cancelled the yearly allowance for Luis. The old conqueror was in Spain, trying to return to Mexico, when death caught up with him in Seville.

Don Martín the elder was now dependent on Don Martín the younger. A soldier by trade, he continued soldiering, earning his keep and accumulating battle scars fighting Spain's wars in Europe. In spite of his mixed racial background, he married a Spanish noblewoman, and by the time he reached middle age, Mexico had become something long ago and far away. It would have been better for him if it had remained that way.

Unfortunately for them all, Don Martín the younger decided to return to his marquisate in Mexico and took his half-brothers Luis and Martín with him. Martín, for his part, brought along his wife and son to participate in a feverish society known as "creole," meaning not 'mestizo', but simply 'born outside the mother country'. Within a couple of years all the sons of Cortés were implicated in "the conspiracy of 1565," a purported attempt by Mexican-born sons and grandsons of the conquerors to stage a coup against Spanish administration of the colony and put the young marquis in power. Creole gentlemen were executed in the repressive aftermath of this folly, but fortunately for Don Martín the younger, his supporters were able to slip him out of the country.

Don Luis, too, escaped, and so, eventually, did Don Martín the elder, but not before he was subjected to the same tortures Diego de Landa had so recently supervised in Mani. There in his native Mexico, Doña Marina's son was stretched on the rack, his limbs wound with cords that were tightened and tightened and tightened yet again, cutting into the scars of the wounds he had received fighting in the service of king and country. Pitcherful after pitcherful of water was forced down his throat, and still he refused to admit that he had ever taken part in a conspiracy against Spanish authority. Finally his tormentors released him, and he left Mexico under banishment, condemned never to return. It is said he continued to support himself and his family by the sword and soon died fighting Moors in the War of Granada.[1]

When his son, Don Fernando Cortés, submitted a probanza in 1605 seeking recognition for the services of his grandmother, Doña Marina, it was the third such petition from her direct descendants. Her daughter Doña María Jaramillo had long since joined the children of the first conquerors in seeking recompense for their parents' deeds.

While Don Martín spent most of his life in Spain except for the excruciating episode in the 1560s, Doña María lived out hers in Mexico. Upon her parents' marriage in 1525, Cortés had endowed Doña Marina and Juan Jaramillo with the fine productive encomienda of Xilotepec located northwest of Mexico City not far from the ancient ruins of Tula. Just a bit over two decades later, when Juan Jaramillo died, his will conveyed the bulk of the encomienda not to his daughter Doña María, but to her Spanish stepmother Doña Beatriz de Andrada—the woman to whom he had been married, according to sworn testimony, for the last twenty years. Doña María, by now a grown woman and married to a Spaniard, was outraged that the reward for her mother's services in the conquest should not come directly and entirely to her, and she and her husband filed suit to contest her father's will. After five years of litigation, the parties settled on a division of the income from the encomienda, part directed to Doña María and her husband, the other part to Doña Beatriz and her new husband.[2]

When Doña María died in 1563, she was not yet forty years old. While her life had been longer than her mother's, it had been narrow and bitter. Her youth had been spent supping the gall of a mestiza stepchild in a Spanish lady's household. After her marriage her young womanhood was consumed in insisting on her right to a legacy. On Doña María's behalf two probanzas were submitted concerning her mother's services. The second one, dated 1581, was raised long after her death by her son. Both documents ended up in the Archive of the Indies in Seville, the same repository that became the last resting place for Gaspar Antonio Chi's probanzas and Francisco de Montejo Xiu's furious indictment of the Franciscans.[3]

The Hispanicization of Gaspar Antonio Chi's Lineage

Gaspar Antonio's daughter Francisca Chinab married a Maya named Antonio Couoh, and in January of 1609 their daughter Francisca Chinab Couoh de Herrera was wedded to a Spaniard in the Mérida cathedral. The following November the young couple's son, duly registered as "mestizo," was given his great-grandfather's name in baptism. Young Gaspar Antonio del Castillo grew up to marry a Spanish woman, and from then on the noble Xiuh lineage Gaspar Antonio had valued so highly grew more and more attenuated as his descendants continued to marry within Spanish society.[4]

The Inconstant Don Francisco de Ayala

By his own account Guaman Poma de Ayala left his wife and children and spent thirty years roaming about the countryside collecting information on colonial abuses while developing his plan for a reformed Peru. Yet he asserts that his oldest son, Don Francisco, accompanied him when he set out over the mountains for Lima to post his report to Spain, and among his illustrations is a drawing of the two of them on the road with a horse and two dogs. On the way he says he argued with other travelers, attracting attention that brought not only criticism and ill treatment, but robbery. Being companion to anyone behaving so provocatively would be trying, to say nothing of dangerous, and perhaps it is not hard to understand how a son—faced with snowy conditions in the mountain passes and the hubbub his father stirred up in the wayside inns—might decide he had to save himself. In any case, according to Guaman Poma, Don Francisco abandoned him, aged and infirm though he was, up there among the peaks. Perhaps it was tit for tat for Guaman Poma's desertion of Don Francisco and his siblings when they were young and vulnerable. The dogs Amigo and Lautaro stayed by Guaman Poma a bit longer than his son, but they too, turned back—as he tells it—and followed the young master home.[5]

Eva's Namesake

Eva's coming of age marked the beginning of the end of her precocious career. By the end of 1663 she had already given birth to two children out of wedlock, which may be the reason the van Riebeeck family did not take her along with them when they left for Java in 1662. Her marriage to the Danish doctor redeemed her in the eyes of the Cape colony, especially since the couple took up residence on the offshore island, far from the wharves where she had sold herself to transient seamen. But widowhood brought her back to the mainland with the three children she had borne her husband before he sailed away to his death in far-off Madagascar. Within a year her outspokenness, drinking, and return to prostitution had brought censure upon her, and following a severe tongue-lashing, she fled, leaving her children behind, but taking their clothes with her. When she was overtaken, she was engaged in selling their clothes to raise the means for her escape.

The authorities banished Eva back to the island, even as they had threatened to do before she ran away, and there she died five years later. Her mulatto children, all baptized, became wards of the church. Eight years after their abandonment, two of her children were taken by a friend of their father to Mauritius, where one of them, Petronella, made a rather splendid marriage with a well-to-do Dutchman. Of their eight children, they named one Eva for her grandmother, and eventually they brought young Eva and her siblings back to the Cape where her grandmother's sad story had begun and ended. No matter what the attitude of the godly residents of the Cape colony toward her mother and no matter what fearful memories from childhood remained with her, Petronella Zaijman had found it in her heart to create a new Eva and bring her up Dutch.[6]

JEAN BAPTISTE CHARBONNEAU

William Clark's determination to separate Sacajawea's charming baby "Pomp" from his mother was hardly unprecedented. Already in the mid-1700s the Reverend Eleazar Wheelock had devised a rescue plan directed to Indian boys that eventually gave rise to Charles Eastman's alma mater, Dartmouth College. An excerpt from an 1811 biography of Wheelock conveys a vivid sense of how people of Lewis and Clark's time perceived Indian society, mentioning as it does "the barren minds of the savages," "their several barbarous languages," and "the suspicions they entertained that white people in all their proposals, had a design to enslave them or obtain their lands." Wheelock's biographers, unaware of the boarding schools the Franciscans had founded long before, ascribed to him "a plan, which was new and till then never attempted." Wheelock would remove Indian boys from their parents and "from all connection with their countrymen; and in this period of their lives when impressions are most lasting," he would instruct them in learning, civilized behavior, and Christian religion. "By keeping them a number of years, under these advantages, and until they should be qualified to teach their brethren," his biographers wrote, "he hoped to form them to such habits, as would effectually secure them from degenerating into the idle, wandering, and vicious manners of their own nation."[7]

This seems to be what Clark had in mind for Jean Baptiste. (And of course it was also the philosophy of the Indian boarding school where Comanche and Shoshone children later met and concluded that the woman known at Wind River as "Bazil's mother" was their common kin and that she was, in fact, Sacajawea.) Clark's whole attempt to save Jean Baptiste from inevitable ruin turned on separating him from his savage mother. But Clark was no educator, so he paid out money to others to train and civilize Jean Baptiste.

The Franciscans had lost confidence in the children in their schools. Indeed, Diego de Landa was maddened by the suspicion that the young Maya chapel masters he helped train led others in the veneration of idols. Wheelock, too, had been disappointed by his Indian students. They were difficult to manage, broke things, preferred sitting on the ground to sitting on chairs, and greatly disliked the clothing they were expected to wear. Despite his efforts, when he sent them back to their peoples as schoolteachers, they "unhappily returned, in a considerable degree, to those roving and savage habits, from which it was hoped they were completely rescued."[8]

So it was too, it seems, with Jean Baptiste, who turned his back on his St. Louis education and returned to the hunting and trapping life of his father. It was through his services as a guide for European big-game hunters flocking to the Great Plains to help with the extermination of the buffalo that Jean Baptiste connected with the German prince who took him off to tour Europe.

We don't know whether Clark thought his emotional and financial investment in the boy was a total loss. As for the old woman on the Wind River reservation, she was remembered by all as emotionally closer to Bazil than to Baptiste. Clark's rescue effort may have simply impoverished the relationship of a mother and her son.[9]

CHARLES EASTMAN'S CHILDREN

Eastman sought by diligent instruction and example to make his six children into models of the new Americans he envisioned, individuals imbued with Indian virtues and Indian skills, regardless of their parents' ethnicity. At camp, New England children of any and every background would learn to be Indian in spirit, and the Eastman children would master their father's ways by teaching them to others.

Yet Eastman had been a much-absent father, and he and Elaine Goodale did not present a united front to their children. It was his wife who carried on the children's education at home when the only available schools were Indian schools, and it was probably she who encouraged their daughter Irene in her operatic voice training. Like her father, Irene dressed in buckskins for studio photographs, but family snapshots show her and her sisters in ruffled dresses, stockings, hats, and hair ribbons. Although all of Eastman's children were placed on the tribal rolls, they did not live the lives of Sioux children.

Following on Irene's death, Eastman's son's rejection of his father's cherished life philosophy must have been very painful to both father and son. Ohiyesa II did not willingly participate in outdoor activities and by family accounts seems to have been primarily attached to his mother. In her autobiography Elaine Goodale relates her son's warm support of her writing, and according to his biographer, one of Eastman's grandsons referred to Ohiyesa II as a "mama's boy." [10] Be that as it may, Ohiyesa II did not stay home and tend his mother. After serving in the navy, he attended college and then established himself in Detroit, working in advertising for the Kelvinator Company.

His father must have regarded his job with bewilderment, but Ohiyesa invited his father to stay with him between lecture tours and whenever winter weather made the unheated island cottage too uncomfortable. Even in death, which struck down the son only a year after it had carried off his father, the two men—so dissimilar in their tastes and occupations—continued their uneasy companionship, side-by-side in unmarked graves in an urban cemetery.

NADESCHDA, TATJANA, AND VASLE

Of the foundlings Paraske nursed, we know nothing. When Anu Kaipainen recreated Paraske's career in a novel, she invented a character to soften the hard story: Antrus, a crown's child who grew up to care for Paraske in her old age, rewarding her with filial love and tenderness. In fact there seems to have been no one like Antrus. [11] It was with her own surviving birth children that Paraske lived and died in Sakkola.

Born in 1858, Nadeschda was the first of Paraske's children to survive infancy, but she was far from robust. Living at home, she passed from girlhood to spinsterhood doing what she could, keeping house and singing. Neovius, writing in 1896 when she was not yet forty, described her as in poor health. When Paraske, her own health failing, returned home after her years of living with the Neovius family, Nadeschda accepted unprotestingly the role of sole caretaker of an increasingly incapacitated parent. With no income, she and Paraske were in desperate circumstances, and when she could, she left her mother's side to go begging. At Paraske's death, Nadeschda dutifully wrote to Neovius, telling him of her mother's last days, and then, unwilling to have her mother's grave marked only with an anonymous black cross, she continued to press Neovius for a memorial stone until the South Karelian Youth Society finally erected one.

Tatjana, three years younger than Nadeschda, was the second of the Larila children to receive Paraske's mother's name in baptism. The first Tatjana had been born at midsummer eleven years earlier and withered away like a summer flower. Defying the ill luck that seemed to come with the name, the younger Tatjana escaped the fate of her tubercular grandmother and of her sister whose life had ended almost as soon as it began. And it was more, too, than infection and early death that this Tatjana escaped. By marrying a local Lutheran freeholder she also put behind her the rituals and the songs of Orthodox Sakkola and the struggle to raise the money every year to keep a rundown cottage on a tiny piece of land. At the time Neovius reported on the family, she was thirty-five years old, and she and her husband had four children. In the years when Paraske was more than once put out of Larila, ill, weak, and cold though she was, she did not move to Tatjana's home.

Vasle, six years younger than Nadeschda and three years younger than Tatjana, was twenty-five when he married a freeman's daughter from a neighboring village. Paraske, who just the year before had sung heartbreakingly at Kauril's funeral, arranged a song-wedding for her son and his bride such as had not been held in Sakkola for many years. And then she departed for her years of work and recognition with Neovius in Porvoo and Helsinki.

With the wedding she had tried to establish positive bonds between herself and the young couple, but from the first they distanced themselves from her even more than her new career distanced her from them. Strangers found her art compelling, but Vasle and his wife wanted nothing of her and her ways.

How is this estrangement to be understood? Paraske's audiences heard her songs in comfortable settings—in Helsinki auditoriums or the parsonage in Porvoo—from Paraske at a time when she was healthier, better-fed, and more handsomely dressed than she had ever been in her life.

Visitors like Theodor Schvindt, Edla Hiilos, and Mrs. Clive-Bayley who went all the way to Sakkola didn't go there in the dark and mud of November or the hunger month of March when the last of the potatoes had gone soft and the rye bread moldy. It was otherwise for Paraske's children, for whom the context of her songs was a bitterly hard life in the midst of a great deal of squalor and death.

Vasle had been spared the experience of estate serfdom, but he knew all too well the grinding poverty of Larila: the dying infants—his younger siblings and the Russian foundlings—at his mother's breasts; Kauril's protracted dotage; the crafty indirection and servility of begging; all the stink and starvation that went with his mother's art. Little wonder if he wanted none of it.

Vasle was as discomforted by his mother's lifestyle as Ohiyesa II was by his father's. When Mrs. Neovius brought the enthusiastic English visitor Mrs. Clive-Bayley to Larila, he turned sullen. The following summer he and his wife may have been humiliated when Paraske took their little son along with her to beg from the vacationing Finnish school teacher. They had named the boy Kauril after his grandfather, and now they had an infant daughter too, children for whom they wanted a future. Paraske represented a dark and troubling past.

Like Laurinda Andrade, who was in full flight from a traditional society she believed would destroy her if she let it, Vasle resolutely did not help. He did not work to save Larila, nor did he take Paraske in as her condition deteriorated. He let his sickly sister Nadeschda, the one who sang her mother's songs, go begging and tend their mother to the end.

CONCHA AND HER CHILDREN

In the first decade of the twentieth century Lucio Tapia had promised the parents of Milpa Alta that the new schools in their town would make lawyers and teachers and priests of their children. Instead, the bombed-out ruins of the school buildings became charnel houses of the Mexican Revolution, and Luz Jiménez was denied the chance to take her place before a new generation of children in the classrooms she had so loved. In the end it was her grandchildren who realized her dream of professional employment.

Concha chose a more conventional course for her life than her mother had. At seventeen she was married in a church wedding, and a year and a half later she and her husband had their first child. Seven more were to follow. The cost of raising so many children consumed Concha, her husband, and Doña Luz as well. Everyone worked all the time to pay for food and housing and endless doctors' bills. Doña Luz, who had managed as a single mother to raise her daughter and help care for her widowed mother, gave up her own home to live in with the burgeoning family and help out with housekeeping and childcare during Concha's pregnancies.[12] As the grandchildren grew up, she found them jobs to help out with family expenses. Some of the work was in Anita Brenner's office, working on her magazine *Mexico This Month*, and some was in the art galleries where Doña Luz was so well known.

It might seem that insufficient income was sweeping the family straight back into the situation from which Doña Luz had sought to free herself, but such was not the case, for Concha's children went to kindergarten and then to school and then on to professional training. One son drove a taxi while working his way through medical school. Another went to the university to study chemistry. A daughter became a nurse. Another took secretarial training and got a job with an engineering firm. When they wrote to Charlot and his family, they wrote in three languages: Spanish, French, and English, and they mainly wrote about their studies, their jobs, their marriages, and their own growing families, not the hard litany of poverty and disaster that had characterized letters from Luz and Concha. What Lucio Tapia had envisioned for Luz and her classmates had taken two generations longer to arrive, and when it came, it was in Mexico City rather than Milpa Alta.

CATARINO AND AURELIO, APOLONIA AND VIVIANA

In 1970 María Sabina told Fernando Benítez that she had ten dependents. One of her daughters did sewing, weaving, and embroidery. The other cultivated some maize and beans. Her surviving son, Catarino, was working as a day laborer and fireworks maker and had recently lost four fingers in an accident. Her three adult children contributed to the household, but María Sabina considered herself the primary source of support for the whole family. What would happen to her grandchildren, she asked, when her strength inevitably waned, and she was no longer able to do veladas for the god-seeking foreigners? It would be easier to keep the wolf of starvation from preying on her grandchildren if she could go back to storekeeping.

Of the nine children she had borne, death had claimed most of them young. The sons who grew up brought violence into their home, and their mother wore the scars: bullet wounds in her body and her searing memory of Aurelio gasping out his life in a lake of blood. Her daughters had brought her their personal problems and found no sympathetic ear. Yet Catarino, Apolonia, and Viviana stayed close to home into middle age, and Apolonia had served as María Sabina's assistant in many a velada. How doubly painful it must have been for her that her mother used the healing ceremony for Perfecto to publicly criticize her for her marital difficulties and then later to pronounce that she was ungifted as a Wise One. Perhaps when their mother told Benítez that she was the one supporting their children, María Sabina's adult children could bear no more. Just a few years later she told Alvaro Estrada that they had all withdrawn from her, and she was living a solitary and lonely life.

ERNIE AND PHYLLIS

Of Chloe Grant's eleven children, eight survived infancy. As they grew up, the oldest of them faced the stark fact that the school in their area was for whites only. Then from the mid-1940s, children of mixed Aborigine/white unions were admitted, before the school was finally opened to all children. As a result, Chloe's eldest children received no formal schooling at all. Their younger siblings attended just a few years, while Chloe's youngest daughter received a full primary and secondary education.

Even in the mid-1960s, when about half the enrollment in the local school was Aborigine, getting an education was not a comfortable process in Murray Upper, for the children lived under the threat of corporal punishment if they were caught speaking among themselves in their home language.

Yet the forbidding conditions did not stifle everyone's desire to learn. Chloe's son Ernie continued to live at home with his mother, and when Dixon arrived with his tape recorders and notebooks, it was Ernie who encouraged Chloe to cooperate with him. Ernie, with only two years of formal education, had recently qualified for a private pilot's license, and as Dixon and Chloe pursued their linguistic research together, Ernie worked at teaching himself trigonometry, turning now and then to Dixon for assistance. When the opportunity to buy a piece of land presented itself, and the bank refused him a loan because he was an Aborigine, Ernie left Australia and went to New Guinea to work in the timber industry. There the man who was ineligible for a loan at home because he was considered black was assumed to be white and did not take the trouble to deny it. After a while he returned to Australia, where things were gradually getting better, and now is employed part-time by the Tully State High School as a resource person for their course on Dyirbal language and culture. His niece Phyllis Grant received a scholarship to the Canberra College of Advanced Education and enrolled for a diploma in Museum Studies with the opportunity to return for a baccalaureate degree.[13] Both are beneficiaries of the positive appreciation of Dyirbal in Queensland that derives from the rigorous work Chloe and George Watson did with Dixon.

In the lifetime of Chloe and her children, the local schools moved from excluding Aborigines to employing them to teach children, both Aboriginal and white, about their Australian heritage.

SAM PADILLA AND DAYUMA'S SECOND FAMILY

Ignacio, the son born to Dayuma at the hacienda around 1949, survived many a disorienting experience on his way to becoming a grown man called Sam Padilla. For some time after his father and infant brother died of measles, his mother was unable to care for her surviving child. Then, when she regained some strength, she was obliged to work dawn-to-dusk in order to provide for the two of them. As a result, the little boy was left to himself and didn't learn his mother's native language. Once the linguists Rachel Saint and Catherine Peeke came on the scene, Dayuma's scant free time went to them as they worked to reactivate the language her son did not share.

The Bible translators who worked with his mother did take an active interest in the boy, whom they called Sammy, arranging his schooling and care for him during his mother's absences and also plane trips to interesting places, not the least of which was Arkansas. After Dayuma reestablished herself with her Huaorani relatives, he went along to live with them in the forest at the settlement of Tiwaeno.

These compensations do not erase the fact that as an eight-year-old Sammy watched his mother depart with Rachel Saint for what was supposed to be a short trip to Hollywood and did not see her again for most of a year. Soon he was separated from her again, when she returned to the forest to begin her evangelical work. Early on, when Dayuma provided the only access to the language of the Huaorani, Rachel Saint was unwilling to put her in harm's way for fear of losing the services of the missionaries' unique informant. That their use of her, however, might put at risk Dayuma's relationship with her son was not a matter of first priority to the missionaries, whose overriding concern was the salvation of souls.

During Dayuma's initial trips into the forest, Sammy was sent to school and got to know urban life in the Ecuadorian capital of Quito. Only after Rachel Saint, Elizabeth Elliot, and the Elliots' four-year-old daughter had been well-received at Tiwaeno was Sammy taken in to be introduced to his grandmother and other kin. Operating the phonograph and teaching other children to run it, he finally began to learn to speak his mother's language. Having accompanied two of his forest relatives on a trip out of the forest to learn about the world with which he was already so familiar, he became an accomplished interpreter for the Huaorani. Eventually he made a trip back to the U.S. to appear with them at evangelical rallies and on the *Today* show. In her 1973 follow-up book on Dayuma and the Christianization of the Huaorani, Wallis quotes him relating with enthusiasm how he helped escort deep-forest people to Tiwaeno, and among the illustrations she uses photos with the credit line "Sam Padilla (Dayuma's son)."

When the Basque priest Alejandro Labaca Ugarte undertook his mission to the Huaorani, he kept diaries that were published after he was speared to death in the forest. Here and there in his entries he mentions Dayuma's son, mentioning the service he established in the 1970s to take tourists to see his mother's people. According to Labaca he once made the comment that in Huaorani society women don't count.[14] Rachel Saint, Catherine Peeke, Elizabeth Elliot, and Ethel Wallis would have been disappointed to hear such an opinion, since by and with Dayuma they had endeavored to convey salvation to the Huaorani via womanpower.

What had become of the boy Dayuma had dedicated to their effort? Perhaps their spiritual son had been quoted out of context. Or perhaps, like others of the Huaorani, Sam too had cooperated in their vision for quite a while and then decided they were mistaken. In any case, disaffected Huaorani were not alone in their doubts. Unshakeable in her Christian faith, Elizabeth Elliot nonetheless questioned the enterprise at Tiwaeno, writing, "Gradually I saw, to my dismay, that Rachel's approach to linguistic work, her interpretation of what the Indians did and said, and the resulting reports she sent out were often radically different from my own."[15] In any case, multilingual Sam Padilla and his North American wife continue to operate a rain-forest tour service, employing Dayuma's relatives, while Dayuma and her Huao husband have become prosperous cattle raisers.

The Huaorani, whose numbers had been shrinking throughout the middle of this century, are now experiencing rapid population growth to which Dayuma and her husband contributed with three daughters and a son. The birth of their first daughter, Nancy, was so difficult that Dayuma was flown in labor to a hospital. Then their second daughter, Eunie, was born blind. The misfortunes raining down on the Huaorani were not sparing their native evangelist. But their third daughter Eva and their son Solomon fared better. In earlier times, Nancy's hard birth would have been the death of both mother and child, and there would have been no further children of Dayuma. In earlier times, too, the Huaorani would not have invested in the survival of Eunie, who could not be a productive member of their society. But the Huaorani had so changed under the influence of Dayuma's teachings that the child was allowed to live until the river took her life in 1972. More than their efforts to prevent spearings and plural marriages, the influence of the missionaries among the Huaorani is expressed by the photograph in Ethel Wallis's second book of Eunie happily sharing a hammock with one of her relatives and by the fact that Dayuma today has twelve grandchildren.

SURROGATE CHILDREN

Dersu Uzala lost his wife, son, and daughter to smallpox, and from their deaths until he met Arsenjev he chose a solitary life. At the very beginning of their friendship Dersu told Arsenjev of his circumstances, but it was later, when Arsenjev's company made camp near where the family lay buried, that Arsenjev saw his usually outgoing companion turn in upon himself, silent and apprehensive. Only then did Arsenjev appreciate the profundity of Dersu's loss.

There were still Goldi in the taiga, however, who greeted Dersu when he approached and bade him farewell when he moved on. Ishi, on the other hand, never had any children to lose, and every last Yahi on earth died before he did. For him, after his mother died and their two companions disappeared, there were no greetings, no farewells in the only language he had known for the first fifty years of his life. Ishi was even more alone than Dersu.

Both men found in strangers stand-ins for their lost kin, for the sons they did not raise. And who can say whether Arsenjev, Waterman, Kroeber, and Pope may not have been more devoted, more willing learners than born sons could have been? Unlike Ohiyesa II and Paraske's Vasle, they wanted to know and master everything. Secure in themselves in their own worlds, their enthusiasm was unbounded, their affection unreserved.

During the three months in which she took responsibility for the abandoned baby rescued during the heat of battle, Sarah Winnemucca—working in the employ of the army—necessarily left the care of the child to others. Her personal experiences had hardly been of a sort to foster parenting skills. Having given birth to none of her own, she often referred to the Paiutes as her children, but as dispenser of rations and liaison between them and the various arms of the U.S. government, she acted toward them in ways more authoritarian than tender. The Paiutes were not always grateful children, frequently criticizing and shunning her, and in the last years of her life, she gave up on the adults and sought to be a molder and educator of youth. Whether or not she had any talent for mothering, her arguments for keeping children with their families and teaching them in their own language seem humanitarian and sensible today, and visitors to her school came away with the impression of happy children joyfully engaged with their teacher. One can never help wondering what might have been, had her potential been utilized rather than denied.

Laurinda Andrade, too, envisioned herself as a teacher, and she worked long and hard to become one. While still completing her own education, she had taught Americanization classes, but she was middle-aged before she had a regular appointment. There were consequently fewer years left for teaching, and in fact, just two years after receiving a master's degree from Columbia University, she took early retirement from the New Bedford school system, excusing herself for reasons of health and to give young faculty the opportunity to move up.

In an interview on the occasion of her retirement in 1966, she complained of her students that because of television they lived "in a fictitious world," so passive that their teachers were forced to become frantic entertainers. Protesting that she really did enjoy her classes and that some of those she taught were "exceedingly good boys and girls," she nonetheless concluded that respect for teachers had eroded, and she called for greater responsibility and self-discipline on the part of students.[16]

As soon as she retired, she set about writing her autobiography, which was completed and published within two years. The section on her teaching career occupies just twenty-six pages out of 240, and although she states that upon leaving teaching, "the mere thought of having to break away from it was real torture,"[17] her actual description of her quarter-century at New Bedford High School is overwhelmingly concerned with internal politics, the administrative details of program building, and contacts with the Portuguese community, branches of the federal government, universities, and international programs. Students seem very abstract indeed, few emerging from her pages with names or personalities.

It seems to me that Laurinda Andrade had little personal inclination to nurture, and that her ambition to be a teacher was inspired not so much by a commitment to young minds as by her own devotion to learning. It must have been hard for her that so few in her classrooms shared her intellectual voracity, yet the large enrollment in her classes and the public recognition of her program testify that she was by no means unappreciated as a teacher. Perhaps it positively contributed to her effectiveness that she was not seeking surrogate children among her students.

Notes

CHAPTER 1. THREE GUIDES

1. Díaz del Castillo, *Discovery*, 174. The English edition of Bernal Díaz from which I have drawn quotations is an abridgment. For full details of his treatment of Doña Marina's role in the conquest of Mexico I have used the complete Spanish edition published by Porrúa.
2. Ibid., 64.
3. Doña Marina appears in all four scenes of the fragmentary Lienzo de Tlaxcala Manuscript held by the University of Texas at Austin.
4. Díaz del Castillo, *Discovery*, 150.
5. Krueger, *Malinche*, 65.
6. Somonte, *Doña Marina*, 131 (translation mine).
7. López de Gómara, *Cortés*, 408.
8. López de Gómara, *Cortés*, 57, states that she was stolen rather than given away. Don Fernando Cortés affirms that she was the daughter of a local ruler but does not mention the circumstances by which she was separated from her family (Somonte, *Doña Marina*, 174). More accurate Nahuatl spellings of these placenames would be *Coatzacualco* and *Xicallanco*.
9. Díaz del Castillo, *Discovery*, 64; López de Gómara, *Cortés*, 56; Oviedo y Valdés, *Historia general*, 230.
10. Cortés, *Letters*, 73, 376.
11. The assertion that her full Nahuatl name was "Malinalli Tenepal" dates from the late nineteenth century and is based on a misunderstanding of a colonial period document. At the beginning of the seventeenth century the historian Domingo Francisco de San Antón Muñon Chimalpahin Quauhtlehuanitzin made a manuscript copy of López de Gómara's biography of Cortés with some extrapolations, including one that states that her name was "Marina o Malintzin Tenepal," a direct Nahuatl translation of Spanish "Doña Marina la lengua." Chimalpahin's annotated transcription, known as the *Historia de la conquista de Mexico*, survives in several copies from the mid-eighteenth century, the earliest being the Browning manuscript in private hands in Yuma, Arizona.
12. The Chontal Maya that Doña Marina spoke was not exactly like the Yucatec Maya Aguilar had learned, and the coastal Nahuatl she spoke was not identical to the Central Mexican Nahuatl of Montezuma, but neither dialectal differences nor formal rhetorical style impeded her ability to communicate.
13. Díaz del Castillo, *Discovery*, 140–141; López de Gómara, 106–107, gives credit for uncovering the intent of the Tlaxcalans to the Cempoalans who accompanied Cortés.
14. Díaz del Castillo, *Discovery*, 185–186; Sahagún, 12: 37.
15. This meeting was unique; by the time the Spaniards arrived in Peru, their epidemic diseases had preceded them, and Inca society was in chaos.

16. Karttunen, "Polite Speech."
17. Díaz del Castillo, *Discovery*, 193.
18. Ibid., 194.
19. Sahagún 12: 49, illustration 51.
20. Ibid., 293; for a Nahuatl account of the horrific effects of smallpox, see Sahagún 12: 83.
21. Díaz del Castillo, *Discovery*, 67–68. *Cacica* is the feminine form of *cacique* 'ruler', a Taino word the Spaniards brought to the mainland and spread throughout the Americas.
22. López de Gómara, 346.
23. Scholes and Roys, *The Maya Chontal Indians of Acalan-Tixchel*, 391–392; López de Gómara, 356.
24. Cortés, 376.
25. López de Gómara, 370.
26. Octavio Paz, *The Labyrinth of Solitude*, 86.
27. Manuscript deposition of Isabel Pérez de Arteaga, Puebla. Owned by the Jay I. Kislak Foundation, Miami Lakes, Florida. A description of the document is in Catalogue 70 of the Philadelphia Rare Books and Manuscripts Company.
28. López de Gómara, 57.
29. Alva Ixtlilxochitl, *Obras históricas* 2: 198.
30. Lewis and Clark, *History*, 256–257. In the interest of readability I have drawn quotations from the 1893 edition of *The History of the Lewis and Clark Expedition* with its standardized spelling and punctuation. The 1893 edition was based on an 1814 version compiled from the journals in consultation with Clark and other members of the expedition. In conjunction with the *History*, I have used the definitive University of Nebraska edition of the journals themselves.
31. Ibid., 192.
32. Minnetaree is a name used for the ethnic group also known by the names Hidatsa and Gros Ventre.
33. Lewis and Clark, *History*, 448.
34. Ibid., 1028.
35. Ibid., 778.
36. Ibid., 1184.
37. Ibid.,1104.
38. Howard, vi, 74, 150. Lewis and Clark make the same point, *Journals* 5: 268, 306.
39. Lewis and Clark, *History*, 376–377, n. 32. "Snake" was another name used for the Shoshone.
40. Ibid., 368–369.
41. Ibid., 510.
42. Ibid., 458–459; Lewis and Clark, *Journals*, 5: 165.
43. Howard, 62.
44. Lewis and Clark, *History*, 557.
45. Ibid., 745.
46. Ibid., 1004–1005.
47. Howard, 20.
48. Lewis and Clark, *Journals*, 8: 224–229. The name was originally Pompy's Tower and was changed to Pompey's Pillar in the *History*, 1151.
49. Lewis and Clark, *History*, 1178.
50. Ibid., 1184.
51. Lewis and Clark, *Journals*, 8: 305.
52. Ibid., 142.
53. For summaries of the Shoshone tradition and Eastman's investigation, see Howard, 175–192; Clark and Edmonds, 103–145; and Wilson, 177–180.
54. Wilson, 178.
55. Howard, 190.
56. Ibid., 185.

57. Ibid., 183.
58. Ibid., 190.
59. Clark and Edmonds, 110–111, 124–125.
60. Ibid., 111.
61. Lewis and Clark, *History*, 742.
62. Howard, 150.
63. Lewis and Clark, *History*, 509.
64. Clark and Edmonds, 104.
65. Howard, 160; Clark and Edmonds, 106.
66. Clark and Edmonds, 115, 126–127.
67. Letter of Sarah Winnemucca to Commissioner E. S. Parker of the Bureau of Indian Affairs, Washington, D.C., 1870. The last page of this letter appears as an illustration in Canfield, 66.
68. Winnemucca Hopkins, 69.
69. Ibid., 23.
70. Ibid., 60.
71. Canfield, 20.
72. Winnemucca Hopkins, 59.
73. Ibid., 92.
74. Ibid., 93.
75. Ibid., 177.
76. Ibid., 204.
77. Ibid., 213.
78. Canfield, 164.
79. Winnemucca Hopkins, 223.
80. Bataille and Sands, 160.
81. Gay, 146.
82. Winnemucca Hopkins, 113.
83. Somonte, 145.
84. Canfield, 164.
85. Lewis and Clark, *History*, 1184.
86. Howard, 141.
87. Canfield, 134.
88. Caffrey, 14.
89. Karttunen and Lockhart, 151, 155–157. These same punishments are represented pictorially in the Codex Mendoza ff. 59r, 60r, 66r.
90. Zorita,136.
91. Clark and Edmonds, 118.
92. Ibid., 126.
93. Ibid., 130–131.
94. Morison, 212.
95. Howard, 151.
96. Winnemucca Hopkins, 228.
97. Winnemucca Hopkins, 48 (emphasis in the original).
98. Ibid., 207. The preface is unpaginated.

CHAPTER 2. THREE CIVIL SERVANTS

1. Blom, *Conquest*, 103.
2. Landa, *Relación*, 41–42. In Darien (the Isthmus of Panama) Spanish settlers and Indians alike were also dying of an unidentified disease in 1514.

3. Morley and Brainard, 570; Roys, *Chumayel*, 138; Bricker, 15, 26–27. The first "Maya Death" of Yucatec tradition seems to have occurred in the fifteenth century, before the importation of European diseases.

4. Landa, *The Maya*, 61.

5. Benítez, *Alma Encantada*, 96 (original Spanish text); Blom, "Gaspar Antonio," 252 (English translation).

6. Landa, *The Maya*, 124.

7. Ibid., 42.

8. Landa, *Relación*, 45.

9. Landa, *The Maya*, 49.

10. McAndrew, 243.

11. Roys, *Indian Background*, 186.

12. There is a partial translation of both documents in Stephens, 170–172. There is a full translation of a copy of the 1557 document in Roys, *Indian Background*, 185–190.

13. Full accounts of the events that began in Mani in 1562 are to be found in Clendinnen, 72–100, and Landa, *Relación*, 76–83. Primary documents about the proceedings are to be found throughout Scholes and Adams, vols. 1 and 2.

14. Landa, *The Maya*, 124. See the discussion in Landa, *Relación*, 77–78.

15. Landa, *Relación*, 78.

16. Scholes and Adams 1:246–248.

17. See Landa, *Yucatan*, 114–115, for a facsimile and English translation of one of these letters. Another appears on 367–368 of *Cartas de Indias*, vol. 1, and is reproduced with interlinear Maya and Spanish text in the frontmatter of the Ciudad Real's *Motul Dictionary*, 59–61. For a textual analysis and the view that the original letters may not be quite what Francisco de Montejo Xiu claimed them to be, see Hanks.

18. Landa, *Yucatan*, 115–117. The Spanish text of this letter appears in *Cartas de Indias* 1:407–410.

19. Letter reproduced in González Cicero, 250 (translation mine).

20. Morley and Roys, 214–215.

21. *Relaciones de Yucatán* 2:83–92.

22. Farriss, 100. Original text in *Relaciones de Yucatán* 2:327.

23. *Relaciones de Yucatán* 1:413, 427.

24. Blom, "Gaspar Antonio," 260. See *Relaciones de Yucatán* 1:183, 375–382.

25. Landa, *Relación*, 45.

26. Jakeman presents a concordance of answers to questions 14 and 15 from the reports that acknowledge Gaspar Antonio's assistance.

27. *Relaciones de Yucatán* 1:428.

28. The abstract of Gaspar Antonio's report and this statement appear in López de Cogolludo, 287–293 (translation mine).

29. The complete English translation of Gaspar Antonio's report appears as an appendix in Landa, *Relación*, 230–232.

30. Guaman Poma, *Letter*, 204–205. The English edition of Guaman Poma's letter from which I have drawn direct quotations is an abridgment. My primary source is the complete Spanish edition by Murra and Adorno.

31. Cobo, *Religion*, 103–104.

32. Garcilaso de la Vega, 1:212–213.

33. Guaman Poma, *Letter*, 100.

34. Cobo, *History*, 230.

35. Spalding, 297–298.

36. Rowe, 268. See Cieza de León, 77.

37. Guaman Poma, *Letter*, 40–41, 93.

38. Guaman Poma, *Nueva Corónica* 1:119.

39. Guaman Poma, *Letter*, 184.

40. Mannheim, 132–139.

41. Urioste, 17–19.

42. Guaman Poma, *Letter*, 169–170.

43. Guaman Poma, *Nueva Corónica* 1 : 39; 2 : 349, 380, 382, 390, 521; 3 : 894.

44. Adorno, *Writing and Resistance*, 27–32 and passim.

45. Guaman Poma, *Letter*, 184.

46. Adorno, "Waman Puma," 16 n. 5.

47. Guaman Poma, *Letter*, 230.

48. Ibid., 194.

49. Guaman Poma, *Nueva Corónica* 1: xl, 4–5, 11.

50. Guaman Poma, *Letter*, 241–242.

51. Adorno, "Waman Puma," 14.

52. Ibid., 14.

53. Guaman Poma, *Letter*, 208.

54. Ibid., 203, 211.

55. Ibid., 59.

56. Ibid., 194.

57. Ibid., 211.

58. Ibid., 132, 201.

59. Ibid., 194, 209.

60. Ibid., 172.

61. Silverblatt, 14–19.

62. Guaman Poma, *Letter*, 177.

63. Ibid., 177.

64. Guaman Poma, *Nueva Corónica* 2 : 507.

65. Guaman Poma, *Letter*, 216.

66. Ibid., 113.

67. Guaman Poma, *Nueva Corónica* 2 : 342–343, 3 : 1139.

68. Guaman Poma, *Letter*, 141.

69. Ibid., 169.

70. Ibid., 228.

71. Eastman, *Indian Boyhood*, 288.

72. McDermott, 18.

73. "My father," Eastman related, "wrote to me in the Dakota language for my encouragement" (*DeepWoods*, 48).

74. Eastman claimed, "Although I could not understand or speak much English, at the end of the second year I could translate every word of my English studies into the native tongue, besides having read all that was then published in the Sioux" (Ibid., 49).

75. These "Big Bellies" were the surviving remnants of the same Hidatsa people known to Lewis and Clark as the Minnetarees. Although their language belongs to the same overarching Siouan language family as Eastman's Santee and the Dakotah/Lacotah dialects, it is a different language, unintelligible to Eastman.

76. Goodale Eastman, 155.

77. Goodale Eastman, 164; Eastman, *Deep Woods*, 111; Wilson, 58–59; Harjo, 9; Waldman, 158–159. Another version of what happened, based on interviews immediately after the event, blames a Sioux signal, a handful of dust tossed into the air, for the beginning of the shooting (Mooney, 118).

78. Eastman, *Indian Today*, 33, 43, 51.

79. Mary Eastman, 52.

80. Mary Eastman, 64–66; Eastman, *Indian Boyhood*, 181–187.

81. Mary Eastman, iii, v, 104.

82. Goodale Eastman, 34–35, 85, 93.

83. Ibid., 68, 104.

84. Mary Eastman wrote of wife-beating, "I have sometimes thought, that if, when a warrior, be he chief or commoner, throws a stick of wood at his wife's head, she were to cast it back at his, he might, perhaps, be taught better behaviour. But I never dared to instill such insubordinate notions into the heads of my Sioux female friends, lest some ultra 'brave,' in a desperate rage, might substitute the tomahawk for the log" (xi).
85. Goodale Eastman, 66, 100.
86. Ibid., 43, 58.
87. Mary Eastman, iv, 39.
88. Eastman, *Soul*, 5. Yet Eastman was aware of the mound builders, for Beloit College was built on a mound-builder site, which Eastman describes in his autobiography (*Deep Woods*, 52).
89. Eastman, *Soul*, 5. In a list of distinguished men he met and conversed with while at Dartmouth, Eastman includes Ralph Waldo Emerson and Francis Parkman (*Deep Woods*, 72).
90. Eastman, *Soul*, 10–11; *Indian Today*, 5.
91. Eastman, *Indian Today*, 18.
92. Mary Eastman, xxvii.
93. Goodale Eastman, 78 (used as description as the springboard to a rebuttal); Eastman, *Indian Today*, 12–13.
94. Eastman, *Indian Today*, 17; *Old Indian Days*, 93, 132; *Indian Boyhood*, 245–252.
95. Eastman, *Indian Boyhood*, 17.
96. Eastman, *Soul*, xii.
97. Eastman seemed hardly capable of using the word "woman" without the adjective "beautiful," while Goodale tended to describe women as "intensely feminine."
98. Eastman, *Old Indian Days*, 51–52. Considering that Eastman identified himself with the highest level of Sioux society, it is peculiar that when he describes the initiation of Indian marriages, he chooses the scenario in which young men and women steal away in secret to live together for a period before rejoining the community, although proper unions among the Sioux involved family negotiation, exchange of gifts, and the public delivery of the woman to her husband-to-be.
99. Eastman, *Indian Today*, 88–89.
100. Eastman, *Soul*, 42.
101. Eastman, *Indian Today*, 174.
102. Eastman, *Old Indian Days*, 57, 182.
103. Eastman, *Soul*, 42.
104. Goodale Eastman, 67, 173–174.
105. Eastman, *Indian Boyhood*, 5.
106. Eastman and Goodale Eastman, 187–192.
107. Eastman, *Soul*, 24.
108. See Las Casas, *A Short Account*, passim.
109. Wilson, 115.

CHAPTER 3. THREE NATIVE INFORMANTS

1. Larin Paraske, 93 (translation mine). Etymologically *lillukka* seems to be a diminutive form of 'lily', but the name refers to a member of the rose family. To convey something of the alliterativeness of Paraske's verse, I have favored the form of the word over its reference.

2. Magoun, 47–48.
3. Despite famine in the 1860s followed by heavy emigration, Finland's population tripled between 1800 and 1900.
4. Sussman, 62–67. For information about infanticide in Moscow prior to the founding of St. Petersburg, see Hellie, xvii, 375, 380, 425, 448–459. For a general overview of wet nursing and infanticide in Europe, see Piers, chaps. 3 and 4.
5. For a comprehensive history of Russia's foundling hospitals with figures for mortality rates, see Ransel, passim.
6. According to Piers, 67, two-thirds of the children sent from the St. Petersburg hospital to rural villages died before reaching age six. In "Hittebarnets värld," Engman, 426, states that for the year 1857 69 percent of the 1,212 infants sent to the Finnish villages died before reaching their first birthday.
7. A major concern of the time was that infants with congenital syphilis conveyed the infection to the women who nursed them, who then passed the disease on to other nurslings and in time to their husbands.
8. Engman, *S:t Petersburg*, 144–145; Ransel, 195–196.
9. Paraske's life story appears in a number of versions. Most of the detail is present in the first account of her life, written by Adolf Neovius for a biographical dictionary of Finnish women. Mikko Uotinen retold her life story in a memorial speech and publication in 1911. Väinö Salminen published a biography in 1931, and Yrjö Hirn devotes a chapter to her in a book about folk poets and collectors. Matti Haavio also has a chapter about her life in his book on singers of folk poetry, and Senni Timonen includes a biography in her edited collection of Paraske's poems. Anu Kaipainen wrote a novel about her life, and the novel was adapted for the stage. Letters dictated by Paraske are in several collections.
10. Alho, 92.
11. Haavio, 342, 344, 349; Hirn, 237.
12. Larin Paraske, 151.
13. For the sake of comparison, around the middle of the century a house in another village was purchased for three hundred rubles (Haavio, 85).
14. Tweedie, 119.
15. Virtaranta, 120–121, 126–127 (translation mine).
16. Larin Paraske, 98 (translation mine). The translation is loose in order to convey at least the visual impression of alliteration.
17. Clive-Bayley, 51.
18. Larin Paraske, 157 (translation mine).
19. Larin Paraske, 108 (translation mine).
20. Hirn, 249–251. Hirn reproduces a drawing of Paraske wearing specatacles and reading with Charlotta Molin, and in a footnote reproduces the text of a short letter from Parakse to Neovius inquiring about "old Miss Mulina," to whom she expresses gratitude for her reading lessons.
21. Letter from Krohn to Neovius, written March 11, 1891, in the archives of the Finnish Literature Society.
22. Tweedie, 173.
23. Schvindt, 9.
24. Larin Paraske, 173 n. 6.
25. Clive-Bayley, 279, 283–284.
26. 1,500 marks was about the equivalent of the annual salary a woman could earn working as a clerk, bookkeeper, or telephone operator in Helsinki in the mid-1890s. Tweedie, 179.
27. Larin Paraske, 155.
28. Letter from Krohn to Neovius written March 12, 1907, and letter from the stone

company written July 25, 1907, in the Neovius collection of the Finnish National Archives.

29. Uotinen's poem quoted in Haavio, 300–302 (translation mine).
30. *Mexico This Month*, 13.
31. Jiménez, *Life and Death*, 138–139.
32. *Cantares Mexicanos*, 26r–26v (translation by James Lockhart). A transcription of this song from the *Cantares* is to be found in Bierhorst, 216, 218.
33. Jiménez, *Life and Death*, 138–139.
34. Ibid., 178–179.
35. Morse, 44.
36. Ibid., 41.
37. Charlot, 168.
38. Weston, 1 : 143. (Unconventional spellings are Weston's.)
39. *Mexico This Month*, 12.
40. Personal communication, Zohmah Charlot.
41. Charlot, 166.
42. Letters from Luz to Charlot, one undated but before the wedding, and the other August 18, 1942, Jean Charlot Collection, Hamilton Library, University of Hawaii, Manoa.
43. Letter from Luz to Charlot, November 27, 1964, Jean Charlot Collection.
44. Personal communication, Concepción Hernández de Villanueva (Concha).
45. Charlot, 168.
46. Ibid., 46.
47. *Mexico This Month*, 12. By the 1950s Santa Anita had been absorbed into Mexico City and its canals filled in. The festival then moved to Mixquic, another canal town south of the capital. Xochimilco continues the tradition with a fiesta featuring the selection of the "Loveliest Flower," a coronation, a procession of women in folk costume, decorated boats, etc.
48. Jiménez, *Life and Death*, 166–167. The English translation says "fathers and mothers," which is misleading. In the original Nahuatl and Spanish it simply says "parents." There were no fathers among the refugees.
49. Undated letter to Charlot written in the spring or summer of 1942, Jean Charlot Collection. Edward Weston's Mexico City household had young Indian maids. As he describes openly in his diaries, he used them sexually and grew irritated with them when they became emotionally dependent. Nor did he have scruples about pilfering their savings to pay his bills (Weston 1: 47, 130, 141–142, 149, 156, 192).
50. *Mexico This Month*, 13.
51. Zantwijk, 46.
52. Brenner, *Idols*, 282.
53. Charlot, 168.
54. *Mexico This Month*, 13.
55. González Casanova, 25.
56. Jiménez, *Life and Death*, 104–107.
57. Whorf, "Milpa Alta Dialect," 368.
58. Minutes of the First Aztec Congress in Folder 179, the Barlow Archives, University of the Americas, Puebla-Cholula, Mexico.
59. Letter to Charlot, April 20, 1948, Jean Charlot Collection. A recording of Luz speaking Nahuatl is archived in the Languages of the World collection at Indiana University. Barlow's disc recordings have yet to be located.
60. *Mexico This Month*, 13.
61. Letter to Charlot, September 18, 1958, Jean Charlot Collection; Morse, 76.
62. Unpublished papers of Fernando Horcasitas at the Tulane University Latin American Library, Box 19. The payments are recorded at the bottom of the transcriptions.

63. Letter to Charlot, May 29, 1963, Jean Charlot Collection.
64. Personal communication, Concepción Hernández de Villanueva; letter to Charlot from Concha's son, Alfonso Villanueva Hernández, January 30, 1965, and letter to Charlot from Concha, February 13, 1965, Jean Charlot Collection.
65. In his foreword to *Life and Death in Milpa Alta*, Miguel León-Portilla remarks on a similarity of her narratives to Nahuatl texts of the sixteenth century.
66. Jiménez, *Life and Death*, 179. From the original transcriptions archived among his papers at the Tulane University Latin American Library, it can be seen that Horcasitas put Doña Luz's texts in a particular order and wrote chapter headings while respecting the integrity of her Nahuatl and Spanish narratives, reproducing them as she dictated them without changing them, even when they do not quite coincide.
67. Madsen, 83–84.
68. Zantwijk, 26.
69. Personal communication, Concepción Hernández de Villanueva.
70. *Mexico This Month*, 13.
71. Miguel León-Portilla remarks in his foreword about how few value judgments she makes.
72. Doña Luz expresses concern about this in an undated letter sent before Concha's wedding in 1942, and twenty-one years later Concha does the same. Letter dated August 12, 1973, Jean Charlot Collection.
73. Estrada, 39.
74. Details about María Sabina's personal life are drawn from her autobiography dictated to Alvaro Estrada. The 1981 English edition of her autobiography expands on the original Spanish edition with textual commentaries by Estrada and Henry Munn, as well as a preface by the poet Jerome Rothenberg. Both the Spanish and English editions include a retrospective essay by R. Gordon Wasson. In 1970 Benítez published some biographical information about María Sabina extracted from three interviews he had conducted with her through an interpreter (*Indios de México* 3:205–282). For the most part, it agrees in detail and in style with what she told Estrada directly in Mazatec without an interpreter.
75. Tibón, 50–51, confirms the pattern of marriage between thirteen and fifteen for girls. He also states that because of the surplus of women in Huautla, polygamy was commonly practiced, but María Sabina does not mention the practice in her autobiography.
76. In an interview conducted through an interpreter, Benítez (*Indios de México* 3:233) understood her to say that her first husband died in the influenza pandemic that began in 1918.
77. Estrada, 40.
78. Estrada, 67. Periods of sexual abstinence were also required for rites to protect corn fields. And here too, the punishment for a man who does not abstain is that his testicles will rot (Ibid., 196).
79. Ibid., 47.
80. Ibid., 40.
81. Ibid., 68.
82. First related by V. P. Wasson in the preface to *Mushrooms, Russia, and History* and repeated verbatim in most of Wasson's publications thereafter.
83. Pike, in a letter to Wasson dated March 9, 1953, reprinted in Wasson and Wasson 2:242–245. María Sabina herself compared movies to the mushroom visions (Estrada, 64).
84. Wasson and Wasson 2:250.
85. Ibid., 257.
86. Wasson, "Seeking the Magic Mushroom," 100.
87. Wasson and Wasson 2:288.
88. Estrada, 71. In this account of her first contact with Wasson María Sabina says three blond men came to her house on this first visit, and that one of them performed a

medical examination. "One of the visitors listened to my chest. He put his head on my chest to hear my heartbeat, held my temples between his hands, and put his head against my back. The man nodded while he touched me. Finally he said some words that I didn't understand; they spoke another language that wasn't Castilian. I don't even understand Castilian." She is probably compressing events. Valentina Pavlovna arrived the day after Wasson and Richardson and brought a stethoscope. It was probably she who did the examination.

89. Wasson and Wasson 2: 292.
90. Ibid., 290.
91. Wasson, "Seeking the Magic Mushroom," 109; Wasson and Wasson 2: 302.
92. Wasson and Wasson 2: 289.
93. Ibid., 301.
94. Ibid., 303.
95. Estrada, 80.
96. Ibid., 79.
97. Estrada, 71–72. She may have been mistaken. It was not Vanegas but Aurelio Carrera whom Wasson described in print as "on a much humbler level" of proficiency than she (*María Sabina*, ix).
98. Wasson and Wasson 2: 304.
99. Within days of the appearance of the *Life* article, *This Week* magazine published an article, "I Ate the Sacred Mushroom," by Valentina Pavlovna.
100. Tibón, 130–133.
101. Wasson et al., *María Sabina*, xiii.
102. Estrada, 72.
103. Wasson et al., *María Sabina*, xii, xxiv–xxv.
104. Ibid., xiii.
105. Estrada, 90.
106. Ibid., 86.
107. Ibid., 73.
108. Wasson, *The Wondrous Mushroom*, xvi.
109. Original Spanish text, Cela, 36–37; English translation, Balada, 12, 17–18.
110. Hughes, 33.
111. Estrada, 98.
112. *Mexico City News*, November 23, 1985.
113. Estrada, 56, 84.
114. The less expensive edition for sale to libraries and individuals came with cassettes rather than records.
115. Wasson et al., *María Sabina*, ix; Wasson et al., *Persephone's Quest*, 25.
116. The film was *María Sabina: Mujer Espíritu,* by Nicolas Echevaría.
117. Tibón, 167–168.
118. Estrada, 20 (emphasis mine).
119. Ibid., 19.
120. Ibid., 90–91.
121. *Tiempo*, December 10, 1985: 35; *Mexico City News*, November 23, 1985: 6.
122. Haavio, 251–252 (translation mine).
123. English summary of Calendar of Women's Work, in Tweedie, 162–181. Originally from a column in the Swedish newspaper *Stockholms-Tidningen*.
124. Letters to Jean Charlot, September 18, 1944, and May 29, 1963, Jean Charlot Collection.
125. Honko, 17.
126. Wasson et al., *Road*, 12.
127. In Tweedie we find, "The Finns, though intellectually most interesting, are not as a rule attractive in person. Generally small of stature, thickset, with high cheek-bones, and eyes inherited from their Tartar-Mongolian ancestors, they cannot be considered goodlook-

ing" (10). "She had very high cheek-bones and a wondrous round moon face. . . . Had she been dark instead of fair, judging by the width of her face and the lines of her eyes, she might have been Chinese. . . . Spite of the hard outlines of her face, and her peculiarly small Finnish eyes" (80). Clive-Bayley mentions the Finns' "Turanian speech" (59), and remarks, "All the women's noses seem more or less tip-tilted—generally more!" (89).

128. Timonen, 25.
129. Haavio, 223, 230.
130. Benítez, *Indios de México* 3:249.
131. Brenner, *The Boy Who Could Do Anything*. Letters to Charlot, March 2, 1942, undated (but from context in summer 1942); August 5, 1942; October 11, 1942; November 11 (no year, but from context 1942), Jean Charlot Collection.
132. Letter to Charlot, January 13, 1962, Jean Charlot Collection.
133. Estrada, 79.

CHAPTER 4. MORE LIVES, FAMILIAR STORIES

1. Richard Elphick presents the history of the Khoikhoi and the life stories of Eva and the other interpreters in *Kraal and Castle: Khoikhoi and the Founding of White South Africa*. The original sources for Eva's story include the *Journal of Jan van Riebeeck* and papers in the colonial archives of The Hague.
2. Elphick, 184, 203, 213.
3. Ibid., 94.
4. Riebeeck 2: 286, 289, 328, 359, 366; 3:17.
5. Elphick, 107; Riebeeck 2: 170, estimated that Eva was fifteen or sixteen in the fall of 1657.
6. Or perhaps she was her cousin. Riebeeck 2:362–364.
7. It wasn't just women who eked out an income from seamen in the harbor. Curious Europeans paid Africans of both sexes to exhibit themselves and especially to expose their genitalia, which were rumored to be different from those of Europeans (Elphick, 180–181, 196–197).
8. Ibid., 165, 201–203.
9. The visually lovely and moving movie *Dersu Uzala*, a joint venture by the Japanese filmmaker Akira Kurosawa and the government of the Soviet Union, follows Arsenjev's journal closely until near the end, in which three significant changes are made. First, in the movie Dersu goes into a fatal decline subsequent to shooting at a tiger. By Arsenjev's account, Dersu's depression had to do with his failing eyesight, and the shooting incident with the tiger had happened long ago. Second, Arsenjev is portrayed as having in the Russian town of Khabarovsk a household with wife and son to which he takes Dersu. Arsenjev was married at the time, but according to the journal, he and Dersu shared bachelor quarters. And third, Arsenjev is implicated in Dersu's death by having sent him off to the taiga with a new rifle for which robbers murder Dersu. These changes impart a tragic structure to the movie but somewhat misrepresent the relationship between the two men. Arsenjev's attachment to Dersu, which in the journal appears as intense devotion, seems more like paternalism in the movie.
10. These people are currently known as the Nanai. They belong to the larger grouping of aboriginal peoples of eastern Siberia and Manchuria known as the Tungus.
11. Arsenjev, 97, 143. Visiting the Goldi of Manchuria two decades later, Lattimore (32) observed the prevalence of tapeworm infestation.
12. Arsenjev, 207.

13. For the contents of Dersu's backpack, see ibid., 114–115; concerning Goldi multilingualism, Lattimore writes that many spoke Russian and Chinese "with perfect readiness" (70).
14. Arsenjev, 188.
15. Ibid., 189–190.
16. Lattimore (53–55) expresses a very different view of shamanism from Arsenjev, saying that it possesses "religious ideas of a very high order" and characterizing it as "essentially an aristocrat's religion."
17. Arsenjev, 273.
18. Ibid., 14.
19. Ibid., 129–130.
20. Ibid., 333.
21. Ibid., 339.
22. Theodora Kroeber (45–78) relates the details of the decimation of the Indians of North California in the first section of her biography of Ishi. Primary documents upon which she drew have been published in Heizer and Kroeber, *Ishi the Last Yahi: A Documentary History*. Of several documentary films, the recent one by N. Jed Riffe and Pamela Roberts with funding from the National Endowment for the Humanities—also entitled *Ishi the Last Yahi*—is especially accurate and well-made.
23. Heizer and Kroeber, 232–234.
24. Dixon, *Aboriginal Languages*, 1–3, 33, 35.
25. Ibid., 159.
26. Ibid., 133.
27. Dixon, personal communication.
28. Dixon, *Aboriginal Languages*, 240.
29. Dixon, personal communication.
30. Quotations from George Watson are from a recording he made for Dixon.
31. Dixon, *Aboriginal Languages*, 170.
32. Andrade, 41, 168.
33. Ibid., 56.
34. Ibid., 102–103.
35. Ibid., 149–150.
36. The Spanish spelling of this name is Huaorani; an alternative is Waorani. *Huao/Wao* (pronounced something like "Wow!") is the name the people use for themselves, and the suffix *-rani* makes it plural, so Huaorani literally means 'Huao people'.
37. Dayuma retold biblical stories on a record produced for evangelical work among the Huaorani. English summaries of a number of traditional stories and biblical stories Dayuma recounted are included in Wallis, *The Dayuma Story*, and the full texts in Huao of three stories told by Dayuma appear with English translations in Pike and Saint.
38. Wallis, *Dayuma Story*, 130.
39. Ibid., 224.
40. Ibid., 78.
41. Ibid., 176.
42. Ibid., 255.
43. Ibid., 234.
44. Ibid., 255–257.
45. Wallis, *Aucas Downriver*, viii (map), 74.
46. Ibid., 115.
47. Ibid., 100.
48. Elliot, 272–273.
49. Labaca, passim.
50. Kimerling, 56, 87–95.

CHAPTER 5. WHAT WAS WON AND WHAT IT COST

1. Farriss, 99.
2. Lockhart, 384–385.
3. Eastman, *Indian Today*, 16–17.
4. Haavio, 246, 248–250, 260–264.
5. Sahagún 10:165–197.
6. Laughlin, "Drama of Maya Women."
7. Karttunen and Lockhart, 155–157; Berdan and Anawalt, *Codex Mendoza*, ff. 70v-71r (Nahuatl text in Vol. 3, English translation in Vol. 4).
8. Sahagún 6:102.
9. Díaz del Castillo, *Historia* 2:69–70.
10. Goodale Eastman, 49.
11. Eastman, *Deep Woods*, 144–145.
12. Letter to Charlot, March 2, 1942, Charlot Collection.
13. Andrade, 135, 156.
14. Ibid., 188.
15. Ibid., 98–99.
16. Ibid., 224–225.
17. Ibid., 79.
18. Ibid., 155.
19. Ibid., 161.
20. Ibid., 77.
21. Somonte, 145. There are drawings of her to be found in the *Florentine Codex* and the several versions of the *Lienzo de Tlaxcala* as well as numbers of other illustrated documents.
22. Lewis and Clark, *History*, 189–190 n. 13.
23. Andrade, 148–149, 173.
24. Kroeber, 162.
25. Eastman, *Deep Woods*, 70, 90.

EPILOGUE. THEIR CHILDREN

1. *Diccionario Porrúa* 1:743; Benítez, *Century*, passim; Somonte, 169. Somonte's source seems to be family history conveyed to him by a descendent of Don Martín.
2. Gerhard, 383; Somonte, 141–144.
3. Archivo General de las Indias (Seville): Patronato Legajo 58, Num. 3, Ramo 4 (1547 probanza); Patronato Legajo 76, Num. 2, Ramo 10 (1581 probanza). Somonte gives the text of the 1547 probanza.
4. Morley and Roys, 241; Rubio Mañé, 108. Gaspar Antonio had other children besides Francisca.
5. Guaman Poma, *Letter*, 229, 233, 235–236.
6. Elphick, 201–203.
7. McClure and Parish, 18–19.
8. Ibid., 39.
9. As for other children of Sacajawea, the mystery of how long she lived casts all into

confusion. The woman who died at Luttig's outpost left a daughter named Lizette, and the guardianship papers approved the following summer are for Lizette, now a year old, and a ten-year-old boy named Toussaint, not an eight-year-old Jean Baptiste. No more is heard of Lizette, although one of Sacajawea's biographers suggests she may have grown up to be a married woman living in Westport, Missouri, in the 1840s (Howard, 162). In subsequent years Clark made educational payments sometimes for "J. B. Charbonneau" and sometimes for "Toissaint Charbonneau." Again controversy turns on whether Jean Baptiste was sometimes called Toissaint after his father or whether Clark had taken on the care of two of the elder Charbonneau's children in addition to Sacajawea's son. In the same list in which Clark lists Sacajawea as dead and Tousssaint Charbonneau as "Mand," he also writes "Tousant Charbon in Wertenburgh, Gy.," apparently referring to Jean Baptiste, who was off in Europe with the German prince (Howard, 189).

10. Goodale Eastman, 173–174; Wilson, 188.
11. Anu Kaipainen, personal communication, 1985.
12. Letter from Luz to Charlot, April 20, 1948, Charlot Collection.
13. Dixon, personal communication.
14. Labaca Ugarte, 29, 77, 109.
15. Elliot, 272.
16. "Laurinda Andrade, Pioneer Teacher of Portuguese, Retires This Year," *New Bedford Standard Times*, December 25, 1966.
17. Andrade, 234.

Bibliography

Abrams, H. Leon. "Robert Haywood Barlow: An Annotated Bibliography with Commentary." In *Katunob: Occasional Publication in Mesoamerican Anthropology* 16. Greeley, Colo.: University of Northern Colorado, 1981.

Adorno, Rolena. *Guaman Poma: Writing and Resistance in Colonial Peru*. Austin: University of Texas Press, 1988.

————. "Waman Puma de Ayala: 'Author and Prince.' " *Latin American Literature and Arts Review* 28 (1981): 12–16.

Alho, Olli. *Orjat ja isännät: Tutkimus inkeriläisistä maaorjarunoista / Serfs and Masters: A Study of Ingrian Serf Poetry*. Helsinki: Suomalaisen Kirjallisuuden Seura, 1979.

Alva Ixtlilxochitl, Fernando de. *Obras históricas*. Edited by Edmundo O'Gorman. Vol. 2. Mexico City: Universidad Nacional Autónoma de México, 1985.

Andrade, Laurinda C. *The Open Door*. New Bedford, Mass.: Reynolds-DeWalt, 1968.

Arsenjev, Vladimir Klavdiejevitch. *Dersu, the Trapper*. Translated by Malcolm Burr. New York: Dutton, 1941. Originally published as *Dersu Uzala,* 1923.

Balada, Leonardo. *María Sabina: A Symphonic Tragedy*. Text by Camilo José Cela. Music by Leonardo Balada. Dobbs Ferry, N.Y.: General Music Publishing Company, 1969.

Barlow, Robert. "Un cuento sobre el día de los muertos." *Estudios de cultura náhuatl* 2 (1960): 7–82.

Barry, Kathleen. *Susan B. Anthony: A Biography of a Singular Feminist*. New York: New York University Press, 1988.

Bataille, Gretchen M., and Kathleen Mullen Sands. *American Indian Women Telling Their Lives*. Lincoln: University of Nebraska Press, 1984.

Benítez, Fernando. *The Century after Cortés*. Chicago and London: University of Chicago Press, 1965. Originally published as *Los primeros Mexicanos: La vida criolla en el siglo XVI* (Mexico City: Ediciones ERA, 1962).

————. *El Alma Encantada: Annales del Museo Nacional de México*. Mexico City: Fondo de Cultura Económica, 1987.

————. *Los indios de México*. 4 vols. Mexico City: Ediciones ERA, 1970.

Berdan, Frances F., and Patricia Rieff Anawalt, eds. and trans. *The Codex Mendoza*. 4 vols. Berkeley and Los Angeles: University of California Press, 1992.

Bierhorst, John. *Cantares Mexicanos: Songs of the Aztecs*. Stanford: Stanford University Press, 1985.

Blom, Frans. *The Conquest of Yucatan.* Boston: Houghton Mifflin, 1936.

————. "Gaspar Antonio Chi, Interpreter." In *American Anthropologist* 30 (1928): 250–262.

Boas, Franz. "Cuentos en Mexicano de Milpa Alta D.F." *The Journal of American Folk-Lore* 33 (1920): 1–24.

Boas, Franz, and Herman K. Haeberlin. "Ten Folktales in Modern Nahuatl." *The Journal of American Folk-Lore* 37 (1926): 345–370.

Brenner, Anita. *The Boy Who Could Do Anything and Other Mexican Folk Tales.* 1942. Reprint. Hamden, Conn.: Shoestring Press, 1992.

————. *Idols behind Altars.* 1929. Reprint. New York: Biblo and Tanner, 1967.

Bricker, Victoria Reifler. *The Indian Christ, the Indian King: The Historical Substrate of Maya Myth and Ritual.* Austin: University of Texas Press, 1981.

Caffrey, Margaret. *Ruth Benedict: Stranger in This Land.* Austin: University of Texas Press, 1989.

Canfield, Gae Whitney. *Sarah Winnemucca of the Northern Paiutes.* Norman: University of Oklahoma Press, 1983.

Cartas de Indias, Vol. I. Madrid: Biblioteca de Autores Españoles, 1974. Originally published Madrid, 1877.

Cela, Camilo José. *María Sabina y El carro de heno o el inventor de la guillotina.* Madrid and Barcelona: Alfaguara, 1970.

Cerwin, Herbert. *Bernal Díaz: Historian of the Conquest.* Norman: University of Oklahoma Press, 1963.

Charlot, Jean. *The Mexican Mural Renaissance, 1920–1925.* New Haven: Yale University Press, 1963.

Cieza de León, Pedro de. *The Incas of Pedro de Cieza de León.* Edited by Victor Wolfgang von Hagen. Translated by Harriet de Onis. Norman: University of Oklahoma Press, 1959.

Ciudad Real, Antonio de. *Diccionario de Motul maya-español.* Edited by Juan Hernández Martínez. Mérida,Yucatán: n.p., 1929.

Clark, Ella E., and Margot Edmonds. *Sacagawea of the Lewis and Clark Expedition.* Berkeley and Los Angeles: University of California Press, 1979.

Clendinnen, Inga. *Ambivalent Conquests: Maya and Spaniard in Yucatan, 1517–1570.* Cambridge: Cambridge University Press, 1987.

Clive-Bayley, A.M.C. *Vignettes from Finland: Or Twelve Months in Strawberry Land.* London: Sampson Low, Marston and Company, 1895.

Cobo, Bernabé. *History of the Inca Empire.* Translated by Roland Hamilton. Austin: University of Texas Press, 1983.

————. *Inca Religion and Customs.* Translated by Roland Hamilton. Austin: University of Texas Press, 1990.

Colección de documentos inéditos relativos al descubrimiento, conquista y organización de las antiguas posesiones españolas de Ultramar. Second series, vols. 11 and 13. Madrid: Real Academia de Historia, 1898–1900.

Cordy, Donald. *Mexican Masks.* Austin: University of Texas Press, 1980.

Cortés, Hernán. *Hernán Cortés: Letters from Mexico.* Translated and edited by Anthony Pagden. New Haven: Yale University Press, 1986.

Crosby, Alfred W. *The Columbian Exchange: Biological and Cultural Consequences of 1492.* Westport, Conn.: Greenwood Press, 1972.

———. *Ecological Imperialism: The Biological Expansion of Europe, 900–1900.* Cambridge: Cambridge University Press, 1986.

Díaz del Castillo, Bernal. *The Discovery and Conquest of Mexico.* Translated and edited by A. P. Maudslay. New York: Farrar, Straus, and Giroux, 1956.

———. *Historia verdadera de la conquista de la Nueva España.* 3 vols. Mexico City: Editorial Porrua, 1955.

Diccionario de Porrúa de Historia, Biografía y Geografía de México. 3 vols. Fifth ed. Mexico City: Porrúa, 1986.

Dickey, John Sloan. *Eleazar Wheelock (1711–1779), Daniel Webster (1782–1852), and Their Pioneer Dartmouth College.* New York: The Newcomen Society in North America, 1954.

Dixon, R.M.W. *Searching for Aboriginal Languages: Memoirs of a Field Worker.* Chicago: The University of Chicago Press, 1989.

Eastman, Charles. *From the Deep Woods to Civilization: Chapters in the Autobiography of an Indian.* 1916. Reprint. Lincoln: University of Nebraska Press, 1977.

———. *Indian Boyhood.* 1902. Reprint. Boston: Little, Brown, 1921.

———. *Indian Scout Talks: A Guide for Boy Scouts and Camp Fire Girls.* Boston: Little, Brown, 1915.

———. *The Indian Today: The Past and Future of the First American.* Garden City, N.Y.: Doubleday, Page and Co., 1915.

———. *Old Indian Days.* New York: The McClure Company, 1907.

———. *Red Hunters and the Animal People.* New York: Harper and Brothers, 1904.

———. *The Soul of the Indian: An Interpretation.* Boston: Houghton Mifflin, 1911.

Eastman, Charles, and Elaine Goodale Eastman. *Wigwam Evenings: Sioux Folk Tales Retold.* 1909. Reprint. Boston: Little, Brown, 1918.

Eastman, Mary. *Dahcotah: or, Life and Legends of the Sioux around Fort Snelling.* Minneapolis: Ross and Haines, 1962.

Elliot, Elizabeth. *Through Gates of Splendor.* Wheaton, Ill: Tyndale House, 1981.

Elphick, Richard. *Kraal and Castle: Khoikhoi and the Founding of White South Africa.* New Haven: Yale University Press, 1977.

Engman, Max. "Hittebarnets värld i 1700- och 1800-talets Europa—Findelhuset i S:t Petersburg och Finland." In *Historisk Tidskrift för Finland* 3 (1990): 399–445.

———. *S:t Petersburg och Finland: Migration och influens 1703–1917.* Helsinki: Bidrag till Kännedom av Finlands Nature och Folk, Utgivna av Finska Vetenskaps-Societeten, 1983.

Estrada, Alvaro. *María Sabina: Her Life and Chants.* Translated by Henry Munn. Santa Barbara, Cal.: Ross-Erikson, 1981. Originally published as *Vida de María Sabina, la sabia de los hongos* (Mexico City: Siglo Veintiuno, 1977).

Farriss, Nancy. *Maya Society under Colonial Rule: The Collective Enterprise of Survival.* Princeton: Princeton University Press, 1984.

Fuentes, Patricia de. *The Conquistadors: First-Person Accounts of the Conquest of Mexico.* New York: Orion Press, 1963.

Garcilaso de la Vega. *Royal Commentaries of the Incas and General History of Peru by Garcilaso de la Vega, El Inca.* 2 vols. Translated by Harold V. Livermore. Austin: University of Texas Press, 1966.

Gay, E. Jane. *With the Nez Perces: Alice Fletcher in the Field, 1889–1892.* Edited by Frederick E. Hoxie and Joan T. Mark. Lincoln: University of Nebraska Press, 1981.

Gerhard, Peter. 1972. *A Guide to the Historical Geography of New Spain.* Cambridge: Cambridge University Press, 1972.

González Casanova, Pablo. "Cuento en Mexicano de Milpa Alta, D.F." *The Journal of American Folk-Lore*, 37 (1926): 25–27.

González Cicero, Stella María. *Perspectiva religiosa en Yucatan 1517–1571.* Mexico City: El Colegio de México, 1978.

Goodale Eastman, Elaine. *Sister to the Sioux.* Lincoln: University of Nebraska Press, 1978.

Guaman Poma de Ayala, Felipe. *El Primer Nueva Corónica y Buen Gobierno por Felipe Guaman Poma de Ayala [Waman Puma].* Edited by John Murra and Rolena Adorno, with translations and textual analysis of the Quechua by Jorge L. Urioste. Mexico City: Siglo Veintiuno, 1980.

————. *Letter to a King: A Peruvian Chief's Account of Life under the Incas and under Spanish Rule by Huamán Poma.* Translated by Christopher Dilke. New York: E. P. Dutton, 1978.

Haavio, Martti. *Viimeset Runonlaulajat* (The Last Verse Singers). 1943. Reprint. Porvoo, Helsinki, and Juva: Werner Söderström OY, 1985.

Hanks, William. "Authenticity and Ambivalence in the Text: A Colonial Maya Case." *American Ethnologist* 13 (1986): 721–744.

Harjo, Suzan Shown. "A Hard, but Good Day." In *Native Nations* 1, 2 (1991): 9–12.

Hebard, Grace R. *Sacajawea, a Guide and Interpreter of the Lewis and Clark Expedition.* Glendale, California: Arthur H. Clark, 1933.

Heizer, Robert F., and Theodora Kroeber, eds. *Ishi the Last Yahi: A Documentary History.* Berkeley and Los Angeles: University of California Press, 1979.

Hellie, Richard. *Slavery in Russia: 1450–1725.* Chicago: University of Chicago Press, 1982.

Hirn, Yrjö. "Larin Paraske, Suuri runonlaulaja." In *Matkamiehiä ja tietäjiä* (Travelers and Seers). Edited by Yrjö Hirn. Helsinki: Kustannusosakeyhtiö Otava, 1939.

Honko, Lauri. "The Kalevala process." In *Kalevala 1835–1985: The National Epic of Finland.* Helsinki: Books From Finland, Helsinki University Library, 1985.

Howard, Harold P. *Sacajawea.* Norman: University of Oklahoma Press, 1971.

Hughes, Allen. "Mexican Cult of 'María Sabina' is a Poetic Premier at Carnegie." *New York Times*, April 18, 1970: 33.

Jakeman, M. Welles. *The "Historical Recollections" of Gaspar Antonio Chi: An Early Source-account of Ancient Yucatan.* Provo: Brigham Young University Publications in Archaeology and Early History, No. 3, 1952.

Jiménez, Luz. *De Porfirio Díaz a Zapata: memoria náhuatl de Milpa Alta*. Edited by Fernando Horcasitas. Mexico City: Universidad Nacional Autónoma de México. 1968.

—. *Life and Death in Milpa Alta: A Nahuatl Chronicle of Díaz and Zapata*. Translated and edited by Fernando Horcasitas. Norman: University of Oklahoma Press, 1972.

—. *Los Cuentos en Náhuatl de Doña Luz Jiménez*. Edited by Fernando Horcasitas and Sarah O. de Ford. Mexico City: Universidad Nacional Autónoma de México, 1979.

—. Unpublished letters to Jean Charlot, 1942–1965. Jean Charlot Collection, Hamilton Library, University of Hawaii, Manoa.

Kaipainen, Anu. *Poimisin heliät hiekat* (I Would Gather the Bright Grains of Sand). Helsinki: Werner Söderström, 1979.

Karttunen, Frances. "Conventions of Polite Speech in Nahuatl." *Estudios de Cultura Náhuatl* 20 (1990): 281–296.

Karttunen, Frances, and James Lockhart. *The Art of Nahuatl Speech: The Bancroft Dialogues*. Los Angeles: UCLA Latin American Center Publications, 1987.

Kimerling, Judith. *Amazon Crude*. Washington, D.C.: Natural Resources Defense Council, 1991.

Kroeber, Theodora. *Ishi in Two Worlds: A Biography of the Last Wild Indian in North America*. Berkeley and Los Angeles: University of California Press, 1976.

Krueger, Hilde. *Malinche: or, Farewell to Myths*. New York: Arrowhead Press, 1948.

Labaca Ugarte, Alejandro. *Crónica Huaorani*. Quito: CICAME, Vicariato Apostólico de Aguarico, 1988.

Landa, Diego de. *Landa's Relación de las cosas de Yucatan*. Translated by Alfred M. Tozzer. 1941. Reprint. Millword, New York: Kraus Reprint Company, 1975.

—. *The Maya: Diego de Landa's Account of the Affairs of Yucatán*. Edited and translated by A. R. Pagden. Chicago: J. Philip O'Hara, 1975.

—. *Yucatan before and after the Conquest, by Friar Diego de Landa*. Translated by William Gates. New York: Dover Publications, 1978.

Larin Paraske. *Näin lauloi Larin Paraske* (Thus Sang Larin Paraske). Edited by Senni Timonen. Helsinki: Suomalaisen Kirjallisuuden Seura, 1982.

Las Casas, Bartolomé. *A Short Account of the Destruction of the Indies*. Translated by Nigel Griffen. New York: Viking Penguin, 1992.

Lattimore, Owen. "The Gold Tribe, the 'Fishskin Tatars' of the Lower Sungari." *Memoirs of the American Anthropological Association* 40. Menasha, Wisc.: American Anthropological Association, 1933.

Laughlin, Miriam. "The Drama of Mayan Women." *Ms.* 2, 1 (1991): 88–89.

"Laurinda Andrade, Pioneer Teacher of Portuguese, Retires This Year." *New Bedford Standard-Times*, December 25, 1966.

Lewis, Meriwether, and William Clark. *Journals of the Lewis and Clark Expedition*. Edited by Gary E. Moulton. Vols. 2–8. Lincoln: University of Nebraska Press, 1986–91.

—. *The History of the Lewis and Clark Expedition under the Command of Lewis and Clark*. 3 vols. Edited by Elliott Coues. New York: Dover Publications, 1965.

Lockhart, James. *The Nahuas after the Conquest: A Social and Cultural History of the Indians of Central Mexico, Sixteenth through Eighteenth Centuries.* Stanford: Stanford University Press, 1992.

Lockhart, James, Frances Berdan, and Arthur J. O. Anderson. *The Tlaxcalan Actas: A Compendium of the Records of the Cabildo of Tlaxcala (1545–1627).* Salt Lake City: University of Utah Press, 1986.

López Cogolludo, Diego. *Historia de Yucatan, escrita en el siglo XVII.* Mérida, Yucatan: Imprenta de Manuel Aldana Rivas, 1868.

López de Gómara, Francisco. *Cortés: The Life of the Conqueror by His Secretary.* Translated and edited by Lesley Byrd Simpson. Berkeley and Los Angeles: University of California Press, 1964.

"Luz: Her Legend." *Mexico This Month* 10, 10 (March 1965): 12–13.

Macleod, David I. *Building Character in the American Boy: The Boy Scouts, YMCA, and Their Forerunners, 1870–1920.* Madison: University of Wisconsin Press, 1983.

Madsen, William. *The Virgin's Children: Life in an Aztec Village Today.* Austin: University of Texas Press, 1960.

Magoun, Francis Peabody, ed. and trans. *The Kalevala, or Poems from the Kaleva District.* Cambridge: Harvard University Press, 1963.

Mannheim, Bruce. *The Language of the Inka since the European Invasion.* Austin: University of Texas Press, 1991.

Martínez Marín, Carlos. *Tetela del Volcán.* Mexico City: Universidad Nacional Autónoma de México, Instituto de Investigaciones Históricas, 1968.

McAndrew, John. *The Open-Air Churches of Sixteenth-Century Mexico: Atrios, Posas, Open Chapels, and Other Studies.* Cambridge: Harvard University Press, 1965.

McClure, David, and Elijah Parish. *Memoirs of the Rev. Eleazar Wheelock, D.D.* New York: Arno Press, 1972.

McDermott, John Francis. *Seth Eastman: Pictorial Historian of the Indian.* Norman: University of Oklahoma Press, 1961.

Mexico City News. November 23, 1985: 6.

Mooney, James. *The Ghost-Dance Religion and the Sioux Outbreak of 1890.* Chicago: University of Chicago Press, 1965.

Morison, Samuel Eliot, ed. and trans. *Journals and Other Documents on the Life and Voyages of Christopher Columbus.* New York: Heritage Press, 1963.

Morley, Sylvanus, George W. Brainard, and Robert J. Sharer. *The Ancient Maya.* Stanford: Stanford University Press, 1983.

Morley, Sylvanus, and Ralph Roys. *The Xiu Chronicle.* Washington, D.C.: Carnegie Institution, 1941.

Morse, Peter. *Jean Charlot's Prints: A Catalogue Raisonné.* Honolulu: University Press of Hawaii and the Jean Charlot Foundation, 1976.

Mushroom Ceremony of the Mazatec Indians. Recorded by V. P. and R. Gordon Wasson. New York: Folkways Records and Service Corporation, 1957.

Neovius, Adolf. "Paraske (Paraskena [sic] Nikitina)." Entry in *Biograafisia tietoja Suomen naisista eri työaloilla* (Biographical Information about Finnish Women in Various Areas of Employment). Helsinki: Suomen Naisyhdistys (1896): 131–133.

Oviedo y Valdés, Gonzalo Fernández de. *Historia General y Natural de las Indias: Islas y Tierra-Firme del Mar Oceano.* Vol. 8. Asunción del Paraguay: Editorial Guarania, 1944.

Paz, Octavio. *The Labyrinth of Solitude: Life and Thought in Mexico.* New York: Grove Press, 1961.

Peterson, Robert W. *The Boy Scouts: An American Adventure.* New York: American Heritage, 1984.

Piers, Maria W. *Infanticide: Past and Present.* New York: W. W. Norton, 1978.

Pike, Evelyn G., and Rachel Saint, eds. *Workpapers Concerning Waorani Discourse Features.* Dallas: Summer Institute of Linguistics Publications, 1988.

Ramírez Castañeda, Isabel. "El folk-lore de Milpa Alta, D.F., Mexico." In *International Congress of Americanists. Proceedings of the XVIII. Session, London, 1912.* London: Harrison and Sons. 1913.

Ransel, David L. *Mothers of Misery: Child Abandonment in Russia.* Princeton: Princeton University Press, 1988.

Relaciones histórico-geográficas de la gobernacion de Yucatán. 2 vols. Mexico City: Universidad Nacional Autónoma de México, 1983.

Riebeeck, Jan van. *Journal of Jan van Riebeeck.* Edited by H. B. Thom. 3 vols. Capetown and Amsterdam: A. A. Balkema, 1952, 1954, 1958.

Rowe, John Howland. "Inca Culture at the Time of the Spanish Conquest." In *Handbook of South American Indians*, ed. Julian H. Steward, 2: 183–330. New York: Cooper Square Publishers, 1963.

Roys, Ralph L. *The Book of Chilam Balam of Chumayel.* Norman: University of Oklahoma Press, 1967.

———. *The Indian Background of Colonial Yucatan.* Washington, D.C.: The Carnegie Institution, 1943.

Rubio Mañé, Jorge Ignacio. "El Cronista Maya Gaspar Antonio Chi, 1531–1610." *Memorias de la Academia Mexicana de la Historia Correspondiente de la Real de Madrid* 15 (1956): 102–108.

Sahagún, Bernardino de. *Florentine Codex: General History of the Things of New Spain.* Books 6, 10, 12. Translated by Arthur J. O. Anderson and Charles E. Dibble. Salt Lake City: University of Utah Press, 1969, 1961, 1975.

Sánchez de Aguilar, Pedro. *Informe contra los idólatras de Yucatan escrito en 1613.* Mexico City: Imprenta del Museo Nacional, 1892.

Scherer, Joanna Cohan. "The Public Faces of Sarah Winnemucca." *Cultural Anthropology* 3 (May 1988): 178–204.

Scholes, France, and Eleanor B. Adams. *Don Diego Quijada, Alcalde Mayor de Yucatan, 1561–1565.* Vols. 1 and 2. Biblioteca Histórica Mexicana de Obras Ineditas 14. Mexico City: Antigua Librería Robredo, 1938.

Scholes, France V., and Ralph L. Roys. *The Maya Chontal Indians of Acalan-Tixchel: a Contribution to the History and Ethnography of the Yucatan Peninsula.* Norman: University of Oklahoma Press, 1968.

Schvindt, Theodor. *Ompelu- ja Nauhakoristeita* (Embroidery and Ribbon Decorations). Helsinki: Suomalaisen Kirjallisuuden Seura, 1982.

Silverblatt, Irene. *Moon, Sun, and Witches: Gender Ideologies and Class in Inca and Colonial Peru.* Princeton: Princeton University Press, 1987.

Somonte, Mariano G. *Doña Marina, "La Malinche."* Mexico City: n.p., 1971.

Spalding, Karen. *Huarochirí: An Andean Society under Inca and Spanish Rule.* Stanford: Stanford University Press, 1984.

Stephens, John L. *Incidents of Travel in Yucatan.* Vol. 2. Norman: University of Oklahoma Press, 1962.

Sussman, George D. *Selling Mother's Milk: The Wet-Nursing Business in France, 1715–1914.* Urbana: University of Illinois Press, 1982.

Tibón, Gutierre. *La cuidad de los hongos alucinantes.* Mexico City: Panorama Editorial, 1983.

Tiempo. December 10, 1985.

Timonen, Senni. "Lönnrot and his singers." In *Kalevala, 1835–1985: The National Epic of Finland.* Helsinki: Books from Finland, Helsinki University Library, 1985.

Tweedie, Mrs. Alec. *Through Finland in Carts.* New York: The Macmillan Company, 1898. London: Adam and Charles Black, 1898.

Urioste, George L. "The Spanish and Quechua Voices of Waman Puma." *Latin American Literature and Arts Review* 28 (1981): 16–19.

Villagutierre Soto-Mayor, Pedro. *History of the Conquest of the Province of the Itza.* Culver City: Labyrinthos, 1983.

Virtaranta, Pertti. "Katri Peräläinen, inkerilainen kielenoppaani" (Katri Peräläinen, My Ingrian Language Guide). In *Kertojat ja kuulijat* (Tellers and Listeners), edited by Pekka Laaksonen. Helsinki: Suomalaisen Kirjallisuuden Seura, 1980.

Waldman, Carl. *Atlas of the North American Indian.* Oxford and New York: Facts on File Publications, 1985.

Wallis, Ethel Emily. *Aucas Downriver: Dayuma's Story Today.* New York: Harper and Row, 1973.

———. *The Dayuma Story: Life under Auca Spears.* New York: Harper and Brothers, 1960.

Wasson, R. Gordon. *The Hall Carbine Affair: A Study in Contemporary Folklore.* 1941. Reprint. New York: Pandrick Press, 1948.

———. "Seeking the Magic Mushoom." *Life*, May 13, 1957: 100–120.

———. *The Wondrous Mushroom: Mycolatry in Mesoamerica.* New York: McGraw-Hill, 1980.

Wasson, R. Gordon, George and Florence Cowan, and Willard Rhodes. *María Sabina and Her Mazatec Mushroom Velada.* New York and London: Harcourt Brace Jovanovich, 1974.

Wasson, R. Gordon, Stella Kramrisch, Jonathan Ott, and Carl A. P. Ruck. *Persephone's Quest: Entheogens and the Origins of Religion.* New Haven: Yale University Press, 1986.

Wasson, R. Gordon, Carl A. P. Ruck, and Albert Hofmann. *The Road to Eleusis: Unveiling the Secret of the Mysteries.* New York and London: Harcourt Brace Jovanovich, 1978.

Wasson, Valentina Pavlovna, and R. Gordon Wasson. *Mushrooms, Russia, and History*. 2 vols. New York: Pantheon Press, 1957.

Weston, Edward. *The Daybooks of Edward Weston*. Vol. 1. Edited by Nancy Newhall. Millerton, N.Y.: Aperture, 1973.

Whorf, Benjamin Lee. "The Milpa Alta Dialect of Aztec, with Notes on the Classical and the Tepoztlán Dialects." In *Linguistic Structures of Native America*, edited by Harry Hoijer et al. New York: Viking Fund Publications in Anthropology, 1946.

————. "Pitch Tone and the 'Saltillo' in Modern and Ancient Nahuatl." Edited by Lyle Campbell and Frances Karttunen. *International Journal of American Linguistics* 59, 2 (April 1993): 163–220.

Wilson, Raymond. *Ohiyesa: Charles Eastman, Santee Sioux*. Urbana: University of Illinois Press, 1983.

Winnemucca Hopkins, Sarah 1883. *Life among the Piutes: Their Wrongs and Claims*. Edited by Mrs. Horace Mann. Bishop, Cal.: Chalfant Press, 1969.

Zantwijk, R.A.M. van. *Los indígenas de Milpa Alta*. Amsterdam: Instituto Real de los Trópicos, 1960.

Zorita, Alonso de. *Life and Labor in Ancient Mexico: The Brief and Summary Relation of the Lords of New Spain*. Translated by Benjamin Keen. New Brunswick, N.J.: Rutgers University Press, 1963.

Index

Knee, 56, 147–148; attacks on, 149, 150, 166, 287, 293, 298, 299; professional longevity, 167–168; death, 163

Eastman, Irene (daughter of Charles Eastman), 151, 162–163, 311

Eastman, Jacob (Many Lightnings, father of Charles Eastman), 137, 139–141, 325 n. 73

Eastman, John (brother of Charles Eastman), 140–141, 150

Eastman, Mary (wife of Seth Eastman), 137–138, 152–155, 157, 159, 168, 326 n. 84

Eastman, Mary Nancy (Goddess, mother of Charles Eastman), 137–138, 163

Eastman, Ohiyesa II (son of Charles Eastman), 151–152, 162–164, 311

Eastman, Seth (painter, grandfather of Charles Eastman), 136–138, 142, 144–145, 160

Ecuador, 274–285, 316–318; Quito, 317

Edelfelt, Albert (painter), 187, 190–191

education, schooling: boarding schools, 40, 70–73, 91, 145, 150, 153, 161, 265, 267, 309–310; of Paiutes and Bannocks, 46, 48, 50–51, 55, 58–59, 66, 70–73, 319; of Maya, 91–95, 105–106, 109, 165–166; of Guaman Poma, 122–125, 129, 165; of Charles Eastman, 135–136, 140, 141–143, 165; of Paraske, 184–185; in 19th-century Finland, 185–186; in Milpa Alta, 193–195, 200–201, 203–204, 209; of Luz Jiménez's grandchildren, 314; of Chloe Grant's son and niece, 315–316; of Laurinda Andrade, 269–273; Laurinda Andrade as teacher, 319–320; of Dayuma's son Ignacio, 282, 316; of Jean Baptiste Charbonneau, 37–38, 310; in Australia, 315–316

Elliot, Elizabeth (missionary), 281, 284, 317

embroidery, 178, 183, 184, 186, 188, 190, 194, 199, 220, 238

encomienda (grant of Indian labor), *encomendero*, 17, 92, 95–98, 102, 104–112, 165, 169, 307

England, 142, 162, 249, 266

English (people), 132, 136, 151, 179, 181, 189, 209, 212, 221–244, 249, 289, 290, 293, 297, 313; (language), 34, 38, 40, 45–46, 48, 50, 52, 70, 74–75, 112, 115, 137, 140, 141, 143, 145, 149, 151, 154, 166, 211, 238, 240, 246, 265, 270, 271, 272, 292, 314

epidemics, *see* infectious disease

Estrada, Alonso (conquistor), 21

Estrada, María de (conquistadora), 12, 15, 17

Estrada family (Mazatec: Alvaro, Eloina, Natividad), 235, 237–240, 315

Eva (Krotoa), 248–252, 287, 288, 292, 294–295, 298–299, 302, 308–309

famine, *see* hunger

Farriss, Nancy (historian), 287, 293

Felipe and Martín (Quechua interpreters), 121

Finland, 171–176, 179, 181, 185, 187, 192, 241–243, 312; Gulf of Finland, 173, 175. *See also* Helsinki; Porvoo; Sakkola

Finnish (language), 173, 180, 290, 330–331 n. 127

Finnish Literature Society, 185, 189–192

Finns, 171, 175–176, 182–183, 186, 242, 244, 290–291, 313, 330–331 n. 127

Flandreau, S.D., 140–141

Florentine Codex, 2, 11, 103, 290–291, 299, 333 n. 21. *See also* Sahagún, Bernardino de

folklore, folklorists, 23, 68, 137, 158, 169, 182, 183–186, 196, 199, 202–205, 211, 242, 244, 291, 302

folk poetry, 175–177, 182–183, 185, 189, 289. *See also* song

folktales, *zazanilli*, 196, 204–205, 210, 211, 241

United States presidents, 27, 45, 82, 294; as Great Father, 36
University of California, Berkeley, 260, 262
University of Hawaii, Manoa, 214
Uotinen, Mikko (poet), 191–192
Usher, Frederick, 235, 240
Uspensky Cathedral, 187
Ussuria (maritime province of Siberia), 252, 254
Ute (people), 40

Vancouver Barracks, 66
Vanegas, Evaristo (Mazatec), 228, 232
Vasle (brother of Larin Paraske), 177
Vasle (son of Larin Paraske), 178, 181, 188–189, 242, 312–313
Vassar College, 58, 67
Velasco, Viceroy Luis de, 125, 128
Veps, Vot (people), 171, 173
Veracruz, 5, 7, 12, 13, 87–88
vigils, *veladas, see under* Sabina, María
Villalpando, Luis de (Franciscan), 92, 94, 165
Virginia City, Nev., Sutcliff's Music Hall, 51, 142
Viviana (daughter of María Sabina), 237, 315

Walla Walla River, 34, 44, 51
Wallis, Ethel Emily (biographer), 278–279, 318
Waorani, *see* Huaorani
Washington, D.C., 27, 36, 39, 41, 46, 54, 58, 60–61, 63–66, 69–72, 150, 161, 167, 265, 269, 273–274, 298, 303
Wasson, Masha (daughter of R. Gordon Wasson), 223–224, 226
Wasson, Peter (son of R. Gordon Wasson), 223–224, 231
Wasson, R. Gordon, 221–236, 238–247
Wasson, Valentina Pavlovna (wife of R. Gordon Wasson), 221–224, 226, 228, 233, 236
Waterman, Thomas (anthropologist), 260–262, 318

Watson, George, 266–269, 292–294, 299
Weitlaner, Robert, 221, 223, 238
Wellesley College, 142
Weston, Edward (photographer), 195–196, 199, 201–202
wet nursing, 29, 138, 170–174, 178, 313. *See also* foundlings
Wheelock, Eleazar (missionary educator), 141, 309–310
whipping, 99–101, 107–108, 131, 176–177, 192
White Sea, 175–176, 288
Whorf, Benjamin Lee (linguist), 203–205, 207–208, 212, 243
Wilbur, James H. (Indian agent), 62–63, 65–66, 69
Wild West shows, 144, 258
Wind River reservation, 24, 28, 33, 39, 40, 42, 44–45, 75, 78–79, 81, 163, 167, 298, 310
Winnemucca, Elma (sister of Sarah Winnemucca), 50–52, 66, 70, 73, 81
Winnemucca, Lee (brother of Sarah Winnemucca), 46, 57, 60–61
Winnemucca, Mary (sister of Sarah Winnemucca), 49, 52
Winnemucca, Mattie (sister-in-law of Sarah Winnemucca), 60–62, 65, 76
Winnemucca, Natchez (brother of Sarah Winnemucca), 46, 50–53, 55–57, 59–63, 70–73
Winnemucca, Nev., 56–57, 66
Winnemucca Hopkins, Sarah: education, 46, 48, 50–51, 166, 292; marriages, 54–56, 58–59, 64, 66, 68–69, 71–74, 76, 81, 160; domestic service, 49–50, 72, 249, 265; army service, 46, 53, 55, 60–62, 66, 74–76, 168, 283, 318; Indian agency service, 57, 59, 65, 299; as hospital matron, 56; as teacher, 54, 58–59, 63, 66, 70–73, 143, 145, 265, 319; as author, 45, 67–68, 72, 293, 302; as critic, 54, 56, 58, 63, 67–68, 80, 82–83, 147, 214, 252, 288, 293, 295, 303; as public speaker, 45, 51–52,

ABOUT THE AUTHOR

Frances Karttunen is a linguist in the Linguistics Research Center at the University of Texas. She is the author of *An Analytical Dictionary of Nahuatl* and co-author of *Nahuatl in the Middle Years: Language Contact Phenomena in Texts of the Colonial Period.*